To Charles & Elsie
with cordial regards
of Francis C. Taylor

# LIFE OF
# WILLIAM SAVERY

THE MACMILLAN COMPANY
NEW YORK · BOSTON · CHICAGO · DALLAS
ATLANTA · SAN FRANCISCO

MACMILLAN & CO., Limited
LONDON · BOMBAY · CALCUTTA
MELBOURNE

THE MACMILLAN CO. OF CANADA, Ltd.
TORONTO

WILLIAM SAVERY, TANNER, AGED 40

# LIFE OF
# WILLIAM SAVERY

## OF PHILADELPHIA

### 1750-1804

BY

FRANCIS R. TAYLOR, A.M., LL.B.

New York
THE MACMILLAN COMPANY
1925

*Printed in the United States of America by*
J. J. LITTLE AND IVES COMPANY, NEW YORK

# PREFACE

I first undertook writing the Life of William Savery from family interest. Having begun, the work grew, almost in spite of me, as I came to a fuller appreciation of his importance as an historical figure. I became really embarrassed with the wealth of material that developed, not only in Philadelphia and London, but in Boston and Detroit as well.

Soon after starting, the sale of the library of the late Samuel W. Pennypacker, former Governor of Pennsylvania, very unexpectedly brought to light most of the original manuscript of William Savery's Journal. It was acquired by Governor Pennypacker from a source unknown to me, in 1913. It had been published in part in 1837, under the editorship of Jonathan Evans of Philadelphia, who, in that edition, avowedly left out many items of secular interest, and, as the recovered manuscript proves, took extensive and serious liberties with both form and matter.

Though I have used the manuscript freely, I have made but comparatively few quotations. Rather have I tried to conform to modern historical methods by first elaborating the background and then fitting the individual narrative into that setting. Only by so doing is it possible to evaluate the thoughts, motives, actions and aspirations of persons in a given period.

Many kind friends have helped me with suggestion and reference. Of these Norman Penney and M. Ethel Crawshaw, of Friends' Reference Library, Devonshire House, London, have opened up the wealth of accumulated material in their charge with their wonted courtesy. On this side of the water, Albert J. Edmunds, of the Historical Society of

[ vii ]

# PREFACE

Pennsylvania, Rayner W. Kelsey of Haverford College, and Miss G. B. Krum of the Burton Historical Collection of Detroit, have aided me with their treasures and experience without stint. In addition, Rufus M. Jones has kindly read the entire manuscript and helped me with suggestions.

Without diminishing the sincerity of these acknowledgments, I would grant priority to the inspiration received from the late Isaac Sharpless, formerly President of Haverford College, whose peculiar and happy faculty it was to instill his own enthusiasm for scholarship of sundry kinds into the experience of many of his students. In him, modern interest in historical Quakerism first revived in Philadelphia and to his efforts to interpret the past, without adulation, for the use of the present, may be justly attributed much of the late reawakening in Quaker circles. Especially is this true, in the accurate perspective, available in educational matters through his efforts.

Regarding William Savery himself, I can only plead the importance of his life in his own period as an excuse for the length to which the book has grown. His fifty-four years reveal a remarkably all-round man whose story is of moment to people and communities far beyond the pale of the Society of Friends. He touched the turbulent life of his period as minister of the Gospel, business man, traveler, observer, missionary and ambassador of the Prince of Peace, and in all these varied callings his experience was fraught with events and conclusions of interest and importance to Christians of today. That some additional elements of perspective may result from this study of him and his times is my earnest hope.

Francis R. Taylor.

Cheltenham, Pennsylvania,
November, 1924.

# CONTENTS

[ ix ]

# CONTENTS

# ILLUSTRATIONS

# LIFE OF
# WILLIAM SAVERY

# LIFE OF WILLIAM SAVERY

## CHAPTER I

## QUAKER PHILADELPHIA IN 1750

The Philadelphia of 1750 was a unique City. Provincial in all but its culture, self-sufficient to a large extent, the center of thriving foreign trade and commerce, wealthy and well educated for the three generations of its previous existence, it was an ideal environment for the youth of the time, born to see and experience the changes in store for the next half century. In this City on Seventh Month 14, 1750, was born little William Savery.

The life and service of the little lad are, more than is often the case, only fully understood in the light of his City and his parentage. In all the changes of his life and under every circumstance, William Savery was a Philadelphian. Time and again in his Journal, he refers affectionately to his native City and with a pathos, rivaling that of Penn, he recounts her blessings and advantages. By his parentage, under the "birth-right" system, then and now one of the peculiarities of the Society of Friends, he became automatically a member among the Quakers.

The time of his birth marks also one of the most fateful transitions in American Quaker history,—that from great political activity to absolute withdrawal from it. The year 1750 may, in fact, almost be termed the end of Quaker political aspirations. Even the most casual student of Pennsylvania history can feel, almost by intuition, the varying connotations of the names associated with its distinctive periods. Penn died in 1717, Thomas Lloyd in 1694, David Lloyd in 1731, and James Logan in 1751. This quartette are distinctly of the Provincial period.

Isaac Norris, Jr. (1776), Israel Pemberton (1779), and James Pemberton, whose great age carried him to 1809, are as distinctively Colonial.

Both of these groups were active in Church and State. Almost without exception they combined a broad general learning with the ministry or eldership and politics. Their great crux, in every recurring crisis, was the issue of war and peace, and on that issue they maintained a fairly consistent front until, under John Kinsey, in 1756, the flood tide of the French and Indian War submerged them and they thereafter, almost to a man, refused membership in the Assembly.

In importance to Quakerism, this date, 1756, ranks with 1682, the founding of Pennsylvania, and 1827, the Hicksite Separation. It is not without significance that in 1756 the Meeting for Sufferings was established in Philadelphia Yearly Meeting. It was appointed by the Yearly Meeting to care for sufferers for conscience sake; and busy it was on these concerns during the subsequent periods of warfare. Due to the belligerent agitation, the Society of Friends recoiled as if struck. The Quaker worthies of the subsequent chronicles are an entirely different type of men, and, of even more significance, of women. American Quakerism from 1756 bred its leaders, if the paradox is permissible, to the ministry and the ministry alone. The names of Nicholas Waln (who died in 1813), Thomas Scattergood (1814), George Dillwyn (1820), Arthur Howell (1816), John Woolman (1772), and William Savery (1804) connote little profound learning, of the profane type, and absolutely nothing of politics. The elder statesmen had an actual background of English education. The third generation was American born and taught. The powerful men of this Federal period, if it may be so termed, knew their

Bibles and read little else, except the approved writings of Friends. While diligent in business, it was to them a very inferior portion of their lives, in some instances a positive burden of necessity. While some of them were quite successful in business, their Journals and Memoirs regard it rather as a snare, if mentioned at all. Such wealth as they had was inherited rather than acquired.

But even more remarkable was the development of the women ministers of the period. Strange to say, during the Provincial and Colonial periods, covering about a century of American Quakerism, there was no woman minister, of more than local repute. Following the Revolution and coincident with the withdrawal from the political field, came a remarkable coterie of powerful women preachers, of wide influence. Most of these centered around Philadelphia. Rebecca Jones, Hannah Cathrall and Sarah Dillwyn were some of the able and consecrated women called into the work of the Church in this new period when the ideals of the Quaker world were being quickly and subtly transformed to an ecclesiastical approach to every problem.

There was no loss of a social consciousness. On the other hand, it was greatly quickened, and that, too, with a holy fervor. The political and cultural acquirements, aspirations and ideals of Penn, Logan, the Lloyds, the Norrises, the Pembertons and Kinsey evaporated almost overnight, in the great withdrawal of the Friends, as a body, from the Assembly in 1756.

The new bent of the social consciousness was both the cause and effect of the extreme introspectiveness of its prophets. The quavering, tearful Journals of Job Scott and Thomas Scattergood are in strong contrast to the polemic writings of their Philadelphia forebears and of the "First Publishers of Truth." Back of the whole transition was a shifting of values, an unexpressed and tacit abandonment of the political, and almost of the educational, method. The Holy Experiment had failed; the learning

[ 3 ]

of its promoters had proved a seductive veneer. What was needed in the eyes of these newer prophets was a return to the power of a religious experience as the only salvation of society. All else was superficial; hence the essentials were a common school education, an intensive application to the "state of society," and little of inspirational matter beyond the Bible and the preaching in the meetings for worship. The learning of the universities was openly distrusted. The search for knowledge was restricted to the few and they were no longer the spiritual leaders.

It must not be supposed, however, that this change, abrupt as it was, contained no positive features. The flow of Quaker idealism had received a check in direction rather than in intensity. It was to burst forth afresh in an itinerant ministry of apostolic fervor; in a denominational use of the spiritual power of women; in a spiritual attack on deep-seated social evils and in a realization of the corporate responsibility of the denomination for them, the import of which we are but now beginning to appreciate.

In social life, too, the Philadelphia of 1750 was undergoing a change. Only those who have experienced the loneliness of social isolation, bred in war time, when the individual, or a relatively small group of individuals, impelled by conscience, stand fundamentally opposed to the prevailing and overwhelming sentiment of the rest of the community, can really sense the social timidity which overtook the Society of Friends in America as a result of the final breakdown of their efforts for a consistent endeavor in politics. Ostracism is an insupportable burden for sensitive natures. Provincial Pennsylvania had been full of such natures, permeated too with the idealism of Penn's Experiment and desperately striving to the end, to harmonize the commercial and frontier morality with the Christianity they professed. They failed and the French and Indian War was the dramatic climax that proved to them themselves that they had failed. Having withdrawn, they unconsciously assumed the stigma, so familiar to conscientious objection, of impracticality.

In 1756 neutrality was not construed as hostility. In the Revolution of 1776, however, it was and the nonpartisan Quaker, and in some instances rightly, was considered as a Tory and British Loyalist. The social sensitiveness resulting from the French and Indian War was given its logical completeness by the Revolution and both periods mark the formative years of the life of William Savery.

## CHAPTER II

# YOUTH AND EDUCATION

Like most Friends who indulged in Journals, William Savery has recorded very little of his youth, and the editor of the Journal, who knew him well, has added but little regarding that period. His father, William Savery, Sr., was a consistent Friend and a member of Philadelphia Monthly Meeting. Throughout his life he was associated with its activities, centering around the "Great Meeting House," located at the southwest corner of Second and Market (then High) Streets. His origin is a matter of interesting speculation, upon which the usually meticulous records of the Monthly Meeting shed no light.

A collateral reference, among the manuscript records at Devonshire House Library, London, and an obituary notice in Philadelphia coincide with the strong family tradition in ascribing a French origin to both the London and Philadelphia Savery or Savory families. The Devonshire House manuscript was written by "S. R.," as related to her by Martha (Savory) Yeardley, with the note, stating that her

"great-grandfather and William Savery's grandfather were Brothers. They were of the Hugenots (sic) and left France at the Revocation of the Edict of Nantes."

The other reference appeared in the *American Daily Advertiser*, of Philadelphia, after his death in 1804, attributing William Savery's peculiarly easy and unreserved temperament, perhaps to

"a spark of national vivacity (for he was descended from a family of French protestants that had been exiled from Mont-pellier, during the persecution under Louis 14th)."

[6]

# YOUTH AND EDUCATION

Liberty of conscience had been granted by Henry IV of France, by the Edict of Nantes, promulgated in 1598. Under it the Huguenots, as the French Protestants were called, flourished, especially in the south of France. This liberal policy was completely reversed by Louis XIV, by his infamous Revocation in 1685, due to which thousands fled the country and France thereby lost a most substantial class of citizens. It is probable that the name was spelled Sévérît or Savary in France. The name became prominent in French history in the person of Anne Jean Marie René Savary, Duc de Rovigo, who was active in the French wars after 1790. He later became one of Napoleon's most trusted and successful generals, during the period of William Savery's travels.

If credence be granted to the collateral references above quoted, it is hard to see why the two brothers should have parted, particularly as the next few years are covered by no certain data. The first step was undoubtedly to England, where one brother, adopting the name Savory, remained, as do many of his descendants today. Family tradition in Philadelphia again asserts that the other brother went to Barbadoes. The Savery name certainly appears in the records of Barbadoes, in connection with the Society of Friends, but there is nothing to substantiate the tradition beyond that meager fact.

Of more significance is the appearance of a William Savery, as test to the will of Ezekiall Jackson, probated November 10th, 1696, in Cecil County, Maryland, as stated in the "Calendar of Maryland Wills." Maryland was a Catholic Colony, under Lord Baltimore, but Protestants were in a great numerical majority. Cecil County lies next to Pennsylvania and the exact line between Pennsylvania and Maryland was then and for long afterward in dispute between William Penn and Lord Baltimore, so that there need be no inconsistency in a French Protestant seeking refuge near to the Quaker Colony, founded

[ 7 ]

in 1682, shortly before the Revocation of the Edict of Nantes.

From the records of the Maryland Land Office comes another entry of extreme interest:

"An Inventory of the goods and chattels, rights and credits of William Savory Senr Late of Kent County Deceased this Twenty Second Day of June 1739."

Kent County, Maryland, is directly south of Cecil County, and the identity of the William Savery of 1696 in Cecil with the William Savory of 1739 of Kent is easy to assume. The inventory covers four pages of modern typing and foots up £-301/14/1. Headed with five negro slaves, it runs the complete gamut of plantation gear,— cattle, horses, wheat and tobacco constituting the bulk of the estate. The household chattels reveal a good cross-section of a self-sufficing home of the Colonial period. If this William Savory *was* the Frenchman (as I believe) the William Savory, presumably his son, who became Administrator, was no Quaker, for he "made oath on the Holy Evangels of Almighty God." *If* (and again I so believe) this younger William later became the cabinet-maker of Philadelphia, he must have become a Quaker between 1739 when he took a judicial oath and April 19, 1746, a date on the books of the Monthly Meeting of Philadelphia, when William Savery certainly married Mary, daughter of Rees Peters, in Friendly manner, she being of Welsh extraction. It is passing strange that there is no entry of William Savery's reception into membership, either by convincement or birth or certificate from another meeting among those thoroughly reliable records.

The Kent County inventory of 1739 further discloses "Nathll Ricketts and Ester E. Salter," the latter signing by her mark, as "two of the nearest of the kin" of the deceased William Savory, from which it may be safely assumed that the Frenchman married after his arrival in Maryland, or there would not likely have been kin of different surnames mentioned.

There is but one difficulty in aligning the future Philadelphian as a son of the Frenchman in Maryland. The Philadelphian died, as disclosed by the Meeting records, in 1787, at the age of sixty-five years. He must therefore have been born in 1721 or 1722, and if so, would have been but eighteen years old at the Frenchman's death in 1739, and probably too young to administer an estate. The only possible answer is that eighteen may have been legal age in Maryland at that time.

Based on the above facts, so far as they are such, it is my belief that the three William Saverys, the first of Montpellier, France, fleeing to Maryland and dying there in 1739; the second, born in Maryland and eventually settling in Philadelphia, and the third, the tanner and minister and the subject of this book, are grandfather, father and son. Certain it is, under any circumstances, from the statement of Martha Yeardley, that the minister was the grandson of the French refugee.

The second William of this triumvirate was a cabinet-maker. He has, of late, acquired considerable fame among antiquaries and furniture collectors through the Palmer collection of antique furniture, now permanently lodged in the Metropolitan Museum of New York. The exquisite high and low boys and tables of this collection represent "the workmanship of one of our greatest colonial cabinet-makers, William Savery of Philadelphia."

To quote from an article in the December, 1918, Bulletin of the Metropolitan Museum of Art:

"The uprooting from ancestral homes in the vicinity of Philadelphia of certain pieces of extraordinarily beautiful furniture of the middle of the eighteenth century has long led to the belief among our collectors that a cabinet-maker of preëminent ability had successfully conducted his trade in the City of Brotherly Love. The identity of this hitherto unknown cabinet-maker, William Savery, has been disclosed through the finding of a tiny label attached to a superb lowboy now in the Manor House at Van Cortlandt Park, a charming little colonial museum furnished, cherished and guarded by the Colonial Dames of the State of New York."

Several of these little paper labels are still in existence. They read:

"All Sorts of Chairs and
Joiners Work
Made and Sold by
WILLIAM SAVERY
At the Sign of the
Chair, a little be-
low the Market, in
Second Street.
PHILADELPHIA."

An alternative to this form reads "In Second Street, near the Market." From searching the real estate records of the period, this property proves to be the present No. 17 South Second Street. As stated above, the Great Meeting House stood at the southwest corner of Second and High (now Market) Streets. Little William Savery was born in 1750. His father bought the Second Street house on September 12, 1753, so the lad grew up under the shadow of the principal meeting place of his sect, directly across the street. The Market, to which the labels refer, was a long, one-story structure, running along the middle of the High Street, from Front to Fourth Streets, and equipped with stalls on either side of its central aisle.

Of the early boyhood of William Savery little is known save the statement in his published Journal that he "received an education in the principles of the Christian religion" or, as it is stated in the testimony of the Monthly Meeting, "in the principles of the Christian religion, as professed by us." It is a matter of great regret in the vast majority of Friends' Journals that these early periods of adolescence and the youth or young womanhood are too often passed over or even glossed over, as topics to be

avoided in a narrative meant for the profit of the youth of
a later time.   If the youthful history and struggles of the
Apostle Paul were to be deemed profitable only after his
experience on the road to Damascus, the world would
be the poorer both in religious psychology and spiritual
experience.

A man as well equipped, intellectually and education-
ally, as William Savery was in after life, must have had
a good schooling in his youth.   His manuscript Journal and
more than a score of his letters, still extant, show a firm
and steady, though not easy hand.   Their diction is constantly good and the sentence structure accurate.   The
facility with which he later mastered French and German,
of which mention will be made hereafter, evidences a considerable classical training and a remarkable linguistic
ability.   Bemoan it later, as he did, his extensive reading
must have broadened him greatly.   Said he in a sermon in
1796, regarding his early habits:

"I know that I for many years so abused my time in reading
novels, romances, plays and a variety of trumpery of this kind, that
I had no relish for the Scriptures."

To that disparaged period can undoubtedly be attributed
the quotation, in the same sermon from Shakespere's "King
Henry VIII" of Cardinal Wolsey's lament.   In this same
collection of printed sermons he quotes from Socrates and
Seneca and maintains that his contention is as "clear as
any axiom in Euclid," all of which references undoubtedly
hark back to those school days in Philadelphia.

From a valuable monograph [1] recently published, it is
possible to state with very great probability of accuracy,
the educational influences surrounding little William up to
his fourteenth year, when he left school for an apprenticeship.   He may very probably have attended the Penn
Charter School, as it is now called, it being at that time the

[1] Thomas Woody, *Early Quaker Education in Pennsylvania.*

principal school under the care of Friends and close to his
father's home. His name does not appear among those of
the pupils annually listed in the minute books of the Overseers of the Public Schools. These lists, however, may not
have been inclusive and certainly many of them referred
only to needy students whose parents could not pay the
modest schooling charges. In his mature years, William
Savery was elected one of the Overseers of the Public
Schools, in charge of the Friends' School System of that
time. The building in which this school was then kept was
the new one, authorized in 1744 to be built on the south
end of the lot devised, for school purposes, by William
Forrest, at the southeast corner of Fourth and Chestnut
Streets. The present Forrest Building at 119 South Fourth
Street, marks the site of this Quaker school where a building sixty by thirty-five feet, two stories high and with a
cellar, rising three feet above the ground surface, finished in
1746, at a cost of £794, was supposed to be commodious
enough to house all the Quaker youth for some time to
come.

Three schoolmasters of more than passing importance are
associated with the period of William Savery's school
days,—Anthony Benezet, Alexander Seaton and Robert
Proud. With the advent of Benezet, in 1742, the Friends'
school system may be said to have really begun. Though
ill health kept him from his duties some of the years between 1757 and 1764, it is a reasonable conjecture that it
was from him that the rudiments of French were imbibed
by the youth who was afterwards to return to his forefathers' France as a missionary of the Gospel. Benezet's
gentle and successful disciplinary methods are well known
even in this generation and his long incumbency, at a time
when service was usually short and teachers were even
scarcer than now, is evidence of his consecration to his
profession and his qualifications for it.

Alexander Seaton was head of the "English School" from

1754 until his death in 1763. He was responsible for "writing, arithmetic and mathematics," and under him, as "ushers" or assistants were, at various times, Moses Patterson, Phineas Jenkins and George Smith. Latin and Greek were, until 1760, under Charles Thompson, a teacher of long training who in that year forsook the calling for business and later became Secretary of the Revolutionary Congress of 1775. His place was filled and augmented by Robert Proud, who came from England on the recommendation of John Fothergill and John Hunt. His name is now better known as the historian of Early Pennsylvania, but his teaching was most acceptable to his constituents. He, more than any of his contemporaries, had profound learning and profound respect for all learning. If William Savery fell under his influence during the last four years of his schooling, he can be counted as a student of the greatest of early Quaker schoolmasters.

The Friends' schools were under the care of Overseers, appointed by the Monthly Meeting, in much the same way as at present. The care extended varied with the different committees, but the strict regimen of the school and the severity of its requirements are evidenced in the rules adopted in 1748 and doubtless in effect in William Savery's time. Promptness was enjoined and absence, without parental permit, forbidden. Strict obedience to the monitor, with right of appeal to the master, was required as was also decorum in coming to and leaving school. Civility and the use of the plain language to all persons were a part of the requirements and "ranting games" and quarreling were ranked with keeping company with the rude boys of the town, among the forbidden pursuits. The Rules closed with encouragement to play with their own school fellows and to attend meeting on Fifth Day.

Such, in general outline, must have been the atmosphere of those school days. The attendance at Penn Charter School, then more widely known as Friends' Public School, after the English idea of "Public Schools," is indeed better than conjecture. It being the only Friends' school to which general attendance was attracted in the central portion of the then City, and being located within a few blocks of his home, it is hard to imagine any other possibility from which an "education in the principles of the Christian religion as professed by us" could have been acquired.

It may or may not be significant that in 1759, when the little lad was nine years old, his father, William Savery, was appointed by Philadelphia Monthly Meeting for the first time in a long series to "the care to prevent the rudeness of the Boys at Evening Meeting in the Galleries and to hire Constables to attend at the Doors to prevent Disturbances there." For two decades after this time the father was appointed with unfailing regularity on the committees charged with unruly conduct among the boys. In 1763, besides being appointed "to sit in the Boys' Galleries and to use their endeavors to prevent the disorders complained of at our Public Meetings," they were also "desired to meet together to consult upon the most suitable means of performing the service effectually."

These recurring appointments may indicate special fitness for the service or, as results seem to have been lacking, unfitness for it. Whether the conduct of the little son in meeting had any bearing on the appointment of the father can only be left to surmise.

Again from the Journal we learn that he "was placed with a Friend in the country to learn the tanning business." No further details of this important step in the boyhood of the future minister are permitted in this narrative. From the bare records of Philadelphia Monthly Meeting comes an excerpt (the first of the many, many minutes that were afterwards to chronicle the activities of this dedicated man) stating, "Wm Savery the younger, asks for a certificate to Goshen, he being placed apprentice there." At the next session, Eighth Month 31st, 1764, the certificate was produced, approved and signed. We may well imagine the little lad, aged fourteen, faring forth into his "land of Goshen" and the prayers of the pious parents, following their eldest boy. The Goshen records do not disclose, as do many of the time, the name of his master. In after years, when William Savery himself was taking apprentices, the Philadelphia records show several boys in his care and their received certificates duly record the fact.

It would be most interesting to know just where these seven years were spent. Goshen Monthly Meeting at that time was a large and important one, comprising the territory of the modern Newtown Square, Goshen and Uwchlan Meetings. The ancient Goshen meeting house is still a familiar object at the corner of the West Chester Pike and Chester Road. It is safe to surmise several things, however,—his master would have been a safe influence, for the boy was of well-to-do parents who could exercise a choice and who were concerned Friends themselves; that the young apprentice got a good training among the vats and hides and in the woods with the tan-bark, for he followed the calling as his own for the rest of his business life; that he here first met Sarah Evans, whom he afterwards married, and finally that he may have formed some acquaintance with the farm of James Gibbons in the neighboring Township of Westtown, where later was founded the Boarding School, in whose origin he was vastly interested.

Apprenticeship to a trade was then almost universal and was commended as a part of any real education. It was, moreover, frequently a matter of intimate meeting concern, through the Overseers. Sons of families of every station in life underwent the process. For desirable apprenticeships the fathers sometimes paid considerable sums, and the youths fortunate enough to be placed in establishments of first rate standing, often commanded a prestige at the end of their term, commensurate with that of the master. It is interesting, incidentally, to note that in the triple system of apprenticeship, bound service and slavery there was, in a sense, the same fundamental feature. None of the three now exists, but the factor at the basis of each, namely, an avowed inferiority (whether of age, means or race) to the master, is at least an element to be conceded to early society, in any examination or criticism of its slave-holding tendencies.

Beyond this meager mention, the period of the apprenticeship is a blank. In 1771, the boy, now of age, returned to Philadelphia and his old Monthly Meeting recorded,—

"Certificate produced for William Savery, Jr., who served his apprenticeship in Chester County, from Goshen Monthly Meeting, dated Twelfth Month 6th instant."

CHAPTER III

## MANHOOD AND CONVERSION

Following William Savery's majority and his return to Philadelphia, another period of seven years elapsed of which but little can be ascertained today. Of the importance of these years, however, in William Savery's life, the known results are sufficient evidence.

In her Diary, under date, January 30, 1772, Elizabeth Drinker records:

"This morn'g about 7 o'Clock a fire broke out at Thos West, in second Street which communicated to those of John Wallace, one Smith next door, and to Wm Savery's—the roofs and upper Appartments of these 4 Houses, with a great quantity of Furniture and Merchandize were consumed."

It is safe to guess that the youth, only a few weeks returned from his apprenticeship, was in his father's home and that he experienced, with the rest of the family the loss and inconvenience resulting from the fire, but this slight incident throws no light upon the more important facts to which his biographer refers and upon which William Savery himself enlarges in an account quoted in the printed Journal, the original of which is now lost. We learn, however, that when the youth returned from his apprenticeship he entered upon a course of worldly pleasure "with those who like himself, were much inclined to vanity and folly." These are the words of the editor of the Journal. It is hard to estimate at this time just how serious his shortcomings were. He himself mentions as a part of this life, the frequenting of taverns and places of diversion, the relating of adventures and tales to provoke mirth and often, for the embellishment of them, straining beyond the truth.

Fortunately we are not left entirely to deductions from William Savery's own account. Thomas Eddy was born of Irish Quaker parents in Philadelphia in 1758. As a New York Friend of after years he became one of the most prominent advocates of prison reform that the Society of Friends has ever produced, being affectionately termed the "John Howard of America." His story of his younger years runs, in part:

"From the age of sixteen to twenty years, my most particular and intimate friends were Charles Mifflin and William Savary, with whom I daily associated. The former was well educated and of a fine understanding, with sound principles and a marked integrity. The latter was a most valuable character, and a highly pleasing and entertaining companion. We were all fond of such subjects and pursuits as were most likely to promote mirth and pleasantry, yet the wise and excellent sentiments communicated to us by Charles Mifflin were one means of preserving us from much harm; and happy would it have been for me, if I had through life, more imitated his excellent character. He possessed fine literary talents and as a poet was pleasing and instructive. His family connections were wealthy and generally fashionable. He was more particularly during the latter part of his life, a truly religious and good man.

"Of William Savary, it would be difficult for me to say too much. No two persons could entertain a more near and tender regard and affection for each other, than always subsisted between us. He was a man of uncommonly strong mind and good understanding. When about twenty-five years of age he became a minister; and perhaps there never was one more highly esteemed and beloved. He was admired by all classes, and openly opposed to everything in the least marked with bigotry or superstition. As a preacher, he was in the first rank. His manner of delivery was pleasing and solemn, his mind was cultivated and improved, and he was uncommonly liberal in his sentiments towards those of other societies. I have often thought there never was a character, so nearly perfect within my knowledge, in our Society; and none that more extensively inculcated and effectually diffused true, practical, Christian principles.

"I could do no less than pay this brief tribute to the memory of these two excellent men, who were the friends of my youth, and who early instilled into my mind opinions and sentiments that have been instructive and useful to me through life."

About Charles Mifflin a few other facts are ascertainable. He was born December 13, 1753, so he was more than three years and Thomas Eddy eight years younger than William Savery,—considerable discrepancies among intimate youths. Charles Mifflin was a first cousin of young Thomas Mifflin, later Major General in the Revolutionary War and first Governor of Pennsylvania, under the Federal Government. Charles Mifflin was an Episcopalian by birth, but later joined Friends and married Mary Waln in 1777. For a time he taught school, Elizabeth Drinker recording, July 7, 1781:

"Charles Mifflin broke up school, ye weather being hot and ye girls tired."

His death occurred in 1783.

Such companions as these, particularly in the light of their sober after lives, would not be considered dangerous according to modern standards. They were undoubtedly lively youths, and William Savery's greater age and his social temperament would doubtless throw upon him the chief responsibility for their waywardness. And yet at that time, just preceding the Revolution, the Society of Friends was not as puritanical or as strict as it became very soon after. Temperate drinking was almost universal and brewing was still an accredited occupation among Friends. The frequenting of taverns was discouraged, but more from the standpoint of the associations involved and the temptation to excess than from the potations served.

We know that the taverns of Revolutionary Philadelphia were the centers of a radical political and social philosophy that effervesced into the business and religious life of the City. We also know that they harbored much hard drinking and a seamy social life entirely in contrast with that which Friends at all times have upheld. There can be no doubt that William Savery tasted of this and found it pleasant, at least superficially. "Activity of spirits, loose discourse and noisy mirth, were my sad refuge to drown serious reflection," he writes of this time. It may be safe to assume that this was written in after years, when the intensity of religious experience and the conservatism of age had magnified the sins of youth. It is also, I think, a safe surmise that these shortcomings were venial and that no gross or deeply immoral acts marred the after-thoughts of the young man. So frequently do the Journals of this period and of the type of men to which William Savery, Job Scott and Thomas Scattergood belonged, speak with deep contrition and regret of the waywardness and frivolity of their misspent youths, that the modern interpreter can but dilute the self-condemnation with the fact that Quaker tendencies were leading to a disapproval of any degree of levity or genial relaxation in any relation of life. The humorous vagaries of Nicholas Waln, a prominent minister of this period, are bywords to this day, not only for their intrinsic merit, but because they were more and more frowned upon as his generation yielded to a sterner, more forbidding one.

I am inclined to believe that the waywardness of whatever degree was more the reaction of a youth returning to the attractions of town life after seven years in a country region, under strict discipline and at hard and unremunerative work, than an expression of any particular depravity. Adolescence was past, manhood was upon him and the necessity of taking up the business to which he had been trained was the next step. A desire to mix with the world, to appraise its influences, to estimate its currents and to fraternize with future business acquaintances, is easily discernible in the two tendencies of which he writes. He was, on the one hand, carried along with the new current of convivial and lively companionship, while on the other his deeper nature was constantly warning him and reminding him of spiritual desires that his developing personality found unsatisfied. He was undoubtedly yielding to dangerous tendencies, but he was never without a sense of his situation and his gayety was often followed by bitter remorse. He records:

"The Lord * * * followed me to my chamber, and upon my pillow has drawn tears of sorrow and contrition from me, * * * so that my days of joy and laughter have often produced nights of sorrow and weeping. Still I continued sinning and repenting and turning the grace of God into wantonness for a number of years, being at times favored to see in part, the beauty there is in holiness, but fearful of incurring the scoff and scorn of the world's deluded votaries should I turn my back upon it."

This period of spiritual conflict lasted, in its intensity, until 1778. In those years the momentous events of the Revolution were in progress around him. What were his reactions to the revolutionary propaganda, everywhere evident, not only in the taverns but in the City and country at large; what influences played around him to encourage or to restrain him in the line of military service on one side or the other in the struggle with the Mother Country; how active were his parents in their oversight of their son and in the choice of his associates; these and many other queries of great interest in estimating his experiences, must probably remain forever unanswered, through the oblivion that time has cast around them. Most particularly is this regrettable regarding the war.

There is only one well authenticated incident, belonging to this period of wartime. In the "Life of Thomas Eddy," to which reference has already been made, appears the following paragraph:

"In 1777, the British troops took possession of Philadelphia and soon after their entering the city, the American army attacked them at Germantown. I rode out with William Savary to that place, before the battle was entirely over, and had a view of the killed and

wounded on the ground. When we arrived, the Americans had retreated, and the British army had advanced as far as Chestnut Hill.

William Savery's presence, behind the British lines and
in company with an avowed Loyalist like Thomas Eddy, is
pretty strong indication that his own sympathies were
mainly with the British cause. To this may be added Dr.
Lettsom's account of William Savery's conversation with
George III, twenty years later, when he told the King of the

"high esteem which the people very generally entertained for him;
and that the Society of Friends had always preserved an inviolable
attachment to his person and family, to the last moment of the
American Revolution."

a statement that may very possibly have been colored by
Dr. Lettsom's sympathies and wishes in reporting it.

From his own intimacy with Thomas Eddy another surmise is possible. Thomas Eddy was a brother of Charles
Eddy, who, in September, 1777, just before the Battle of
Brandywine, was exiled with twenty-one other Friends,
many of them very prominent in the Society, to Hopewell,
Virginia, for their alleged Loyalist sympathies. Of the
sympathies of the Eddy brothers there can be no doubt, as
both went to New York with the British, upon the evacua-
tion of Philadelphia. As late as 1802, when the "Black
List" was published in Philadelphia, giving the names of
those "attainted of treason" for Loyalist activities, both
Charles and Thomas Eddy were included.

The twenty-two Friends were exiled to Virginia by the
Executive Council of Pennsylvania, under authority of the
American Congress. There was little or no semblance of
legal process in the affair, and feeling ran very high. A
petition, signed by 113 Friends, was presented to the President and Council of Pennsylvania dated "5th of 9th month,
1777," lamenting the "alarming violation of the civil and
religious rights of the community," the remonstrance being
issued "lest by our silence on this very interesting occasion,

Hugh Reinagle Pinx.ʳ

Engraved by J W Steel

**FRIENDS MEETING HOUSE MERION.**

Pub.ᵈ by Childs Engraver 80 Walnut St. Philadelphia ____ 1830

it should be understood that we acquiesced therein." The Savery family was very deeply stirred by the incident as William Savery, Sr., and his two sons, William, Jr., and Thomas, then 28 and 27 years old respectively, were three of the signers.

The tension was increased by the sequel, when two other Friends in good standing, John Roberts and Abraham Carlisle, were tried upon charges of treason, convicted and hanged in Philadelphia. The record of their trials makes sober reading in the state papers of the United States. John Roberts had been accused of having sent word to General Howe, approaching with the British army to take possession of Philadelphia, that the Friends, exiled to Virginia, were then en route to Reading, and suggesting to the General that he send a detachment to intercept the detail in charge of them and return them to their families in Philadelphia. After his execution in 1778, John Roberts was buried at Merion and my surmise is that this was the occasion of William Savery's conclusive experience at Merion Meeting House. The funeral was certainly largely attended and Nicholas Waln and others preached. Thomas Eddy records his own attendance and it is entirely likely that William Savery, his boon companion, was among the large number from the City. It was certainly at a meeting at Merion, held after an interment, that he was most deeply impressed with serious thoughtfulness and this event certainly happened in 1778. No other interment of that sad period could have made a more terrible appeal than the funeral of John Roberts. I rarely pass this ancient house of worship, perched high on its bank by the Montgomery Pike, without reverting in mind to William Savery, who found his road to Damascus in the graveyard to the rear.

Two other events in 1778 marked this dubious period of alternate sinning and repenting. He married that year Sarah Evans, a member of Bradford Monthly Meeting, as the meeting record discloses. He must have met her during his apprenticeship, probably at her grandmother's home at Edgemont, within the limits of Goshen Meeting. She was of a serious and pious disposition, so far as we have any record of her, and closely sympathetic with him in his early spiritual troubles. She seems to have had less unity with his prolonged absence later, in Europe, as she left Philadelphia and returned to Bradford, in spite of his repeated and pathetic requests for her to resume her habitation in the City. In 1841, Stephen Grellet wrote the following in a personal letter, about the Saverys:

"His memory continues precious to many. I have often thought of a little circumstance in the early part of his setting out in life, which it would be well for many of our young people in like manner circumstanced to put into practice. When he married he was very gay, yet it appears he was looking towards an advancement in better things, therefore he said to his intended bride, 'My dear, in preparing for our house-keeping, we had better provide ourselves with plain furniture, such as we shall not be ashamed to have, when we grow better, which we must entertain the hope to become.'"

With a father who was at that time at the peak of his artistic effort in creating sumptuously elegant furniture, such a resolution was surely evidence of changed conditions.

The other momentous event of 1778, in William Savery's personal fortunes, was that "he settled in business in Philadelphia," though the strict accuracy of this statement is hard to reconcile, since he must have been occupied in some business between 1771 and 1778. Probably he became a master tanner for the first time in 1778.

All the while it was a sobering time for young and old in the Society of Friends. The British army occupied Philadelphia from September 26, 1777, till June 19, 1778. While Washington's troops were freezing at Valley Forge, the British, under Howe, gave Philadelphia the gayest winter of its existence and allowed Washington the time he needed to perfect his plans for their final discomfiture the next spring. For the Friends that winter was painful from a moral standpoint, as the theaters, balls, pageants and wantonness of the British army sorely strained their ideas of propriety. From all other aspects they were better treated than by the Continentals. Few chapters of history have so deeply impressed the Society and from still fewer has it drawn so little credit. The very attempt to maintain neutrality simply brought disrepute and misunderstanding. With charges of treason, disloyalty and Toryism being bandied about; when Friends' houses were attacked, windows smashed and doors broken in for refusing to illuminate in celebration of victory on either side and with twenty-two of the foremost Friends of the Yearly Meeting in exile, it is small wonder that the Society, and especially the young men, were deeply affected. Some went off with the "Free Quakers," joined the American army and proved their mettle in the field. Others (and William Savery was evidently one of these) underwent a transition of another type, proving themselves in the harder test of contumely and ostracism.

Those who have experienced the perfervid intensity of war mania will easily appreciate the appeal of the war spirit and the corresponding, albeit inconsistent outbreak of a certain type of emotional religious expression, almost exotic in its nature. William Savery went through this sort of public fever and his nature was undoubtedly influenced by it, save that in his case, as with Thomas Scattergood and Daniel Offley, resulted one of those spiritual conversions that deepened and broadened as he grew older. In his later service in the war-torn countries of Europe, his mind must frequently have harked back to the Revolution and the tumultuous political and social ferment of which he was a spectator. His earlier experience would have given him a perspective, through which to evaluate the stern poverty of the Flanders and Germany, which he afterward saw.

His own account of his spiritual condition at this time tells of earnest efforts toward a more circumspect life:

"being pretty careful in my conduct and conversation, and just in my dealings among men, and I was willing to believe I had attained to great matters, and that I might now take up my rest; for by my own strength, abilities and contrivance, I could not only keep up a fair, upright character among men, and make my life happy and myself respected, but also that it would, at the close of time here, gain me an inheritance in the regions of purity and peace, among all those that are sanctified."

Following this period of smug satisfaction came an intense, but comparatively brief time of deep spiritual travail. He was shaken from his false rest only to find nothing substantial in his former degree of experience:

"This brought great distress and anxiety of mind over me, and sometimes I was ready to doubt the truth of these divine revelations; and was exceedingly desirous to find, if possible, an easier way to peace and happiness, than by submitting myself to the cross, of which I had as yet experienced but little. I was much tossed and distressed, as one who was in a dark and howling wilderness, where I could see no way out, either to the right hand or to the left."

Of the climax to this struggle, it would be vain to use other than his own words:

"Oh! these were times of baptism never to be forgotten in mutability. One evening, sitting in my house alone, great horror and trouble seized me—I wept aloud, and shortly after went to bed; but my distress was so great, that it almost overcame me, and I thought I tasted of the misery of fallen spirits. Not being able to contain myself, I arose and walked the room. My spirits at length being nearly exhausted, I threw myself on the bed again, but had not lain long, before I grew cold like one near death, a clammy sweat covered me, and I was to appearance stupid. In this state I was, through adorable mercy, released from the horror that before surrounded me, and was comforted with a sight and feeling of a state of inexpressible happiness and joy; and when so far come to myself to have utterance given me, I cried aloud on this wise, 'Oh! now I know that my Redeemer liveth!'

"Oh! the sweetness I then felt, in being favored with such an evidence of the goodness and mercy of God! It far surpassed everything I had before experienced, and was such that I hope to bear it in remembrance as long as I have a being here. Tears of joy ran freely down my cheeks, in so much that I could not restrain them nor scarcely utter a word for a considerable time; and my dear partner, who shared with me in my affliction, was also made a partaker with me in my exceeding great joy."

Following this time of intense struggle, William Savery spent much of his time, when not engaged in his tanning business, in retirement at home. He was favored with the loving care of some sympathizing Friends, and may be said from that time on to have attained an experimental realization of the depths of religious life that his former complacency had rendered impossible. Subject as all are to depression and the sense of sin and shortcomings, he never again was without a sure sense of his Savior's sufficiency in spite of his own weakness, to aid and redeem, whatsoever the circumstances were.

CHAPTER IV

# EARLY MINISTRY

In the manuscript records at Devonshire House, London, appears a narrative, related by "M. Y. to S. R.," probably Martha Yeardley and Sarah Rawes. It agrees in all essential details with a favorite story of Sarah H. Cresson's, a story frequently related to her great-nephews in Philadelphia. The Devonshire House record is as follows:

"When young, Wm Savery and his brother Thomas, were very different characters. T. S. appeared in the ministry, much to the dissatisfaction of his brother, Wm. They sat together in meeting on a cross form, and one day, W. S. said to him,—'Tom, if thou stand up again to preach, I'll pull thee down by thy coat lap.' Thomas turned to him in a solemn manner and said,—'If thou do, I hope the burden may rest upon thee.'

"At, I think, the next meeting, Thos Savery stood up in testimony, when Wm pulled him down. From that time Thos never felt it required of him to appear in this line, but very shortly after, a very great change took place in Wm, who appeared in the ministry very acceptably to his friends & Thomas became a valuable and weighty Elder."

As already related, this sudden and vital change in William Savery took place in 1778, and his first appearance in the ministry, in accord with the above story, soon followed. Jonathan Evans, writing of this period, states it was "about this time," in 1779, "as far as appears," when William Savery accompanied another Friend on a visit to the meetings of Virginia and Carolina, that "he was engaged to speak a few words in meetings, by way of Gospel ministry." Perchance like other timid prophets he felt best able to develop his gift away from home, where he might not be without honor.

One incident of this journey, in the last days of the Revolution, give an interesting sidelight on William Savery's peace views. A Friend, conscientiously opposed to war, had been drafted and, upon refusal to serve, had been tried by court-martial and sentenced to be whipped. He received forty lashes on his bare back from a cat-o'-nine-tails, in the presence of some thousands of persons, suffering the punishment with meekness and patience. Of this incident, William Savery wrote:

"Great endeavors were afterwards used, both by threats and persuasions, to induce him to comply with some service in the military establishment, such as waiting upon the sick, or in some other employ that they might take hold of, so as to answer their purpose: but remaining steadily fixed, he could have no freedom to countenance their measures, let the consequence be what it might. I think it is worthy of remark, that his prudent wife appeared to be more concerned on account of an evil report that her husband had been brought to a compliance, than for all his suffering, or all they were worth in the world. After the time had expired, for which he had been drafted, he returned home."

Whatever faltering or doubt there may have been in his youth, there is in this reaction to conscientious objection and suffering, a clear note of entire coincidence with the Friendly viewpoint on war, and another indication that the Quaker attitude brought ostracism and loneliness in those days as surely as it did in more recent times. It is impossible to avoid the inference that the aftermath of war wrought powerfully on the minds and hearts of men of good-will in those times, as it has in our own. Time and again, in the course of this study of William Savery and his times, I have been struck with the similarity of the impetus and of the stimulus, arising from the common danger, the common suffering and the consequent outpouring of responsibility for their fellow men, as such, and without distinction as to race or nationality,—the similarity to the concern felt by English and American Quakerism today, under circumstances differing in degree rather than in kind. Back of the quickened conscience of the decades from 1790 to 1810 lay the sinister days of ostracism and social ingrowth, leading to a narrowness of vision, a distrust of everything worldly, cultural or broadly educational, that terminated in the tragedy of the separations of 1827-1830. The incessant wars from 1776 to 1815 carried the iron into the soul of the Society of Friends. This experience produced towering individuals, fired with the cure of the world's evils, through the preaching of the message of the Kingdom, from a strong doctrinal standpoint, but it produced on the part of the Society at large a lethargy and numbness as to things social, that opened it to internal dissention, disintegration and loss of influence that a century has not repaired.

In the present, when we are again at a period of great possibility, it is well for us to study the after effects of the war stimulus on our testimony, not only in the Revolution but in the Crimean and American Civil wars. If, in so doing, we do not build more wisely than our Fathers, our fault is only so much the greater by reason of our superior opportunity to learn and to judge.

William Savery was peculiarly the child of this environment. His was the age of appreciation of political growth by the nation and a corresponding distrust of all things political by Friends. It was also the age of French immigration, during which some of the choice spirits of French culture and refinement sought refuge in America. Among these came our own Antoine Bénézet and Étienne de Gréllet du Mabillier, neither of whom, however, would have cherished his name thus written. They were part of the bond that tied the newly-born Republic of the West to the struggling France, in which, in spite of its orgies of revolution and bloody excess, America, of all creeds and of none, saw a drama being enacted that boded good or evil, in superlative measure to the nations and peoples of a war-sick world. These French immigrants carried with them a glamor and romance, born of suffering and exile, that caught the imagination of all classes. Especially was this the case with the exiled nobility of whom Stephen Grellet was typical. With world problems pressing for solution on a mammoth scale and on every hand, it was only probable that the concerned members among Friends should first endeavor to make clear their own action and then carry to the world the Gospel message that appeared to them all sufficient, in itself, for the healing of the nations.

Fortunately, they had cleared themselves of negro slavery just prior to the Revolutionary War. After that, negro and Indian education and religious work were first-hand obligations, broadening, as the world wars developed in scope and intensity, to a peculiarly acute concern for Europe,—as well the Continent as the British Isles. There was no attempt to organize this movement or to make it more than the operation of an individual concern. The greater experiment was left for its first faint tryout in the Crimean War, when British Friends found practical relief for the wants of the body to be effective means of introducing a message of good-will,—a method vastly elaborated in our own day.

Like few of his fellow laborers, William Savery went through both the domestic and foreign fields of service. His first heavy undertakings, as we shall see hereafter, were to the Indian tribes, which the Friends still considered their peculiar wards. Thereafter came the great and extensive service in Europe. Of the decade of preparation, between his precipitate acceptance of a religious life and his extensive travels, we have but the most meager facts.

His fidelity to his ministerial gift was, however, noteworthy, as he was acknowledged a minister only two years later, in 1781, at the age of thirty-one years. It was in these younger days that William Savery and Thomas Scattergood performed together a service of peculiar and startling nature. It is the first recorded of the many joint undertakings of these devoted friends who in after years sat side by side in North Meeting.

The story was told by Thomas Scattergood, many years after, to a London Friend. Capital punishment was then more common than now and executions were always a public spectacle, on the ground that such horrors would have a deterrent effect on the community. Thomas Scattergood learned of two men who were to be executed and felt a strong impulse to be present. While the concern was hardly a religious one, he called upon William Savery in his currier's shop and found him disposed to accompany him.

As the tumbrel, carrying the convicts, approached, the two young men joined the crowd in its wake. They were then powerfully impressed with a deep sense given them of the state of mind of the criminals and under this influence climbed upon the cart and rode with the condemned. Riding thus over the rough streets, in the face of a gaping crowd, the two Quakers felt dreadfully hardened. At the scaffold under the same impelling conviction, they unhesitatingly ascended the ladder after the poor men and witnessed their execution so close at hand. Immediately after the dread accomplishment, William Savery addressed the multitude around the platform, his sense of the hardened guilt of the men changing into a deep compassion in which his whole soul welled up in a fervent outpouring of spirit, so that he could with difficulty restrain his tears.

When he ceased, many among the crowd were weeping and Thomas Scattergood immediately followed in a powerful and impressive appeal against the evil of yielding to the first temptation, closing the unusual service with earnest supplication. The quietness with which the crowd dispersed, after an hour's stay at what may well be termed the strangest execution in Philadelphia's criminal history, bore testimony to the solemnity of the occasion. After this incident both young men were concerned that the time had been too short for them to consult Friends before undertaking the service, but they found, to their relief, that there was very general approval and satisfaction in it.

The activity of this decade was very considerable, an activity that was preparing a man, young enough to stand the brunt of travel such as the world of today has little conception of, and yet mature enough to serve in camp, council, meeting and royal court with meekness, urbanity and acceptability. In 1785, with the concurrence of his Monthly Meeting, William Savery attended Baltimore Yearly Meeting, which, curiously enough, did not have complete autonomy in those days. Both Maryland and Virginia Yearly Meetings then appointed representatives to Philadelphia Yearly Meeting. It was probably this circumstance that led to William Savery's concern in those parts, for both Maryland and Virginia had petitioned Philadelphia to transfer to them sundry meetings within their own territories. This matter lasted over for several years, and in the interim, William Savery attended New York and New England Yearly Meetings in 1787, as well as several of the meetings within their limits. In 1789 he went again among the meetings of Pennsylvania and Maryland, the while a committee of Philadelphia Yearly Meeting was considering the petitions from Maryland and Virginia. The attitude of this committee was broad and statesmanlike. The whole Friendly situation, from Maryland to the Carolinas and Georgia, was reviewed with the result that in 1789 it was recommended that Warrington and Fairfax Quarterly Meetings be transferred to Maryland (now Baltimore) Yearly Meeting. A new committee of eleven Friends, headed by James Pemberton and William Savery, then thirty-eight years old, was appointed to aid in the transfer. In 1790 they reported the completion of the project and thereafter Maryland never appointed delegates to Philadelphia Yearly Meeting.

Another item of service to which William Savery was appointed with others in 1790 has a distinctly modern tone. A new militia law was before Congress, offering exemption to persons conscientiously refusing to serve, upon payment of $2.00 yearly toward defraying the expenses of civil government. The committee prepared an address, opposing the provision as inconsistent with a religious objection, "it being a fine in lieu of personal service,"—so early was the distinction recognized and the difficulty of pacific citizenship realized.

It was a continuance of the concern for the Southern Yearly Meetings that led William Savery again into the field the next year, 1791, in an extensive journey by sea, with Charleston, South Carolina, as the prime objective, but including other parts of the southern states as well. At Charleston he found only fifteen Friends. With a presage of his later work in Europe, he found most of his work among those of other denominations. His meetings were frequently held in Methodist or Baptist meeting-houses, of the crude frontier type, and in this way he came into close touch with the Evangelical movement, in the days of its early power. It is interesting to note, thus early in his experience, this willingness to coöperate with other denominations and to use their houses, a rare trait among Friends in those days. Two other aspects of this journey are of outstanding importance,—his melancholy sadness over and abhorrence of slavery and the evidently appreciated power of his preaching. In the degradation of the blacks he suffered much. He chose rather to expostulate with the hard-hearted masters than to leave them, as John Woolman had done, though he found little relish in food, over which an "unfeeling wretch" asked a blessing after having just before ordered a negro boy flogged till his back was raw and then salted. The next morning, as William

Savery stood musing in the doorway, he heard the lashing of a whip and pleading cries for mercy. He ran toward the sounds and found one negro lashing a boy of fourteen so unmercifully that the blood was already running to his heels. The feelings of the young Quaker, which had been "roused" the evening before, now carried him into action. Stepping between the boy, who was tied to a post with his toes barely touching the ground, and his assailant, he ordered him untied immediately. With some reluctance and astonishment this was done, whereupon William Savery betook himself to his host and in the face of "horrid execrations and threatenings upon all the Northern people" berated him unsparingly for his cruelty; so much so that a bystander with a muttered oath, declared he should be "popped over."

This incident in Beaufort County at the extreme southern tip of South Carolina, had its sequel the following day in the great droves of slaves, working in water to their waists, both men and women, practically naked, in the rice swamps. With gloomy sadness the Friends pressed on to Charleston, and the Journal gave a little forecast of the Civil War in the words:

"O Christianity and humanity, how are ye disgraced! Where will such astonishing horrible conduct end?"

It was, however, in the vast numbers that attended the meetings that he had his greatest and most humbling experience. This journey is the earliest of which we have a detailed account, and from his expressions it is probable that he appreciated for the first at this time the power of the ministry that had been entrusted to him. Time and again, to his "humbling admiration," large meetings were held and attended by people of all ranks and professions. At Augusta, Georgia, alone, were the efforts unsuccessful, and there the Friends' attitude on slavery and a dissipated group of pleasure seekers prevented the success of the meetings. At Mendenhall, Georgia, a meeting was held that evoked scenes similar to those of ancient Quakerism:

"A large number of Methodists and Baptists attended. Two women fell on their knees and trembled and shook and prayed and exhorted. I could scarcely account for such an extraordinary appearance, as they continued in these agitations some time after meeting broke up. Several wept and most of the people appeared serious. I stept in among them again and advised the women to stillness; and then thought I had a more favorable opportunity to speak to the people than before."

During this period William Savery's ministry was increasingly acceptable in Philadelphia. A refreshingly candid and intimate running comment on his ministerial activities is contained in the Journal and letters of Ann (Head) Warder, who accompanied her husband, John Warder, to Philadelphia from England in 1786. Although she never returned to England save for a year's visit, such was her expectation and for nearly three years she kept a Journal which was sent piecemeal to her mother and sister in England.

Soon after her arrival she heard of the death of her infant child, left behind in England, and it was to her in this sorrow that William Savery first appealed, although without then knowing her or her grief. She refers to him under date of Seventh Month 2, 1786, for the first time:

"I rejoiced in attending (meeting) partly on account of a minister, whom I thought, exceeded most I ever heard and my mind from affliction seemed humbled which no doubt was contributed by the comfort of his testimony which was long and eloquent."

The estimate thus casually given was never revised downward. In fact, the intimacy between William and Sarah Savery and John and Ann Warder lasted till the death of the minister and was of ever-increasing intensity. A fortnight after she first heard him preach, Ann Warder attended the Bank Meeting and William Savery "long addressed us in such a lively manner I scarce ever heard; indeed he is a wonderful man and though wrong to follow preachers, I would like to more frequently attend his meetings."

Ten days later, while visiting at Cousin Sukey Trotter's on Cable Lane, she met William Savery for the first time. Her narrative is interesting:

"William Savery, the Friend with whose ministry I am afraid of being too much captivated, was standing at his own door opposite. I expressed my great desire to have a little of his company, they called him over, when a short time convinced me he was a man whose conduct was consistent with his profession. He could not stay so long as we wished from a meeting appointment."

Of these meeting appointments, the minutes of his Monthly Meeting and of the Yearly Meeting bear mute testimony to this day. One of them of about this period appears in Elizabeth Drinker's pages, chronicling the meeting at her home of a committee, appointed to visit families, a kind of appointment, incidentally, never made in these days. She refers familiarly to the worthy Friends, then mostly young, as S. Emlen, S. Hopkins, Billy Savery, C. West and Caleb Cresson, Mar'gy Norton, H. Cathrall and R. Jones.

The daily entries of these two liberally educated and spritely women, Elizabeth Drinker and Ann Warder, are full of references to William Savery and of his varied activities. He was especially desired at weddings and was as frequently in service at funerals. Two other peculiar forms of service in which their pages show him to have been very active were the numerous Youths' meetings and the meetings held for the negroes. Ann Warder was young enough to qualify for the Youths' meetings and frequently refers to "my favorite, William Savery" and to his message, which, though short, "conveyed much affectionate love, sympathy and tenderness toward us all." Her lively account of the wedding of Elliston Perot and Hannah Sansom in 1787 finds William Savery at the meeting where he gave a long and fine testimony. Whether he attended the festivities thereafter does not appear, but the occasion was the more memorable because many of the gowns were "almost ruined" by black paint too recently applied to the scurting board, and the bride's brother, "Josie Sansom," covered himself with contumely and his sister's dress with wine and bitters, when a decanter slipped from his control. We will meet "Josie" again, later, in these pages.

In 1787 also occurred the death of William Savery, Sr., "a very hearty old man," as Ann Warder records, "out last Sixth Day at meeting in usual health, but struck with an apoplexy soon after."

On the last day of 1788 a funeral was to be held at Darby and the Warders essayed to go. After four miles of very bad roads to the Schuylkill bridge (probably Grey's Ferry) they found it was in too much danger of driving before the great cakes of ice that were sweeping down, to risk the crossing. The women consequently returned, but John Warder, being joined by William Savery, went across and they attended the funeral. Returning, they found their apprehensions justified, as the bridge had been swept away. They rode to several ferries in a vain attempt to find a safe crossing and after twenty miles' wandering at last got across and back to their homes.

Just at the close of this active decade of preparation we can glimpse a typical First Day program through Elizabeth Drinker's chronicle. She went to the Bank Meeting in the morning. William Savery opened it with prayer after which Samuel Emlen and he both appeared in testimony. In the afternoon, William Savery went to Chestnut Hill with "Daddy" (Henry Drinker) to a meeting which he had appointed, both returning home after dark.

During this period also, William Savery was evincing the power of influence over individuals, particularly young people, that became so conspicuous a part of his ministerial gift in later years. Isaac T. Hopper was one of the young men upon whom this influence was early exerted, the preaching of William Savery being recorded as "more powerful than all other agencies" in his spiritual experience. Quoting from "The Life of Isaac T. Hopper":

"* * * at evening meetings * * * the Spirit is said to have descended upon him (William Savery) and his hearers in such copious measure that they were reminded of the gathering of the apostles on the day of Pentecost. * * * He (Isaac Hopper) never forgot those refreshing meetings. To the end of his days, whenever anything reminded him of William Savery, he would utter a warm eulogium on his deep spirituality, his tender benevolence, his cheerful, genial temper, and the simple dignity of his deportment."

Another young man of totally different antecedents who felt this influence for good was Jacob Ritter. The slender little volume of his "Memoirs" introduces him as the son of poor German Lutheran parents. In spite of incipient conscientious scruples, he fought with the Continental army at Brandywine, at twenty years of age, and was captured by Hessians after Washington's defeat and lodged in the military prison at Philadelphia. Here, with 900 other prisoners, he survived, as many others did not, the atrocities perpetrated by the British in the infamous shambles that that prison became. Liberated most unexpectedly through some influence that he never fully understood, by the efforts of "a plain looking Friend," whose name he never learned, Jacob Ritter finally drifted into the Bank Meeting House one day, as the result of an impression that he should go there. Through manifold difficulties and after much persecution from his former Lutheran associates, he persisted in attending Friends' meetings and received much inward satisfaction therefrom.

"About this time," he records, "William Savery took notice of me; he would come and sit by me, when I was at work, and was a strength to me. I told him I now felt peace and believed I was safe. He said, 'Oh! Jacob, thy work is only pretty well begun yet, but keep in good heart, keep the faith.' "

Jacob Ritter soon after applied for membership in the Society of Friends. The committee appointed kept his case open for two years, visiting him a great many times, and sitting in silence with him.

"I told William Savery one day, 'I thought Friends were very slow.' He said, 'Never mind, Jacob, all is right enough: keep the patience, thou art just as well off as if thou wast a member.'"

He was finally admitted and in due season spoke a few words in German in meeting, after which he got away as soon as possible:

"One day I saw two young men getting into a gig, who laughed out loud and said, 'There goes the man that preached to us in Dutch.' So I felt discouraged, but William Savery came to see me and said, 'Jacob, thou preaches to us in Dutch; can'st thou not preach in English, we can't understand Dutch.' I said, 'My English is very imperfect.' He said, 'But thou can try, Jacob. I want thee next time to try and preach in English as well as thou can.' So the next time I sphoke as well as I coot, part Tutch and part English."

And so, in a continued round of meeting appointments and public and private service, the early years of William Savery's ministry passed and he ripened into the mature man, tender and affectionate in his bearing, eloquent and powerful in his delivery, and, withal, humbled in admiration at the results the Lord was accomplishing at his hands. His talents were soon destined to find occupation in wider fields of service.

## CHAPTER V

## BUSINESS LIFE

We have seen that William Savery returned from his seven years' apprenticeship in Chester County in 1771, at the age of twenty-one years. It may be presumed that he there became a master tanner, as he followed the calling the rest of his life. Jonathan Evans, who edited the Journal, says that he "settled in business in Philadelphia" in 1778. He must have been active before, however, as he purchased a tanyard on June 2, 1777, for £900, on "the old German-town great Road, leading from Delaware Front Street into the Liberties." The location of this yard was not far from the present Second Street and Girard Avenue, and also near the fabled site of Penn's Shackamaxon Treaty with the Indians. It fronted one hundred and thirty-three feet on Germantown Avenue and extended back to the modern Hancock Street. It was just north of Cohocksinck Creek, a forgotten stream that now flows in a great sewer, under the present tortuous Canal Street. The lot had a full complement of buildings and sunken vats, as they are mentioned in the deed. The brief of title, recorded with the deed, vividly recalls the British campaign of 1777 that ended in the occupation of Philadelphia that fall. It recites that "the records, being removed to Lancaster, the title could not be made," and, in fact, the deed itself was not recorded till 1785, after the troublous days were over.

The tanyard must have been a precarious possession. The British defeated Washington at Brandywine, on September 11, 1777, and entered Philadelphia soon after. They were attacked by Washington again at Germantown on October 4, and though they repulsed him, they were so thoroughly alarmed that their lines were drawn much closer to the City than previously. The Cohocksinck was bridged at Germantown Avenue, at that time, and William Savery's tanyard, hard by, must inevitably have been affected by the line of defense, described by Watson: [1]

> "While the British army occupied Philadelphia, in the years 1777 and '78, they dammed in all the Cohocksinc meadows, so as to lay them all under water from the river, and thus produced for themselves a water barrier of defense in connexion with their line of redoubts, across the northern end of the city. Their only road, and gate of ingress and egress northward, was at the head of Front Street, where it parts to Germantown, and by Kensington to Frankford."

"Front Street, where it parts to Germantown," was but little below Cohocksinck Creek, and the bridge-head, which was most sedulously guarded, was almost on William Savery's property. The tanyard may have been flooded during these operations, although there is no record save Watson's of the situation. John Hill's map of Philadelphia, dated 1796, clearly shows a slight eminence, above the meadows, at the site occupied by the tanyard, and it may have escaped the inundation. Be the facts what they were, William Savery undoubtedly lost interest in the locality very quickly. Its strategic importance and the military surroundings must have been very disquieting to him. On November 5, 1779, after holding title a trifle over two years, he conveyed the tract to another. The British had in the meantime evacuated Philadelphia on June 19, 1778, so military inconvenience could not have been the sole reason for the sale. The price for which the tanyard was sold is mentioned in the recorded deed as £15,000, superficially a neat wartime profit over the £900 paid in 1777. Once again our friend, Watson [2] dispels the illusion. Both

[1] *Annals*, I, 479.
[2] *Ibid.*, II, 299.

prices were quoted in Pennsylvania currency. During the dark days after Brandywine, Germantown and Valley Forge, "a fast trotting horse could not keep pace with its depreciation." Counting quotations of December, 1776, as par sterling, upon the basis of relative values, William Savery really bought his tanyard at £750 and sold it for £650.

The sale of the Cohocksinck tanyard did not interrupt the business of the proprietor. The site of the next venture is not determined, but it could not have been far distant from the first, as William Savery bought him a home in 1784, for £520, at No. 14 Cabel Lane. In olden time, the narrow thoroughfare that bore this intriguing name had been a rope walk, and from the usage the name was derived. It was one of several rope walks that flourished along the Philadelphia river front in early days. Cabel or Cable Lane ran north from Vine Street, east of and parallel to Second Street. It is today known as New Market Street. Just around the corner, running in from Front Street as a blind alley, was Brooks Court, with its famous pump and its more famous mistress, Rebecca Jones, the best beloved among the many beloved ministers of old North Meeting. The Meeting House itself stood hard by, in Keys Alley, now New Street, a dark, little, slum-ridden street, wide enough for only one vehicle. But that House was the center for as powerful a meeting as Philadelphia has ever produced. Over those narrow sidewalks came and went the plain groups of that generation, mighty for good in the aggregate,—interesting and lovable as individuals, and yet the place of their assemblage, today, knows them no more and their local influence has seeped and ebbed into nothingness. Rare, indeed, is the Friend of today who knows even the location of old Keys Alley Meeting House.

New Market Street, too, is a slum. Livery stables, garages and tenements face the cluttered street, where once shone the brick fronts and marble steps of the original Quaker householders. William Savery's house no longer stands. The site is now No. 310 New Market Street. Upon its seventeen feet front a four-story dwelling was erected about 1860. The sign of a Polish shoemaker is nowadays displayed from its first floor. Kayser's Alley runs alongside to a court in the rear, crowded with two story hovels, where was William Savery's garden for the last twenty years of his life.

From 1783, a series of apprentices entered William Savery's business and of these, George Baker, a young Irishman from Cork, and Thomas Sykes, of Upper Springfield Monthly Meeting, were the first. They both presented certificates from their meetings and were received into North Meeting, then recently established. George Baker returned to Ireland in the following spring. There seem to have been several such employees, both in William Savery's service and that of his parents. In 1797, when he visited Cork, he met the widow, Ann Harris, the mother of a certain Hannah Baker. She was

"exceeding glad to see me, having often heard me and my family mentioned, especially my dear Mother, whose attention to H. B. * * * she acknowledged."

At Youghall, another such acquaintance, John Mac-Donald, who "boarded a considerable time in the year 1786 at my Father's," met William Savery and sent kind remembrances to the Savery family in Philadelphia. He had probably been in the joining or cabinet work with the elder William Savery, and may have been partially responsible for some of the furniture turned out from his "Sign of the Chair." Thomas Sykes was afterwards to render his master signal service, in a time of trouble, as will appear later. In 1787 Timothy Abbot and in 1788 Clayton Gaskill, both of Upper Springfield Monthly Meeting, joined the tannery and North Meeting, so that, presumably, the business was increasing and its proprietor thriving.

A story that has gained much currency of late years, in connection with William Savery's business, is that of his dealing with a man who had stolen some hides from his tanyard. It originally appeared in a "Life of Isaac T. Hopper" and thereafter in Pike's "Historical Anecdotes," published at Nottingham, England, in 1880. In "A Book of Quaker Saints" and "The Child's Story Garden," both of recent publication, it appears again, though somewhat developed to add color and setting. In all the accounts the name of William Savery's wife is erroneously given as Mary, instead of Sarah, as it should have been. His mother's name was Mary.

The story is simple enough. Some hides having disappeared from the tanyard, William Savery suspected one of his shiftless, intemperate neighbors. He consequently advertised in the public prints that he had a sincere desire to be the friend of the thief, if he would reveal his identity, and that if poverty was the reason for his false step, that means would be found to give him honest employment. As a result, the suspected neighbor brought back the hides and through the gentle and affectionate efforts of William and Sarah Savery, gave up drinking. He entered William Savery's employ in the tanyard and was one of his trusted employees for many years. His identity was never revealed, nor did William Savery ever tell the story until long after the man's death. Even then he did so to point the moral of overcoming evil with good, rather than in the spirit of lauding his own action or that of his wife.

During a part of every year for a long time, William Savery was absent from home on religious service, and consequently away from his business. He resigned, in February, 1793, his position as one of the Overseers of the Friends' Public Schools, to which he had been elected just three years before. His release was requested and granted because, as stated upon the minutes of the Overseers, he apprehended

"that his other religious engagements are such as prevent him from devoting as an Overseer so much time and attention to the business of the Schools as the importance thereof requires."

It proved a well-timed exercise of discretion. His frequent absences in the years following would have rendered his membership purely perfunctory.

Reference has already been made to the extensive ministerial journeys in the early years, after 1779, when William Savery was twenty-nine years of age, including the labor in the meetings to the south, in the years following. In 1793, a period of over four months was consumed in attendance at the first Indian Treaty. In 1794 the second Treaty required two and a half months and soon after his return from that, William Savery set out on another journey to Virginia Yearly Meeting in company with Thomas Stewardson. In May, 1796, he left home for Europe and did not return until October, 1798, and thereafter until his death in 1804 he was frequently away under like service.

It is from the busy pen of Elizabeth Drinker that we learn that William Savery had a partner in his business. Under date, July 30, 1796, slightly more than two months after he had sailed for England, she records:

"Tho's Stewardson called on H. D. to go out with him on William Savery's business, his partner being lately deceased."

This intelligence did not reach William Savery until he received Philadelphia letters on October 31, in Germany. He wrote:

"* * * contained the acc$^t$ of my Partner, C. Rosin's death, the —— which excercisd me much and my mind was very heavy, being sensible it must bring an increased burden upon my dear Sally & my other friends."

Distance and the impossibility of doing anything evidently solaced William Savery's mind. He makes very rare references to his business in the score or more letters still extant, written from Europe. The first hint of concern in them occurs at the end of a long letter of July 19, 1797, to his wife, several months after he had the news of his partner's death, in which he says:

"With respect to my business, I can say but little, I hardly dare give myself liberty to think of it, but I rest in confidence that if I am permitted to return, Providence will kindly point out a mode of obtaining all I want (the necessarys of life) either in that line or some other. Friends in Europe are kind and I hope, I have money enough with me to carry me through, and I beg, my Dear, thee may want for nothing—all we have is thine."

It would seem, however, from these letters, that Sarah Savery took little concern for the business, as she seems to have spent most of her time during her husband's absence away from Philadelphia, much of it being spent at her old home in Bradford Township, Chester County. She also abode at times with Thomas Savery, her brother-in-law, at whose home Richard Jordon and Mary Pryor, itinerant ministers, met her when in Philadelphia. Her apathy seems almost heartless, from the homesick, yet tender tone of William Savery's letters to her. He hoped she might "be made equally comfortable by resuming our house again," or at another time, "I have requested thee, my dear, in more than one letter to resume our house, before the next Yearly Meeting at Philadelphia and I would not have thee neglect it," and still later, he hoped his continued absence "may not hinder thy getting into our house as before requested."

He had, however, faithful friends in the emergency. He wrote several letters to Henry Drinker and Thomas Stewardson on business, though the contents are not available today. In a letter to his wife, dated August 11, 1797, he wrote:

"Thee says nothing, my dear, about the Tanyard, neither can I say anything, only express a hope, that T. Sykes and all my friends who have kindly interested themselves about it, may be so good as to continue some attention towards it a little longer—my love to them all."

There can hardly be any doubt that "T. Sᴋes" is the apprentice lad of 1783, now perhaps independently established but with evident good-will toward his former master.

Once again, in a letter dated October 4, 1797, from Edinburgh, he refers specifically to the Friends:

"When I give way to thinking of my business and the Burthen the present state of it must lay upon thee, my Dear, upon T. Sykes, T. Stewardson, H. Drinker, T. Savery & other friends, I feel much anxiety to be at home. Give my dear love to them all that are concerned for me. I hope I shall not trespass on their patience much longer."

William Savery, Sr., died in 1787, possessed of what would then have been considered an ample estate. In 1780 he had been assessed an annual tax of £149/16/6 on a property value of $46,000, and he probably increased this in the years following. His widow survived him longer than his son, William, Jr., and to her the bulk of his estate was left, but his four children inherited small amounts at his death in 1787.

It is impossible to tell just how much William Savery's travels drew upon his own resources. At the beginning of his journey, his passage to England was paid by the Yearly Meeting, as Elizabeth Drinker recorded, under date of May 14, 1796:

"Philip Atkins, master of the ship, Sussex, for Liverpool, was here this evening. H. D. paid him 210 pounds, equal to 120 guineas, for the passages of Sam'l Emlen, William Savery, Deb. Darby, Reb. Young, Phoebe Speakman and Sarah Talbot, H. D. being treasurer of the Yearly Meeting."

This reference, with the prior quotation as to the kindness of Friends in Europe, would indicate that the major portion of his expenses was borne by the Society. On the other hand, he stated in London Yearly Meeting of 1798, that he had spent over 100 guineas of his own money, in traveling on the Continent, in Gospel service.

William Savery in 1790 was forty years old and at his full maturity. A description of his personal appearance at this time, when broader fields of service were opening before him, will be of interest:

"He was in person about five feet nine or ten inches in height, was of firm make, and for one inclining to corpulency, had a good figure. His features were comly, and although his complexion was not fair, it was good and healthy. The expression of his face was usually placid, and when he was sitting in silence, in meeting or the social circle, it was dignified and sedate. But when in conversation, his countenance would often suddenly brighten up, and a smile, the most benignant and attractive would play over it."

Among the papers of John Parrish, preserved by the Historical Society of Pennsylvania, is a lock of chestnut brown hair, still bright and glossy, attached to an acrostic, in eulogy of William Savery, whose hair it was.

## CHAPTER VI

# THE INDIANS AND THE UNITED STATES

The close of great international struggles always presents problems of reconstruction and rehabilitation that last for years, but the results of which, in the light of history, look comparatively simple, so thoroughly does the event obscure the process. In the actual experience, situations seem insoluble to the participants; to the next generation, when history records not only the question but the answer, the whole seems easy, if not automatic in the outcome. Too often, events are the result of circumstance, swept by the passions engendered in the strife, and but slightly subject to intelligent guidance or righteous inclination.

Such was the case with the Indians and Indian affairs after the French and Indian and the Revolutionary wars. The main combatants settled their differences without much regard for their savage allies, and after each the victor had to settle minor wars with the Indians, regarding territory, over which the Indians claimed rights superior to either main belligerent.

The Society of Friends was gravely concerned over these side issues that so closely involved the Indians. The details of this concern will appear in later chapters, but to understand them a brief résumé of Indian history is essential.

From the earliest times the French colonial schemes had followed the St. Lawrence, the Great Lakes and the Mississippi. The British had occupied the Atlantic seaboard, west to the Alleghenies. After the French and Indian War, by the treaty of Paris of 1763, France ceded all her American territory to England, including such grants

[ 50 ]

as she had obtained from the Indians, throughout the whole extent. To confirm titles to these, came the inevitable Indian wars, ending for the nonce, in the great Treaty of Fort Schuyler or Fort Stanwix of 1768, whereby the Iroquois, or Six Nations, then defeated, ceded to the British all land south of the Ohio. At this Treaty, the Indians probably realized for the first, the insatiable land hunger of the whites. The Treaty became a classic among them and is more referred to than any other in their history.

After the Revolution, the British claims on the Indian territory south of the Lakes were surrendered to the new United States. Little trouble was experienced from the Iroquois in New York State. They were composed of the six tribes or nations,—the Senecas, the Mohawks, the Oneidas, the Onondagas, the Cayugas and the Tuscaroras, all of whom, save the Mohawks, had sided with the Colonies in their struggle. The exception, however, was noteworthy, as the Mohawks were led by Thayendanegea, better known as Joseph Brant, probably the ablest Indian that ever lived, both as warrior and statesman. He was reputed to be the half-breed son of Sir William Johnson; had been well educated and had, at various times, held secretarial positions of importance. With all these, he was an Indian in his appearance, his thought and his viewpoint. To him is to be ascribed the aspiration toward an Indian Federation, binding together all the Indian tribes of North America, an ideal that took strong hold of the leaders of Indian thought at the time, but which proved ephemeral, due largely to the pettiness of inter-tribal jealousies. Brant was a captain in the British army during the Revolution, was well acquainted with all the leading British officers and to the end of his life kept up a large correspondence with many of them. He was the leader in the massacres of Wyoming and the Minisink, and thus contributed two of the bloodiest incidents in American history.

Brant was in constant touch, after the Revolution, with the chiefs of the tribes, north and west of the Ohio. The Miamis, Delawares, Shawanese, Ottawas and Wyandots, who occupied these regions, recognized no grants or treaties of any kind that had to do with their territory. Covering all of the present states of Ohio, Illinois, Indiana and Michigan, this "Northwest Territory" was the most attractive and at the same time the most dangerous frontier open to the new nation. It was from the Ohio River that the hostile tribes determined to make their stand against white encroachment, and Brant's idea of a Federation of Indian Tribes was a nucleus around which the Indian opposition crystallized.

Under the Articles of Confederation affairs went badly between the United States and the Indians. Congress lacked power in this as in many other regards and the States dealt with the Indian difficulties as local interests and prejudices dictated.

Many attempts at harmony were made and a number of treaties were held. The chief difficulty with these was that the attempt to settle with tribes by payment of money (William Penn's old method, now no longer available, as we shall see) succeeded so long as one tribe received money for lands claimed by another; it being almost impossible to convene enough tribes in one place at the same time to effect anything like a general treaty. This feature led to continuous disavowal of treaties, made with every evidence of sincerity, but with some tribe claiming rights, not present, or perhaps represented by inferior sachems only. Congress was also handicapped by its own inconsistency in recognizing the tribes as sovereign bodies and treating with them, while it at the same time claimed that all title to their lands had been forfeited by their adherence to the British side in the Revolution. The difference was really one of practice rather than theory, and the main object was to remove the Indian menace to the westward migration of the white men, whether by treaty or by force.

In 1784, a second Treaty was made with the Iroquois at Fort Stanwix, whereby they ceded to the United States all their claim to lands in Ohio, Indiana and Illinois. Shortly after similar treaties were effected at Fort McIntosh with the Wyandots, Delawares and Chippewas and in 1786, at Fort Finney, with the Shawanese. There still remained the Kickapoos, Pottawattamies, Miamis, Weas and Eel River tribes who would make no treaties and who declared the Ohio River the boundary between the Long Knives and the Red Men, beyond which no white man should ever settle with impunity.

By the end of 1790 it was pretty generally acknowledged that desultory Indian warfare was raging upon most of the northwestern frontier. In true Indian fashion, the hostile tribes struck here and there, with no plan or design, and it became impossible to foretell which community would next feel the weight of savage ferocity.

In the summer of 1790, General Harmar went down the Ohio to Losantiville. His scouts, returning to him, gave such alarming reports of the Indian temper that he at once returned to Cincinnati to organize resistance. By October he had mustered a force of regulars and militia and set forth with 1,453 men to attack the Maumee villages. The force was a ridiculous agglomeration of squabbling, jealous officers and undisciplined men. The net result was the destruction of some Indian corn, the burning of five Indian villages and the death of about twenty Indians. The return of the so-called "army" was little short of a rout. But most disastrous of all, the Indian tribes on the Wabash River were aroused to a pitch of fury that brooked no defense in their revenge. The Indians made their chief attack on the village of Big Bottom, a small settlement on the Muskingum River in Ohio, and wiped it out. The effect on neighboring settlements at Marietta and Belle

Prairie (now Belpre) was instantaneous, through the desertion of most of their inhabitants.

The President's message to Congress in December, 1790, gravely noted the Indian troubles but the only action taken was of a military kind. In the spring of 1791 General St. Clair started a string of forts from Cincinnati to the site of the modern Fort Wayne, Indiana. Only three were actually completed by November when the force, reduced by desertion, sickness and starvation, was attacked on a branch of the Wabash River by an inferior force of Indians under the same great war chief, Joseph Brant or Thayendanegea, and driven pell-mell back to Fort Jefferson with the loss of over half their men. The Indian atrocities, following the defeat, were as terrible as any recorded in Indian warfare, and the victory was the most crushing ever won by the Indians.

The stir in Administration circles was tremendous. President Washington's wrath descended upon St. Clair, in common with that of the public as a whole and the old General resigned. Washington put General Anthony Wayne at the head of the United States forces and Congress began an endless discussion of a Bill for the Protection of Frontiers. In Philadelphia and the East generally, there was strong sentiment in favor of abandoning the whole miserable Indian business. There was land enough and to spare for generations to come, and, said they, the future of the country lay in overseas commerce rather than in western prairie lands. The frontier Congressmen, however, dilated upon the undoubted treachery of the Miamis and the cowardice of deserting the frontiersmen who had moved into the Ohio territory in entire good faith.

As usual, a modification of both views prevailed. The military preparations went forward unabated, but a fairer appreciation of Indian rights became noticeable in the public attitude and discussion. In December of 1790, after Harmar's disastrous defeat, as noted above, the Cornplanter, the principal chief of the Senecas, came to Philadelphia in the interests of peace. Probably no chief of the time was better known to Friends or more acceptable to them. At the solicitation of Washington's Administration, he was induced to go with Colonel Proctor of the Indian Department on a mission first to the Six Nations (of which the Senecas were one) and then to the Miami country in northwestern Ohio. Through their efforts a council of the Six Nations was successfully held at Painted Post, in southern New York, by Colonel Pickering in June, 1791, largely to hold the Mohawks, who alone of the Six Nations were hostile to the Americans, in line for peaceful negotiations. From there Proctor and the Cornplanter pushed on to Buffalo Creek (Buffalo) to a Council headed by Red Jacket, a Chief of the Senecas, only to find that Brant, of the Mohawks, had gone west a few days before of his own initiative to sound out the Miami chiefs before meeting the Americans. In his absence, Fish-carrier, the leading chief of the Cayugas and Brant's right-hand man, refused to treat and openly disapproved of the Cornplanter's mission. Proctor insisted on following Brant to the Miami country and requested permission of Colonel Gordon, of the British army, to charter a vessel for the purpose. In view of Brant's expressed threat that any white man following him would be put to death, Colonel Gordon, who was one of the few British officers sincerely desirous of peace between the Indians and the United States, peremptorily refused the request, and Proctor had no alternative but to return home.

Another attempt to effect peace by negotiation at this time is worthy of mention, although it did not succeed. Colonel Pickering next tried to persuade Captain Hendrick Aupamut, of the Muhheconnuck or Stockbridge Indians, to undertake a mission to the Miami country in the interests of peace. This too came to naught. Aupamut is undoubtedly the man who afterwards wrote the Friends in

Philadelphia and to whom they referred as "Captain Hendricks."

It cannot be doubted that the jealousy and enmity of the British officers along the Great Lakes was the chief cause of the failure of peaceful negotiations. From the correspondence of some of these, now published, it is possible to realize the hopelessness of the attempts at peace, while the United States, on the one hand, continued its active preparation for a renewal of the war, and the British officers, on the other, furnished an unfailing supply of munitions to the Indians and actively inflamed them with reports of American duplicity. There are strong indications that this course was inspired from London, in the hope that the territory between the Ohio and the Great Lakes, from which the British, in spite of treaty obligations, had not yet entirely removed, might still be retained under a British protectorate of the Indian inhabitants, provided the latter were successful in their resistance.

Though this phase of the matter was not unknown to the Administration, it seems likely that all the preliminary dealings in the years 1790-1793 were undertaken in all sincerity by it. Washington wrote Lafayette in August, 1790,

"The basis of our proceedings with the Indian nations has been, and shall be, *justice*, during the period in which I have anything to do with the administration of this government."

The caliber of the Commissioners whom Washington chose, and the record of their actions and speeches when in that service, all bear out the impression that peace failed largely because of the duplicity of Governor Simcoe, of the Canadian Government, and of active emissaries of the type of Simon Girty and Colonel McKee, both of whom were Tory refugees of the Revolutionary period, who harbored bitter hatred against their quondam country. From this list, as has been already stated, should be excepted Colonel

Gordon of the British post at Fort Erie, who was at all times a consistent friend of peace.

Following Proctor's failure to negotiate peace through the mediation of Cornplanter and Aupamut, Colonel Pickering pressed the invitation which he had extended to the chiefs of the Six Nations in June, 1791, to hold a council in Philadelphia. Brant, the most important and most elusive of these chiefs, had not been present at Painted Post when the invitation was given and yet was essential to the success of the proposal. Elaborate efforts were put forth to assure his attendance. After extended and flattering correspondence, chiefly bearing upon the dignity of the escort and reception that would be accorded him, the wily chief accepted, but did not actually arrive until June 20, 1792.

Meanwhile the main Council had been held with fifty sachems of the Iroquois present in Philadelphia from March 13 till the end of April. It is of participants in this Council that Elizabeth Drinker wrote in her Diary:

"March 14 1792,—Near 50 Indians, chiefs from six nations, arriv'd in town this afternoon, escorted by ye militia with Drum & fifes."

A week later she records the death of one of the chiefs and his burial, "with great parade." The pomp and ceremony with which the Administration greeted and entertained the visiting chiefs was in line with the promises to Brant and in contrast with the usual method of receiving visiting Indians. It was no unusual thing for bands of red men to visit Philadelphia, to meet the "Great Father" and to see the metropolis, but their accommodations were usually of the crudest. The dusty cavalcades of horsemen usually arrived with squaws, papooses, tepees and other camp material on pole drags, and always in charge of military escorts to assure peaceable intentions to the countryside.

Again on April 4, 1792, Elizabeth Drinker writes:

"We had 20 persons to dine with us besides our own family, Isaac Zane and his daughter, Sally, John Parish, W. Savery, Ben Wilson, 13 Indians and 2 interpreters. They dined in ye back parlor and had a talk after dinner in the garden; went away about 5 o'clock."

These small incidents would indicate that Friends were fully alive to the situation and were the close confidants of the sachems.

The six weeks of negotiation resulted favorably. The Six Nations being friendly, after elaborate discussion, agreed to send a delegation on a pacific mission to the hostile Indians in the Miami country (Ohio and Indiana) to explain the attitude and purposes of the United States.

Their departure was delayed until mid-September, 1792. In the meantime Brant's visit to Philadelphia had been made and he had been induced to become a part of the pacific mission. In justice to him be it said, that he at all times declared himself "for the interests of His Majesty and the credit of my nation," and later wrote his friend, Colonel McKee, that he had small hope of peace as the hostile Indians were flushed with two victories, suspicious of the unceasing military preparations of the United States and no other terms were being offered to them than those which they had already rejected.

A Grand Council was held at the Au Glaize, on the Miami River, near Lake Erie in the autumn. The Cornplanter, with forty-eight chiefs of the Six Nations and fifty Mohawk chiefs and warriors were present, but Brant (of the Mohawks) was ill and unable to attend. The western Indians were in a decidedly hostile mood. They flaunted the declaration that the United States "solemnly disclaimed any design of taking a foot more than had been ceded in the Treaty of Muskingum in 1789," by stating that Duintate, the chief who had negotiated that treaty was dead and had always declared that he had been imposed upon

[ 58 ]

and did not know that the cession of the country was involved in it.

The Shawanese were resolute for war and taunted the
Six Nations for having first proposed a great confederacy
and now having come to Council "with the voice of the
United States folded under their arm." Red Jacket of
the Senecas replied and better counsels prevailed so far as
to agree upon a suspension of hostilities for the winter of
1792-1793, and the holding of a Council with the United
States the following spring. These conclusions were based
upon the proviso that the United States should withdraw
its troops from west of the Ohio and that the Ohio should
be conceded as the boundary as fundamental in any negotiations. It is important that these features be stated
clearly, as they color all the subsequent affairs and lend a
consistency to the action of the Indians that does not appear
unless they are understood.

Upon their return, the Six Nations convened in council
at Buffalo and wrote President Washington:

"You sent us to the Westward, with a message of peace to the
hostile Indians.

"We proceeded accordingly to your directions, and was protected,
going and coming by the Great Spirit.

"We give thanks to the Great Spirit that we have all returned
safe to our seats.

"While we was at the westward, we exerted ourselves to bring
about peace. The fatigues we underwent are not small. Now it is
our desire for your people on the Ohio to lay down their arms, or
otherwise it is all in vain what we have done.

"Now if you wish for peace you must make every exertion, and
proceed through this path we have directed for you. If peace does
not take place, the fault must arise from your people.

"Now we desire you, Brothers, to send forward agents, who are
men of honesty, not proud land-jobbers, but men who love and
desire peace. Also, we desire they may be accompanied by some
Friend, or Quaker to attend the council.

"Wish you to exert yourself to forward the message to the Western
Indians as soon as possible; and we are taken by the hand, and have

agreed, next Spring, to attend the Council at the Rapids of Miami, when we shall hear all that takes place there."

To this, Washington replied evasively. In sooth, he could hardly do otherwise, in view of the apparent incompatability of the Indian demands and the acknowledged aims of the American Government. His effort was lost, however, on the Indians, who replied reaffirming their stand that they would listen to no proposals not based upon the Ohio as the boundary and the removal of the American forts from the Indian territory, and as a further precaution, that they would hold a private conference at Miami Rapids before meeting the American Commissioners at Sandusky, and would not meet them at all, unless clothed with authority to accept the terms thus prescribed.

It was to this Conference that the Meeting for Sufferings sent John Parrish, William Savery and John Elliott of Philadelphia, Jacob Lindley of Chester County and Joseph Moore and William Hartshorne of New Jersey all of whom traveled under individual concern and with minutes from their respective Monthly Meetings.

Washington chose Colonel Timothy Pickering, General Benjamin Lincoln and Beverly Randolph. As after events proved, these were men of sane and patient temperaments, well versed in Indian ways and dilatoriness, and sincerely desirous of peace. They went forth on an impossible mission, but their failure cannot be laid to their door as circumstances beyond their control and beyond that of their Quaker companions had gone too far to allow a peaceful adjustment.

## CHAPTER VII

# THE FRIENDS AND THE INDIANS

We have already seen that the French and Indian War of 1756 ended Quaker participation in governmental affairs. It also inaugurated a series of sporadic and desultory wars that did not yield to the treaties of the greater powers involved, but smoldered on in frontier raids and reprisals.

While Friends had washed their hands of government, they could by no means absolve themselves from the consequences of the changed circumstances. In fact, there is little of credit to the Society of Friends in this attitude of withdrawal and of shirking responsibility under stress of acute situations. The incident is one of the most important in that period of Quaker history that is mostly marked by negation and introspection. The adoption by the de-Quakerized government of an active policy of military repression must have struck Friends with little short of dismay. The Quaker Peace, based upon a policy as old as the Colony, was actually over. The Government had a policy, a military one, but the Friends had none, and worse still, there was very little constructive leadership in the Society looking toward any definite policy. From 1756 till the close of the century all the concern for Indian work fell upon individuals. There is much upon the minutes of the Yearly Meeting on the subject but beyond memorials to Congress and the President, the concern for Indian work consisted almost exclusively of preaching or of such material aid as was possible through the frequent visits of the Indians to Philadelphia, while it was the national Capital.

An exception to the drifting policy resulted from the activities of "The Friendly Association for Regaining and Preserving Peace with the Indians by Pacific Measures." It is impossible to understand the Indian relations of Philadelphia Friends for the latter half of the eighteenth century without reference to its activities. It was largely the conception of Israel Pemberton, that doughty and aggressive pacifist whose wealth and social position made him not only a bulwark for the Society of Friends but a prime target for all its enemies. The Seven Years War, or the French and Indian War, as it was called in America, had given opportunity to the French to alienate the Delaware and Shawanese Indians, formerly the particular friends of William Penn, from the British interest. Injustices from the Proprietaries (the Penn heirs) began with the infamous Walking Purchase of 1737. Thereafter the land hunger of the whites brooked no longer the slow process of barter and payment for territory and the Governors of Pennsylvania, representing the Penns absent in England, lent themselves frequently to nefarious schemes that rankled more and more in the savage breasts of the retreating redmen.

The Yearly Meeting of 1756 had refused to consider any official interference with "public affairs" and as a result, the Friendly Association was organized on November 2, 1756,—the first of a long line of ably conducted volunteer associations, that, until the present day, have exerted Quaker influence upon public affairs when the Society officially lagged behind. A mass meeting of Friends was called at the Great Meeting House. Among the eighty contributors and organizers was William Savery, Sr., who remained an active supporter for several years after.

William Denny was then Governor, and though he too was associated with the predatory interests of the Proprietaries, things went better than under his predecessor, Governor Morris. It is also interesting to find members of the German pacifist sect of Swingfelders (Schwenkfelders) coöperating with the Friends as did the Mennonists and Brethren during the Great War. Athwart the policy of aggression, Israel Pemberton and his colleagues threw themselves with all their weight of religious, legislative, economic and social prestige,—elements of no mean consequence in a Province predominantly Quaker in faith and attitude.

The importance of the Friendly Association, in the life of William Savery, Jr., then six years old, lies in its method of working on a delicate and serious problem. In fact, this Association was the training school for the later group of Indian workers.

Large sums of money were raised annually and spent by the Trustees of the Friendly Association in presents for the Indians and for expenses of delegations in attending Treaties at Easton and Reading. At one time Israel Pemberton dispatched a messenger on a pacific errand to Fort Duquesne, now Pittsburgh, with £2,000 worth of presents, a contribution largely from his own pocket. Another element evident in the work at this time as well as in that of the later Quaker ambassadors was its entire detachment from the national interest. How complete this detachment of interest was, is evident from an interchange of communications between Governor Denny and the Friendly Association. On July 11, 1757, Governor Denny wrote:

"Gentlemen:—The Proprietaries have acquainted me that the Earl of Halifax has communicated to them, with strong expressions of dissatisfaction, a treaty held with the Indians at Philadelphia, by the people called Quakers, which his Lordship was pleased to think the most extraordinary procedure he had ever seen in persons who are on the same footing only with all others of the King's private subjects, to presume to treat with Foreign Princes; and further, as the suffering any one part of the King's subjects, whether of a different profession of religion, or however else distinguished, to treat or act as mediators between a Province in which they live and any independent people is the highest invasion of his Majesty's Prerogative Royal and of the worst consequence."

The letter then concluded by forbidding presents to the Indians, and stating:

"It would be prudent to decline going in a body, your attendance at treaties as a distinct Society, having given great offence to the ministry."

Perhaps no more courageous paper ever emanated from members of the Society of Friends than the following answer, dated Seventh Month 14th, just three days later:

"We apprehend our duty to God and the King have engaged us in this business: and some of the good effects thereof have already appeared. * * * The business to be transacted there is of so much consequence to the lives, liberties and properties of the people of this Province that should we omit to attend there and depend upon the Governor and the King's agent receiving all the information on this important occasion from the Proprietaries' agents and others, who have for some years past been concerned in transacting Indian affairs, we should be deficient in our duty as Christians and Englishmen,—denominations we hold more dear to us than any other titles or appellations whatsoever."

This bold defiance was followed by another interchange of letters showing increased acrimony on the Governor's part and a courteous but firm insistence by the Friends. As a result, some of the Friends attended the Treaty and some of their presents were sold to the Commissioners to be given to the Indians at that time.

As the war drew to a close, its chief operations against the Indians were shifted to the Mohawk Valley, far away from Philadelphia. The Friendly Association gradually dissolved about 1764. The Treaty of Fort Stanwix, in 1768, ended for the time being Indian depredations, especially with French backing. In it, the defeated Indians were completely outdone, and in the next few years they turned repeatedly to the Quakers as the only whites in whom they retained confidence.

# THE FRIENDS AND THE INDIANS

The American Revolution happily, did not involve the Indians in the same active participation that had marked prior warfare among the whites. The Indian problem did not become very acute again until after the establishment of the Federal Government and the beginning of the great emigration into the Northwest Territory. Consequently, it was not until about 1790 that the seriousness of the Indian affairs on the frontier began to affect Philadelphia Yearly Meeting in earnest and in a corporate capacity. The problem involved not only the Indian tribes but the smoldering jealousies between the British and the Americans as an aftermath of the Revolution. Each was entirely willing to fan any latent trouble on the other's frontier into activity. Time and again in the negotiations of 1793 and 1794 the Indian sachems sarcastically reminded the American Commissioners that they had much to explain in the Fort Stanwix conclusions and that the best earnest of sincerity in the Indian dealings would be a cordial attitude toward the British, inasmuch as they were told that the chain of friendship between England and the United States had been brightened and all rusty spots removed.

The near-policy of the Yearly Meeting about this time seems to have been an amplification of Penn's policy of purchase of land. In reality, as we have seen, the French and Indian War and King Philip's War, followed by the Treaty of Fort Stanwix, rendered that policy archaic. Thenceforth the difficulty lay, not so much in terms for the purchase of territory, as in persuading the Indians even to consider such sales. The purchase of Manhattan by the Dutch and that of Pennsylvania by Penn for a few baubles were no longer analogies, in view of the ever increasing pressure of the white emigration. This change of circumstance was a disconcerting element to the Friends in adopting a policy. It really deprived them of any very effective plan, save the hope, as Jonathan Evans expressed it:

[ 65 ]

"that they might be instrumental in calming the minds of the natives, and in inducing both parties to accede to such reasonable propositions as might facilitate the settlement of the subjects in dispute, stay the effusion of blood, and restore amicable relations."

It was at best a difficult situation. For the whites, the land was an essential; for the Indians, resistance to the tide was the only salvation, and for the Friends there was the unwelcome task of intermediation in a situation that no longer lent itself to the old panacea of purchase. As we shall see, the first attempt, in 1793, resulted in a deadlock and the second, in 1794, in a peace that recognized boundaries resulting from conquest, rather than consent, and then only with the Six Nations which, of all the Indian tribes, were the most friendly to the United States. Even to this peace, the Friends declined to be parties, and refused to sign the Treaty, though earnestly requested so to do, because it confirmed the right of the United States to large tracts of land obtained by conquest, without making the Indians what Friends deemed adequate and just compensation for it. Of these Treaties we shall learn in detail in the following chapters.

## CHAPTER VIII

# THE ATTEMPTED INDIAN TREATY OF 1793

While affairs on the part of the National government were taking the course already narrated, the Friends were by no means apathetic to the general crisis. In 1792 there were conferences between the Friends and the Indian chiefs in Philadelphia and the subject was constantly before the Meeting for Sufferings. The latter body that same year addressed a Memorial to the President and Congress, then both in Philadelphia, recommending such just and pacific measures as might arrest the devastating border wars and establish peace upon a firm basis. This sentiment was entirely in accord with that of many citizens, but lacked concrete suggestions of a practical character.

In February, 1793, word reached the Meeting for Sufferings that a Treaty was to be held the following fall at Sandusky, on the southern shore of Lake Erie, now in the State of Ohio. From the Western Country came messages from Captain Hendricks, a justly celebrated Chief of the Stockbridge or Muhheconnuck Indians, who in 1785 had removed from Massachusetts and become a part of the Oneidas, and his two brothers and a letter from Hopackon, a Sachem of the Delawares, anxiously desiring Friends to attend the Treaty, and in confirmation, sending three strings of white wampum. It is regrettable that the letters and the wampum were not carefully preserved among the archives of the venerable Meeting for Sufferings.

The service requested was of peculiar danger, not only from the hardship of the journey, but even more from the uncertainty of life in the event of unsuccessful negotiations.

It was a call requiring a rare degree of consecration and much physical endurance, as well as close appreciation of the Indian temperament and nature.

Five Friends volunteered for the arduous undertaking, namely, John Parrish, William Savery, John Elliott, Jacob Lindley, Joseph Moore and William Hartshorne. They fared forth on May 3, 1793. They bore with them a letter of introduction from the Meeting for Sufferings, the representative body of Philadelphia Yearly Meeting. In its appreciation of Indian allegory and figurative speech, it is probably unique among the staid epistles issued by that body. For that reason, it follows in full.

"*To the Indians living on the North-Western and Western borders of the United States, and all others whom this writing may concern:*

"BROTHERS,

"Hearken to the speech which your friends called Quakers, assembled in Philadelphia, from several parts of Pennsylvania, New Jersey, &c., now send to you by their brethren, John Parrish, William Savery, John Elliott, Jacob Lindley, Joseph Moore, and William Hartshorne.

"Brothers,—When our grandfathers came with Onas over the great waters to settle in this land, more than one hundred years ago, they kindled a large council fire with your grandfathers, and sat together around it in much good-will and friendship, smoking the calumet pipe together; and they told your grandfathers that they were men of peace, and desired to live among you in peace and love, and that their children might also be careful always to live in the same love one with another, as brothers of the same family.

"This council fire was kept burning with a clear flame many years, which gave a good light to all around the country, and the chain of friendship which was made at the same time, was kept clean from rust by our fathers and your fathers; until about forty years ago, an evil spirit whispered bad stories in the ears of some of your people and of some of the white people, so that the light of the ancient council fire was almost put out, and the old chain of friendship was made dull and rusty.

"Brothers,—Our grandfathers told your grandfathers, that the Great and Good Spirit who made them and all people, with a design that they might live on this earth for a few years, in love and good-will one toward another, had placed his law in the hearts of all men, and if they carefully attended to its inward voice, it would keep them in love and friendship, and teach them to shun everything that would occasion them to trouble and hurt one another.

"Brothers,—Do you not find that after you have been angry and quarrelsome, or done any bad action, you are made uneasy and sorrowful; and that when you are sober and serious, and do good actions, your minds feel pleasant, easy, and comfortable? It is the law from the Good Spirit, who is all love, and who placed it in your hearts, which gives you such peace and comfort when you do well, but when you do evil things, it reproves you and makes you feel uneasy and sad.

"Brothers,—We wish you to consider and remember, that the Great Spirit sees and knows all the thoughts of your hearts, and of the hearts of all mankind, and all their actions. And when their bodies die, such men of all colors and all nations, who have loved, served and obeyed the holy law of the Good Spirit, placed in their hearts, He will receive their souls, which are never to die, and they will live with Him in joy and peace for ever: but the souls of bad men who have lived wickedly in this world, must live, after their bodies die, with the bad Spirit in a state of distress and misery.

"Brothers,—We make profession of the same principles with our grandfathers, which teach us to love you and all men; and in that love we feel our minds drawn to send you this speech, with a great desire for your good.—We were made glad when we heard that the sober, good people among you were disposed to promote peace and brighten the old chain of friendship, with the white people of the United States; and that many of you have a desire that you may be instructed in tilling the ground, and to live after the manner of the white people, which we believe you will find to be more comfortable for you and your families, than to live only by hunting; and we think it will also be good for your young people to be learned to read and write, and that sober, honest, good men should be sent among you for teachers.

"Brothers,—We have often told some of your chiefs when we have had the opportunity of taking them by the hand in this city, that we are not concerned in the management of the affairs of government, which are under the direction of the President of the United States, and his counsellors, but that we should, at all times, be willing to do anything in our power to promote love and peace.

'Brothers,—We greatly desire that the commissioners who are

now sent by the President, and also your counsellors and chiefs, may look up to the Great Spirit for his wisdom and help, that you may all be made wise and strong to light up the council fire, and brighten the chain of old friendship, that all things may be settled to satisfaction, and a lasting peace established, so that there may be no more difference or war between your people and the inhabitants of these States.

"We desire you may receive our friends, by whom we send this writing, in love, as brothers who are disposed to encourage you in all good things.—And, in the ancient love which our grandfathers felt for each other, we salute you, wishing you happiness in this life, and that which is to come, and remain your friends and brothers.

"Signed by forty-four Friends.

*"Philadelphia, fourth month* 19*th,* 1793."

Washington's instructions to Jefferson, then Secretary of State, are interesting from a public standpoint. He wrote on March 22, 1793:

"As it has been suggested to me that the Society of Quakers are desirous of sending a deputation of their body to be present at the aforesaid treaty, which, if done with pure motives, may be the means of facilitating the good work of a peace, you will consider how far, if they are approved characters, they ought to be recognized in the instructions to the Commissioners, and how proper it may be for them to participate therein, or to be made acquainted therewith."

This attitude eventuated in the formal instructions, given by Secretary of War Knox to the three Commissioners: [1]

"The Society of Friends have, with the approbation of the President of the United States, decided to send some of their respectable members, in order to contribute their influence to induce the hostile Indians to a peace. They are not, however, to confer with the Indians upon any subject of importance, until they shall have previously communicated the same, and received your approbation."

How laxly the last prescribed inhibition was regarded by the Commissioners will be apparent in the narrative, as the Friends were not hampered in the least in their intercourse with any of the Indians, either singly or in groups.

[1] American State Papers, V, p. 341.

# THE ATTEMPTED INDIAN TREATY OF 1793

A few days prior to their departure, at Jacob Lindley's suggestion, a conference was held with President Washington, James Pemberton accompanying Jacob Lindley, William Savery and John Elliott. They met a favorable reception and had a "full opportunity to relieve our minds; which we thought tended to his satisfaction as well as ours." [1] The details of this interview would be interesting today, if available, for the anomolous position of the Quakers in the undertaking, rendering them neutral in the pending negotiations, would have been apparent to Washington, who, like the two other great war Presidents in American history since, had a keen appreciation of the Society of Friends. Their feeling of detachment from the American program in the treaty negotiations is evidenced by their statement to the British Commander at Detroit, that they were "totally distinct and separate from the Commissioners," and yet they were keenly alive to the dignity of their country, as Jacob Lindley remarked when an old, emaciated horse was provided for General Lincoln at Albany, in lieu of the many fine horses at hand:

"This treatment roused my feelings for the honor of our Government, and the regard due to its respectable officers; of which I consider him (General Lincoln) as one—especially on the present intended peaceful mission."

Incidentally the General was provided with a better horse. The Friends had some inkling of the delicacy of the task ahead of them early in the service, and the sense of it increased as the service developed. Jacob Lindley well expressed their quandary:

"Notwithstanding our disinterested and universal principles of love and good will to mankind, we are sensible our path is narrow and our situation delicate,—the eyes of four different interests being open towards us,—British, United States, Indians and the reputation of our religious Society."

[1] J. Lindley, Journal.

# LIFE OF WILLIAM SAVERY

At a time when the Society of Friends had officially withdrawn from public life and effort, here were Quakers officially endeavoring to influence the course of diplomatic measures of their Government toward a peaceful event. It is one of the few, if not the solitary instance of its kind between the aloofness and detachment of the early Friends from the factional wars of the Commonwealth and the same attitude of modern Friends in the reconstruction and relief work during and since the Great War. In the earliest and latest instance, however, the activity of the Society was entirely apart from any diplomatic significance; in 1793 it was essentially diplomatic in its character, and therefore unique in Quaker annals.

Minute and detailed accounts of the journey and of the negotiations were written by William Savery, Jacob Lindley, Joseph Moore and General Lincoln. The Savery Journal was published in Philadelphia in 1837 and afterwards in London in two editions; the Lindley and Moore accounts in Friends' "Miscellany" and republished in Michigan Pioneer and Historical Collections, XVII, in 1890.

Pickering and Randolph went directly across country by land, traversing the wilds of Pennsylvania and New York to the mouth of the Niagara River. With them went Parrish, Elliott and Moore. Savery and Lindley went to New York, being there joined by Hartshorne, and all three accompanying General Lincoln, who was in charge of the supplies, to Albany. The route via Albany and the Mohawk River was as nearly as possible an all-water route. Eight batteaux, built by Government contract, awaited the party at Schenectady, two of them being covered in the middle with painted canvas, nine feet long and furnished with a table. Mattresses were supplied for all, but General Lincoln indulged in the luxury of a bed.

The party numbered about eighty men as it set out on May 9th, breasting the strong, rapid current of the Mohawk and frequently striking bottom. With the group went John Heckewelder, a Moravian missionary of long experience with the Indians and a man in whom they had much confidence.

The accounts of Savery and Lindley are full of interesting details of the whole journey, and in particular of the Mohawk Valley and its people, for which space does not suffice here, save to note that the travelers were keen observers. On the 13th, boats and baggage were portaged around the falls (Little Falls, N. Y.) and the night was spent at Fort Herkimer. Arriving at Fort Stanwix, famous for its Indian Treaty of 1768, the party left the Mohawk and portaged over the watershed to Wood Creek. En route they crossed the battlefield of a few years before and found skulls of the victims of Indian warfare, upon which the marks of tomahawk and scalping knife were still visible.

As Wood Creek was but six inches deep, most of the baggage was carried in wagons to the junction of Canada Creek, a distance of seven miles which the passengers walked. Down this Creek they went to Oneida Lake and thence to Fort Brewington (modern Brewerton). From there down the Onondaga or Oneida River to Oswego Falls, around which the boats were drawn on rollers by hand and then down a rapid, rocky current to Oswego Fort, which, though on American soil, still contained a strong British garrison. Alternately sailing and rowing, they crept cautiously along the southern shore of Lake Ontario and in five days reached Fort Niagara at the mouth of the Niagara River. Here they landed at the formidable fortification, where the great, square, stone "Castle," built by the French in 1726 and captured from them by the British in 1759, still housed a British garrison, although it was, by treaty, American soil. It still stands today, a silent testimonial to the border warfare of three nations and their savage foes and allies.

They soon crossed to Queenston on the Canadian side,

having found the fort "a dark, noisy, confused, dirty place," in the language of Jacob Lindley. Here they met Pickering and Randolph and Governor Simcoe, "a plain man and much beloved in government." The Friends found him very easy of access, and cordial in his reception. While walking in his garden, he told them their undertaking did their Society great honor. He entertained the Commissioners "at his house in Navy Hall," but the rest of the company took boat to the Landing, so called, seven miles up the Niagara River and but four below the Falls. While on the way they were hailed from the bank by John Parrish, Joseph Moore and John Elliott, who were already at the Landing. It was a joyous reunion, but they were soon sobered on May 26th by a visit from the Commissioners and Governor Simcoe, who informed them that the Treaty could not possibly take place before July 1st. It was the first of the many delays that were in store for them.

Brant, the powerful Mohawk Chief, of whose good faith at that time one can rightly entertain strong doubt, had left for the West, with a body of other Mohawks, a few days before. He was accompanied by Colonel Butler, the British Indian Superintendent at Niagara. Their object was to attend the preliminary conference at the Rapids of the Miami or Maumee River in northwestern Ohio, prior to the intended Council at Sandusky. There was nothing for the Commissioners to do but to await further word before proceeding, a circumstance that much annoyed them.

The Friends were deeply chagrined and discomfited by this turn of affairs. They discussed whether it would be better for them to return home or to attempt religious work among "the scattered sheep in Canada." On the 29th, in company with Heckewelder and Captain Hendricks, the Indian, they went down the River and conferred with the Commissioners and Governor Simcoe, as a result of which the missionary possibilities of the situation overcame their

TALK WITH THE INDIANS AT BUFFALO CREEK IN 1793

1 Col. Timothy Pickering    3. Beverly Randolph    7. ...... British Officer
2 Gen. Benjamin Lincoln     4. coloured Chairman    W. Quakers
                            5. Interpreter
                            6. Indians Chiefs

low spirits and they decided to go on to Detroit, in advance of the Commissioners. It is also probable that the Friends thought they could effect more if in closer touch with the scene of action and in a position to confer with the hostile Indians, should occasion or opportunity arise.

It was probably at this time that the conference with the Indians at Buffalo Creek (modern Buffalo) took place, as pictured herein. The sketch was made on the spot by Colonel C. A. Pilkington, of the British army, who, being transferred to Gibraltar, gave it to a Mr. Henry of Massachusetts in 1819. In the group of Quakers, the second from the left has a youthful face, which, in its fullness, corresponds well with the descriptions of William Savery. Certainly the five depicted are the Friends of the mission to Detroit in 1793 and the picture itself is of rare interest in Quaker history because of the diversity of the human elements shown in it.

On May 30th, Lindley, Moore and Elliott visited the Falls for the first time. Jacob Lindley's accounts of his two close inspections of the greatest natural wonder on the continent are as accurate as they are appreciative. He was thrilled and awed by the spectacle; he marveled at the majesty and power of the scene and gazed upon it in wrapt attention. His account is especially valuable as it is among the earliest authentic documents left by an eye witness. The three Friends descended into the gorge from a point on the Canadian side near where the suspension bridge now terminates. Their path was supplemented by Indian ladders of clumsy but effective construction. All the notable features, though not by their modern names, were mentioned,—the roar of the water, the mist, floating off over fields, more luxuriant on that account, Goat Island, the American and Horseshoe Falls and the Upper and Lower Rapids. Above the Falls they were guests for a time of Squire Birch, who had mills driven by the Upper Rapids. Could Jacob Lindley see the mammoth power projects of today, located at this precise point, he would find his surmise justified, in deeming the Squire's location

"perhaps one of the grandest situations for water works in the world; and I think, if he opens his front door, he need never pay the clergy for preaching. He is kind to Friends, having in early life contracted an esteem for Samuel Emlen at sea."

The printed Journal of William Savery makes only slight mention of the Falls. On the way out he felt uncomfortably close to them when their boat was breasting a strong current, half a mile above. On the return trip, when they "stopped a few minutes at the Falls of Niagara," he mentioned a curious expedient to which the farmers resorted to keep their ducks and geese from being washed over the cataract.

"They pluck the feathers entirely off their breasts, about the size of a dollar, and keep it constantly bare. The water so affects them in this part, that they stay in but a few minutes."

If the manuscript of this part of the Journal were available, it might disclose other observations, in keeping with the elaborate notes on other less outstanding subjects, but for this part of the journey Jacob Lindley's pages give the fullest and most satisfactory account.

On June 5th, the Friends and John Heckewelder packed their bedding and stores and went on board the *Dunmore* at Fort Erie opposite Buffalo Creek, now the City of Buffalo and sailed away to Detroit. There were just ninety souls on board, half of whom were Indians, including Captain Hendricks, who was one of the first Indians to invite the attendance of the Friends at the Treaty.

The Commissioners remained at Queenston until July 26th, when they too went up the River to Fort Erie. While there Colonel McKee wrote from Detroit that the Indians were ready and requesting them to repair to Sandusky. They prepared to do so but were detained by contrary winds. Lincoln's Journal records that "reports have been bruited about, that should the Council break up without making peace, it was the determination of the hostile Indians to fall upon the Commissioners and sacrifice them."

A similar feeling was prevalent at the other end of the Lake, as recorded by William Savery:

"We have need to ask for both faith and patience to support us under our long detention, and the continual alarming reports of the disposition of the Indians, who are collecting for the treaty. Most of those who pass this place are said to go prepared for war, if the commissioners do not comply with their wishes: they are in a haughty spirit, being elated with their successes. There are many among the inhabitants here kindly disposed towards us, who appear to be very doubtful for our personal safety at Sandusky, and seem rather to desire we would not venture. We are thankful in being preserved so far in quietness and confidence, trusting in the Omnipotent arm for preservation. We cannot admit a doubt of the propriety of our coming, nor of the motives which led to it; yet I may say, it is the most trying situation I was ever brought into."

The depressing effect of the constant reference to the danger involved in the prospective service, without being able to be at it, was soon evident to all. Joseph Moore felt the entire appreciation and good will evidenced by the advice frequently given them: "For God's sake, gentlemen, don't venture yourselves to Sandusky," a conclusion in which Jacob Lindley concurred in his statement:

"It evidently appears a serious business, and little, if anything, short of offering up life by those who attend (the treaty)."

In spite of these untoward signs, matters progressed until the sudden return, on July 5th, of Brant to Fort Erie, with Colonel Butler and the fifty Mohawks who had accompanied him West. Matters then stopped. Brant and his confrères reported that the western Indians, assembled at Miami Rapids, were suspicious lest General Wayne, who was at Fort Washington (Cincinnati), should advance during the absence of the chiefs and warriors and take the Indian villages, and also lest the Commissioners were not empowered to stipulate that the settlers should fall back behind the Ohio, as an established boundary.

The Commissioners replied in elaborate form that they had full power as to boundaries and that General Wayne was quiet and would remain so. With this assurance Brant set sail again, on July 14th, across Lake Erie with his deputation to Miami Rapids, but notwithstanding, the Indians kept their runners out constantly, to watch the motions of Wayne's army.

In spite of their assurance, the Commissioners were worried. Lincoln wrote Washington on July 10th, dispatching the letter express to Philadelphia:

"If the reports which circulate here from different quarters are in any way true, General Wayne must have violated the clearest principles of a *truce*. * * * The Commissioners could not have painted to themselves any hope of personal security but in such a belief. For if there is no *truce* existing they are just throwing themselves into the hands of the savages at open and active war. The Commissioners are not so apprehensive for themselves, as for the honor of the United States and the success of their mission."

Under the shadow of this apprehension the Commissioners set forth for Detroit, and it is a reasonable surmise that the presence of the Friends there was a comfortable anticipation to them in the newly realized danger,—a danger to which, as we have seen, the Quaker deputation was fully alive, in spite of their neutral character. There was, to be sure, considerable irony in the Quakers having preceded the Commissioners to Detroit,—an irony more apparent in their fine disregard of Secretary Knox's instructions that the Quakers should not confer with the Indians without the approbation of the Commissioners.

DETROIT WATER FRONT, 1794

## CHAPTER IX

## RELIGIOUS LABOR AT DETROIT

The Friends and John Heckewelder arrived at Detroit on June 10, 1793, and then ensued many weeks of dolorous waiting, in anxious expectation of the arrival of the Commissioners. The town was even then of considerable importance, both as a trading post and a fort. Like the other fortified places on the Lakes it was still in the hands of the British.

The approach up the river had afforded the travelers

"a beautiful prospect of continuous houses, farms, windmills, luxuriant meadows and orchards, which had a very pleasing effect, having seen nothing like it since we left the Mohawk River."

It is remarkable that, barring the windmills, the approach to Detroit today presents much the same appearance as it did in 1793.

Upon arrival, the Friends immediately presented the passports, given them by Governor Simcoe, to Lieutenant-Colonel Richard England, the British Commander of the Post, and thereby met a man who became at once their warm and loyal friend. Jacob Lindley describes him as "a cheerful, open-countenanced, masculine soldier, who received us like a gentleman, and kindly offered civilities to us,—for which we acknowledged obligations to him." Among these civilities was the use of his garden, and thither the Friends frequently resorted, using a pleasant arbor for rest, conference or reading.

Among other acquaintances readily made were their publican, Matthew Dolson and Hannah, his wife. In spite of the high price of two dollars a day, without board, and prices of foreign articles triple that in Philadelphia, the Dolsons won a firm place in the Friends' hearts and it was with regret that they eventually left their hospitality.

The town itself was confined within high pickets, with four gates leading into it. The streets were miserably narrow, generally about fifteen feet in width. Joseph Moore's complaint that they were much confined "within the limits of this small garrison town where the streets are unhealthy for the want of air," is more readily understood when we read that the one hundred and fifty or two hundred houses were closely huddled together, and that the only drinking water was brought from the river and soon became insipid. Their attitude toward the water and strong drink in particular was indicated by Jacob Lindley's comment on Captain John Drake, "remarkable for using no kind of drink but water, yet is a healthy, robust man." Dust and hosts of flies by day, and fleas and bugs by night, varied with drunken brawls of Indians and the lewdness and obscenity of the town generally, made Detroit no haven of rest to temperaments used to the decorum of Philadelphia.

The river bank was a bluff, perhaps fifteen feet high, and extended into the modern city to Woodbridge Street. At a point on Woodbridge Street, just east of the modern Cass Street, and then fronting directly on the River, was the King's Shipyard, where stood a building, old even in those days, containing a sail-loft. Here were held the first Friends' meetings in Detroit, a fact that is the more interesting because of the recent establishment of a Monthly Meeting in the city.

The concern for holding these meetings was one of the first things that occupied Friends' attention. William Savery's account of it is as follows:

"After informing the Colonel (England) of our intention to hold a meeting here to-morrow, to which he cordially assented, we viewed two places which were offered for the purpose; but they being somewhat inconvenient, the King's ship-builder offered his boat-house, which being large, and in a fine airy place on the side of the river, we accepted it. Attended the meeting at ten o'clock forenoon. The colonel having dispensed with the accustomed military exercise, which is practiced at that hour, a large number of soldiers and most of the officers were present, besides a considerable collection of the inhabitants of the place of both sexes; and as the house was in a large open lot, great numbers stood out of doors. This being doubtless the first meeting of our Society at Detroit, curiosity was greatly excited; their behavior at first, as might be expected, was a little restless, talking, taking snuff, &c., but upon one of our company endeavoring to set before them the nature of our mode of worship, with a request they would join in our manner, they were very attentive and became still; some of them, especially among the poor soldiers, were reverent and thoughtful. The service, which was considerable, appeared to be received with openness, and I believe the opportunity ended to mutual satisfaction."

The meetings continued to be well attended throughout the summer, the officers, soldiers and townspeople coming in numbers and many from the country round about. The only place of worship in the town was a Roman Catholic Church and the Protestant element in the vicinity, although not of a very deeply religious type, welcomed the opportunity and the few deeply spiritual individuals they found were truly refreshed by their fellowship. The most memorable of the meetings arose out of the greatest weakness, when all of the Friends save Joseph Moore and William Savery were away, the latter being ill. The meeting was postponed till evening, when William Savery had measureably recovered, and the disheartening beginning gave way to the triumph of the spirit of Christ over the group.

Aside from the holding of the meetings, the Friends had a lively concern for the community,—a service that justified and relieved the strain of waiting for the treaty.

The morals of the town were loose and the Friends suffered much in spirit, believing "it would be a vain expectation for us to think to reign where Truth so evidently suffers." Time and again the libertinism of the frontier settlement, "this dark and wicked place," and the drunkenness and debauchery of Indians and whites alike, with the consequent fights, riots and murder, were borne in upon them so vividly that their mission seemed almost transformed into a gospel message to convert the town. Finding that "open debauchery is too generally practised on the frontiers and so common that white men of the first rank do not appear ashamed of it," they sought an opportunity for "conversation with the most libertine part of the company, who glory in their debaucheries; but it was like casting pearls before swine, they turn again and rend you."

In company with John Heckewelder sometimes and more often in groups of their own number, the Friends traveled up and down the Detroit River, visiting communities and appointing meetings. Several meetings were held at River La Rouge, six miles below Detroit, one of them in the home of Judge Powell, chiefly attended by Mennonists and French and German emigrants. Later the group penetrated five miles up River La Rouge to a new grist mill, and another meeting called forth the expression:

"O happy Philadelphia, what privileges thy inhabitants enjoy! Mercies unthankfully received or unimproved, will increase condemnation."

Many of the attenders of these meetings came long distances on foot and showed great interest in the exercises that developed as the meetings progressed.

Still later, when with the Commissioners the Friends were encamped at the mouth of the River Detroit, meetings were held at the home of Simon Girty, the wily interpreter, whose wife was "glad of our meetings." The Girty home, like that of Captain Elliot, was very near the mouth of the River, on the Canadian side, in a place that was excellent for strategic purposes. To the meetings held there people flocked from far and wide and Generals Lincoln and Chapin and several other officers and a number of Indians were present, the latter behaving soberly.

A final appointed meeting was held at Grosse Isle in the Detroit River in the afternoon. All the Friends but William Hartshorne attended in spite of the great heat of a mid-August day. From the boat landing they trudged four miles to the meeting place and found a crude but appreciative gathering. Of it William Savery wrote:

"These poor frontier people have very seldom any opportunity of assembling for religious worship; and though many of them in their dress and manners, as well as their information, are very little above the Indians; yet they esteem it a favor to have the benefit of a free ministry, travelling far on foot to attend meetings. Some are rude and restless at times, but others appear like thirsty ground, which I trust the great Lord of the harvest will in his own time water."

The fort and the officers were naturally the chief social centers of the garrison town. From Colonel England to the petty officers, all the military men were cordiality itself to the Friends. The fort lay to the rear of the cluster of houses on the river bank. Called in the early French days Fort Pontchartrain du Detroit, it had been redubbed Fort Lernoult by the British. The high pickets entirely surrounding the little town connected with the near wall of the fortifications. With prudence, bred in the bloodshed of the desperate assault by Indians, at the time of Pontiac's Conspiracy, watchmen were placed at the four gates of entrance to the town and at night the gates were shut. On one occasion the Friends, returning late, had to abide the night outside the pickets, entrance being granted to none. On the ramparts and bastions of the fort, sentinels called the rounds every fifteen minutes from nine o'clock in the evening till three in the morning. Under the strain of savage uncertainty, it seemed almost sacrilege to the Friends to hear the "All's well" of these sentinels and the invariable "All's very well" of the last to give the refrain.

In the hospitality offered to them by the officers, the

Friends found "plenty and elegance at least equal to the most fashionable houses in our city." Potations were an essential part of the entertainment, and the Friends were appreciative of the quality of the beverages. Jacob Lindley described one of these banquets with sixteen young British officers, a luxuriously sumptuous entertainment, with flesh, fish, fruit and vegetables, a variety of wines and excellent London porter. The conversation ran on religion, governments (the United States were still a despised democratic experiment), war, peace and theatricals. At the end temperance, in the true sense of the word, was upheld by Friends' objection to toasts as liable to lead to intemperance. All were dispensed with, therefore, save a toast to the King's health, and then in excellent good part the officers drank, "Success to the Quakers in their present honorable and disinterested undertaking," a courtesy extended and accepted with equal urbanity.

As the time wore on and the deputation saw more and more of the evil effects of strong drink on the Indians, they inclined to lay most of the border difficulties to it.

"The elimination of rum is a reform which loudly calls for the united efforts of our government and that of Great Britain, together with the endeavors of all Christians and lovers of mankind."

The endeavors to persuade some sort of restraint or limitation to the traffic in rum elicited no more from the officers and British Indian agents than a respectful hearing, all declaring it to be inextricably involved in frontier trading. The concern went deep into the hearts of the Quaker group, but progress in it was not to be realized in their day.

The ease with which the Friends associated with army officers, both British and American, contributed no little to the confidence reposed in them. Writing of it William Savery records:

"Their respectful, polite behaviour to Friends marked their character as gentlemen and merited our acknowledgement. They permitted us to use great freedom with them, and I hope we kept our places."

When the Friends had been a week in Detroit, some of the officers requested William Savery to outline the hopes Friends had in their business with the Indians. This he gladly did, spending an hour with four of them. What the definite plan of the Friends was, he nowhere clearly indicates in the Journal, but the officers expressed the belief that much respect would be paid to the sentiments of Friends, and that many of the insinuations as to personal safety were dropped by those who were interested in the continuance of hostilities.

Of the three Commissioners, they knew Pickering best, he being a frequent visitor at the homes of some of the Friends in Philadelphia. He was also the leader of the delegation and thrown with them in conference more than the others. It was General Lincoln, however, that they grew to know and esteem the highest. He would engage in religious conversation with them and his sentiments on these weighty subjects appeared to them just and valuable. He also associated more with the Friends. On the occasion of a visit one evening to the home of James Colwell, on the river bank in Canada, Joseph Moore refers to him as "our good old general." Lincoln also frequently attended the Friends' meetings and seemed to appreciate them for their solemnity. On the return trip, William Savery and Joseph Moore chose a longer and more tedious route, more largely, perhaps, to be with Lincoln than for any other reason. Beverly Randolph is not mentioned in any of the Journals, except in references to the Commissioners as a group. The general impression of the Friends was summed up by Joseph Moore in stating,

"Colonel Pickering and General Lincoln, through the whole of the journey, so far as I have seen them, have conducted as men of religion and sobriety."

And so the summer wore away, with diplomacy mixed with ministry and much complaint on all sides at dilatoriness and inability to come to conclusions. Detroit was, by nature, the gateway for all the Indians coming to the treaty from the northwest and the Friends were able to see their future conferees in advance and at close range. The experiences were neither pleasing nor encouraging. Says William Savery:

"Many Indians came to see us, but most of them being intoxicated, we had little conversation with them. * * * Almost wearied out with the importunities of the Indians for rum, we however put them off. Some of the Chippeways having arrived last evening from Michillimachinack, and encamped outside the picquets, we paid them a visit, but they had drunk much rum before we went, were very rude, called us ill names, and appeared very angry. All the Indians I had ever seen were far short of these in their extraordinary terrifying painting, and the appendages of their dress; any description I am capable of giving, must afford a very faint idea of the ferocious appearance of this nation. On leaving them, one followed and took hold of the arm of one of us, crying very harshly, 'come back, come back.' A ship-carpenter who was near, and understood their language, said he believed if we had returned to them, they would certainly have killed us, which most likely they would; this made us more cautious of going into their company afterwards, especially when heated with strong drink. A number of Indians frightfully painted, passed through the town, dancing the war dance, some of whom having knowledge of us, came to our lodging to pay us a compliment; but I wish to be excused from a compliment of the like kind in future. The frightful painting of their faces and bodies, which are almost naked on such occasions, their terrifying whoops and yells, their ferocious countenances and actions, together with the tomahawks and scalping knives in their hands, form so horrid a scene, that every truly Christian mind must recoil from it with disgust and sadness."

Jacob Lindley is even more specific in his description of these Chippeways from the far reaches of upper Superior. Their paint was of red, blue, green and black; they wore turbans on their heads with pikes and prongs of skin, feathers, hair and sticks projecting eighteen inches from their heads, and tails of wild beasts extending from their heads down their backs. Some of their canoes were decorated with from fifteen to thirty scalps on poles, and one grisley savage in particular attracted attention by a scalp of beautiful, fair curly hair tied to his ear. These Chippeways, when sober were good-humored and pleasant, and carried no bows and arrows, which would have indicated warlike intentions. They had crude flutes with them which, at the request of the officers, they would play, blowing either through their noses or mouths. Truly, they had Christian faith who thought to assuage the evil genius of such as these, with the spirit of the Man of Galilee!

They received many visits from chiefs of the various tribes, most of whom were well disposed, but the rank and file of Indians were suspicious, giving them

"angry looks and drawing away their hands when we offered ours— calling us Schomochoman, or long knives, by which they distinguish all who are citizens of the United States."

The Friends frequently dined with the chiefs and their table manners were agreeably surprising. This was especially so with the Shawanese, one of whose young chiefs is described as behaving at table with great gentility and being garbed in a new silk hunting shirt, with at least one thousand silver brooches bedecking it.

Toward some Oneidas the Friends were able to act as friends indeed. Eighteen of them had come West on the Lake, with sixty other Indians, to go to Miami Rapids to the Grand Council. Of the party was also the British Colonel Butler, who, knowing the temper of the Indians at the Rapids, and that the Oneidas were esteemed in the American interest, declined to allow them to land and brought them on to Detroit, to go forward in due time to Sandusky with the Friends. The Oneidas were one of the tribes of the friendly Six Nations and their chief was unpopular with the war chiefs of the assembled Indians.

Early in July a letter was received from Captain Hendricks, complaining of the short allowance of provisions; whereupon the Friends sent them a barrel of flour, some pork, five dollars in money, tobacco, etc., and wrote an answer. On July 9th and 10th a really important interview was held with the famous Shawanese war-chief, Blue Jacket, fresh from the Rapids. Having been in command of the Indians at the defeat of General St. Clair, he naturally carried a deal of prestige with him. He was dressed in scarlet with gold tassels and wore a laced hat. The Friends thought him "a brave, masculine figure of a man." His Indian name, "Wawiapieschenwa," signified a whirlpool. He proved to be a good politician, and though appearing to be a man of understanding, preserved an impenetrable taciturnity, stating that he had given his sentiments at the Council.

The British were as much at sea over Blue Jacket's visit as were the Friends, and his objects were undisclosed to both. Thomas Duggan writing to Colonel McKee, at the Rapids, under date of July 17, 1793, said:

"I have as you desired * * * a very good look-out after Blue Jacket and the other Person whom I have had repeatedly at my house since I received your caution. * * * He invited Blue Jacket three or four days ago to dine with him and the Friends-Quakers, but he disappointed him and the Friends, he got merry before dinner time & thought himself better engaged."

It would be interesting to know just what the wily chief had in mind and why he was under suspicion by the British.

Later, the same day, the Friends were

"visited by several Indians, some of whom understand a little English, and appeared pleased wih our views in coming here. The Shawnese, Wyandots, and Delawares, all appear to have more or less knowledge of Friends, and acknowledge that they have confidence in the Society, because we are peaceable and just. We have seen some of almost every nation, which are collected at the council, and have been more or less conversant with them every day since we arrived."

In spite of all these conferences no hint appears in William Savery's pages of the elements of the Friends' plan. The nearest approach to it occurs in the following after-dinner discussion:

"Dined at James Abbott's, who being much acquainted with Indian affairs for thirty years, expressed his opinion that no treaty would take place at present; or if it did, no peace would be obtained; with which our two interpreters joined; all agreeing that the Indians must first be chastised and humbled. Friends urged their pacific sentiments towards the natives, and that kind, lenient measures, accompanied with justice, would prove more effectual than the sword; but without much effect. Men who are in the spirit of war, we have found in many instances in this place, cannot possibly see as we see. A long and truly afflicting recital of Indian cruelty and perfidy was brought into view, of which we have been obliged to hear enough before to fill a large volume. I could, several times, have been glad to have stopped my ears from hearing of blood, as I am confirmed in opinion that it has a tendency gradually to eradicate the tenderest feelings of humanity."

The Quakers were so continually regaled with these stories of atrocities, seemingly as well authenticated as they were horrible. Though loath to credit them, they were forced to do so by their apparent authenticity.

Early during the stay at Detroit an interesting meeting took place with some of the so-called "Good Indians," particularly with John Killbuck, they being introduced by John Heckewelder, the famous and successful missionary of the Moravians. William Savery's narrative gives the details:

"J. Heckewelder returned yesterday from the Moravian town, on the river Le French (modern Thames River) and brought with him Gabriel Senseman, a missionary, and six or seven Indians, among whom was John Killbuck, and his son, who had been educated at Princeton College, but has again resumed Indian habits and manners. These poor Indians, who do not go to war, have been driven about, from place to place, and much distressed. Governor Simcoe has now granted them ten miles square of land, which they are beginning to cultivate; but at present their situation was represented to be very distressing, for want of provisions, having scarcely anything to subsist on, but roots, until their corn grows. Heckewelder and Senseman requesting our attention to them, Friends took it into consideration, and no other resources appearing, we thought it right to procure corn and flour for them, to the amount of one hundred dollars; part of which they immediately took off in their canoes."

A Shawanese chief was next in conference with the Quaker delegation, he being a quiet, cautious man, whose sentiments respecting the treaty they could not obtain save that he thought it would not be over before frost. He had come from the Miami Rapids conference desiring to see the Friends. Two other early visitors were chiefs of the Wyandots, one of whom was blind. The other remembered some long and broad belts of wampum that had been given to Friends in former treaties, stating that they

"were intended to bind us together by the hands and arms, so that no small accident in the future should be able to make a separation; and notwithstanding all that had happened, the Wyandots felt some of the old affection to remain."

The Friends were in almost constant communication with the Indians at the Rapids. They were also impressed with the reiterated statement that it was the hunting grounds and not the money for them, that the Indians wanted, for without them they could not subsist and for their recovery they would risk their lives. A Shawanese who came from the Council presented their predicament in a narrative worthy of preservation for its picturesqueness. He stated what he had at times heard from old men concerning the first coming of the white people:

"The wise men among the Indians, at that time, foresaw what has now happened, and warned their brothers not to countenance each other in receiving gifts from the white people; saying, that the Great Spirit had made the land over the great lake for white people, and this island for the yellow people. They then refused to drink rum, and told the whites, the Indians did not want the bitter water; that it was only drink for white people, and that the Great Spirit had given the brooks and springs to the Indians for their drink; and foretold the consequence of Indians receiving that, and knives and hatchets, which would be the ruin of them. He remarked, that now several of those original tribes were extinct, and yet the Indians had not adverted to the advice, but had continued parting with their lands for these things, until they were almost driven to where the sun set."

And so the time dragged on, with visits from members of practically every tribe represented at the Rapids, with religious meetings, social calls, conferences among themselves and writing of letters. All the time the talk of atrocities and of personal danger in attending the Treaty increased, until William Savery recorded:

"If we attend to the various opinions and sentiments we hear, we are likely to be kept in continual fluctuation."

## CHAPTER X

# THE END OF THE DRAMA

In the Province of Ontario, Canada, where the Detroit River empties into Lake Erie, were located in these days the manorial home of Captain Matthew Elliot and the more modest dwelling of the renegade interpreter, Simon Girty. The large and attractive stone and log mansion of the Elliot family is still standing today, though in utter and weedy dilapidation. Later it was notable in history as the shelter of Chief Tecumseh, during the War of 1812, and as the Canadian haven of Eliza, of "Uncle Tom's Cabin" fame. At the time of our story, it was the proudest and most sumptuous mansion in the neighborhood, and was the center from which the British distributed stores and trinkets to the savages. Captain Elliot was in charge of this service, the importance of which in holding the red men steadfast to the British can be estimated from Governor Simcoe's statement to the Friends, that it cost the British Government £30,000 per annum for doles and gifts to the Indians.

Elliot's ménage was elaborate. A political rival described his plantation as follows:

"He lives as I am informed in the greatest affluence, at an expence of above a thousand a year. He possesses an extensive farm not far from the garrison, stocked with about six or seven head of cattle & I am told employs fifty or sixty persons constantly about his house and farm, chiefly slaves."

This opinion was, to be sure, intended to infer graft in Elliot's administration of the Indian stores, an intimation that was finally successful in removing him from the Indian service, but its main outlines are probably correct, as the old house still standing below Amherstburg, Ontario, bespeaks an opulence that must have been rare on the frontier. General Lincoln mentions it as the "best I have seen in the country by far."

It was to this place that the scene was now shifted. On July 21st, the United States Commissioners arrived at the mouth of the Detroit River, and immediately sent word to the Friends to join them. General Lincoln rather whimsically records that the "Commissioners could not obtain permission to visit (Detroit) although we were within eighteen miles of the garrison." More explicit was Jacob Lindley, stating that the Friends would gladly have seen the Commissioners at Detroit but understood "neither they nor any others from a foreign state under military characters, are admitted within the limits of this garrison." Perhaps no better commentary could be made on Anglo-American relations than this picture of an official embassy of the United States, excluded from a British garrison within the treaty limits of the new Republic. In contrast were the greater liberty that had been unstintingly accorded the Friends and the letter they bore from Lieutenant Colonel England, reviewing their residence at Detroit, and stating:

"Those Gentlemen while here have conducted themselves very correctly so far as came within my knowledge * * * and I understand from them that they are totally distinct and separate from the Commissioners."

This difference in treatment must have impressed the Commissioners, but the Friends were overjoyed to hear of their arrival and lost little time in responding to the call to meet them at Elliot's. Fourteen tents were pitched before the house, in two wings, on a fine green sward, sloping toward the river. They were soon occupied by the Friends, the interpreters, two British officers, General Chapin and others. William Savery and Joseph Moore occupied one of the tents together. A number of Indians camped alongside, while the Commissioners were entertained in Captain Elliot's house. The first night proved unfortunate. A violent thunderstorm deluged the camp and drove all its occupants into the house and barns adjacent. Barring the rains and mosquitoes, the scene was a picturesque one, easy to reconstruct mentally, even in spite of the unkempt overgrowth that today covers the quondam lawn. In front of the tents were the trees under which the Council fires were lighted and the calumet pipes smoked, in anticipation of the grave ceremony of official converse. The Indians seem to have had no real function in the treaty making, but they, in company with some of the whites, spent many nights, dancing, singing and yelling, with an accompaniment of wild Indian music. A Wyandot Indian stayed much with the Friends, and hunted for them, bringing them plenty of all sorts of wild game. As he spoke many Indian dialects he was quite useful and they paid him well for the game.

With another Indian, William Savery had a disagreeable experience:

"In the evening, two Indian canoes having come down from Detroit, each having a keg of rum, some of our new visitors (Indians) got drunk, and came into our camp, just as we were going to bed, making a great noise, and going from tent to tent. Much persuasion being used, I at length prevailed on the worst one to let me lead him away some distance: he frequently called me brother, and seemed pleased with my attention; but after I returned, it appeared to me to have been a very dangerous undertaking, as he had a long knife at his side, which he had before drawn out and brandished in our camp; but Providence preserved me. They still kept at the distance of about a quarter of a mile from us, yelling and whooping; several of our company offered to be watchmen, which we thought prudent; and an uneasy night it was, as they passed frequently backward and forward by our camp; but no mischief was done to any. Early in the morning I was awakened by one of them, who had gotten into the middle of our encampment almost naked, very frantic and noisy, with his knife drawn, which he vapored in the air, and beat on his breast. Some of the servants and others would have seized him, but this would have been imprudent. After troubling us about half an hour, an old Indian, who was sober, came and led him away."

Captain Elliot was assistant to Colonel Thomas McKee in the British Indian Department. He was hospitality itself to the visitors, but was under strict orders as to their activities. He absolutely forbade their nearer approach to the Rapids. As the British controlled the Lakes and all the shipping, no boat could be chartered for the purpose without his consent. The Commissioners were nearer the scene of action but by no means nearer the solution of the interminable delays in bringing on the Treaty. They had no other recourse than to settle down again, though at closer range, to the tedium of waiting and palavering.

Very soon after the Friends arrived at Elliot's, they had a conference with the Commissioners, who gave them the substance of what had transpired at Niagara, between them and Brant, all of which "appeared favorable" to the Quaker deputation. It is interesting to trace the fluctuations in the opinions of the Friends, during the negotiations that were to follow, in the sincerity of the Commissioners and of the United States. After the first favorable impression, "believing our worthy Commissioners had nothing but upright views in their proceedings, consistent with the trust reposed in them by the Government of the United States," and were "sincerely disposed for peace," their confidence was shaken by the long delay and the tenacious dealings. Midway of the proceedings, they became apprehensive as to the Commissioners' power and that the Government had had no intention that they should yield anything. Even more direct and bold was the conference, described by Jacob Lindley, with a frankness which William Savery and Joseph Moore never entrusted to paper, in which the Friends frankly disclosed their doubts to a group of Shawanese, one of whom was a "very solid man." Through an interpreter, they "let him know what our views were in common, and also what our apprehensions were in the sincerity of the government in the present embassy."

It would be hard to find a more pronounced example of world patriotism than this,—a sitting in judgment over the partisanship of nations and rightly dividing the element of truth, irrespective of consequences and of natural inclination toward the cause of one's own country. There must have been more of such counsel than the Journals admit, particularly in William Savery's case. He hints at sophistication beyond his expression. He certainly realized that the task was one involving great discretion, and he did not abuse that discretion by printed words which might lead to unforeseen consequences. He was probably the readiest talker among the Quakers; certainly he was the spokesman of the group, and this may have given him the conservatism that responsibility often develops. All of the Friends must have been keenly alive to the four interests that centered their attention upon the action of the Quakers, and the impartial decorum with which they behaved both in public and private.

The apprehensions as to the sincerity of the parties involved increased,—not indeed, through suspicion as to the individuals, but because it became more and more apparent that the Commissioners were dealing with forces which, with the best of intentions, they could not control, because they had not originated them. So it always is in strife. Negotiators and peace makers find their best efforts fruitless, due to an inherited chain of evil precedents. Justice and liberalism are throttled before they can be tried out, due to the vicious history that precipitated the difficulties that the peace should heal.

It is not surprising, therefore, to find the Friends increasingly aware of a feature, probably unknown to them at the inception of the task, that they were witnesses and participants in the game of nations, in which the Indians were pawns and the stakes an empire. Truly did Jacob Lindley voice this feeling, well on in the dealings:

"My mind has often involuntarily been impressed with the secret sorrow and sense of the want of true sincerity in these poor people, in which I see different schemes and opposite interests are engaged, while the poor Indians have been exposed to their sufferings, as grim sufferers under an undue influence."

To relieve the strain, Captain Elliot offered to go to the Rapids and to bear a message from the Commissioners to the Indians and to his superior, Colonel McKee. He returned from this mission on July 29th, bringing with him twenty-five or thirty Indians, among them "Carry-one-about," a Wyandot chief, Ocohongehelas, the great war-chief of the Delawares, and Colonel McKee, Simon Girty and an interpreter, Smith. The party was wary of too close intercourse and encamped on an island, Bois Blanc, in the river, opposite the Elliot mansion. This island is the modern Bob Lo, under which contorted name it now furnishes recreation to the pleasure seekers of Detroit.

If no other reason were assignable, the presence of McKee and Girty at the Indian Conference at the Rapids would be sufficient to explain the failure of the negotiations. Probably no more unscrupulous and wily politicians ever influenced the red men than this pair. Whether the Americans realized that fact, does not appear in any of the accounts of the Treaty, but we can know today what they could not,—that the British Government, through Canada, was semi-officially striving to undo some of the concessions to the new United States, under cloak of Indian sovereignty, with the hope, doubtless, that a new turn of events might in some way regain for her the vast valley of the Mississippi, down to the Spanish possessions. William Savery and Joseph Moore hardly mention political considerations at all, and Jacob Lindley only indirectly. General Benjamin Lincoln constantly refers to them. His far-seeing eye was on the future and his record of the expedition is a continuity of observations on possibilities of national expansion, dealing with routes, watersheds and Indian traits. Most of all was he exasperated by the continuance of British garrisons in the forts in territory ceded to the United States, along the southern shores of the Lakes, and retained by the British, upon the pretext that they were not yet safe in American hands from Indian ravages.

McKee and Girty and their Indians merely brought another address, delivered by the Wyandot chief, "Carry-one-about," stating that their envoys at Niagara had not been sufficiently explicit, nor had the Commissioners been unequivocal in their reply. This time the reply, like the address, was to be in writing. Once again the elaborate formalism of question and answer, involving endless summaries and repetitions, and all the punctilia of Indian etiquette and conference were gone through. The Indians simply propounded again their old questions, whether the Commissioners had power to arrange boundaries and, if so, whether the boundary would be reëstablished at the Ohio, as stipulated in the Treaty of Fort Stanwix. With inexhaustible patience the Commissioners wrote their reply, detailing again the treaties and cessions since Fort Stanwix and the impossibility of recalling emigrants who, in good faith had entered on lands ceded by these later treaties. They concluded that for a confirmation of these cessions the Indians would receive "such a large sum in money or goods as was never given at one time for any quantity of Indian lands since the white people set their foot on this island" and also a large annuity for many years to come.

The Indian deputation withdrew to their island, Bois Blanc, to consider an answer. Among them were representatives of ten nations and several of them were great men among the Delawares, Shawanese and Wyandots. The latter said they knew Friends and were acquainted with their motives in coming. Whereupon William Savery presented five of the principal men with neat tobacco boxes, well filled, which they said would constantly remind them of Friends. The interval between councils gave much opportunity for conversation and Friends appear to have made full use of it, the original instructions from Knox to the Commissioners to the contrary notwithstanding.

The next morning the Indians returned, "and after the fire was kindled, and they and we had smoked our pipes on the benches under the trees," the Shawanese chief, Kakai-palathy, arose to deliver the answer, with Simon Girty interpreting. The chief stated that they would return to the Maumee and deliver the Commissioners' document to their fellows, and (so Girty interpreted) the Commissioners might "now go home." Such a statement was almost an insult, and certainly was an ultimatum. It was the tensest moment in all the long weeks of negotiations, for in the abrupt dismissal was involved all the failure that had been looming larger as time went on. To Captain Matthew Elliot belongs the quick intelligence and action that for the time, at least, saved the situation and unmasked Girty. Elliot immediately repeated Girty's interpretation to another chief, declaring it wrong, in which the Indian agreed. Girty insisted that he had truly interpreted, but the American interpreters having heard differently from other chiefs, the spokesman was recalled and promptly disavowed having made such a statement, adding that he had requested the Commissioners to remain until they had consulted the head warriors. And so it was adjusted, though Girty was insistent upon his correct interpretation, and, as Heckewelder states, "supported his insolence by a quill or long feather run through the under part of his nose cross-ways."

Even his biographer admits that "the evidence is strong that the declaration was wholly the work of Girty." But one can surmise that the experienced old Moravian, Heckewelder, with his intimate knowledge of Indians and their various languages and dialects, was better able than the Friends to penetrate the guile that Girty typified. Perhaps the Friends were more discreet and wrote less of their real sentiments in their Journals, or perhaps they were really less suspicious of the duplicity of men of Girty's stamp,—at any rate the old Moravian missionary sensed the danger and stinted nothing in voicing and writing his distrust. He learned that there were fifteen hundred warriors at the Rapids of the Maumee and no women. The latter circumstance was especially suspicious to him as in his experience the women and children were invariably brought along to treaties so that they could claim the more presents in the distribution of bounty. He saw nothing but war in the atmosphere, and he laid the blame for it clearly on the British, who would not allow the Indians to act freely and independently, but provided them with evil advisers.

The Friends had their own special concern in the matter and an anxious time this drift in the negotiations caused them. There could be little doubt that an ultimatum was pending and in its wake they as clearly as any could foresee another chapter of horrible border warfare with all its attendant atrocities. They had conversation upon the trying situation and realized "the necessity of asking for fresh supplies of wisdom and patience to enable us to answer, as much as in us lay, the objects of our journey." The best that appeared possible under the circumstances was to send the address from the Meeting for Sufferings and a letter from the six Friends by Captain Elliot and Colonel McKee for delivery and interpretation. In addition to that, as William Savery notes, closer and more dangerous contacts were discussed:

# THE END OF THE DRAMA

"Friends consulted together on the propriety of some of our number going with these chiefs to the council. The concern and fervent engagement of our minds that the poor Indians might be wisely directed in the present juncture, produced a resignation in my mind to be one, though it appeared to me there would be some risk of our lives; but upon laying it before the commissioners, Captain Bunbury and Thomas M'Kee, they were not easy we should attempt it, as the Indians had positively forbid any American citizen to come on the ground, while the grand-council held; we therefore declined it."

One cannot but admire the meek bravery of this attitude toward a possible avenue of service. No men were more unused to physical prowess than these Quakers in a wilderness with painted savages, frontiersmen and army officers. They had left home under deep concern for these savages and had heard and seen enough to dampen any ardor, save a spiritual concern. They had not, as is painfully evident, any very concrete program or any practical solution for the impasse, but they had an abiding faith in spiritual forces, and believing themselves rightly called into the service, they doubtless thought that He who had sent them into the wilderness would give them the words they had need of when the emergency arose. But they never reached the Council.

Then ensued, from August 1st to 14th, another period of waiting. With failure all but certain it must have been a dispiriting experience that William Savery chronicled:

"Very rainy, and much wet in my tent; arose about three o'clock, bundled up my mattress and tied it in a painted cloth, and sat up till sunrise."

Meanwhile at the Rapids, debate ran high. Frequent reports of the struggle were brought to the meadows below Amherstburg, Ontario. Several parties of Indians, returning to the northwest, passed through, their clothes worn to rags. They were tired of waiting and alarmed at the sickness and mortality prevailing at the Indian Camp. Seventeen Indians had died, among them three chiefs, and they were about to remove the camp to the side of the Lake. The Six Nations and the Seven Nations of Canada were for peace; incidentally, their boundaries were not in question. The Shawanese, Wyandots, Miamis and Delawares were unalterably opposed and it was their territory that was immediately in controversy. Brant and Cornplanter of the Six Nations were indefatigable on behalf of peace, and on the 11th had spoken twice in favor of it, and were about to speak again. Brant was reported as determined to speak a fourth time, in the face of Indian usage to the contrary, if it were necessary. Indians whom Heckewelder knew personally informed him that "the combined nations had charged both the British and the five nations as the cause of these troubles, they having put the tomahawk into their hands."

On the 14th, the Commissioners demanded that the British grant them passage to the Rapids in person, a demand more promptly refused than made. Two more long days ensued, in which the Friends were "often looking towards the point (Grassy Point) twenty miles distant, with a spy glass, desirous of discovering a boat." The Commissioners, baffled in their attempt to go in person, sent two swift Indian runners to the Rapids, about forty miles by land, for information, and all hands nursed their impatience as best they could. On the last day of the suspense, William Savery had a conference with Colonel Pickering (the only mention of him in the Journal) who was "desirous of giving me more information than I had yet received, of the treaties held by the United States with the Indians, and the nature of their uneasiness." The occasion was apparently satisfactory to both and was marked by much candor on Pickering's part. William Savery was "sensible of the confidence he reposed in me, by showing me the commissioners' books and papers."

One can but wonder whether Pickering, realizing that

the negotiations were about to fail, was buttressing his case for the return to Philadelphia and an anxious public, no small part of which, in the Capital, was composed of Quakers. The only alternative being, as all knew, a renewal of the war, it is probable that the Commissioners all felt as did Lincoln,—"Knowing the upright and liberal views of the United States, * * * we trust impartial judges will not attribute the continuance of the war to them." If there were any "impartial judges," the Quaker deputation contained them.

Finally, on August 16th, a canoe with two Indian deputies, who proved to be Wyandots, was discerned coming around Grassy Point and the long wait was over. The messengers bore a long letter, which Heckewelder pronounced

"both impertinent and insolent, being intended to put an end to the treaty business. The language in the speech was such, that no person having knowledge of the Indians and their modes of expression, would believe it an Indian speech."

Whatever its linguistic inspiration, it was at least consistent in disavowing on the part of the Indians, any treaties save that of Fort Stanwix, stating that money was no consideration to the Indians, and with fine irony suggesting that the vast sums promised should be used in compensating the settlers beyond the Ohio for the retaking of their lands.

The letter ended with a noble and pathetic note, all the more so because throughout the entire negotiations the Indians had not varied an inch from their previous statement that the Ohio as a boundary was the *sine qua non* of their willingness to treat at all. They said, in conclusion:

"Brothers: We desire you to consider that our only demand is the peaceable possession of a small part of our once great country. Look back and view the lands from whence we have been driven to this spot. We can retreat no further, because the country behind hardly affords food for its present inhabitants, and we have therefore resolved to leave our bones in this small space, to which we are now consigned."

(Signed)

| | |
|---|---|
| Wyandots (a Bear) | Seven Nations of Canada (Turtle) |
| Delawares (Turtle) | Senecas of the Glaize (Turtle) |
| Shawanese | Pottawattamies (Fish) |
| Connoys (Turkey) | Munsees |
| Miamis (Turtle) | Nantikokes (Turtle) |
| Ottowas (Fish) | |
| Chippewas (Crane) | Mohigans (Turtle and Turkey) |

To the modern reader, the impertinence, contempt and insolence of this address, even if written under the British influence, is hard to see. The effect upon the group at Elliot's was, however, instantaneous. It was immediately patent to all that the end had come. The Commissioners answered by a line or two, the disconsolate and scared Wyandots slunk away and the lawn resounded with the noise and turmoil of striking the tents and packing baggage. Hostility was in the air immediately. The luggage was ordered on board the *Dunmore* at once; some removed to the ship to sleep, while others huddled into the house for safety, as night approached. In spite of the alarm and hubbub, be it said to the credit of the Friends, in the language of Jacob Lindley, that they "slept in their tents as heretofore, I believe with little fear."

It was a gloomy evening to the Quaker delegation. They got together in a solemn little group, to feel for any duty that might open up. None appeared; in fact, they were struck with consternation, because two of them had heard General Lincoln state that "they had received just such an answer as he could have wished for." They did not dare to analyze the meaning of that statement, but they, as well as any, knew that the warriors were on their way back home, or were lurking in the vicinity, ready for some act of savage reprisal, before returning to meet Wayne in the campaign that was now a certainty, with the opening of the next spring.

# THE END OF THE DRAMA

"We felt much shut up and as we had never been called in the counsel with the Commissioners nor had any public conference with the Indians, we were obliged to bear our own burdens and submit the awful subject to the interposition of the Divine hand."

So great was the haste that the whole party, thirty-one passengers besides the crew and the marines, and two bears, belonging to Captain Bunbury, sailed off in the *Dunmore* before noon the next day.

This attempt at a treaty, in its failure, marks the last stand of any importance of a considerable body of Indians to stop by peaceable council the encroachment of the whites. The race was a doomed one. Its fate was inevitably sealed. There was no man wise enough to propose a suitable peaceful solution. Humanly speaking the issue was insoluble, not only as between Indian and American, but more so because of the British policy of fanning the existing discontent. Of Girty and his ilk, we may say with his biographer, that though he "aided powerfully to frustrate negotiations, it cannot be said that he alone secured the failure." The combined effect of the British interference did, however, secure that failure, and the bloodshed of the following year, and much of that in the War of 1812, can be attributed more justly to Simon Girty, Colonel McKee and Governor Simcoe than to any other human beings.

Does it seem chimerical to those of us who lived through the "War to End War," and have witnessed the pitiable reaction; or does it even seem unduly idealistic that these apostles of peace had gone forth into the wilderness, strong in the power of their God, to effect righteousness, and were forced to return empty handed? Have we of today garnered any richer results from the human agony of the Great War; or has mankind, even yet, learned to control those events that jeopardize and prejudice the peace, even before the fighting is begun?

Jacob Lindley had told a British Officer

"that when the broils in France should subside, the African slave trade be abolished, and a permanent peace be concluded with our American Indians, all this globe might be at peace, and that swords (of which he had one by his side) might be beaten into plowshares."

How fatally pregnant with prophetic meaning seem these three desiderata, and how full of bloody foreboding for the generations to come! Twenty years of warfare for the French and British before Waterloo laid Europe prostrate in bankruptcy and degradation comparable only to that of today; four years of Civil War before slavery followed the slave trade into the discard, and eighty years of border warfare, from Little Turtle and Tecumseh to Geronimo and his Apaches, before a "permanent peace" was concluded with the red man,—all these things accomplished, and still we have not peace. "No more War!" As well say, "No more fires, no more famine, no more sickness!" say the cynic and the pessimist. But then as now the spirit of righteousness and justice, the unquenchable idealism of the revelation of the Prince of Peace, swells up in the hearts and souls of the men of good-will, until we of today cry aloud with William Savery, when he reviewed the wretchedness, the wickedness, the atrocities and the duplicity, of which he and his associates, the long summer through, had been the unwilling witnesses:

"O ye professors of the benign and heavenly doctrines of the Gospel, that breathes nothing but peace and good-will to men, how will ye appear in the awful day of retribution, when our Divine Master shall come to judge the world in righteousness, if any of you have been promoters of the great devastation, wretchedness, and misery, which mark the footsteps of war?"

## CHAPTER XI

# THE JOURNEY HOME

A remarkable and in a sense, an inexplicable feature of the Indian Treaty of 1793 was the route by which William Savery and William Hartshorne returned home. Sixty souls, including the Commissioners' retinue, boarded the *Dunmore* at once, apprehensive of the danger of longer tarriance, being desirous of spreading the information of the failure of the treaty before the Indians had time to do mischief without warning. The whole party traversed Lake Erie together, but upon arriving at Fort Erie, Jacob Lindley borrowed a horse from the Commissioners and John Parrish, John Elliott and Joseph Moore, having had their horses sent to them, set out across New York and Pennsylvania for home, visiting families of Friends en route.

There were not horses enough to go round, so the rest had no alternative but to proceed by water. Pickering and Randolph returned by the Mohawk River and Albany, the route by which Lincoln and his party had come out.

Lincoln elected to return via the St. Lawrence and Lake Champlain. It is probable that he, as a New Englander, was interested primarily in the water-ways projects with which his mind was certainly busy on the way out. Early in his Journal he speculated on the possibility of connecting the waters of the Hudson and the St. Lawrence by canals and his vision also forecast the great Barge Canal of today in its utilization of the waters of the Mohawk River. It may be, too, that he wished to see again the beauties of Champlain and to revisit the Forts and Stillwater and Saratoga where he had assisted in the capture of Burgoyne.

Lincoln was accompanied by the Secretary of the Commission, Charles Storer of Maine, Dr. McCoskry of Carlisle, Pennsylvania, Heckewelder, the Moravian, and William Savery and William Hartshorne, the latter, as it proved, being twice able to save the lives of the whole party in the stress of storm.

Whatever were Lincoln's motives, we have no slight allusion to those of William Savery and William Hartshorne in choosing this route. The former merely records:

"I felt heavy at parting with them (the other Friends); but seeing no alternative, wrote by Jacob Lindley, informing my wife of my intention to return by Montreal."

If the motive was a religious one it certainly was not fulfilled by preaching, as the perilous journey and the swift traveling presented no opportunities. It may have been personal attachment on William Savery's part to Benjamin Lincoln, to whom he referred in 1794, as "my old, generous Friend, Gen'l Lincoln."

Leaving Fort Erie, the travelers went by batteaux to Winternut's Tavern and Chippeway and thence by wagon to Queenston.

On the 30th of August they sailed at 3 A. M. in a small sloop eastward on Lake Ontario, making the remarkable distance of one hundred thirty miles, and the next day arriving at Kingston and proceeding twenty-five miles in a batteau toward Lachine. With a crew of four Frenchmen and nine passengers the batteau proceeded down the St. Lawrence all night, the travelers wrapping themselves in their blankets and sleeping as best they could. September 1st took them through "the greatest number of islands I ever saw in a river, which are called the Thousand Islands" and through a long rapids into Lake St. Francis, a journey of over one hundred miles in the day. Of the squall that struck them at this point, William Savery's vivid description can best tell:

# THE JOURNEY HOME

"The wind being fresh, it was doubtful whether we could cross it or not in the night; but our Canadians concluding to venture on, we all laid down as in the preceding night. The lake is about fifteen miles long and six broad. I slept none; the clouds appeared wild and threatening for a night voyage. About ten o'clock, the helmsman seeing a gust rising, roused all up; and in a few minutes a terrible hurricane came on, with tremendous lightning and thunder, and very dark; but by the flashes of the lightning, we judged we were about a mile or a mile and a half from shore. The rain poured down in torrents, and it appeared almost a hopeless attempt to reach the shore; but some of our company, possessing considerable fortitude and skill, were active in directing and encouraging the men to persevere in rowing—notwithstanding all which, such was the impetuosity of the waves and violence of the winds, added to a deluge of rain and perpetual thunder and lightning, that one of our best hands threw down his oar, and cried out in French, 'We shall all perish,—we shall all perish!' But Providence, whose tender mercies were over us, had more gracious designs concerning us, and at length brought us safe to shore, which happily proved to be sandy, or we might still have been dashed to pieces. Having a piece of painted cloth on board, as many of us as could got under it, as it continued to rain very hard. About twelve o'clock it cleared away, and, being very cold, we concluded to go on shore, and walk about to warm ourselves, being thoroughly wet, and shivering with the cold. It was thought impossible to kindle a fire, as everything was so wet; but one of our Friends striking to light our pipes, we were enabled to kindle one, which was a great relief to us, and, sitting round it till daylight, were enabled to prepare something for breakfast, and set sail again. I believe all of us were thankful for our deliverance."

Heckewelder's account is more specific in its denunciation of the superstitious crew, with faith, that soon waned, in "some pieces of consecrated host, which they carried in leather bags in their bosoms," but who in the first breath of the storm laid down their oars and quailed in fear as the boat drove at the mercy of the winds. One is reminded of another shipwreck and another lay-pilot of apostolic times in the rest of his account:

"In this precarious situation, the quaker preacher, William Hartshorne, of Shrewsbury, New Jersey, who had in former times frequently made trips to the West Indies in small vessels, became the visible instrument of our preservation. By dint of urgent and encouraging appeals to the boatmen, he prevailed upon them, with the exception of one, who was so terrified that he trembled all over, to take up the oars; and he himself assumed the command of the boat, in which he was supported by the secretary of the commission, Mr. Charles Storer, and a New England gentleman. Our boat was steered to the opposite shore, through the most frightful breakers, and rocks above and below water, amidst the darkness of night and the raging storm. * * * In the morning we saw with awe and loud thanksgivings to Providence, the numerous rocks projecting out of the water like hay stacks in a meadow, through and over which our boat had been successfully conducted without receiving any material damage."

A new tavern at the end of the Lake failed to have the fire they had anticipated, so they set out again and ran two rapids with tremendous speed, the first of them, nine miles in thirty-five minutes and the next of several miles in four minutes. Upon arriving at Lachine at 3 P.M. William Savery was very ill, but even a restless night in addition to his illness did not stop the journey. The baggage was put in carts and a calash provided for each pair of the travelers, and so over an extremely bad road they drove to Montreal.

Like Detroit, Montreal was a stirring frontier town and quite populous. Its old world market with dog-drawn carts, about twice the size of a wheel-barrow, laden with fruit and vegetables, was said to be the cheapest in America. The evident Catholicism struck William Savery and prepared him for the European experiences that were to be his later on. The fabulous wealth of the churches, accruing from a one-ninth levy on all land sales at public auction, at the church door, the devotions of the people, kneeling in public in the chapels, the richly endowed nunneries and the nuns, in their long black robes and hoods, were all strange sights to the Philadelphians. The kindness of the commanding officer in providing two carts and four calashes for their convenience the next morning provoked alike their gratitude and their astonishment. The conveyances were commandeered by arbitrary demand under military authority, such being "the effects of military government."

Leaving Montreal at 6 A.M., they breakfasted at Chambly and then, through a beautiful country, twenty-seven miles to St. Johns, on the Richelieu River. In spite of the continued illness of William Savery, Captain Scott and several others of the company, the rapid journey proceeded. Fifteen embarked in a small boat but not being favored by either wind or current they stopped for the night at an undesirable house, the character of which and of the people frequenting it was bad. Another sleepless night ensued and still they pressed rapidly on, passing the American custom house on the New York side, and entering the foot of Lake Champlain. Those who have seen the dangerous and lowering beauty of Lake Champlain in storm will appreciate the rashness of the next part of this remarkable journey, which could only have been inspired by reckless ignorance or an over-weening desire to get forward.

The master of the boat fell sick at this point, and they had to leave him behind, having only a sixteen-year-old boy, who knew the Lake, to steer and manage the boat. Once again William Hartshorne's nautical skill was of value. He took command and with a fine wind they sailed all day but came to grief in the dark evening in attempting to run in to Gillis' Creek for the night. Says William Savery's account:

"None of us being acquainted with the entrance, we ran upon shoals and rocks, and the sea and winds being high, our little bark thumped as though the bottom would have been beaten out. In great danger we continued on the shoals near an hour; at length, with much difficulty, we got off, and anchoring in sufficient depth of water, were obliged to lay here the remainder of the night, and a painful one it was to me; it being rainy and a high wind, and no light to find our blankets. I laid down on some casks and trunks, but slept none, and my disorder returned upon me with double force in the morning."

The day following was one of continuous sickness for William Savery. He had little interest in anything save to get to bed as soon as they stopped for the night at a small house where the only bed was put to his use, although there were many lodging there. On this he got the first sleep for two nights. The rapidity of their traveling is evidenced by their arrival at Skeensborough (modern Whitehall) on the New York-Vermont line and east of Lake George, only two days after they had left the Canadian boundary. Here it was almost necessary to leave William Savery behind, so ill had he become with a high fever. Captain Scott and several others also were suffering and the division of the party seemed inevitable. "Yet I had a great desire to reach home, if practicable," says our traveler, and with that desire he persisted the next day over exceedingly rough roads to Fort Ann where he took a little food and after a rest went on to Saratoga by evening.

A tolerable night put them forward to Still-water for breakfast. General Lincoln, who had been in Gates' army in its capture of Burgoyne in this vicinity, interested the party with reminiscenses of that drama of fifteen years before and so through a pleasant country, they reached Albany.

At Saratoga the party heard for the first of the terrible epidemic of yellow fever that was then at its height in Philadelphia,—the most terrible scourge that has ever visited the City. The news greatly depressed William Savery in his weakened condition and he mourned over his "beloved city" and the vast numbers who died daily and were buried without the ordinary rites.

From Albany the party took a sloop to New York. It arrived there after grounding once in low water and was only got off at high tide by jettisoning a quantity of lumber which was tied in rafts and reacquired several miles below. In the five days occupied with this voyage William Savery had two violent fits of fever, one of them preceded by the

most violent chill of his experience. The anticipation of
entering his own pestilence ridden city in his weakness,
exhausted by travel and worn with fever, must have laid
heavily upon his spirits.

The Philadelphia travelers, having bade farewell to the
rest of the company in New York, reached their homes
about as soon as those who had come across by land. Truly
their way had been unusual and one can hardly surmise the
cause of their haste. To be sure, William Savery was always a traveler, and at forty-three was still young enough
to feel strongly the spirit of adventure. It may be that a
justifiable curiosity to see new lands and strange people,
particularly the French in Canada, had actuated him,
particularly owing to the French origin of the Savery
family. Whatever his desire, his gameness under serious
illness, in persisting in proceeding with the journey and the
fervent sympathy for the fever stricken sufferers in his
beloved city, evince a strength of personality and a recu-
perative ability little short of miraculous. Travel in those
days was hard, very hard, and William Savery experienced
it at its worst on two continents, but his whole spirit was
the apostolic willingness to endure hardness as a good
soldier of Christ Jesus.

## CHAPTER XII

# THE YELLOW FEVER, 1793

William Savery reached Germantown, near Philadelphia, on September 19, 1793. Though he left no record of the next few months, it is probable that he did not go into the doomed City. Joseph Moore by his different route arrived in Germantown the same day, and there found Sarah Savery, who had fled the City and taken lodging at Caspar Haines', where William Savery joined her. "Wyck," the ancient and present home of the Haines family, is still standing on the Main Street, Germantown. As stated above, he had heard that Philadelphia was in the grip of the yellow fever, as the returning travelers came through Saratoga, but he could not have known its seriousness until he arrived home, spent and weary, and ravaged with fever and ague, and learned from his own family the extent of the scourge.

Philadelphia was then a City of 50,000 people. The malady first appeared in Water Street, between Arch and Race Streets and thence gradually spread, mostly along the water front (then largely a residential district) until the deaths and consternation almost depopulated the City. It began at the latter end of July, and during August the average daily number of deaths was eleven. By mid-August the exodus of citizens began toward the higher elevations north and west of the stricken town, and the deaths increased to a daily average of fifty in September. The business life of the City ceased, the streets were almost deserted and burials were largely conducted by negroes (they being immune to the contagion) who went through the streets calling, "Bring out your dead; bring out your dead." Trenches were dug in the burial ground at Fourth and Arch Streets and the bodies put in by rows without careful designation, record or distinction. The present meeting house, built on that site in 1804, covers many of these rows and on that account the cellar has never been entirely excavated.

Well authenticated accounts are extant of the desperate straits of stricken people, left to die alone by mercenary nurses, or deserted by their families, and discovered, days after their death, in conditions too horrible to relate. Joseph Moore, who died of the dread disease three weeks later, described the Friends' Burial Ground at Fourth and Arch Streets,—

"The sight was awful and alarming, to behold the many new graves, and others digging, with the hearses standing, and some coming and going, most of which were attended by black people, whom, it is said, the fever did not reach."

Of the Guardians of the Poor, all fled but three,—James Wilson, Jacob Jenkins and William Sansom. A public meeting was called to procure substitutes and as a result twenty-three persons volunteered to aid the three faithful Guardians of the Poor. Of these many were unable to work on account of illness or death and the main burden fell on twelve persons of whom were Daniel Offley, Stephen Girard, Thomas Wistar, John Letchworth and Thomas Savery, the brother of William Savery. Thomas Savery took his wife and four children to the country, bade them a tender farewell and returned to the stricken City to labor throughout the rest of the pestilence. Testimonials on parchment were issued by public authority after the epidemic had passed away to each of these benefactors, bearing the names of all who bore a part in that obnoxious and dangerous service. As stated in these testimonials, a hospital was provided at Bush Hill for the reception of the stricken, where Stephen Girard and Peter Helm were peculiarly active in providing every possible comfort for the sick and decent burial for the dead. No more appropriate example of heroic service without the glamor of pomp and circumstance can be found than the quiet, unostentatious actions of those devoted men, whose names are set forth in the testimonials. That it was dangerous service is shown by the casualty list, six out of a total of twenty-six,—among the dead being two of the Overseers of the Poor, James Wilson and Jacob Jenkins.

As in the Influenza Epidemic of the fall of 1918, many of the victims were young people. Daniel Offley, a member of the Volunteer Committee of Health, was stricken and died, aged thirty-seven; Charles Williams, who like Daniel Offley was a recommended minister in the Society of Friends, died at twenty-nine. Joseph Moore, who had accompanied William Savery to the Treaty, died of the fever within three weeks of his return. Rebecca Jones and Stephen Grellet were both of them given up for dead, and their recovery was little short of miraculous. Throughout the whole time, two doctors stood out heroically, Doctor Physick and Doctor Cathrall, refusing to follow the lead of less courageous men into the country.

In October the epidemic reached its peak, with a daily average of sixty deaths, the highest number being 119 in one day. By the end of the month, the force of the visitation was nearly spent.

The Friends' meetings for worship had been kept up during the entire period, though but sparsely attended. The Yearly Meeting occurred in September and the business was transacted. Very few Representatives attended, and from three Quarterly Meetings not one responded.

All of the country regions around Philadelphia were crowded with refugees, and of all others this was true especially of Germantown and Darby.

It was at Germantown that the Federal and State Governments were set up. President Washington dwelt in the Perot (later the Morris) mansion on the Main Street; the various members of the Cabinet occupied buildings adjacent and Congress requisitioned the Germantown Academy building, though never actually occupied it. By coincidence, the village was full of French refugees from the West Indies, fled from the St. Domingo massacre, a shiftless and lazy lot, that filled the streets with their queer chatter and queerer costumes. Their noisy manners and ubiquitous gaiety and music were distinctly distasteful to the Friends. Prior to this invasion of summer fever refugees from the City, Germantown (sometimes then called "Longville") had been all that either name implies. As there were no deaths there from the fever, it became popular as a summer retreat, and real estate prices rose rapidly. From that date preaching in English began in the churches, where theretofore, save in the Friends' meeting, the preaching had been in German.[1]

William Savery's name does not appear in the list of the Volunteer Committee of Health along with his brother's, and it is entirely likely that his own severe illness required him to avoid danger of further complications. From the frequent mention of him and his doings in Elizabeth Drinker's pages it is altogether probable that he spent some time in recuperation and thereafter drove to and from the City to attend to business. The Drinker family had gone to Germantown, lodging at the eighth mile stone, just above Hesser's Tavern, across the way. From this vantage point several incidents locate William Savery definitely during these months.

On September 20th, Elizabeth Drinker wrote,—"Wm Savery and young Marshall called here before meeting— Wm just returned from the treaty." On September 22nd, William Savery attended Germantown Meeting and preached and was fervent in "solemn supplication," this

[1] Watson, 2, 63.

being the First Day of Yearly Meeting week. He called again upon the Drinkers on October 4th, reporting many deaths in the City.

At that time it was customary to hold a Youths' Meeting once a year, early in October in Germantown, and William Savery and Thomas Fisher, being in attendance at that meeting, brought the news of the death of Joseph Moore, referred to above. On October 13th he called and on the 14th he accompanied Henry Drinker to Darby, to visit John Parrish, who had taken his family there from the City. Finally, on October 17th and 25th, Henry Drinker and William Savery were together again, on the latter day going "to Tommy Fisher's."

On November 14th the Committee for the Relief of the Sick and Poor published an address to their fellow citizens, stating that the scourge was over, that the death rate had fallen to normal and that return was safe. The population returned with the cooler weather, the City resumed its business, markets reopened and the taverns began again their activities, but the people were sobered. The recollection that this same thing had happened in 1699 brought forth exhaustive medical inquiry and many reforms, both moral and sanitary, but the same sort of pestilence broke out again in 1798. Whatever its origin and cause, the epidemic left a deep impress on the Society of Friends in Philadelphia. William Savery wrote to Sarah Harrison:

"You have been witnesses and some of you partakers, * * * in giving forth warning after warning to a people who have too many of them, been ungrateful receivers of the manifold mercies and blessings of a gracious and long suffering God. * * * more especially, we must mourn on account of that ardor which prevails among many of our fellow professors, after the riches, splendour, vanities and delusive enjoyments of a perishing world, which, but so few months ago, were exhibited in their native colours and emptiness."

## CHAPTER XIII

# THE IROQUOIS AND THE TREATY OF 1794

It will be recalled that upon the failure of the Indian Treaty of 1793, with the representatives of practically all the Indian tribes then in contact with white influences, the Commissioners and their attachés left for home precipitately and by many different ways, to send broadcast the information that no treaty had been made and that Indian depredations might again be expected. The truce was over. General Wayne, whose uneasy passivity had aroused the suspicion of the savages and the ire of the Commissioners, at once took active measures. During the winter months he completed his army and gathered supplies, while the anxiety over the Indian situation eclipsed all other topics in Philadelphia. In November, 1793, a report was bruited about that the Indians had beaten the army and that Wayne himself had fallen. It was an anxious winter.

By spring of 1794, the army advanced to the place of St. Clair's defeat and erected Fort Recovery, a name calculated to reinspire faith in the military prowess of the United States. By August 8th, Wayne had advanced without opposition to the confluence of the Au Glaize and the Miamis of the Lakes (modern City of Defiance, Ohio) and there he threw up breastworks. On the Miamis of the Lakes (modern Maumee River), thirty miles below him, were the Rapids where the main body of Indians had held their Council in 1793. Although this was well within the present state of Ohio, the British still maintained there a fortified post; one of those rankling sore spots that festered the relations of the new government with the British. The bitter hatred indulged by many subordinate officers in the British service who had been royalist refugees from the Colonies during the Revolution found an outlet in cherishing such posts.

Around the British Post had collected two thousand Indians, a larger force than either Harmar or St. Clair had faced in their disastrous expeditions. With them Wayne made one more attempt at a negotiated peace and upon the rejection of his offer he proceeded cautiously down the Miami. The Indians were led by the redoubtable Miami Chief, Little Turtle, or Meshecunnaqua, who had defeated Harmar, and in company with Brant had overthrown St. Clair. Little Turtle was opposed to meeting the Americans in battle at the Maumee, but was overruled by the other chiefs and the battle was joined on August 20, 1794. The Americans charged and held the offensive throughout the engagement, driving the Indians before them with much slaughter, up to the guns of the encroaching British fort. Wayne remained three days on the front, laying waste the homes and the fields of the Indians. His report states that the burning included the

"barns, stores and property of Colonel M'Kee, the British Indian Agent and principal stimulator of the war between the United States and the savages,"—

an interesting sequel to McKee's activities as go-between in the abortive treaty of the year before. Wayne then returned to Au Glaize and destroyed Indian villages and corn fields within fifty miles of the river, drove the Indians entirely out of the district and, for that time and section ended the border wars.

Another year was spent in dickering over the terms of a treaty and active in it, with all the dilatory tactics at their command, were our old British friends, Colonel McKee and Governor Simcoe. Finally on August 3, 1795, at Greenville, Ohio, Wayne concluded peace with the hostile Indians entirely on his own terms.

# THE IROQUOIS AND THE TREATY OF 1794

The difficulty which the Six Nations of New York had experienced at the attempted Treaty of 1793, in being excluded from the private councils of the other tribes, had been on account of their being considered in the American interest. The Mohawks, who lived in Canada, alone, of all the Six Nations, had held out against the United States, largely through the influence of Brant, the most powerful individual in the Six Nations, and his lieutenant, Red Jacket, of the Senecas, the most eloquent and witty orator of the tribes.

British influence was, however, strongly exerted to excite them and to keep things stirred up. Canadian border diplomacy had not yet gone beyond the stage of Indian allies, or rather, tools. It is altogether probable that the Iroquois Treaty of 1794, which the Friends attended, was as largely calculated by the Federal Government to keep the Six Nations busy in New York and thus prevent them from joining the hostile Indians in Ohio against General Wayne as to effect a real peace with them. Certain it is that the Six Nations were becoming restive and suspicious. The Legislature of Pennsylvania, at the instigation of Governor Mifflin, authorized the raising of a company of artillery and three companies of riflemen to protect the western boundaries, as Wayne had taken with him all the Federal troops into Ohio. The Pennsylvanians were put under the command of Major Ebenezer Denny, and sent to Presque Isle (modern City of Erie) ostensibly to protect Commissioners who were laying out towns there and hard by, at Le Boeuf, but also, as Denny wrote, on March 1, 1794,

"to cut off intercourse between the Six Nations, who had become wavering and suspicious, and the hostile Indians and (thus) favor General Wayne, who was preparing to march against the latter."

On October 19th, he heard for the first of Wayne's victory in August, and wrote that the "severe drubbing" would be "very apt to quiet the Six Nations, the instigations of the British to the contrary, notwithstanding."

In view of this proposed treaty with the Six Nations the Meeting for Sufferings in Philadelphia was notified in August, 1794, both by the United States Government and by the Indians that the presence of another delegation of Friends would be welcome. Under these circumstances, four Friends,—David Bacon, John Parrish, William Savery and James Emlen,—offered themselves for the service, under a sense of religious duty, and were appointed; whereupon Peter Yarnall called at Drinkers' at "Clearfield," now Logan, Philadelphia, "smoked a pipe with us on his way home from Meeting for Sufferings" and so informed the Friends.

Of these Friends, John Parrish and William Savery had been in attendance at the abortive Treaty of the year before. Their departure was precipitate, as they were appointed on September 9th and left on the 15th, for Canandaigua, New York State. In his manuscript Journal of this trip, William Savery invariably refers to the place of assemblage as Canadaqua, which may have been the early name for the town, then a frontier settlement.

Their departure was a solemn as well as a social event. Henry Drinker, Thomas Stewardson, Sarah Savery and probably some others accompanied the Friends to Germantown where they stopped for refreshments at Caspar Haines' and took an affectionate leave of each other.

They bore with them a letter from the Meeting for Sufferings to the Indians, certifying them to be

"our friends, whom we greatly love, being true men, whose love is so great to their Indian brethren, the old inhabitants of this land of America, that they are willing to come to see you, with desires to do you good."

William Savery's own reflections on leaving were summed up:

[ 122 ]

"Nothing from without affords so great consolation and strength in undertaking such arduous journeys as a sense that we now are favored with, of the precious unity and affectionate concern of our near connections and brethren."

The journey to northern Pennsylvania was uneventful and is interesting largely for the references to Friends and their settlements en route,—at Joseph Potts' and Thomas Rutter's near Pottsgrove, a mention of an uncle of William Savery's, Samuel Jackson at Reading and a cousin of the same name at "Catawisse"; breakfast was had with Mordicai Lee at Maiden Creek; at "Catawisse," John Mur, John Lloyd and Richard Nesbitt set them on their way. Later they partook of fresh mutton chops and sour metheglin, "an excellent regale," and so came to Muncy, where, then as now, there were "both the means and the will" for the hospitable entertainment of "poor travelers," at the farms of Samuel Wallis and William Ellis. The next day, what with rain and a violent fever on William Savery's part, only seven miles' advance was registered, to Loyalsock, where they lodged at the Widow Mary Harris', she and her large family of grown children being the last Friends encountered for some time. From this point the difficulty of traveling increased. The route led up the Lycoming River and across the watershed into the Valley of the Tioga and thence into New York State. Though on horseback, the travelers found the way exceedingly difficult, with stones, roots and mire and innumerable fords. At the Block House, so-called, a weird night was spent with a Frenchman and his large family. The fare consisted only of flour "which the woman in a very dirty manner kneaded up in the fat of an elk which her husband shot a few days before." A boy and girl were the messengers from this home to civilization thirty miles away, and in coming and going they frequently had to spend the nights in the woods. Both family and visitors, twelve in all, slept on the floor, cheerful and content, with the house open on all sides. This outpost was the only habitation in forty-three miles, and in traversing the region, the travelers saw much wild game, including two bears. Deer, elk, foxes and wolves were very numerous, the last so much so that it was impossible for the settlers to keep hogs or sheep. It is of passing interest that the region so described was very close to the present Elkland Friends' Meeting in northwest Sullivan County, Pennsylvania.

The Tioga River flows north to a junction with the Cohocton at the town of Painted Post, already famous for an Indian Treaty of several years before. Thence the travelers followed the Cohocton, through the new town of Bath, with twenty houses, built in the last eighteen months under the enterprise of a Scotchman, Captain Charles Williamson, who lived there in elegance and who, being the chief owner of all the land for twenty-five miles around, bade fair to be one of the richest men in the country. He was selling the land off at about two dollars per acre. Two days more of riding, mostly through woodland, brought the Quaker emissaries at last to Lake Canandaigua and the scene of their anticipated activities, on September 25th, just eleven days out from Philadelphia.

The Oneidas, one of the Six Nations, were already in camp. As the travelers arrived, they beheld their acquaintances of the year before, Colonel Pickering and General Chapin, holding a complimentary conference with the Oneidas, but they soon freed themselves, welcomed the Friends and directed them to the quarters prepared for them in a private house.

The relative numbers of the Six Nations at the time of this Treaty of 1794 was stated to the Friends to be about 1900 of the Senecas, 800 of the Mohawks, all of whom were in Canada, 600 of the Oneidas, 500 of the Onondagas, 400 of the Cayugas and 300 of the Tuscaroras. The Cayugas came in with slight ceremony, as they were relatively few in number and had no chiefs of much importance.

The Onondagas were next to arrive under two chiefs, Clear Sky and The Eel. The Tuscaroras, although also of less importance, were influential through their chiefs, Captain William Printup and Sword Carrier, in the Treaty, and the latter, as we shall see, is of especial interest to Friends, through his possible suggestion of Tunesassa Indian School. His Indian name is variously spelled Saragousa, Sagaressa, Sagourisky and Sagourissy.

Of the Six Nations, the Mohawks, with their consistently hostile policy toward the United States, were not expected to be present. Indeed, they were not essential, as their land lay across the Lakes in Canada and they resolutely retained their British sympathies and allegiance, under their famous, or from the American standpoint, their infamous war-chief, Captain Brant. The slowness of the tribes in coming to the Treaty boded no good for its success. Said William Savery:

"The old lesson of last year is to be learned over again—that is, Patience, which will always be wanted by those that attend Indian Treaties."

The Senecas were last to arrive, and their preponderance in numbers and the importance of their chiefs required elaborate ceremony. John Parrish and James Emlen set out on October 9th to meet the Senecas and to accompany them into the encampment. So slow were they in coming on, however, that it was the 14th before the ceremonial was complete for their entry. Having spent the entire morning in painting and ornamenting themselves, they finally came on, headed by Farmer's Brother, their Chief Sachem and Little Billy, a well known Chief. Before General Chapin's door, the Oneidas, Cayugas and Onondagas were drawn up, dressed and painted, with their arms prepared for a salute. The Senecas drew up, facing the Oneidas, Colonel Pickering and the many white people present, and immediately fired three rounds, which the other Indians answered with a like number. While the echoes were still reverberating through the woods, the Senecas wheeled into a circle around Pickering and Chapin, and sat down. Farmer's Brother delivered a speech and returned the strings of wampum which had been sent to them with the invitation to come to the Treaty. Pickering, as sole United States Commissioner, returned a complimentary answer and ordered several kettles of rum which were soon disposed of. The chiefs then handed in bundles of sticks, answerable to the number of men, women and children under their respective commands, totaling for these arrivals 472 Senecas. One can well appreciate William Savery's comment upon these proceedings, "They made a truly terrific and warlike appearance." Two days later, on the 16th, Cornplanter, the Head Warrior of the Senecas and the warm friend of the United States and of the Quakers, arrived with a second contingent of 400 Senecas, whose entry was marked by almost identical ceremony, with high dress and paint. There were now about 1600 Indians assembled.

Although over three weeks had already been spent by the Friends in awaiting the beginning of the Treaty, they were still to experience to the full the tedium of such transactions. One can but admire the patience and tact with which Pickering, experienced statesman that he was, handled the very protracted negotiations, and those biographers who attribute to him later, as Secretary of State, considerable crabbed snobbishness, would do well to temper their judgment by a review of his Indian experiences.

Prior to the main Treaty, there were two collateral inquiries that took a deal of time. The first of these was to settle some differences among the Oneidas, with which the Commissioner was busy when the Friends first arrived. With infinite refinements of ceremonial, the first session was merely a recital by the Oneidas of an epidemic that, during the past summer had carried off a large number of their nation. Pickering replied that he himself had just lost a darling son and could fully sympathize with them. Each then unstopped the ears and opened the throats of the other, the latter operation being nominally for candor in speech, but a gallon of rum being at once introduced, its consumption seems to have been the most immediate result.

At the next session, David Bacon and William Savery attended and Captain John, Chief Sachem of the Oneidas, and Peter, the Chief Warrior, presented to the Commissioner the difficulties resulting from disagreements between the sachems and the warriors over the leasing of a large tract of land to one Peter Smith. So heated had been the strife that the two parties of Indians had actually faced each other in arms, and, had not the surveyors desisted, the Oneida nation might have destroyed itself. Peter, the Warrior, spoke first and it became evident to Pickering that the quarrel was not only one over a fraudulent land deal, but that it involved the question of the relative powers of the Sachems, the civil, and of the Warriors, the military elements in the tribe. Pickering assured them he would do his utmost to have the Smith lease annulled, remarking afterwards to the Friends that not only private persons, but the Governor of New York, himself, had given great cause for their complaints.

At a later date, the Oneidas reconvened, and Pickering gave them much solid and fraternal advice in avoiding land frauds. He was followed by Captain John, the Sachem, who thanked him for the good advice but hoped he would also tell them whether the Warriors or the Sachems had been in the wrong; that it would not hurt the Sachems to be told, if they were wrong, and also that the Indians only wanted their lands back and did not care to have Smith subjected to the fine and imprisonment that Pickering had said he was liable to. He also noticed what was said about our mode of government and laws and that the Indians had also their mode which had been handed down by their forefathers, and one custom was for the Sachems only to sit in council on civil affairs, but of late their Warriors appeared jealous and intruded into things, contrary to the ancient custom. Indeed he thought that Peter, the Chief Warrior, was aiming at being something more than the Nation was willing he should be. He concluded by giving a droll rehearsal (which made the Indians smile) of the manner of the white people in persuading them out of their lands.

Pickering repeated his advice as to sales and leases, but did not venture upon the delicate question of prerogative between the Sachems and Warriors. As we shall see later, this jealousy flared up again and nearly wrecked the Treaty.

The second of the inquiries, collateral to the main Treaty, pertained to the Friends alone. A doubt had been felt by Friends as to whether just payment had been made to the original Indian proprietors of the land settled by Friends in the vicinity of Hopewell Meeting in Virginia, and the Quaker deputies had many conferences regarding it. The Oneidas and the Tuscaroras were the chief claimants and the Friends, after consulting Jefferson's notes on the Virginia titles and taking the opinion of Colonel Pickering, decided in favor of the Tuscaroras, and promised to lay the matter before the proper persons after their return. Some time later a deputation of Tuscarora Indians did come to Philadelphia on this business, and after the most careful scrutiny of maps and papers, the Friends decided that no vestige of title had ever been in the tribe. The disappointment of the Indians was so great, however, that a considerable sum was raised and given to them, to their intense gratification.

It was almost a month after the Friends arrived at Canandaigua before the main purposes of the Treaty were approached, and then two days were spent in elaborate ceremony always incident to Indian diplomacy. On October 19th and 20th, the council fires were lit. Pickering, Chapin and three interpreters occupied the center of a circle of grave and thoughtful Indians, presenting a very striking appearance to the Friends as they entered. Captain John of the Oneidas welcomed the western confederates and passed to the Seneca Chiefs much wampum. Fish Carrier, Clear Sky and Red Jacket, for the Senecas and Tuscaroras, replied at length and returned the wampum; then all the Indians informed the Commissioner that the Six Nations were embodied in council and ready to treat. He made a complimentary reply and the fire was then covered as the rum was brought.

At the second session, Pickering outdid the red men themselves in his ceremonial. Referring to the murder of a young Indian by a white man at Venango, the summer before, he figuratively took the hatchet out of the murdered man's head and buried him after the Indian custom. He then covered the ground with leaves, to hide the grave, tore up a large pine tree and buried the hatchet in the hole, then covered it thickly with stones and planted the tree on top so that it should never more be removed. He then wiped the blood from their beds and the tears from their eyes and opened the path of peace which he requested the Indians to keep open at the other end as long as the sun shone. William Savery estimated the value of the strings of wampum delivered to the Indians during this remarkable harangue at about one hundred dollars. After a spirited address by Farmer's Brother to his fellows, the Indians not being prepared to answer Pickering, the fire was covered "and the rum brought in as usual."

On October 21st, a third session was held, full of speeches and exchange of fifteen strings of chequered wampum, representative of the fifteen United States, but little progress was made beyond a formal introduction of the Friends by Pickering to the Indians, as "their old friends, the Quakers, who had come forward at their request and with the approbation of the President." The Friends then read their address which, upon interpretation, was received with frequent expressions of "Entaw!" or approbation. One other incident was noteworthy. Jemima Wilkinson, who called herself the "Universal Friend" and had left Philadelphia with a numerous following to found a colony at Canandaigua, was allowed to attend the Council, largely because Pickering was interested to see so notorious a woman. She prayed and preached to the Indians on the blessings of peace. This seemed about as much as the program permitted and the fire was covered.

The sequel to Jemima Wilkinson's visit was not long delayed. In view of the generally accepted subservience of Indian squaws to the braves, a request from three Indian women to attend the Council next day, must have been a surprise to the assembly. They were admitted and introduced by Red Jacket. They claimed an equal interest in the welfare of their tribes with the men and that it was the fault of the whites that their grievances subsisted, as the whites "had squeezed them up together and pressed their hearts sorely." They added that a woman yesterday had exhorted the Indians to repent, and they, in turn, now desired the whites to repent.

"How long will you oppress us, how long will you press our hearts together! General Washington and the fifteen fires (the United States) grant our request; then the chain of friendship will be made bright and strong."

This conference was held at the house of Thomas Morris, and was attended by chiefs only. Captain John brought his humor into play again by his description of the whites in their land deals, stating that however honest a white man might be in other matters, they were all deceivers when they wanted to buy Indian lands. He then took a shrewd fling at the Friends (upon whom the effect was by no means lost) by referring to the Walking Purchase, whereby

"one of the descendants of Onas (William Penn) deceived them in the long walk in Pennsylvania, having got one of the swiftest runners in the country, who went 67 miles in one day, three times as far as the Indians were easy to part with."

At this select Council, the main topic of the Treaty was finally mentioned,—namely the boundary between the Indians and the whites. The Indians had referred vaguely to a line drawn from a point on Lake Erie to the Moskingum, a river in Central Ohio. If this line had been agreed upon, the Western Indians, who had already been defeated by Wayne, need not have fought. Although Wayne's victory in August was as yet unknown to Pickering, the time was past when any such boundaries would hold the rushing tide of white emigration and the rest of the time was spent in dickering over suggested substitutes. As at Detroit the year before, the Treaty of Fort Stanwix loomed large as the basis of all negotiations, the Indians alleging that they had been imposed upon and the Commissioner refusing to yield an inch from what it had specified.

During the next week the pages of William Savery's Journal relate a tense little drama, which we of today can appreciate but of which he was probably unaware. On October 27th, a Tuscarora runner arrived from Niagara, dispatched thence by Colonel Butler, bringing news of the battle on the Au Glaize, between Wayne and the Indians, but stating the results as doubtful, many on both sides being killed and each side withdrawing from the field. William Savery sensed the situation somewhat in his surmise:

"The Indians appear cautious of letting out the particulars, perhaps considering that if any capital loss has been sustained on the Indian side, it might operate to their disadvantage at this critical period of the treaty, so that the accounts, being very various, nothing can be determined with certainty."

It will be remembered that this Colonel Butler was the British officer who the summer before had been with the Indians at the Rapids of the Miami, when their Councils were being developed adversely to the American interests. The drama unfolded a little farther at Canandaigua by the

arrival, almost simultaneously with this news, of one Johnston in the character of a British interpreter. He brought
a message from the Mohawk, Brant, to the Six Nations and
delivered it to the chiefs at once. The next day he appeared at the Council and was on very intimate terms with
the Indians. It then became known that Brant and our old
friend, Governor Simcoe, of Niagara, had just returned
together from Detroit, where they must have had fresh
and exact information of the extent of Wayne's victory,
and that Johnston had left both of them at Fort Erie
in leaving upon his present mission. There can be little
doubt that the Indian chiefs were thus apprised accurately
of Wayne's victory. From the manuscript Journal of David
Bacon (now in the Haverford College Library) it is almost
certain that Johnston divulged more than he intended, at
least to the Friends, and possibly to Pickering. David
Bacon records that the Western Indians were complaining
because the "British stood by and did not help them, meaning, as I suppose, the battle they had with Gen'l Wayn,"
and this information came from Johnston.

Whatever Pickering may or may not have known regarding Wayne's victory, he at once took decisive measures regarding Johnston. When the Council reconvened, Cornplanter, aware of the uneasiness his coming had produced,
arose to vindicate it. He was surprised that the British
and Americans had evidenced such antipathy to each other
ever since the so-called peace between them and that they
resolutely refused to sit together in treaties with the Indians.
He also said that Johnston had recently returned from the
Western Indians who believed the failure of the year before
was not their fault and suggested a new attempt at Sandusky next year. Granting that Johnston did know of
Wayne's victory, this proposal was one of the baldest pieces
of duplicity ever attempted in Indian diplomacy. Cornplanter finally concluded with a message from Brant reminding the chiefs of their agreement of last year to abide

by a certain boundary, which if established would ensure peace, and also desiring General Chapin to come to him (Brant) at Buffalo Creek, as soon as the Treaty at Canandaigua was completed.

At this audacity, Pickering's anger flared out. He arose and accused Johnston of being a British spy; that he was an insult to him, the Indians, their friends, the Quakers, and the fifteen fires and that his intrusion was a fresh proof of British impudence and insolence. He then outlined at length the perfidy and ill treatment, suffered by the Americans at the hand of the British Government and that either this man must leave or he would cover the council fire, as his instructions from General Washington were to suffer no British agents at this treaty. Wrote William Savery:

"The Indians appeared in amazement at the warmth with which the Commissioner delivered himself and said when he sat down that the council fire grows warm and the sparks of it fly about very thick. As to Johnston, he appeared all the time, for about two hours, like one that was condemned to die. He then rose and left us."

After a half hour's conference the chiefs decided to let him return home, giving him provision for the journey, and a letter, which Pickering did not approve, assuring Brant that they intended to insist upon the line as agreed. That evening the Friends dined with the Commissioner, by candle light, fifteen chiefs being present, and all in a gay mood. The Indians were full of witty repartee, in which Red Jacket excelled them all.

As stated before, Major Denny, at Presque Isle, much nearer the Au Glaize, in Western Ohio, than Canandaigua, heard of the victory of the Au Glaize for the first, on October 19th. Johnston's arrival at Canandaigua, about October 23rd, and that of the Tuscarora runner, about the 27th, would have put a less experienced man than Pickering to speculating on the real results at the Au Glaize. It seems incredible that the Federal authorities did not arrange for quick and authentic dispatches between Wayne and Pickering, irrespective of the results, as the victory of either side was certain to affect the negotiations in favor of the victor in a conclusive way.

It is probable that Pickering and Chapin rightly interpreted the indecisive reports to the Indians and their reticence on the subject as a whole, as indicative of an American victory or at least a draw, favorable to the American arms. Even if it were a draw, it was too late for active campaigning and the hostilities were evidently off for the year.

Whatever were Pickering's speculations, his conclusion evidently was to put on a bold front at once. Johnston having been disposed of, he informed the Friends on the 27th that he was "now preparing the way for a full and general council tomorrow, when he will cut the business short, by decidedly opening the proposals of accommodation" and William Savery adds,—"This is good news to us who have been already much wearied with continual delays."

After another brief, though serious, outburst of jealousy between Little Billy and Cornplanter, because the latter, "being only a war chief," was so frequently in consultation with Pickering, to the exclusion of the sachems, the Council reconvened on October 28th. Pickering handed his commission to William Savery to read to the Indians, which done, he stated that the warriors had proposed a line running from Lake Erie due south to the place where the Allegheny River crosses the Pennsylvania line, thence to the forks of French Creek (near Meadville, Crawford County, Pennsylvania), thence to the forks of the Muskingum River (now Coshocton, Ohio) and thence down the Muskingum to the Ohio River. A glance at the map will show the impossibility of these terms to a Government that had placed thousands of settlers in the Ohio territory already and which was at that very moment laying out a city in the "chimney" or cantle of Pennsylvania on the shore of

Lake Erie. The terms were, if anything, more drastic than those of the year before.

Pickering elaborated upon the grant of King Charles II to William Penn, explained the boundaries of the State, which had been confirmed by the Indians upon payment of $10,000 at the Treaty of Fort Stanwix, years before, and never complained of before, and that it included the cantle on Lake Erie, the title to which had been confirmed by the Indians, upon payment of $2,000 additional at the Treaty of Muskingum, in 1786, after the Commonwealth of Pennsylvania had purchased it from Congress, although in the latter Treaty it was supposed that the east line of the cantle would have extended south from the mouth of Buffalo Creek. As a counter-proposal, Pickering suggested that he would cede back to the Indians all the land east of the Pennsylvania triangle (practically Chautauqua County, New York) and that the new line might begin at Johnston's Landing (four miles above Lake Ontario, on the Niagara River) and including a strip, four miles wide, run along the Niagara River and Lake Erie to Buffalo (now Cattaraugus) Creek, thence directly along Lake Erie to the Pennsylvania Triangle. He ignored, perhaps because of Wayne's victory, any question of western boundaries whatever. He reminded them again that the four-mile path between Lakes Erie and Ontario had long ago been ceded to the British in Sir William Johnson's time and that the cession of it to the United States had been confirmed at the Treaty of Fort Stanwix, so the claims of the United States at the present time were not new, in fact, were less that they were entitled to. Moreover, the Indians would be allowed to hunt upon all these lands, and for the creation of more mutual satisfaction, Pickering would increase the annuity of $1500 to $4500 to the Indians, and that he would also distribute among them forthwith, goods to the amount of $10,000. To this offer the Indians could return no immediate answer and the Council adjourned.

For two days the chiefs were either active in consultation or too drunk to attend to business and the weather being fine the young braves indulged in outdoor sports, that though interesting were tedious to men who wished to get away. Reports from the Council house told of high feeling against Cornplanter, the War Chief, and the inability of the Indians to conceive what he had done with two hundred dollars paid him in Philadelphia by the Pennsylvania Government or what induced the Government to give him a farm of fifteen hundred acres. His fervent desire for peace through compromise was the less acceptable due to these tacit inferences of graft.

Finally, on the last day of October, with winter threatening an early approach, began the last phases of the Treaty, and strangely enough the Quaker emissaries found themselves involved in negotiations, from which they were not able to extricate themselves to their own or the Commissioner's satisfaction. A delegation of four chiefs waited upon them at their lodgings. Came Red Jacket, of the Senecas; Clear Sky, the Onondaga; Sagareesa, of the Tuscaroras, and another of the Cayugas. The Oneidas alone were not represented in the delegation. Realizing that a matter of importance was toward, the Friends and Indians withdrew from the house and, seating themselves upon logs, near the edge of the clearing, the conference of Quaker and Red Man began. From the setting, one is vividly reminded of West's picture of that other Treaty between Penn and the Indians at Shackamaxon. The forest background, the felled timbers and the Quaker apparel, in striking contrast to the dress of the chiefs, would have been much the same as West painted. With the wild and inimitable poetry of Indian oratory Red Jacket began his peroration:

"Brothers,—You see here four of us of the Six Nations, who are assembled at this place, in the will of the Great Spirit, to transact the business of the treaty. You have been waiting here a long time, and often visited by our chiefs, and as yet no marks of respect have been shown you.

"Brothers,—We are deputed by the council of chiefs assembled, to come and see you. We understand that you told Sagareesa, that you should not have come, but at our request, and that you stood ready to afford us any assistance in your power.

"Brothers,—We hope you will make your minds easy. We who are now here are but children; the ancients being deceased. We know that your fathers and ours transacted business together, and that you look up to the Great Spirit for his direction and assistance, and take no part in war. We expect you were all born on this Island, and consider you as brethren, for though your ancestors came over the great water, and ours were born here, this ought to be no impediment to our considering each other as brethren.

"Brothers,—You all know the proposals that have been made by Cunnitsutty (Colonel Pickering) as well as the offers made by us to him. We are all now in the presence of the Great Spirit, and we place more confidence in you, than in any other people. As you expressed your desire for peace, we now desire your help and assistance—we hope you will not deceive us. If you should do so we shall no more place any confidence in mankind."

Red Jacket then took the Friends into the complete confidence of the Indians, desiring that they would retain the disclosures secret. The Indians, said he, were willing to give up the four-mile path from Johnston's Landing to Cayuga Creek, in accordance with the compact with Sir William Johnson, long ago; but were not willing to accede to Pickering's proposal to relinquish the strip from Cayuga Creek to Buffalo Creek, as they wished to retain it for its fisheries. He then attacked the validity of the Treaty of Fort Stanwix, stating that Cornplanter and Brant, "who were only war-chiefs," attended the Treaty and were to submit the proposals for general consideration, particularly for the approval of Old Smoke, a man of great understanding, who was then alive. In spite of this, they were threatened into compliance, upon which Brant had gone off to Canada and left Cornplanter to do the best he could.

The delegation specifically desired to learn from the

Friends, whether they knew, first, what was the will of Congress and the extent of the Commissioner's power, and second, why the Pennsylvania Cantle on Lake Erie could not be given up. Seven strings of wampum were then handed to the Friends and the conference was over.

In the evening, William Savery, in considerable uncertainty of mind, went to General Chapin's lodgings and conferred with him and Colonel Pickering. Under the bond of secrecy as to the Indians' true intentions, he learned that both of the Americans believed the Indians would come to their terms. Thus did the Friends, in a sense unwittingly, become the confidants of both sides in this little episode of frontier diplomacy. It was indeed, as William Savery wrote:

"A weighty and delicate matter to answer their request in our situation."

If they should advise the Indians to hold out for their demands, they would directly oppose the favorable outcome of the Treaty efforts of their own Government. All of them, to a man, appreciated the urgent desirability of a treaty of some nature to stabilize the relations between the States and the Iroquois. Each could also recall with vivid distinctness the unhappy ostracism resulting from the Quaker attempt to remain neutral during the Revolution. Being above all "desirous of dealing honestly with the poor Indians and of keeping a conscience void of offence," the Quakers met and drew up a reply. David Bacon was the only one who reduced it to writing in his Journal, the others probably deeming it more discreet to record as little as possible of the actual advice given. At the best, it seems to be a straddle. The Friends advised:

"We can take no part in war, which is one great reason why we cannot be active in civil government and therefore we are not capable of judging of all your grievances, especially as the transactions at Indian Treaties of late years have not fully come to our knowledge.

You have spoken to us respecting the piece of land between Cayuga and Buffalo Creeks. As we are unacquainted with the Commissioner's power, we can give you no satisfactory answer on that subject. If it appears to be a matter of great importance to you, it would be proper to lay it before him. The land you mentioned along Lake Erie, you have been already acquainted that Congress has sold it to Pennsylvania and we do not suppose the Commissioner has power to relinquish it.

"* * * (After stating that they should judge of their rights) and if your minds are not easy with the proposals that have been made, we have no doubt but the ears of the President and the great council of the United States will be open to hear you and to them we conceive you have a right to appeal."

Such an answer was surely not a very powerful attempt. The one concrete suggestion, the appeal to the President and Congress, was truly a forlorn hope.

The next day, November 1st, William Savery acted as spokesman and handed back the seven strings of wampum after having advised upon three points, which Red Jacket, in reply, repeated. He remarked pithily that though the Friends might account the advice of small value, they did not so consider it, but thought it would afford them considerable strength. Later in the day, when returning home by the Indian Council house, they heard Red Jacket holding forth to his fellow chiefs on Pickering's proposals.

On November 2nd, the Indians were again ready to meet the Commissioner in Council, and a numerous assembly it proved to be on the part of both whites and Indians.

After Clear Sky opened the Council, Red Jacket went straight to the subject of brightening the two rusty places on the chain of friendship with the fifteen fires (the United States). He mentioned Pickering's proposed compromise and added:

"We thought you had a sharp file to take off the rust, but we believe it must have been dull, or else you let it slip out of your hands. * * * Although we are but children, we are sharp-sighted. * * * We wish that in respect to the four-mile path, the Treaty of Ft. Stanwix may be broken. You white ~eople have increased very fast on this Island, which was given to us Indians by the Great Spirit. We are now become a small people and you are cutting off our lands, piece by piece. You are a very hard-hearted people, seeking your own advantages."

After requesting that Pickering relinquish the four-mile strip as the preliminary to peace, he concluded:

"At the time we requested a conference, we also requested that our friends, the Quakers, should come forward, as they are promoters of peace, and we wanted them to be witnesses to what took place; we wish to do nothing in private. We have told you of the rusty part, which the file passed over without brightening it, and we wish you to take up the file again, and rub it very hard; you told us, if it would not do without, you would apply oil."

Pickering, in his reply, evidently sensed that the Indians did not consider their position an ultimatum. One can read between the lines that the insistence upon retaining the four-mile strip was a result of the Friends' advice. Pickering may have felt too sure of his position, for, in opening, he stated that the Indians might increase also, if they would, and that he was their friend, for he wished to see them rise and become a great people. This was too much for Red Jacket who called out, "Keep straight!" and the Commissioner returned to the subject. He agreed to allow the four-mile path between Cayuga and Buffalo Creeks to remain with the Indians, provided the States could build a road through it between the Lakes. This would involve taverns as well, and a harbor and the incidental shops and houses. To this no reply was forthcoming and once again the fire was covered.

So sure was Pickering of his ground now that he had the articles of the Treaty reduced to writing and called upon the Friends, at their lodging, to read them to them. The Friends had been seriously discussing the propriety of signing the Treaty, as witnesses, for several days. Another inkling of their true feelings, aside from their equivocal advice to the Chiefs is apparent in their reply to Pickering:

"We told him, on hearing what was proposed, we apprehended, for reasons given, we could not be free to sign them, which did not appear to be agreeable to him; but we have not now to begin to learn to suffer at Indian Treaties."

The Council reassembled in the afternoon of November 4th, but the Friends not having been notified, the Indians refused to proceed until they were called. Red Jacket, for the Iroquois, declined to agree to the building of houses and a harbor on the strip of land, as such would tend to scatter the Indians and make them fall in the street from drink. Said he:

"I see there are many of your people now here, watching with their mouths open to take up this land; if you are a friend to us disappoint them. Our patience is spent, comply with our request; dismiss us and we will go home."

Pickering did comply, obtaining, however, the right to improve and widen the path that then existed over the strip between Fort Schlosser and Buffalo Creek, but not west of Buffalo Creek at all. The details of the Treaty were then committed to a few chiefs and sachems and all signs pointed to an early agreement. Once again, however, the old antipathies between the chiefs and sachems broke out through renewed charges of receipt of moneys in Philadelphia by Cornplanter and Little Billy, both Senecas. Renewed objection also developed to relinquishing Presque Isle, where Major Denny was already laying out the City of Erie. The dissentions waxed so fierce among the Indians that the conference broke up and many of the chiefs became too drunk to make any progress the next day. There is a vein of stoical humor in William Savery's entry:

"It signifies nothing to say you are tired of waiting. It will not hurry Indians. They will only tell you very calmly,—'Brother, you have your way of doing business and we have ours. We desire you would sit easy on your seats.'"

While the drunkenness of the chiefs impeded progress on November 7th, Pickering called to drink tea with the

Quaker delegation, and spent the afternoon. His attitude confirmed their intention of not being witnesses to the Treaty. One is reminded of his similar call of the year before at Detroit, when he appeared to be trying to justify his position to the Quakers, before returning home. William Savery's comment on his call and his ideas is perhaps the best indication of the Friends' attitude in refusing to sign. He wrote:

"The idea he entertains respecting the lands ceded at Fort Stanwix, is, that as the Indians did the United States a great deal of injury by taking part with the British in the late war, it was strictly just that they should make compensation by giving up the lands which they relinquished at that time. He instanced the case of an individual who had committed a trespass on another; the law determines that the trespasser shall suffer either in person or property, and this law is just. Such is the reasoning of conquerors."

In the next session the sachems, strange to say, meekly stated their willingness to abide by the decision of the warriors. Pickering then patched up matters with the latter and the Treaty was actually engrossed and the Council gathered for signing, when the Friends, noticing the Indians putting their heads down together and whispering, realized that something new was wrong. This continued for an hour, when Cornplanter arose.

Of all the other Indians at the Treaty, Cornplanter was the last who might have been expected to back-fire on the negotiations at this late moment. The burden of his harangue placed the responsibilty for the Treaty upon the sachems, stating that, while the warriors would abide by the decision, they would decline to sign, as he felt that they were being deceived again as they had been at Fort Stanwix. The Eel, of the Onondagas, warmly backed Cornplanter and exhorted the assembly to abide by the decision of the sachems.

Once again Pickering, with infinite patience, had to reconstruct his plans to assuage suspicion toward the whites and jealousy between the chiefs. His reply was at once masterly in its simplicity and sincerity and firm in its unwillingness to sign a peace with the sachems without the warriors. And then again the fire had to be covered.

The evening was spent by the Friends with Colonel Pickering on the present state of affairs and the forenoon of the next day with divers chiefs. There can be no doubt of the value of the Quaker delegation as mediators in this crisis, nor is there room to question their success, albeit along lines they probably did not suggest. When the Council reconvened the opposition collapsed as quickly as it had begun, upon another pathetic and moving speech from the Eel, exhorting the warriors and sachems to unanimity. When Pickering then held aloft two parchments, whereon the Treaty was inscribed, the Indians were ready to proceed. He handed one copy to William Savery to examine while he read the other. William Savery then informed the Indians that both were identical, whereupon about fifty Chiefs and Warriors signed the momentous documents.

Immediately after this ceremony was over, the Friends asked the two Senecas, Farmer's Brother, the Chief Sachem, and Cornplanter, the Head Warrior, to collect the chiefs of the different nations to meet the Friends at their lodgings. This they did and about forty came, accompanied by Jasper Parrish, the interpreter. Over pipes and wine a familiar conversation ensued, covering the Indians' welfare, the Friends' principles and good wishes for the prosperity of the tribes. Presents were then brought and distributed by Jasper Parrish, at the chiefs' request, another glass of wine was drunk and the party dispersed, to meet again the next morning for farewells.

This farewell took the form of a speech from Farmer's Brother, asking the Friends, once again, to sign the Treaty as an evidence of their faith in its rectitude and fairness:

"Brothers, if you think peace is now established on a good foundation, we wish you would come forward and sign the articles, as you are a people who are desirous of promoting peace and these writings are for that purpose, we hope you will have no objection and this would be a great satisfaction to us."

The strange reticence in expressing in writing any opinions on the Treaty whatever prevailed again and William Savery makes no statement of their answer to the request. The official copy of the Treaty printed among the United States Indian Reports shows none of the Friends as witnesses to it, and one can be sure they did not wholly approve it, but saw no alternative.

The journey home commenced at once, and it was time. Early snows had already warned the travelers of the dangers ahead of them. The first night was spent in a cold open hut, with the snow dusting in upon them as they lay. A touch of humor enters the account when the straw bed laid upon rails and supported upon blocks, upon which David Bacon and John Parrish had started the night, gave way beneath them and they were sent sprawling to the floor. Poor John Parrish fell from his horse the next day and bruised his face painfully and, indeed, the whole party rode at the apparent risk of their lives, with bushes, swamps and deep mud-holes strewn all along their road. After another night in an open hut, upon straw and a day of snow, they arrived again in Bath and partook of the hospitality of Captain Williamson and his handsome Boston wife, as a welcome boon to "poor, forlorn travelers." Two more days of hard riding in constant snowstorms, their horses' feet continually balling, eating what they could find at poor houses and sleeping on straw or bark on floors or in bunks, crossing the Tioga River again and again, brought them on the 17th to the foot of the Allegheny Mountain. Here to their delight it cleared and they crossed the high land in ten inches of snow, but with ability to see their way as they went.

William Savery's account of the journey closes abruptly, leaving the travelers in the comfortable home of the Widow

Harris, near Loyalsock, with whom they had lodged on the outward trip. From David Bacon, however, we learn that they tarried once again with Samuel Wallis, at Muncy, experiencing a two days' rain. It is interesting to learn that Wallis' mill-dam was washed away and that the Susquehanna River rose ten feet, a memorable flood for days when the forests were still intact upon the Pennsylvania hills around its sources. As soon as they could cross the river the travelers again set forth, John Parrish and James Emlen returning via Cattawissa and David Bacon and William Savery by Sunbury and Northumberland, reaching Philadelphia on November 27, 1794.

## CHAPTER XIV

# INDIAN CUSTOMS AND LIFE

In his introduction to William Savery's Journal, Jonathan Evans, the Editor, wrote of him:

"In the course of his travels, he was much more particular in the memoranda he made than has been customary for Friends in his station; giving a cursory description of the country, its produce, the value of it, and the habits of the people where he traveled. Some of these details, which may be found in other works, have been abridged."

It is precisely some of those details, available in the manuscript volumes of the Journal, that are of surpassing interest today, and most of all, those details relating to the savage life in our own northwest in the formative days of Indian intrigue and warfare. The experience of the two Quaker deputations covered all the tribes with which the white men were then in contact, from the Onondagas of New York, who followed in bark canoes the batteaux of General Lincoln on the river that bears their name, and caught salmon for the white men, to the Sioux around the head of Lake Superior. The Iroquois, as already stated, were the Six Nations,—the Onondagas, Oneidas, Tuscaroras, Cayugas, Senecas and Mohawks. Their names are written all over the map of New York State, and the Cornplanter Reservation, so familiar in name to the Society of Friends, was already looming before the swiftly declining tribes as an asylum, in the pathetic speeches of the chiefs at Canandaigua. The Mohawks had gone to Canada to come under British protection after their disastrous participation, on the British side, in the American Revolution.

To the west of these in northern Ohio were the first of the so-called hostile tribes, the powerful Shawanese, Wyandots and Miamis; beyond them the Weas and Pottawattomies on the prairies of Illinois and Iowa, and still further to the north and west, the Chippeways, the Pawnees and the big and terrible Sioux of the Woods at the head of Lake Superior. It is hard to realize that even at the time of these treaties, the Indians of the far west, the Sioux of the Plains, the Blackfeet, Dakotas and Apaches, who were to give to future generations the final struggle for supremacy in the far West, were still unknown to the whites. It will probably be of more than passing value to record some of the first-hand observations of William Savery on these children of the plain and forest who were, perforce, his neighbors for several months.

At Fort Niagara, he mentioned eating pigeons, which the Indians shot, flying, with their bows and arrows. Such a reference is reminiscent of Penn's description of the vast flights of wild pigeons in his new Province, all the more remarkable because of the total disappearance of the species from the eastern United States.

Visitors from the eastern Indian tribes were not unusual in Philadelphia during the whole of William Savery's lifetime. His statement, therefore, that the Chippeways from Michillimachinack (modern Mackinaw) exceeded any other Indians he had ever seen in their ferocious appearance, when arriving at Detroit, would indicate the judgment of one qualified to pass upon Indian paint, dress and dances. He marveled at the muscularity of these big northwest Indians, at their hideous painting and at their dexterity in handling canoes. His spirit was continually uneasy over the reports of Indian atrocities in war, too well authenticated to be doubted, and of which the Friends were obliged to hear enough to fill a volume.

"I could several times have been glad to have stopped my ears from hearing of blood, as I am confirmed in opinion that it has a tendency gradually to eradicate the tenderest feelings of humanity."

There were, however, brighter features to the situation. Under the care of John Heckewelder, the Moravian missionary, the Friends met John Killbuck and his son, the latter having been educated at Princeton College, but who had resumed Indian habits and manners. With them were several others of the "good" or Moravian Indians who did not go to war and who suffered much on that account. They dwelt on a small grant of land on the River Le French. Their vices, such as they were, had undoubtedly been accentuated by the deceitfulness of the whites in dealing with them, and the Quaker deputation frequently found themselves in the always precarious position of explaining the sins of the enemy by admitting grave offenses on the part of their own country-men. When some Indians brought in sugar (in which Detroit then did a considerable business) mixed with sand, and were blamed for it, they replied, "You learned us by mixing water with your rum."

The opportunity to become acquainted with the customs and dispositions of all the tribes was a rare one and the Friends' situation was peculiarly close and confidential. They were visited by members of one nation or another almost daily.

In the Michigan Peninsula, the Chippeways and Pawnees were in continual warfare, and the former had established quite a trade in selling Pawnee slaves to the settlers at Detroit, at prices varying from £10 to £100 apiece. About three hundred such poor creatures were in service in Detroit in 1793, the traffic having been under way for twenty-five years. Prior to that time the Chippeways had killed all their captives, being determined to exterminate their rivals.

Another feature of frontier life, to which Detroit, as the doorway to the Indian country, was well used, was the ransom of white captives, taken by the Indians in the many border wars. The stealing of both children and adults was all too customary a thing. The British garrison had standing orders to purchase back such unfortunates, and even beyond the government subsidies, the humane and generous officers spent themselves in their efforts to alleviate the miseries of the derelicts. There are numerous instances of such captives assuming Indian ways and spending their lives in savage pursuits. Add to these the great number of half-breeds, resulting from the many inter-marriages between white men and squaws and the open licentiousness and debauchery, which the Friends found flourishing without shame on the part of some white men of the first rank, and there is some explanation of the exceedingly complicated racial situation that existed.

The great outstanding curse of the frontier was rum. Its use was practically universal, as was the use of the finer grades of liquors in the Society of Friends. The Quaker delegation used rum themselves. It was the chief element of hospitality and cordiality, and as we have already seen, it was present at every session of the treaties. Frequently the chiefs and sachems themselves were too drunk for days at a time to transact business. To this statement there was one notable exception in Cornplanter who was a teetotaler and strove hard that all the Senecas should be also.

In the rank and file of the tribes, drink was already working conclusive havoc. Fire water and firearms were the two most coveted items of Indian trading, and both had reduced the tribes to a tithe of their early quotas. The Friends were also well able to smoke with the Indians, and partook of the symbolism of this rite with due gravity. William Savery presented five chiefs of the Shawanese, Delawares and Wyandots with neat tobacco-boxes, filled with tobacco, which, said the chiefs, would always remind them of Friends. Running out of pipes as presents, they had a lot made from tin by an artificer lately come from Philadelphia.

At the mouth of the Detroit River, the Friends' encampment numbered about forty, including the servants. Hard by, and outside the pickets, was an Indian encampment that was frequently in a drunken uproar, of dancing, singing and yelling at night. These dances were continually disagreeable to the Friends, for though not war-dances, they were accompanied by weird music and were not conducive to sleep.

Much pleasanter in the line of dancing were the sportive celebrations of the Iroquois at Canandaigua, of which William Savery has left the following lively description:

"A fine warm day. The Indians almost all turned out of their cabins. The young warriors, some of whom have good horses have been running races all day with the white people—others playing ball, one nation against as many of another, in which they show surprising activity. Others have been employed in dancing, which is almost a daily exercise. They have a variety of dances,—one called a hunting dance, another the Bride's dance, the war dance and the brag dance.

"The brag dance is very humorous. The dancers, of whom there may be a large number engaged at once, are nearly naked and variously painted in a very laughable manner. In this dance each one that deposits a bottle of rum, has liberty to brag of the feats he has done in war, how many scalps he has taken, what stratagems he has used, in which they are exceedingly romantic, exciting a great deal of mirth. A sensible man, whose name was Osman, being present, after he had deposited his bottle and the others had boasted of many marvellous exploits, made his brag, that he had been a man of peace all his days. In the profession of a physician he had been very industrious and restored many that had been ready to die. He said, all they had bragged of was nothing to this, for any child might kill a man but it required the judgment and wisdom of a great man to save another's life. They all acknowledged the Doctor's brag was the best of all. This was a day of high festivity and would have been a rare scene in the environs of Philadelphia."

There was a close and continuous intimacy between the Friends and the chiefs at Canandaigua. The braves were

expert hunters and on several occasions presented the
Friends with venison, of which an enormous amount was
dressed in the encampments. On one day, after a snowfall,
over one hundred deer were brought in. The elegant home
of Thomas Morris, son of Robert Morris, the financier of
the Revolution, was constantly open to the Friends during
the tedium of the Treaty. Here also the Friends were
accustomed to meet the chiefs and to drink tea. On one of
these occasions two squaws accompanied their husbands, an
incident quite unusual in Indian custom.

Of all the Iroquois, the Oneidas were the most civilized
and best instructed in religion. They even paid partial
regard to the First Day of the week. At Detroit, eighteen
Oneidas had been detained by the British authorities who
feared to allow them to attend the Conference at the
Rapids, because of the unpopularity of their chief and because they were known to be favorable to the Americans.
William Savery has left a highly interesting and picturesque account of a meeting for worship, held by the
Oneidas:

"At 4: in the afternoon, we went to the Oneida camp, having previously apprised the chiefs of our intention of a meeting there,
Parrish the interpreter with us. We found some collected in the
woods, where many trees were felled which served as seats. One of
the chiefs went around the camp with a certain hallo, used as a
signal for all to collect, which they did in large numbers. The curiosity of the white people being raised and some coming from other
motives, we had a large and good meeting which held till near sun-
set. Both whites and Indians behaved decent and quiet. As many
of the Indians had received some knowledge of the Christian Religion
from missionaries and were desirous of beginning the service with
singing of hymns or psalms, which we did not object to, they appeared very devout, and for my part, I never heard, as I thought,
more divine melody. The softness of the Indian language in which
they sang and the sweetness of the women's voices, exceeded by far
all that I had ever heard among the white people, which was the
opinion of all my friends and others. Indeed the place, being in the
middle of the woods, the satisfaction of hearing these poor, untu-

tored people sing, with every appearance of devotion, their Maker's praise, and the serious attention they paid to what was delivered to them, all conspired to make it a solemn meeting, long to be remembered by me. We left them in much love and sweetness, after they had closed our service with again singing hymns, to the astonishment of many present."

With all their advantages, however, the Oneidas, as we shall see, fell short in essentials.

The social opportunities with the chiefs were not neglected. On one occasion the Friends dined with Colonel Pickering, by candle light, with fifteen chiefs as guests, including Cornplanter, Red Jacket, Little Beard, Clear Sky, Farmer's Brother, Fish Carrier and Little Billy. It was a lively meal, with Jones interpreting the witty repartee of the red men. Red Jacket, whose talent in this respect was most conspicuous, was described as a man of pleasing countenance and one of the greatest orators among the Iroquois. At a later date Red Jacket brought his wife and five children to call upon the Friends. The children "were exceeding well clad in their manner, and the best behaved and prettiest Indian children I have ever met with."

Another intimate view of Indian life came through a visit to the camp of Farmer's Brother by John Parrish and William Savery. It consisted of about five hundred Indians:

"They are settled by the side of a brook in the woods, where they have built about 70 or 80 huts, which are by far the most commodious and ingeniously made of any that I have seen. The principal materials are bark and boughs of trees, so judiciously put together as to keep the family dry and warm. The women appeared mostly employed and many of the men. This camp has also a large number of pretty Children, who were in all the activity of health, diverting themselves agreeable to their fancy. The vast number of deer they have killed since coming here, which they cut up and hang around their huts inside and out to dry, with the rations of beef which they draw daily, has the grateful appearance of plenty to supply the few wants that simple nature has subjected them to. The ease and cheerfulness of every countenance, together with this delightful afternoon, which these inhabitants of the woods enjoy with a relish far superior to those who are pent in crowded and populous cities, all conspired to make this the pleasantest visit I ever remember to have paid to Indians and induced me to believe that before they became acquainted with white people and infected with their vices, that they must have been as innocent and as happy a people as any in the world."

In spite of these appearances of innocence and simplicity, all was not ideal with the tribes. William Savery gave much thought to the subject, probably in connection with the proposals that ripened into the Indian School, and was forced to the conclusion that even the Oneidas showed little of the influence of their superior civilization and religious instruction in their manners and morals. Though they cultivated ground, had heard of Jesus Christ and sang hymns and psalms

"in their own soft and engaging language, * * * the great body of the nation had received the Gospel in word only, and not in power. * * * A few excepted, they appear to remain enslaved to all the vices common to the other Indians."

William Savery was very fond of the Indian children, whom he mentions frequently. On one occasion, he sat with an Indian Queen for a time and studied her little papoose, in its carrier cradle, hung with about a hundred small brass bells to soothe the child to rest. The Indian mothers customarily nursed their babies three and even four years, according to Scanadoe, an Indian from whom the Friends obtained much information during the course of the Iroquois Treaty. One old Seneca woman, Granny Wagus, of about one hundred years of age, attended the Treaty, having traveled nearly an equal number of miles to get there.

Later in the course of the Canandaigua Treaty, Old Beech Tree and another chief died and were buried, both in one square box. They were dressed in clean shirts, leggins and moccasins, but the box being closed in the hut, the

[ 153 ]

Friends could not see whether other things were placed in it or not. An Indian walked before the coffin to the grave, with a three-gallon keg of rum under each arm and a bottle in his hands. The chiefs spoke at the grave and then the warriors fired three salutes over it, whereupon the mourners fell upon the rum and got completely drunk before night.

Indian grief at death seemed to have been hysterical, but easily assuaged. A gift of a belt of wampum, or the scalp of an enemy, if taken with that design, were always sufficient to banish the sudden and delirious grief that they manifested. It was also customary after a death to return to the donor any particular present given by him to the deceased in his lifetime. A ceremony of this kind occurred near the close of the Iroquois Treaty, when Red Jacket returned to Colonel Pickering a silver gorget, formerly presented to a chief, recently deceased, by the United States. Farmer's Brother made a speech of condolence and presented some strings of black wampum to the family of the deceased.

Throughout the whole Indian narrative of William Savery there is evidence of a plaintive uncertainty of effort and action. The Friends were deeply desirous of being the friends of the red men; they were also unwilling, albeit sincere witnesses of their weaknesses and vices. In view of the almost insoluble political questions that taxed their best efforts, both at Detroit and Canandaigua, there was with them a constant searching for some deeper remedy that would cut to the cause of the difficulties, rather than effect a patched-up peace. It was the age-old problem and it called for the age-old remedy, the only remedy that is at all available to men and women of good-will under trying circumstances.

There is abundant evidence that this remedy was crystallizing along educational lines in the minds of the Friends, as the Treaty at Canandaigua came to a close. What might well be called the initial session of the Tunesassa Committee, albeit informally, is thus described:

"This evening Friends being quietly together, our minds were seriously turned to consider the present state of these Six Nations, and a lively prospect appeared to attend that a mode might, under solid consideration, be fallen upon, by which Friends and other humane people might be made useful to them in a greater degree than has ever yet been effected; at least for the cause of humanity and justice and the sake of this poor, declining people, we hope so. The prospect and feelings of our minds this evening are not to be forgot, if we are favored to get home."

The Indian chief who seems to have been most instrumental in aiding Friends in obtaining statistics regarding the tribes and in suggesting methods of helpfulness to them was, curiously enough, the Tuscarora, Sword Carrier, or Sagareesa. His name contrasted strangely with the Indian name bestowed upon William Savery in accordance with their ideas of cordial hospitality. Being a man of peace, he was dubbed Sagalogorunka, signifying a buck which had cast off his horns. Thus the men of peace and the Sword Carrier conferred on the possibilities of work in the future for the tribes. Of Sword Carrier's visit, William Savery wrote:

"He appears to be a thoughtful man and mentioned a desire he had that some of our young men might come among them as teachers. We supposed he meant both as school-masters and artisans. Perhaps this intimation may be made use of in a future day. Great good might arise to the poor Indians if some religious young men of our Society, from a sense of duty, could be induced to spend some time among them, either as school-masters or mechanics."

## CHAPTER XV

# EUROPEAN WARS AND POLITICS (1790-1800)

Covering the period between William Savery's return from Canandaigua, New York, at the end of November, 1794, and his departure for service in Europe in May, 1796, there is very little material available. The transition from the American wilderness to war-torn Europe is necessarily abrupt, but it will be less so if conditions in Europe are briefly sketched. For that purpose the following chapter is inserted.

The younger Pitt became Prime Minister in 1784 at the age of twenty-four. His ministry lasted till 1800 and covered all the momentous years of the French Revolution. Until the excesses of the Parisian populace threw the Revolutionary party into disrepute, Pitt had been sympathetic to it, in the main, hoping for a development along constitutional lines. His own ministry to that time had been distinctly liberal. In 1792, however, when the situation in Paris developed faster than could be controlled, Pitt was forced to remold his policy. Edmund Burke, who shares with Pitt the esteem of all Americans, was older than when he formulated his policy of Conciliation with America, and with his age had come a conservatism in politics, that made him the arch-enemy of the French Revolution. In 1790 he had published his "Reflections on the French Revolution." Immediately it became the classic of conservatism. Pitt was forced to forego all the reform and liberal measures that he had been advocating, in company with Charles James Fox. He veered around in his attempt to abolish the slave trade, to repeal the Test and

Corporation Acts and to reform the electorate in some of the rotten boroughs.

The deposition of Louis XVI in 1792, and his subsequent death under the guillotine, electrified England into terror, even less reasonable than that experienced as a "red menace" during and after the World War. Burke had started out "to diffuse the terror." He succeeded beyond all expectation. Pitt, though but thirty-two years of age, refused to be stampeded and held out against the swelling tide of popular alarm and the call for war. France having made war upon Prussia in April, 1792, General Dumouriez defeated the Duke of Brunswick in the defiles of the Argonne in September, while the Royalists were being butchered in the dungeons of Paris. The victory vastly increased the confidence of the French and at the "November Convention" France offered the aid of her soldiers to all nations who would strive for freedom. "All governments are our enemies, all peoples are our allies," said the President of the Convention, in words strangely akin to those of the Russian Bolshevists, a century and a quarter later.

In the spirit of the offer, France then declared war on Holland. This was a cast that even Pitt, with all his profound desire for peace, could not ignore. The Dutch, with their maritime importance, were of prime significance to the English, then as now. Pitt was forced into the war ostensibly to save the Dutch allies, but in reality to down the Revolution and its doctrines of a kind so distasteful to the British. Until the Peace of Amiens, in 1802, England fought against the Revolution more largely by subsidizing the Continental armies than by her own man power. After the short breathing spell of that Treaty, she fought Napoleon, with both men and money, but also with a new motive. The Revolution, which had been rampant in William Savery's time, was dead, and in its place was a dictator who had seized the throne of France and hated the Revolution even more bitterly than England did. It is important to keep this distinction in mind, as our narrative deals only with the first, or Revolutionary stage of the struggle.

The years 1793 and 1794 were the years of the unreasoning panic, which Burke had helped to diffuse. Chief among the agitators of the alarm was Tom Paine, the son of an unobtrusive English Quaker family. His arguments for American independence were set forth in "Common Sense," a pamphlet that had had great effect on this side the water, prior to our Revolution. Philadelphia Friends read and discussed him and, as William Savery later told him, in part agreed with his ideas, if not with his methods, until the publication of his "Age of Reason." By this he was then, and still is branded as an agnostic.

Had Paine's reputation rested upon "Common Sense" and his later book, published in 1791 and 1792, called "The Rights of Man," he would be ranked today with the political seers of the age. The latter was in answer to Burke's "Reflections on the French Revolution," already referred to. Save for its advocacy of real republicanism in England and the abolition of all hereditary rights in Crown or Lords, practically all of the "criminal propositions" for which he was afterwards indicted upon a charge of treason are accomplished facts in England today. In Paine's pages are found early mention of graduated income taxes, school taxes for the education of the poor, old age pensions and maternity benefits.

"The Rights of Man" sold by tens of thousands, upon the issuance of the first part in 1791. The appearance of the second part, where he developed his more radical proposals, in 1792, was the signal for action on the part of the Government. Paine absconded, however, having been warned in time, and after escaping the guillotine in France for espousing the cause of Louis XVI, he fled to America, where he finally died in 1808.

Paine's persuasiveness had permeated English society of a class that theretofore had been little interested in or impressed by politics. The working class, having, as will be remembered, no vote at that time, had taken little concern for affairs about which their opinion mattered less. But the "Rights of Man," like Rousseau's "Contrat Social," of earlier days, had in it just that mixture of philosophic theory and practical politics that made it appeal to the reading, but unenfranchised citizen. It crystallized whatever of positive discontent and radicalism there was, and the fears of the ruling classes magnified that discontent a thousandfold. Of Paine, Pitt remarked, "He is perhaps right; but if I did what he wants, I should have thousands of bandits on my hands tomorrow, and London burned."

By 1793 the "terror" had set in, with symptoms strikingly similar to its analogue of 1919. The Habeas Corpus Act was suspended. A new bill against seditious assemblies restricted the right of public gatherings and the ancient Statute of Treasons took on a lusty, new and enlarged phase of usefulness. Many prosecutions were started against editors and dissenting ministers, whose sermons were declared seditious. The panic came to a head in the trials of Hardy, Thelwall and Tooke, three leaders of the Corresponding Society, for treason. The Society was the first workingmen's political and self-help organization in England. It advocated annual parliaments and universal suffrage in electing them. It professed sympathy for France and was deemed to be republican in tendency. The case was the "cause célèbre" in which Erskine won his first great reputation, and the acquittal of the defendants. Charges of treason, since that case, have never been lightly bandied about in English-speaking countries. The direct effect of the decision was universal jubilation in London and the return of a saner attitude toward things in general. The acute stage of the panic had passed, though political prisoners languished in the jails of England for several years more before the full effects were dissipated. Even then the panic left tangible evidence of its existence in the repressive laws against trade unions, associated in the middle-class mind with Jacobinical doctrines of Paine and the Corresponding Society. Had more foresight prevailed to allow trade organization and education, much of the increasing class bitterness and antagonism arising from the Industrial Revolution would have been absorbed, if not avoided.

In the meantime events were slowly moving along on the Continent. Following England's entrance into the war in February, 1793, with Austria, Saxony, Sardinia and Spain as allies, constituting the "First Coalition," little of an active nature was done. The French Jacobins, under Robespierre, stamped out the counter-revolution in blood. At Toulon, where an English force had been admitted by the French Royalists, they were expelled, in 1794, by a young artillery officer, that being the first appearance of Bonaparte in the military history of Europe. The death of Robespierre soon followed, and the Directory ensued, with a more moderate program, under which the France which William Savery knew and described in his travels was reunited in spirit and aim as never before. The counter-revolts ceased, the war was prosecuted with vigor, victories followed and nationalism became, for the first time in European history, the chauvinistic stimulus that it has ever since remained.

These victories of the French over the First Coalition were very disheartening to the young and pacific English Premier. Spain was first to withdraw in defeat; the Sardinians then retreated across the Alps and the Austrians yielded the Rhine provinces to the oncoming French. The small English army was crumpled back along the Waal and the Meuse, leaving the Low Countries open to the triumphal entry of the soldiers of the Republic into Amsterdam.

It is small wonder that Pitt was anxious for peace. Spain, Sweden and Prussia had made separate peace treaties and England, in her insularity, was left alone to face the enemy, with an utterly incompetent army and no sufficient officers. Pitt's pacific tendencies were largely financial in their origin. He had spent enormous sums for nothing of accomplishment. The Continental levies that British money had called into the battle had vanished like vapor, and the paid princelings would not move without more gold. The nation however, vocal through Burke, was strong for the war. When Pitt, in the face of the disasters, tried to negotiate a peace in 1796, Burke issued his "Letters on a Regicide Peace" and stirred England again as he had done four years before. Peace without victory proved elusive and Pitt was forced to the painful task of erecting the Second Coalition. He was destined to another disillusionment. Bonaparte had taken command of the army of the Alps and had begun, in dominating Piedmont, his meteoric career. The year 1797 saw Spain actually in alliance with France, and Prussia and Austria subjected to new humiliation. England was again alone without an ally and with a very definite threat of French invasion. While William Savery was in France and while Pitt was again attempting, in desperation, to negotiate a peace, in the face of public opinion, Burke, the intransigeant, died. England's fortunes were at about the lowest ebb in her history. With a pitiably incompetent army, with a huge debt that had brought no results and with cash payments suspended by the Bank of England, Pitt at Lille failed again in his peace proposals. The Directory was in no mood to make peace. As did Germany in 1914, France then counted on trouble in Ireland and India to distract English attention from the Continent. Risings took place in both quarters, particularly in Ireland in "the '98," but they did not absolve the British mind from the greater possibility of French invasion, than which, since

1066, no other topic has been of more moment to British apprehensions.

To offset the fear of invasion, the English fleet was uniformly victorious; against the French in 1794, against the Spanish, after their defection, in 1796, and against the Dutch (whose fleet the French had captured and sailed against the British) in 1797. Finally in 1798, the Battle of the Nile clinched British naval supremacy and registered the first signal defeat for Napoleon. It was in these days of depression in London and victory on the water that William Savery and his companions traveled in Europe,—a parlous task, requiring stout hearts and the sanction of a calling far removed from the ordinary pursuits of men. It is essential to realize the condition of these countries at the time to appreciate the quiet bravery of those devoted souls who went abroad, often sorrowing and in distress, to accomplish the Master's business.

The British naval victories and Napoleon's failure in Egypt enabled Pitt to revive once more the Continental Coalition. Russia and Austria took sides with the British and launched armies into the struggle. England sent a force into Holland, under the Duke of York, who had to withdraw faster than he went in and left nothing of British prestige behind.

With the rest of the war we have no immediate concern in these pages. In sooth, a brief sketch alone would run to great length. Suffice it to say, that the Coalition finally suffered severe losses. Napoleon's matchless military genius won victories in all directions, and at home overthrew the Directory. As First Consul in name and absolute master in fact, Napoleon was as anxious as were the British for a breathing spell and the nugatory Peace of Amiens resulted in 1802. The struggle with the Revolution was at an end; its genius in Europe lay prostrate, and democracy, which all Europe hated then as cordially as bolshevism is hated today, was apparently scotched for all time. Save in the radical and rather despised American Republic across the Atlantic, no vestiges of the doctrinaire republicanism and democracy of the philosophers, remained in the world, and even in America two generations were to pass and another great war was to be fought before the world was to be convinced that the democratic ideal would work on a really large and national scale.

## CHAPTER XVI

## TRAVELING IN GERMANY

It is difficult to determine at this time just where and how William Savery's concern for the scattered groups in Germany and France that went under the name of Friends arose. There were Germans aplenty in Pennsylvania, and after the French Revolution an increasing number of French émigrés. Europe was in the same after-the-war frame of mind that she now exhibits, although the wars, then fondly hoped to be nearly over, were in reality only beginning. Men felt then as they do now that the supports of the civilization they had known had been undermined and that the structure was fast crumbling into decay. They were right. New standards and new ideals were in the making. New currents of life and thought were rampant and the spirit of the Friends was as much stirred by these events in those days as they have been in these more recent times.

Of all the French émigrés, who came to Philadelphia, Stephen Grellet was the most interesting to the Friends. His life has made a deep impress upon the Society in that City where he is still quoted as one of the foremost saints in its worthy list. William Savery early made his acquaintance at North Meeting. His recent experiences as a Royalist refugee must have been intimately known by John Pemberton and William Savery. It is probable that this German and French connection in Pennsylvania was a strong stimulus to Friends to meet the crisis of warfare in the places where peace testimonies would be most difficult of application. John Pemberton of Philadelphia went to Germany and in January, 1795, laid down his life there in devotion to his duty. His grave in the Friend's burial ground at Pyrmont is one of the neglected Quaker shrines in central Europe.

William Savery knew and loved John Pemberton well. His death may have been a decisive factor in sending William Savery to the Continent. Certain it is that he applied to North Meeting in Philadelphia at the end of 1795 for a certificate liberating him for service "in Great Britain and elsewhere in Europe." The Committee appointed was quaintly charged "to sit down with him in his family, and if way open with desirable clearness," to draft a certificate. Way opened with desirable clearness.

Although the first European experiences were in England, where William Savery and his companions landed, they went so promptly to the Continent, that it was really the first field of labor. The group for this journey consisted of George and Sarah Dillwyn, David Sands, William Farrer, Benjamin Johnson and William Savery. They left the home of Joseph Smith in London, where a number of Friends had gathered to have a "time of comfortable retirement" with them and sailed from Blackwall, in the ship *Victoria*, Johann Borgis, Master, for Bremen. Below London lay many ships of war at the Nore, chief of which was the vast frigate *Ville de Paris*, of one hundred and twenty guns, "like an enormous castle."

An unexplained part of William Savery's equipment for this journey was his ability to speak German. It is possible that he had picked up a knowledge of it from the Germans near Philadelphia, many of whom were Friends. He had surely acquired it before landing in Germany, for his earliest entry relates that the Secretary of Prince Étienne, of Oldenburg, by whom the Friends were received the day they landed, was pleased upon "finding I could speak German." In less than a fortnight, he preached "and was more favored with the expression in the German than

I could have expected." David Sands and George Dillwyn followed and requested him to interpret,

"which I undertook in fear, but hope nothing suffered, * * * though I feel myself not competent to such a work, and less qualified to interpret for others than to speak my own feelings."

This obligation to interpret placed a double burden upon William Savery. "Much of the labor falls upon me, and people frequently calling upon us, I am kept pretty busy." The use of the language also won him respect from the people that interpretation could not have brought.

As they went, his proficiency and self-assurance increased and near the end of the trip he realized that Henry Lang was interpreting so poorly that he dispensed with his aid. As they entered Holland he was able to record that "none of us converse with the Hollanders as myself with the help of my high Dutch."

It is impossible within the compass of this narrative to give in detail the events of the next few months in Germany. It will be better to treat the subject topically, rather than as a journalistic account. The travelers landed in Oldenburg on August 8, 1796, and remained in Germany until December 19, 1796. Their travel took them first to Bremen, thence to Hamburg and Altona, where they had considerable service. Their next stop was at Hanover and thence by Hameln to Pyrmont, their first main objective, because there a Friends' meeting still existed and there lay buried the remains of their friend, John Pemberton. After much effective labor there, of which mention will be made later, David Sands and William Savery, with Lewis Seebohm, a German Friend of deep experience from Pyrmont, went on to Berlin and Freienwalde, visiting en route the cities of Hildesheim, Brunswick, Helmstedt, Magdeburg, Brandenburg and Potsdam, and returning by the same route, save for a side visit to Halberstadt. After the return, they rejoined the Dillwyns and were occupied for some time in the environs of Pyrmont, Minden, Bielefeld and Lemgo, from which they finally set out, without the Dillwyns, for Holland and France, via Osnabruck, Ibbenburen and Rheine to the Dutch border, where we will rejoin them later.

This extensive line of travel involved incredible hardships, not the least of which were due to the undeveloped state of the country. There were in the Germany of that day about three hundred and thirty constituent states, duchies and principalities. In fact, "Germany" was more of a generic name than a fact. The two dominant states or kingdoms of Austria and Prussia were as often allied against each other in the perpetual wars of the period as with each other. Frederick the Great had died in 1786, and had been succeeded by his nephew, Frederick William II, who was King of Prussia from that date until 1797, dying just a year after the Friends had left his dominions. He at that time controlled not only the Prussia of today, but both banks of the Rhine, including all of Westphalia and Rhenish Prussia. He had, in 1793 and 1795, participated with Russia and Austria in the second and third partitions of Poland, being all the while engaged in a war with France. Mention of this series of wars has already been made in a previous chapter. So much interwoven are they, that it is hard to tell when any part of Germany was at peace, as the armies overran the country.

William Savery and David Sands in their more extensive travels were continually subjected to registration and search by military authority. In some cities, the innkeepers were required to return the names of their lodgers to the burgomaster. Frequently a soldier would escort travelers from the outposts to the inns,

"to whom we must always part with some of our groschers, although he does no service whatever." * * * "They not only take our names as we pass through every town, but also where we came from last, our several places of residence, our business in this country & the character we travel in,—whether Officers, Merchants &c, to which we have learned to answer generally, that we are on a visit and travel as 'particulars,' a word they have taught us that generally satisfies them."

At Berlin this examination assumed unusual proportions. As the travelers entered the Brandenburg Gate at Berlin they were examined by a "very polite and amiable young officer" then by the officers of the customs; then, under escort of a soldier, to the Inspector's office, where "after a good deal of persuasion, they consented to examine our trunks and bags this evening, which at first they did not seem disposed to do, but to lock them up till tomorrow."

The nearer they kept to the French border, the more numerous were the evidences of warfare. The Rhine, as always, was the seat of war. Hanover was a fortified city, Bielefeld was completely walled and Hameln was not only strongly fortified, but was considered the chief stronghold of the Hanoverians.

In Westphalia, where the Friends worked extensively, great numbers of soldiers were billeted upon the inhabitants, 30,000 of them in the vicinage of Herford, alone. In most places the Friends were treated with uniform courtesy by the officers. At Ufeln there was an exception,

"officers and other light people crowding into the room, the people of the house cross and disobliging, evidencing clearly we were no welcome guests."

More customary was better treatment.

"An agreeable young man, a Lieutenant in the King of Prussia's service, who was quartered there was very affable and agreeable; said he could adopt all our principles if he could afford it, but being bred to the profession of war, he had no other way to get his bread, but thought it would be a happy thing for the world if all men were of our way of thinking."

At Lemgo, they lodged in an inn

"crowded with Prussian officers, among whom was Prince Lewis, the late King's brother's son. They were polite and very free in inquiry and conversation with us."

And finally at Minden, where they had one of the largest public meetings that they held in Germany, some of the officers of the army were in attendance.

Lest we think conscientious objection a modern development, the following account of a soldier in the Prussian army, who attended a meeting at Bielefeld, is interesting:

"He had been with the King of Prussia against the French: was in several battles and skirmishes but never fired off his gun. One was a general engagement of the two armies. The night before it happened, he being upon guard on the out-picket, perceiving a general attack likely to take place in the morning and feeling great repugnance in his mind to the shedding of his fellow-creature's blood, he kneeled down and besought the Lord to preserve him through the coming day. Which He mercifully granted. His company being divided into five divisions, who were to follow one another successively as they were called out, those who remained alive after expending their ammunition returned and were succeeded by another. He being in the second division was providentially transferred to the last through a concurrence of circumstances. Many of his comrades were killed and the last division being called for, was prevented from getting into action by the night coming on. So his prayer was answered. There being several religious men in the regiment he belonged to and another that was in the same brigade, during the campaign they frequently met together to edify one another in the spiritual life."

Still more modern were some of the evidences of warfare in the lives of the various peoples. In Holland, an ancient Reformed Church building had been taken by the French and used for stabling their horses, much to the dismay of the inhabitants of Deventer. At Rotterdam lived Cornelius Lloyd, a wealthy English merchant of Friendly inclinations, and his wife. She had been so terrified by the noise of the cannon when Dumouriez and the French army had been across the Meuse from the city, that she had lost her memory and could not retain anything in mind more than a minute at a time.

Near Potsdam the Friends attended the religious meeting of some earnest people who had two letters from the seat of war near the Rhine, containing "very affecting accounts of the sufferings of the people in many ways, by the French particularly at their taking possession of a city." All these accounts, with names in some cases transposed, could be made applicable to the Great War, but the following does not even need changing. Well might one think himself reading a modern press dispatch:

"We found several Jews, one of them a Rabbi, who had fled out of Poland at the division of that unhappy kingdom & on going to Copenhagen were not suffered to settle there but sent away. They looked poor pitiable objects, dressed little better than the American Indians & little if any, more polished in their manner. Our landlord informed us they had seen great droves of the poor Polanders driven along like cattle, having little clothes on & some of them in skins of beasts & their living only the coarsest rye bread and water. In this condition they were taking them to the army."

In so conglomerate a group of petty kingdoms as the German states of that time represented, it was impossible for the traveler to give an accurate description that would cover all. Perhaps the chance expression, "country of darkness and wooden shoes," comes as near a generalization as William Savery found. He traveled through the Hanoverian dominions which still owed allegiance to George III of England, where a casual acquaintance was surprised that one born in America should be as white as a German. They thought too that America was on the other side of the world and asked if the sun rose and set as it did in Germany and whether the wild people there believed in a God. Here too,

"one of the religious people of influence suggested to me whether some way might not be found to lay before the Elector of Hanover, King of England, the manner in which many of his subjects were groaning & under a state of discouragement, for want of that liberty of conscience which his English subjects enjoyed."

It is not too much to surmise that this aspect of things duly reached the ears of King George in the interesting interview that William Savery had with him, later in his journey.

It was in that same Germany, in Brunswick, where the travelers sought an interview with the Duke. In his absence, they were received by the Duchess of Brunswick,

"a noble countenanced woman, somewhat approaching to the masculine, about five feet, ten high, dressed in a lead colored silk gown, hat & ribbons—seemed pleased to see us, conversed freely (on) various subjects—told us our people were as much attached to her brother, the King of England, as any of his subjects & if all were like us, there would be no troubles or wars in the world; asked if General Washington was easy in his mind after his exploits, if we were as happy under the present Government as before. We told her Friends were never happier than under the Government of England, but we were bound by our principals to love all men, and were quiet under every Government."

Continental royalty was comparatively easy of access. The Duchess of Brunswick thought the King of Prussia would see the Friends, but told them that he was opposed to the Brunswick interest. Later, in Berlin, the royal family was much in evidence,—on one occasion the Queen, with most of her family and Prince Radsivil of Russia, the cidevant Prince of Poland, the Landgrave of Hesse-Cassel and many of the nobility, "who made a very pompous appearance." The King of Prussia then reigning, was Frederick William II, nephew of Frederick the Great. The Friends had a strong desire to meet him and William Savery especially laid this concern to heart. He saw the King on the street once, but he was only in Berlin for a short time, to attend the baptism of the Crown Prince's son (afterward Frederick William IV).

Upon his return to England, William Savery, in recounting some of his Continental experiences, had Sarah Rawes in his audience. She carefully wrote down many of the things he said, and her record is extant today. The following has bearing upon the King of Prussia:

"Having a desire to see the King of Prussia when they were at Berlin, which at first he found some difficulty to obtain, but on presenting one of the pages with a dollar, he found that sufficient to gain his point and was shown upstairs where the King was likely to pass from one room to another. He was soon gratified by the King's appearance. He had some of the family with him. He stood there conversing with a person and then passed on. I think William said there was no notice taken of his hat."

The incident does not reflect much credit upon William Savery, either from the means used to gain access, or from the standpoint of the hat. One can hardly attribute much religious significance to remaining covered when the audience was obtained by a tip and the King unconscious of the visitor's presence. The incident is not mentioned in the Journal and one can easily surmise that William Savery would not have been very proud of it.

The best the Friends could do was to send to the King a copy of Barclay's "Apology," bound in red leather. The gift went by the hand of Major Marconnay, who, though long in the King's service, and a man of note, had taken a great liking to the Friends and was in close sympathy with them in doctrine and spirit. Through his acquaintance with the Prime Minister, Marconnay arranged an appointment for the Friends with Frederick William, but the word came a day late, as the travelers had left. The Minister dispatched a courier after them to Potsdam, but so fast had they traveled that they were not overtaken. William Savery considered this failure the one great omission of his Continental experience and mourned over it as such. "We cannot charge ourselves with willful omission, and therefore hope it will not be laid to our charge," writes he, but the topic would not down, and weeks afterwards he was wrestling in spirit over undertaking again the six hundred mile journey back to Berlin.

In regal splendor, Prussia exceeded all the other states of Germany. Her roads vied with Brunswick's for excellence, while almost all the other districts had roads so poor as to render traveling in wheeled vehicles extremely dangerous. Prussia had no beggars; the other states had them, in places by swarms. In one other item was Prussia preëminent:

"The King of Prussia suffers no smoking in the streets of the City or villages, under penalty of 50 Dollars, or being sent for some months to work at the fortifications,—this is trying to Germans."

As William Savery took an occasional pipe himself, the comment is the more pertinent.

The magnificence of Berlin and Potsdam especially excited the admiration of the travelers, but finally palled upon them. Potsdam

"is the most magnificent city we have seen by far & may contain 30,000 inhabitants, including a great number of soldiery."

The New Palace, with its one hundred and forty-eight rooms, and Sans Souci, which

"taken together, so far exceeds anything to be seen in England and all the ideas I had ever formed by reading, of human grandeur, that an attempt to describe it would be vain."

The spires of Berlin appeared soon after leaving Potsdam, over a paved road, lined on both sides with Lombardy poplars. Entering by the Brandenburg Gate, then recently built, they were appalled by the grandeur of it and the statuary and architecture of the city. The bridges, public buildings and palaces of the nobility, the large houses, with imposing fronts, covered with plaster, the great number of coaches, with splendid equipage, and flunkeys and footmen on all sides, obsequious to a fault,— in all, so jumbled and confusing an evidence of regal pomp and display, that the Friends turned from it in disgust. Quoth William Savery:

"It will be wisdom in us to turn our minds away from these things & endeavor to stay them upon God who alone can strengthen us to finish the important work he has required of us. * * * The more those who love the humble path of Jesus see of the greatness and glory of this world & how empty & vain it is, the more they will be constrained to draw nigh unto Him, who is their Dignity, their Riches and will finally be their Everlasting Glory."

Other cities there were in that journey, more typical of the various kinds of German life than the capitals. Hamburg, Free City and extensive seaport, with its shady walks, swarming with people, diverting themselves on the First Day of the week, with music, singing, dancing, gaming and drinking, Bielefeld and Osnabruck, with their linen manufacture, ancient Halberstadt, with its "seven cloysters for nuns and fryars," and its mercenary priests, poor trade and appearance of better days gone by. Bremen, with its vast trade in wine,—a trade carried on, be it noted, even in those halcyon days, for the public benefit, long before municipal ownership and state control worried some and pleased others. The public wine cellar was one of the sights of the town, with its many vast tuns, containing forty to one hundred hogsheads apiece, each tun marked with the date of vintage and some of them upwards of one hundred years old, and only to be tapped by consent of the magistrates. Herford,

"which is like many others in this country, dirty narrow streets, no foot-ways & paved with round pebble stones; the houses with the gable end towards the street, generally of a mean appearance; the people poor, few that have a decent or * * * genteel appearance, except the officers of the army; the town crowded with soldiers, billetted on the inhabitants, as all the adjacent towns and villages are."

There was, too, the ancient city of Hildesheim, with its wall, and

"hanging from the wall on the outside of the gates, is an iron cage, in which they put criminals, convicted of small offences, and whirl them round and round, with so much velocity for a considerable length of time, till they are sick almost to death. This is one of their modes of punishment."

Later, near Berlin, William Savery fell in with the President of the Chamber of Justice. Their conversation turned upon crime and punishment and the Quaker minister, with his facile ability to measure himself with men of other callings, soon told of the abolition of corporal punishment in America, with which the German Judge "seemed pleased, but had his doubts whether it would answer the desirable end in view."

Such examples could be multiplied from the intimate and careful observations of this meticulously complete Journal. Germany was in flux, and far more diverse and volatile in her composition than was France. The one had never had unity, save under the nebulous Holy Roman Empire, which, as Voltaire remarked, was neither "holy" nor "Roman" nor an "empire." France had had unity and strong central control, but was disintegrating, for the time being. Germany was experiencing centripetal and France centrifugal political action, but both were far from the modern states called by the same names.

If the political features of the country were diverse, the social were even more so. In England there was an undertone of internal consistency, that persisted in spite of variations. In Germany the variations were bewildering. Cocked hats, queued hair and brave clothes were much in evidence among the upper classes; ragged beggars, coarse living, "potatoes and salt, and rye bread, as coarse as if it had been made of bran," and the utmost servility toward the military, clerical and governing classes, were the predominant features of the masses.

"Vast numbers of the people of this country live, their houses nearly as dirty as pig-stys, and indeed, pigs, goats, cows, geese, &c, live together with the family and much alike."

Naturally one does not derive a completely rounded picture of social Germany from William Savery's pages. His incidents were of necessity spotty, but at the same time they have an interest arising from their very casual nature.

[ 175 ]

Mention has already been made of the apparent poverty and contrasting opulence of the two social extremes in Germany. Wages, prices and rents as they applied to the poorer people receive some small mention. In Lewis Seebohm's "Friedenstall" near Pyrmont,

"These young women who are in families and work either in or out doors as occasion requires and very hard at times, are paid about seven dollars a year & a bright, solid young man, a Friend, tells us if he makes his pair of shoes pr day, he earns abt 2s 6d, our money, a week, and found board & washing—yet he keeps himself decent like a Friend of our country. Provisions & clothing are abt 2/3 of the price in America, but they make a little diet and mean diet do. Several of them express their desire to go to America, but we dare not encourage it to unsettle them."

The desire to emigrate to America seems to have been prevalent in all parts of Germany. Poverty alone prevented a general hegira. A waitress at Halberstadt "said if I would be so good as to take her with me to America, she would be a faithful servant to me. She desired much to go." From Hanover, William Savery did assent to such an appeal and wrote recommending Sophia Crammer "to the attention of my Sally, she being very desirous of going to America."

The lowest paid man around the tool factory received about the equivalent of one shilling Pennsylvania, a day, upon which he maintained a wife and four children. The Friends were considerably concerned to improve the industrial possibilities of these simple Pyrmont folk, and conferred with them about introducing spinning and weaving involving a better living and less exposure. As will appear in a later chapter on the industrial situation in England, production of goods, everywhere, was largely upon a cottage basis. Lewis Seebohm's "factory" must have been far in advance of the Germany of his time, as even England had few real factories. Perhaps the Prince of Waldeck, in patronizing the project, was really subsidizing an infant industry with the hope of stimulating others to a like endeavor, for the benefit of his subjects. But even then it cannot be considered as a factory in the modern sense, as it must have had a modicum of machinery and a maximum of hand-work,—manufacture, in the strict and liberal sense.

The mixture of monetary standards used by William Savery is confusing, and the values of the coins quoted has varied much since his time, but the following summary would indicate a pitiably low level of living, even at the best:

"Women in this country are obliged to labour very hard, both in doors and out, for abt 1/0 Pennsylvania cur^y a week & abt 3/0 if they find themselves. Men get abt 2/6 Penna, a week and their diet and lodging, which are both, in a general way, very poor and probably do not cost more than half a dollar."

In spite of these low wages, the young women of Pyrmont, who became very fond of the Friends, were examples of neatness:

"I admire their neatness & decency. The young women wear white, quilted caps & there is scarce any bonnets among them; indeed bonnets or hats are little used by any of the women of this country."

The only reference to rent and taxes upon German lands occurs in connection with the holdings of the Reckefus brothers, near Herford. They tilled thirty acres of land for which they paid forty dollars annually to a nobleman. Their whole property was valued at six hundred dollars, "but the various demands upon them of a public nature, for some of which they suffer distraint, keeps them poor and bare." It is interesting to note that in this same section, near Ufeln,

"we passed thro the finest piece of woodland we have seen in Germany,—the timber almost as tall as America, which is not common."

The political and priestly levies to which the Reckefus brothers were subjected (in spite of which, says William Savery, "they appear peaceful, contented and easy") were common throughout Germany, with the possible exception of Prussia. Strange to say, Hanover, under the benign rule of George III of England, was rated as the worst by the travelers. It was there that

"poverty, the effect of arbitrary power, appeared in a striking point of view to Americans,"

and where

"the people are shamefully fleeced, both by the government and the priests, beyond anything I have ever heard of."

Surely William Savery, as an American, a former subject of King George and a visitor to him and his sister, the Duchess of Brunswick, must have needed the wisdom of the serpent and the harmlessness of the dove to tell both individuals what, in sincerity, he thought of political conditions in America, England and Europe.

It was this same Hanover, between Bremen and Harburg, a distance of sixty-six miles, that elicited the following description:

"Travelled over a very poor country, one-third of which is a heath, where they keep boys and girls to tend cattle, and the miserable sheep, we see everywhere, as we pass along. Some of the land is sown with rye, barley, oats, buckwheat and some wheat. Hundreds of the poor peasants are employed in mowing and hauling in; the women bearing an equal share of the burden with the men. The grain was poor, compared with England or America. The villages generally have a miserable appearance, being composed of clay huts without chimneys. They use turf for fuel, and the people are very laborious, living hard; coarse, black rye bread, milk, and some vegetables being their principal diet. Their horses, cows, &c, live under the same thatched roof with the family."

Contrasting with this dismal picture was the prosperity of Saxony, then a part of Prussia, where, between Helmstadt and Magdeburg they passed through a very fine country, with many villages and good roads. The ground was covered with wheat and rye stubble, it being

[ 178 ]

"the greatest grain country any of us have ever seen, raises abundant of sheep and geese; the face of the country beautiful & with gentle rises and the land excellent."

This prosperity continued, as the travelers moved on. At Magdeburg, on the River Elbe, were many flat-bottomed boats and shallops for communication with Hamburg, and "a number of curious grist mills that float upon large boats, and are worked by the stream. This is worthy of attention in some parts of America." From Brandenburg flowed a branch of the Elbe, a hundred yards wide, upon which also were some good mills, and there, too, were many stocking weavers, plying their handicraft, on the cottage basis. Most curious trade of all, but peculiar apparently even in those days to Germany, was the raising of canary birds and nightingales. Near Potsdam

"were a man, his wife and daughter, about sixteen, * * * with about 200 canary birds & nightingales which they had raised and were carrying them to Berlin, about 200 miles to sell, expecting about one dollar apiece for them. This was really a curious sight and laborious * * * but Germans, especially women, are fitted for incredible hardships. I gave the young girl some groschers to chear her spirits."

The superior economic position of these parts, then all under the King of Prussia, is a tacit but significant commentary upon the history of the next two decades. The Rhineland had been devastated by incessant warfare and was not to be free from it for long. Only England, France and Prussia were economically strong and those giants were to dispute the mastery of Europe between themselves, until Waterloo found Blücher and Wellington supreme over Napoleon. No historian, however, realized in those days what is now patent to all,—that Napoleon's maxim, "An army marches on its belly," was but the same thing as acknowledging the potency of economic resources in warfare.

With few exceptions, the roads were poor. There were

a few turnpikes, notably near Brunswick, Osnabruck and Springe:

> "There are but few such in Germany; the Princes not willing to spend their money on the roads, and the people generally being too poor, the roads are generally left in their natural state, and little or nothing done to mend them."

Throughout the extent of their travels, the comment on the roads varied between "sandy and tedious" in the Brandenburg-Potsdam district, to "miry, deep and disagreeable" in the vicinage of Minden. At times the going was so rough that the travelers alighted and walked. As winter set in, these discomforts increased. Near Herford, where they experienced the "worst roads we have traveled," they made but four and one-half miles in two hours, and the wagon was so damaged that they had to stop and have it mended. Between Osnabruck and Ibbenburen, they encountered so much ice and snow that they had the wheels shod with sharp iron spurs. These ancient non-skid devices were soon rendered unnecessary, however, as a sudden thaw converted the ice into mud.

The travelers had their own wagon, but even the best were heavy and inconvenient. The modern reader needs to reconstruct his ideas of travel to appreciate properly the enormous burden of long journeys in that time. For eighteen days, in a circuit out of Minden, Christopher Reckefus, a German Friend, acted as guide and postilion. His four horses were in their service during the entire period and the Friends became much attached to him. In the war zone, where Prussian soldiers overran the countryside, feed for the horses was very expensive, oats a Spanish dollar a bushel near Herford.

Even with private horses the troubles of the road did did not vanish. Outside of Herford, in mid-November,

> "Our wagon stuck fast in the mud, and though all our company was out of it and went principally on foot, the horses were not able

to move it with all the baggage out, so our good driver, C. Reckefus, was obliged to go back about ¾ of a mile to a village to get a chain to draw it back. This detained us an hour and a half in the cold. We walked about 1½ miles to a tavern on the road."

The next day William Savery hired a horse of the land-lord and took a man to Hameln to return it, sallying forth ahead of the rest on his journey. The landlord, who with his wife had been as agreeable and courteous as their limited facilities warranted, remarked, regarding the horse, that

"he would not do so by common travelers, but he could trust us with anything,"

whereupon William Savery added the comment that

"Germans are generally suspicious of strangers."

The Friends well nigh used up their wagon in the German travels and in Holland, exchanged it

"for a handsome coach which will be safer and warmer & we hope to travel with two horses instead of four; gave seven guineas for it. Our coach now stands us thirty guineas, suppose it would bring sixty in America."

In Amsterdam, William Savery dickered for two fine mares, which he tried out in harness, through the city. The owner asked five hundred and fifty guilders and two ducats, halter-money, equivalent to £45 sterling, for them, a price which the Friends deemed too high. Later, in Rotterdam, he again tried out more horses and presumably purchased them. His knowledge of horses seems to have been equal to their needs. Months afterwards, upon their return to England, the coach, bought in Holland, was shipped to America, to fulfill a further period of usefulness, doubtless in the streets of Philadelphia. William Savery paid J. Blake, in Great Holborn, London,

"£6 6d sterling, expenses of the carriage, owned by W. F., D. S., B. J., and myself, shipd from Amsterdam to America,"

Blake being agent in London for John Vanderwerf, a

Dutch merchant to whom the Friends were much indebted during their stay in Amsterdam.

Their travel in Germany preceded these arrangements, however. In the various sections of that country they were almost entirely in the hands of innkeepers and their post riders or postilions. The standard speed was about three and one-half miles an hour, "and there seems no inducing a German driver to exceed that gait." The regulation equipage consisted of four horses to the carriage. The postilions were, as a class, well qualified to try the patience of their victims. Approaching Zell,

"we were obliged to stop on the road for our postilion to take his bread, herring and milk, which they do in the middle of every station, for which, and the feed of the horses, passengers must freely pay, or be used worse than they are. The horses eat the same bread as the drivers."

The postmaster (in the old and original sense of the word) was also an individual to be conjured with. If in a bad humor, he could autocratically detain the post and the public could fume but do little else. The postilion was under strict orders, but not averse to extra groschen, "the only argument with his fraternity," by the use of which the Friends reached Magdeburg one night when the regulation pace would not have accomplished it. At another time, in approaching Pyrmont, the common post road meandered too widely among the valleys to enable them to reach their bourne by evening. The postilion was unable to leave it, so they paid him the full fare for his station, four and one-half German dollars, and agreed with the landlord to take them over the hilly, but shorter route, at a cost of seven dollars additional. This road proved very rough and at times they were above the clouds, with the valleys below obscured. Crossing the Weser, "a very beautiful stream, about one hundred yards wide," in a boat, they rejoined their friends at Pyrmont, before dark.

More serious was the experience between Hanover and

Minden, of which the following is William Savery's narrative:

"We rode about ten miles to a poor snap house. Our postilion having taken up a man & woman without our consent, when we came to this house they called for drink and victuals, which the landlord charged to us. We told him it was an imposition which we were not free to submit to. Being a man of violent passions, he stormed and swore we should pay it. It was his practice to charge all to the heersschaft & let the poor of the company go free. So for peace sake we were obliged to submit. He was in such a rage I heard him tell the postilion he would do right to over-set us on the road, which he faithfully executed about one-half mile from the end of his stage. It was extreme cold, windy and snowing, and the night coming in when we overset. David's shoulder was bruised, B. J. & W. F. had their faces cut against the irons and were other ways bruised. I only escaped with little or no damage. A great difficulty we had & were kept in the cold snow and wet more than half an hour, before we could get our wagon up. By this time it was dark."

They walked to the nearest village, not caring to entrust themselves again to the postilion, and there Benjamin Johnson and William Farrer who were "in a bloody pickle from their wounds," found attention. It was near noon next day before the top of the wagon was repaired and the travelers off again. Thereafter, they were constantly in fear lest their top-heavy wagon should offer another chance for harm to a designing or disgruntled postilion.

From the above narrative it is evident that the innkeepers were also a power in the German social system. William Savery is more specific in his mention of the inns and innkeepers of Germany by name than he was elsewhere in his Journal, and his characterizations of the various hosts and their families (for the family was often an important part of the hospitality in those days) is enlightening. The inns varied greatly in their facilities and accommodations:

"We must pay high at the best inns in Germany. There is a surprising difference between them and their lowest taverns, in their charges, and yet the difference in living consists principally in the superiority of the beds, the attendance of servants, of whom they keep a profusion & the mode of serving up the provisions. We wish to study economy, but lodging in the low houses would be attended with so many inconveniences and subject us to noisy, riotous company, dancing &c, that we cannot believe it right to submit to it. The great inns in Germany are remarkably decent and quiet."

The extortionate rates charged travelers, especially those from afar, were a matter of much concern and chagrin to the Friends. At Magdeburg, where they paid six louis, including fees to the servants, for three nights for five of them, William Savery "thought it an enormous bill." At Hamburg they took three rooms at a dollar and a half a day, but in leaving

"our landlady imposed upon us by an unjust charge, which for peace sake we were obliged to pay, though it was contrary to our agreement. This is a land of impositions on strangers."

At Ufeln, in a poor inn, crowded with soldiers, the publican was cross and disobliging, plainly evidencing that the Friends were no welcome guests. They were finally told that they must discharge their reckoning and depart. They stood aghast at the bill. William Savery records the incident with details as amusing now as they were irksome then:

"This (the order to leave) excited in us some admiration as well as disgust, which was not altogether suppressed by me. I found the old Adam still alive & if I had been travelling in any other character than a Gospel minister, probably I should have done more hurt than good by resenting it."

Fortunately, however, all the innkeepers were not of that ilk. Zeisburg, whose genial presence pervaded "The Sign of the Golden Hart," at Berlin, "in the street going in at the Brandenburg Gate, called Unter den Linden, the public walk lined with trees being before the door," became a true host. Of his service, William Savery records:

[ 184 ]

"Our kind landlord & all his family, children, servants, &c, embraced us and evidently manifested the place we had in their minds with tears. They have been very kind and attentive to us all the time of our stay; have forwarded our meetings with great cheerfulness, preparing seats, showing up the people, &c, so that we believe there was a divine hand in sending us to this house."

Others there were who helped the travelers. At Zeisar, "the people of the inn were rather above ye common level of inn-keepers & fond of conversing with us." William Savery bought a very fine hare, and they had it roasted for supper, the first he had ever tasted. Upon leaving, the publican asked the favor of his address in Philadelphia, with his seal or coat of arms, "supposing us to be some great people." At Rinteln, in the dominions of the Landgrave of Hesse, of unsavory memory in the American Revolution,

"the landlord spoke English, having been with the Hessian army to America. He and others looked pleased to see Americans and Quakers. * * * All the soldiers and officers that we meet with, who have been to America, speak well of Friends and treat us with respect."

At Bielefeld and Lemgo the inns were kept by widows, who, with their families, were all that could be desired, in affectionate attention, though their houses were inferior to most, and at Lemgo crowded with Prussian officers.

And so they fared, sometimes well, sometimes ill. At Magdeburg they lodged at "The King of Prussia," and found the people

"more courteous & engaging in their manners than any town we have been in & our company are of the judgement they exceed any other place in the comliness of their persons, especially the women. They are mostly fair complexion. Upon dissecting the name of the city, Magdeburg, it is, in English, the City of Maidens."

At Hanover they patronized two inns, "The Stadt Strelites" and the "Sign of Amsterdam." In the December twilight, the vast inn at Bunde, of one hundred and twenty feet front, proved a haven of rest with good accommodations for the weary pilgrims. In Halberstadt, "The Golden Angel" welcomed them and at their headquarters, Minden, their home was in the "Stadt Bremen." But of all other public houses, the "Grune Elboge" or "Crooked Elbow" at Osnabruck is most carefully described, with a Chaucerian tang that indicates how slightly society had progressed in four centuries. The Friends always preferred to eat their meals apart from the public table. For two days at Osnabruck they submitted to the public table and the curious stare that inevitably followed them. The second evening was worse than the first:

"though all the guests behaved respectfully to us. Among them was a stout, rosy-looking lady abbess, who was the head of a convent in the City of Cologne; had been on a visit to her friends & was returning to her station with a young man, her relation. Her behavior gave us very little idea that she was fond of a recluse life. * * * The most trying occurrence at the table d'hote was six musicianers who was playing so that the guests could not hear one another during almost the whole time. We told the priests and landlord our objection to it and some of the company finding us uneasy, took up the subject. An elderly man who sat by me told the company and landlord he thought it a great imposition upon many to please but a very few, and though he had lodged there for some months, if it was continued, he should be under the necessity of shifting his quarters. So we left them to settle the matter & retired to our own room where we were quiet."

Another bit of diplomacy that adhered to the postilion's position was the choice of hotels where there were more than one. Upon his discretion his passengers had to rely and he sometimes retaliated for scant treatment by landing them at an inferior hostelry. The meals varied from the roasted hare, already mentioned, to elaborate menus that sound epicurean to the modern. Early in their travels the Friends were all sick from the food they had to eat.

"Sour wine, sour beer, bread, meat and vegetables form the principal articles of diet; the meat cooked till it is ready to fall to pieces.

Coffee which the Germans make to perfection and drink it several times in a day, seems to be almost the only good thing at their tables. Meat is mostly poor and veal killed when it is about a week old."

At Rinteln the veal was only two days old, and that fried. With two or three little fish, this veal made the supper, but the Friends being unable to stand the combination, they had milk and anticipated better things for breakfast. As they neared the Dutch border the prices advanced as the cleanliness increased. At Delden they paid "an enormous bill, . . . but truly all over this country travelers are fleeced without mercy, especially foreigners." As their accommodation had included a roast fowl, bread, cheese and a bottle of wine in the evening, and "a little poor beer" and coffee in the morning, and post horses for the next stage of twenty-seven miles, the charge of three pounds sterling would not seem excessive today for four people.

The Friends used their rooms frequently as places of assembly, and nearly always held conferences there with religious people who sought them out. The thick feather puffs which, even to this day, decorate the beds of Continental hostelries, without providing warmth to both extremities at the same time, invoked William Savery's ire. "We everywhere meet with a feather bed covering and * * * could not be furnished with blankets enough to keep us warm." At times the ministers would abide in very poor houses, with straw beds, or even with straw upon the floor and cloaks for covering in cold nights. For such emergencies they carried their own sheets. It was rough traveling and disheartening service, which required a strong and constantly renewed sense of a divine call to encourage adherence to the task.

Perhaps no better generalization of conditions in these public houses could be drawn than is indicated by an incident at the "Golden Hart" in Berlin:

"Two Jews came up into our rooms, one after the other, wanting to trade with us, either to buy or sell or exchange money. I mention this because in all the large towns, strangers will find them and such kind of people exceeding troublesome, for custom seems to have given them and women with fruit & trinkets, barbers & other people of that class, to come into the inn, open your doors, lift up the curtains of your beds and impose themselves upon you, when they please, & they are so importunate that it is hard to get rid of them. Custom has taught some of the women to come into our bed chambers who appear not to have the same sense of the impropriety of it that the American women have."

One can hardly wonder that the little band of itinerants was nothing loath to leave this "land of darkness and of wooden shoes," for the cleanlier inns of Holland, even with the kindly parting greeting of numerous innkeepers ringing in their ears,—a farewell that, says our chronicler, was very common with landlords who were pleased with their guests,—

"Lieben sie wohl, gluckliche reise—commen sie bald wieder."

The various hosts may be granted a greater sincerity than the accuracy of German idiom might indicate.

## CHAPTER XVII

# RELIGIOUS LABOR IN GERMANY

It was in Germany that the Friends first tried out their religious concern on an extensive scale. Their method was singularly spontaneous and unplanned. And yet it became very effective. When one considers that William Savery and George Dillwyn acquired, during this European mission, so extensive a reputation as itinerant preachers and observant travelers, that they were received, upon their return to England, by the King and Queen,—an honor then rarely vouchsafed to Friends,—the novelty of the service and the importance of the contacts become apparent.

They traveled with the simple plan of entering a city, and then inquiring for religious people of a seeking temperament. They were convinced "of the possibility of a Divine call to travel with the Gospel message now, as well as in the apostles' days." Time and again William Savery records that one or another of their number would saunter out from their lodgings and return with reports of some rencontre or other, that led to simple and religious souls, or else to a bumptious charlatan, "full of himself and of talk," or "full of visions" as it was variously styled. It was lonesome and disheartening work:

"* * * like solitary pilgrims in the midst of a strange people. It is not easy to conceive the state of mind and mortification that poor travellers have to pass through daily, but more especially on entering large cities and towns, * * * where the manners, religion and pursuits of the people are so entirely different from ours."

Every town had its assortment, known to the townspeople, of residents interested in religious subjects, and these the Friends soon found by inquiry. It was personal work, soul to soul, of a type that would seem impossible today. It often led to public meetings, but not so frequently as in England, where religious liberty prevailed to an extent unknown in Germany. In Hanover, particularly, this method of publicity was successful:

"The news of our being here, being spread through the city, people came to their windows and doors, to look at us passing the streets, yet nothing rude or scoffing appeared, but kind, bowing & pulling off their hats, respectfully. * * * The school-masters in this place make it a practice to inform their children any interesting intelligence that occurs. Several of them having been to see us, afterwards, as we were informed, told their scholars that we were come from America, a long ways off, to preach the true religion to the people of Germany, without asking any pay for it. The children telling their parents, spread the news fast and accounted for the City being so generally informed."

Among these seekers, were many in full sympathy with the fundamental doctrines of Friends, but weak, in the face of ecclesiastical opposition in maintaining them. Of these, Christian Bacher of Bremen was typical. He and small groups of his ilk, all over Germany, with whom he had correspondence, were called Mystics, fully acquainted with the Friends' doctrine of the inner light, and devout followers of Jacob Behmen and Lady Guyon. He was, however, a bit too talkative for the Friends, and also, like many of the thoughtful Germans, felt there was no need of a visible Church, having all too much experience with the visible forms of the Church in everyday life. "As they know us to be a gathered people," says William Savery, they were the more inclined to be shy of Friends.

Of a similar type were Charles Wellman, a wealthy linen merchant of Bielefeld, and his wife, "very free in conversation, deeply acquainted with the Mystic authors, high in reasoning & seem much in their strongholds." At Zell, "a man looking pleasantly on us, we turned about and spoke to him, with which he seemed glad and took us into his house." He was a Behmenist and strongly, albeit tacitly, opposed to the priests. He proved full of visions and found God in minerals and everything else. Each acquaintance was a vantage point for another and gossip frequently found other persons anxious to meet the strangers from America, who traveled at their own expense, with no other motive than the spiritual welfare of their fellow men. A little boy, hearing of the Friends, told his father, a Calvinist minister, of them. An invitation ensued and William Savery accepted it. A delightful interview followed. The father of thirty-five and the lad of twelve were much interested and at the close the father told the boy,

"that I was one of the people called Quakers, from America; that I did not think it right to pull off my hat in honor to any man, but did it only in reverence to the Divine Being; that I and my brethren never went to war, nor took an oath, our yea being yea, and our nay, nay."

The plain clothes of the Friends attracted attention to them, often to their discomfiture. They were rejoiced to find at Hanover, a tailor, named J. Buck, who, late in their journey, refurbished them after their wonted fashion. They had some of their clothes turned and mended and three of them bought great coats of rugged gray cloth, "with a hood like a fryar's for winter which comes on fast." The cloth for these cost 6d Pennsylvania an ell, the making, thread, etc., about 7/6, with a total for the coat of a guinea. J. Buck was tenderly scrupulous about clothes and the Friends emphasized his concern by coinciding with it. A great part of his trade was in making "fashionable and superfluous clothes," and neither he nor they were able to see his way to a livelihood without making them.

Their dress made them spectacles to the Germans, who "doubtless look upon us as a strange, outlandish people." At Helmstad their curious interlocutors variously estimated them as Catholics, then Brabanters, Frenchmen, or Lutherans, but when told they were from America, simply looked surprised and said it was very far off.  At Magdeburg, as at Hanover, they received very respectful attention, but at other places they were vilified.  At Ufeln

"we were nowhere so much stared at as in that place, nowhere so illy treated nor so much depressed in our minds, * * * the people following us with their eyes and throwing up their windows till we got out of town."

One contributing cause of this unwelcome attention was unwillingness to doff their hats in places of worship, which, nevertheless, they persisted in entering.  In a Roman Catholic chapel in Helmstad, they aroused the resentment of the bystanders, who asked "if we thought we were in a hog-sty."

"However though they looked sour, we continued inside of the door one-quarter of an hour.  The priests were mounted on a stage like play actors, and were acting their part much in the same manner, the place crowded with ancient imagery.  We turned away sorrowful at the wickedness of the priests & darkness of the people."

The Friends also retained their hats in assemblies of other people with whom they worshiped, "telling them our reasons, with which they appeared satisfied" in one meeting, but in another "somewhat prejudiced and not pleased." The travelers interviewed the Governor at Pyrmont.

"The people who saw us with him with our hats on, appeared astonished, for the great men in Germany are approached with much servility."

There can be no doubt that this conscientious feeling regarding hat-honor was a great drawback in some of the approaches in Germany, and would hardly seem to indicate a liberal spirit when applied in a chapel where their attendance was not wanted, still less requested.

Another difficulty experienced was in the singing in some of the religious meetings they attended.  One recalls William Savery's favorable reaction to the singing among the Indians at Canandaigua, but at Magdeburg he was not so catholic in his sympathies and the Friends, feeling "some objection to going among them in the time of their singing, tho they invited us," decided to attend an hour later and then held a meeting after Friends' manner.

In most of the towns through which they passed, on the first day of the week, the Continental Sunday was in full blast. At Bremen,

"the afternoon proved distressing to us, on account of the people making it a time of merriment; drinking, singing, playing at bowls, etc., which appears to be the general practice."

The short space between Hamburg and Altona, having some shady walks,

"swarmed with people, who according to the inconsistent custom of the country, were diverting themselves in a variety of ways, with music, singing, dancing, gaming and drinking."

At Zell, where the Protestant influence was predominant, the itinerants found one of the few quiet Sabbaths they enjoyed on the Continent,

"everywhere exceedingly still and orderly · few people being in the streets or on the public walks."

At Magdeburg, occurred an incident singularly reminiscent of the Middle Ages. Apparently the superstitious people had frequently been the dupes of those claiming the occult arts. The philosophy stone had recently been in vogue and after the Friends entered the city, they soon encountered the followers of a magician. He had the alleged ability

"to converse with departed spirits and angels, had the art of turning metals into gold (and) could cause celestial spirits to appear before him to give him information of things he desired to know."

One of the men had seen and conversed with a venerable spirit with a long beard, raised by the magician, whose powers were attributed by his followers to his experience of the new birth and to particular gifts from Heaven.

With the same apostolic fervor that Paul applied to confounding Elymas in Cyprus, the Friends sought out this modern sorcerer, who assumed an air of consequence and began mumbling incoherent expressions with great rapidity. Lewis Seebohm with difficulty slipped in a few words, deprecating the magician's willingness to live upon other people's charity through his sycophancy, and then, addressing his disciples, told them the man was an imposter and that the golden dreams he had promised them would never come to pass:

"This touched him to the quick; he flew out the door of the room in an instant, saying he should not now esteem L(ewis) S(eebohm) as a brother. Lewis called him back but he did not return. So the false prophet was manifested before several witnesses and they convinced of the delusion."

This incident, trivial though it seems today, was a source of much concern to the travelers. It was in harmony with the superstitious survivals still in evidence in places, and their routing of the magician was a spiritual triumph in the sight of his quondam followers. When they returned through Magdeburg, weeks afterwards, they were most gratefully received by these disillusioned people and told that the magician had been completely discomfited.

The meetings held among the Germans were uniformly small, owing to the strict surveillance to which any religious assemblies were subject. At Magdeburg in a private home about sixty or more persons gathered and a strong time of worship followed, in which David Sands, William Savery and Lewis Seebohm were all engaged, the latter interpreting for both the others. The Friends desired a larger opportunity, but fear of "the jealousy of the priests and government in this country" prevented it. A similar gathering met at a pewterer's in Brandenburg, ending as most of these Continental meetings did, with embracing and salutations of affection.

In Berlin, especially, this working through small gatherings was adopted. Three meetings of this kind were held, the last being attended by one hundred twenty people. Here, too, they were helped by the sympathy and assistance of Zeisburg, the landlord of the "Golden Hart," already mentioned, and by a remarkable man, Major Marconnay, who, though long in the service of the King of Prussia, had retired and led a life of piety and meditation. He became very dear to the Friends and felt close fellowship with them.

The stay in Berlin was of considerable length. The early adventures along religious lines were very discouraging, largely through an unexpected back-fire from Magdeburg. In the latter city one of the most affectionate and appreciative individuals had been a tutor in the college. In leaving, the Friends gave him a copy of Barclay's "Apology," which he at once read to their apparent undoing. For upon arriving in Berlin and asking for one Herman, to whom they had been recommended from Magdeburg, what was their surprise in receiving back the books which they had left with the tutor. A letter accompanied them stating that though he had received comfort and satisfaction from their preaching, "in reading in our books, he finds we hold erroneous opinions, reject baptism and the Supper and do not hold the Scriptures to be the Word of God." Herman having received this letter was little inclined to welcome the travelers and as he was a man of great religious influence, they were sorely troubled. Lewis Seebohm conversed with him at great length, and softened him a little, but he could not at once overcome the influence of the Magdeburg tutor.

It was a time of serious concern:

"We sat together in a low discouraged state and almost wished ourselves away from them all. However we concluded that here we must stay and endeavor to clear ourselves and contend for the faith as ability might be given. * * * We continued thoughtful where it would end, as we were among strangers whose laws we were not acquainted with and things might spread among them to our disadvantage."

They adopted a policy of extreme caution, declining an offer soon after, for an appointed meeting, lest it lead more to "contention than edification." Soon after, Marconnay made his appearance with several others of standing and position. Then followed a meeting which David Sands and Lewis Seebohm attended by invitation, the others remaining at the hotel to meet possible callers. About thirty men and women attended this first meeting and though they were at first shy of the Friends, because they kept their hats on, it ended well, and to the relief of the Friends, without singing. "We make our way by inches in this place, the people being very wary, afraid of being interrupted and meeting with suffering as some have done," wrote our chronicler.

Gradually other individuals became interested, largely through the good offices and influence of Marconnay. The harm threatened through the Magdeburg tutor began to evaporate. At another meeting William Savery met a Lutheran parson, Jeneike, in whom he found "something lovely and valuable," and finally, after a trip to Freienwalde, beyond Berlin, they met Charles Albinus, formerly Kriegs Rath, but who had retired from his lucrative office for conscience sake, although only forty years of age. He was a man of great humility, of good education and polished manner, and one whose "countenance and spirit bespoke him to be a brother beloved in Christ." He clave to the Friends almost by instinct. For four weeks he traveled with them, covering three hundred miles and

"was much broken at parting, * * * and very near to us and we to him, in the love of truth."

The conversion of this polished gentleman was almost as spectacular as the later convincement of Elizabeth Gurney. Two days after he had met the Friends, in the evening, the

conversation turned upon the almost universal custom of
the religious people of Berlin of wearing their hair queued
and powdered.

"Albinus said he had not used powder several years and that he
felt his queue a burden to him for some time and was very desirous
it should be cut off to-night. We desired him to feel his way in it &
if he was fully convinced it was his duty to do it, we united with
him. He sat down and W. Farrer trimmed it, with which he felt
relieved and easy. It will make him the ridicule of his light
acquaintance."

The next day, with his cropped hair, Albinus (for the
Journal rarely refers to him, save by his surname only)
went out and met Jeneike and some others. The Magdeburg letter, however, had been circulated. The accusations
that Friends did not recognize water baptism and the
Supper had been laid before the Superior Clergy, as well
as a new charge, that Friends' teaching "tended to draw
people from their teachers." More disconcerting still was
the report that the Clergy had considered appealing to the
magistrates to send the Quaker delegation out of the city.
Jeneike gave them his personal support, but told all his
parishioners of the cloud under which the Friends rested.
Upon the approach of First Day, they decided to hold a
meeting in their four rooms at the "Golden Hart" that
evening, for the public, after a more select meeting in the
morning.

With the evening meeting came their triumph in Berlin.
As usual with these German meetings many came an hour
ahead of time. The four rooms were soon filled and of the
two hundred attenders were many of rank and standing in
the city.

"A solemnity prevailed over the assembly in a very uncommon
manner such as I have seldom seen in my own country among a
mixed multitude of strangers and great brokenness was among them.
Although the meeting continued three hours and many had to stand
in a crowded situation the whole time, nothing like restlessness

appeared. * * * The Lord causes all things to work together for good to them that fear Him, so that we had reason to believe that this meeting was increased even by the opposition that we had met with from Herman and others."

Thereafter many opportunities opened up. They were besieged by earnest people. One brought them money toward their expenses, which they declined with a tender explanation regarding a free Gospel ministry; a poor woman sent in a pot of honey and some cakes; a Roman Catholic "hearing there were some priests here, from a foreign country, inquired if we received the confessions of the people"; books were distributed till they had no more and they were glad that those left at Magdeburg had been returned to them; parents brought their children for counsel and visits to sick and poor took up much time and effort:

"Time will not admit of particularizing the manner of our almost continuous engagements in this great City, where we find a great number of seeking souls. * * * We never were among people to whom the love of God more richly flowed than to many in this place, nor any that were made more near to us in the Love & Life of Christ."

And so, after two more favored meetings and the farewell already quoted to Zeisburg, their landlord, they closed their work in Berlin, and with Albinus, who now "seems fully convinced," turned back toward Potsdam and Magdeburg, with the particular aim of seeking out the schoolmaster, who, wrote William Savery, in words similar to those which Paul applied to Alexander, the coppersmith, "had endeavored to do us much harm in Berlin." They sent word to the tutor, inviting him or his friends "to meet us with the Bible in their hands," but he apparently did not accept the invitation. They spent two days in the town and met several new people of pious inclinations, including two brothers by the name of Reich, who were most affectionate. Then after two small meetings they continued their journey, feeling satisfied with their efforts.

Toleration of religious belief was greater in some sections than in others, but even in Oldenburg and Hanover, where Lutherans and Calvinists seem to have been most openly acceptable, they had crucifixes and the effigies of saints in their places of worship. At Hildesheim, with its strong but rather decadent Catholic influence, there was one Lutheran church, but the country round about was thickly set with crosses and crucifixes. In Berlin, however, Protestantism came into its own. The Lutherans had thirty-three churches and Calvinists, Catholics, Moravians and Jews all had their own for their relatively smaller portions of the population. All other denominations were forbidden to hold public meetings in the dominions of the King of Prussia, as the Friends found to their sorrow later in Minden.

As in England, so in Germany, the Church still controlled many functions that are today relegated to the State. Every burial called for a stipend to the local priest. A Friend at Minden, not feeling free to bury his wife in the local graveyard, interred her in his garden, whereupon the local priest collected six dollars as his due. Still more drastic was the action taken with a child of Christopher Reckefus. It had been interred in his garden for six months, when the priest exhumed the body, buried it in the public graveyard and promptly collected his charge.

Another of the exactions, almost universally made, was the charge for administering the sacraments. As all the poorest people partook, the levy was most effective as a money raiser. At Halberstadt, where the travelers found Catholicism most intrenched and most decadent of any other place they visited, they met a "loving young priest," who vainly regretted that he was destined to take orders, as he felt no call to the ministry and deplored associating with the mercenary priests of his acquaintance. They gave him Barclay's "Apology" in Latin and had long talks with him, leaving him finally with affectionate embraces and every manifestation of love toward them. Another young aspirant for the priesthood was Henry Nicolais of Hanover. He eked out a miserable existence as a tutor for three boys and occasionally preached as a supply for another parson at six groschen per sermon. He ate little but dry bread and was altogether a pitiable object. The Friends' message took strong hold upon him and they left him unsettled as to his future, and with several books, including Penn's "No Cross, No Crown" in French.

The travelers were constantly aware of a tacit hostility on the part of the various governments, and more especially of the jealousy of the priests. The term "priest" included in their vocabulary the ministers of all denominations. They found this latent opposition wherever their message could be interpreted as unfavorable to a paid ministry, and that was well nigh everywhere. It was, however, only in the experience at Berlin, already described, and in Hanover and Minden, that they actually incurred the active resentment of the authorities.

At Hanover two small meetings were held in the hotel rooms before any notice was taken of them. George and Sarah Dillwyn, who had rejoined the party, had rooms in the "Amsterdam," outside the city gates. They proposed to hold the next meeting there, as the civil pressure was less and the landlord had been most obliging. As the people collected, a different aspect presented itself. The landlord had heard of the opposition of the magistrates and forbade the meeting, turning back the people. In spite of his efforts, about thirty pressed upstairs and a meeting was held. "The Lord favored and it proved a solid, contriting time; most of them were broken into tears." It is no small evidence of the power of the meeting that the Spirit so overcame the patent opposition, all the more so as an officer, "like our constables," was present during the service. After the meeting, a violent altercation ensued between the constable and the landlord's wife, he proposing to fine the house twenty dollars for allowing the assemblage. She in high dudgeon declared she would never pay a groscher, but that the Friends should pay, as she had forbidden the meeting and was free from responsibility. William Savery assured her they would settle the claim and all the Friends save George Dillwyn went into Hanover, conversing with the constable en route. He became very friendly and finally took one of their American passports, with which in an hour he returned to their Inn, stating that all was clear with the Magistrate, but advising that the meetings be held

"in a private way, as some Separatists did, that the magistrates and priests might not come to a knowledge of them. We told him we had a testimony against hiding ourselves in the manner as some others did, and must hold our meetings openly."

The constable then became very friendly, embraced all in leaving and "so the storm blew over."

The opposition in Minden was very similar in nature and evaporated almost as quickly. The Consistorial Rath, "Director of things relating to the Church, as well as a Priest of the first dignity," forbade holding any more public meetings in an orphan school, and was reported to have said things "which reflected hard upon us and the Society." David Sands, Lewis Seebohm and William Savery immediately visited the Rath, who attributed the order to the Edict of the King of Prussia, limiting public assemblies to a few accepted modes of worship, which he believed to be no abridgement of liberty of conscience. Once more the propriety of visiting the King of Prussia appealed to William Savery, but this time with the hope that the concern might "light upon dear G(eorge) D(illwyn). For my own part, I feel my mind relieved from it at present." When asked to explain his accusations against the Friends and the Society in general, "he appeared startled that it had come to our knowledge, * * * he colored in the face and evidently began to be confused and warm," but told the Friends it was a matter of little consequence and that they should rejoice when evil was falsely spoken against them. "We parted in a more calm and friendly manner than I expected, his wife and daughters with himself, shaking us by the hand and wishing us a good journey."

One cannot leave this German ministry without a vague sense of regret. One feels that William Savery and his fellows did not understand the Germany they were in. It was entirely different from anything they had previously experienced,—its religious systems, thought and methods were not akin to the American and English ideals; there was such acute and abject poverty and such regal and ostentatious wealth, that the social consciousness of an American of that period could not readily comprehend them. William Savery deplored the ignorance, squalor and depravity of the populace, but his Gospel was not socially applied. He preached, but the Journal evinces no social implications in the preaching. His thought and method seem to have been to attempt to reach the learned and the rulers, and through them to ameliorate the conditions that were a patent mockery of Christ's Kingdom. Even in this, there is a disconcerting intimation that the ministry of this group of Friends was more of a disputatious and doctrinal nature than a Gospel message in its simplicity. They labored valiantly over sacraments, forms, ritual and minor testimonies, but the German experience contained few of the close, heartfelt interviews and the intimate yearning that the later ministry of William Savery discloses, after he entered England. It was not so much that the work was not personal, because the Friends had many interviews. The conferences seem strangely to lack the quality of the later ones. They seem argumentative and authoritative rather than tender. It seems strange in these days that so much importance was placed upon "thee and thou," avoiding titles and hat honor. Mayhap the servility of the populace and its destitute condition in places called for a more rigorous protest, from the modern viewpoint, than attempts to introduce the English cut of Quaker clothes, which to the travelers seemed to be essential. Reform in dress was evidently acceptable to many, as others besides Albanus cut off their queues and doffed large cocked hats with buttons, transforming them, by new creases, to "plain and friendly ones."

In England, as we know from his published sermons and incidental references, William Savery had a distinctly personal message. It may be that his limited use of the language and the patently corrupt connection between religion and politics on the Continent left him no alternative, —especially in view of the accepted Quaker attitude, which deprecated any knowledge of or acquaintance with politics or political systems. Certainly many of the ills of the times were part and parcel of the priest craft of the Continent, and an argumentative opposition to this may, after all, have been the best approach to a people who knew not freedom of religious thought and who, though they lived in the country whence Protestantism sprang, were, more than most others, hard-ridden by militaristic and ecclesiastical power mongers. Therein may lie the explanations of and excuse for the difference in the message that William Savery and his companions had for Germany.

## CHAPTER XVIII

# THE SOCIETY OF FRIENDS IN GERMANY

Both before and after their journey into the interior, William Savery, David Sands and Benjamin Johnson spent some time with the little group of Friends at and near Pyrmont in Waldeck and after their return, at Minden, in Westphalia. They left George and Sarah Dillwyn with the Pyrmont Friends as they turned their steps toward Berlin, in company with Lewis Seebohm, as we have already seen.

The Society of Friends and its tenets had been no novelty in the Continental countries in the early days. Quakerism at that time had a world vision and made a strong appeal to the Dutch and Germans, particularly. In 1677, when Fox, Penn and seven others went thither, they found Quakerism well established in places. Penn's mother had been a Dutch woman and his interest in the country never abated. When the party proceeded into Germany, "life ran as oil and swam atop of all," said Penn. Later he recorded that some objected to the odium of the name, "Quaker" and hesitated to adopt it, but, wrote he, as all the Germans called any type of sobriety "Quakerism," that ought to remove the stigma,—an evidence of the repute that the sect had attained so early in its history.

Penn advertised his new colony in America very extensively in the Rhenish Palatinate and the Low Lands, with a resultant influx of Germans to Pennsylvania. At Rotterdam and Amsterdam, strong meetings were established. English Friends paid considerable attention to these until about 1720. Thereafter events upon the Continent assumed features unfavorable to any sect with pacific ideals. With the accession of Frederick the Great, in 1740, newer military methods and the early stages of conscription and citizen soldiery were introduced. Wars abounded. Peace became an ideal, known more as an abstraction than a fact. Modern history was beginning, and the map of Europe, from Paris to Berlin, was being dotted with the names of battles, soon to be augmented by those of the Napoleonic era.

It is no part of this biography to trace the rise and decline of early European Quakerism, though the field is a fruitful one, as yet untilled. It became an almost impossible faith in the Europe of the latter Eighteenth century, simply because conscription and warfare drove beyond seas practically all of its youth. Cryptically stated, such was the cause of its decline and such was the period and the condition in which William Savery and his fellows found it.

The Friends were told of people in various places that were called Quakers. In Bremen they found such, though there was little except "the circumspection of their lives and manners, and their frequent meetings together to strengthen and build one another up," that denoted any difference between them and other Christians. At Altona was another old man (for all called Quakers were old), Heltman by name, who was a preacher among a small group of separatists. He was very acceptable to the Friends and admitted himself as in entire accord with their principles. Another ancient man, Buckholtz of Lemgo, considered himself a Quaker and had suffered for his lonely faith. With him, too, the Friends had close fellowship. Like William Penn over a century before him, William Savery deprecated the use of the name "Quaker." In Osnabruck, an intelligent Italian marveled that the Friends adopt and use a name given them in derision. William Savery wrote:

"Foreigners must be greatly at a loss for a reason why we continue the name of Quakers. This sensible man's remarks are not new; they have been made frequently in our travels & been much a subject of regret to me for years, as I cannot see that either reason or religion require it and if Society itself had not have continued to keep it alive, it is very probable the name of Quaker would hardly have been known at this day. It is high time when the Light is spreading through the Nations that have hitherto scarcely heard of our Society, to drop this appellation. Every foreigner must be at a loss what is meant by 'Quaker,' 'Zitterrer' or 'Trembleur.' "

When he arrived in Berlin, "beyond where our Society is known," he felt sorry to distribute books containing the name to people who knew not its origin.

It was in northwestern Germany, however, where in geographical obscurity, the borders of Westphalia, Lippe, Brunswick and Waldeck march, that the only organized Quakerism in Germany existed. Even then, the organization was most notable for its lack of harmony. The Friends had come with full knowledge of this condition, for John Pemberton had written a Journal prior to his death the year before and William Savery had read it. A very serious controversy had broken out among the Friends in the two little communities at Pyrmont, in Waldeck and Minden, thirty miles away in the northern extreme of Westphalia. Pyrmont had been the place of all others to which William Savery's mind had been turned. Into this controversy, though "feeling but little hope of a reunion," he threw himself, with the other Friends, and, being so occupied, he felt "at home for the present and desirous of bearing my part of the burden while we stay."

Just what the nature of the controversy was does not appear, although it seems to have been personal. William Savery carefully avoids any unnecessary detail, even though the matter was closest to his heart of all things in Germany. The leader of the separation was Emanuel Brown, a man whom the Friends did not meet until the very close of their German work. His influence for schism proved,

contrary to their fears, easy to overcome. The Friends
spent a month in Pyrmont and later, about a week at Minden, in each place being instrumental in effecting a complete
and joyous reconciliation.

At Pyrmont, Herman Shutamire, Henry Munthang and
Anthony Shonning, all men of religious experience, were
the chief objectors. Lewis and Frederick Seebohm were
the mainstays of the group that still occupied the meeting
house and mourned over their decline. The meeting house
had been built in 1790. The burial ground was hard by,
and thither William Savery soon repaired to stand by the
grave of his friend, John Pemberton. He wrote:

"When I think of this brother, being brought, in so singular a
manner, to lay down his life among this handful of professors, who
are like the first fruits in Germany, that saying mostly occurs,—'the
blood of the martyrs is the seed of the church.' He is remembered
here with much sweetness."

It might be said in passing that the Pyrmont meeting
house still stands, having been sold by English Friends
about 1895, though they still retain title to the graveyard.
The house is well preserved, being used as a riding school.
Pyrmont has become a popular resort for summer tourists
and presents a lively spectacle during the season.

The actual separation was of about seven months' standing. One of the first events after the arrival of the Friends
was the presentation by Shutamire, Munthang and Shonning of a paper, giving reasons for their defection. The
next day came a similar address stating the causes for the
disunity of those "in strict connexion," from the separatists. "We found it was likely to prove a very exercising
affair to us and were much discouraged."

Weak in faith, but strong in resolve, the Friends set about
the task of reconciliation. Their work was blessed far
beyond their most sanguine hopes. They began with a
series of family visits with the separatists, followed by the
regular meetings for worship, beseeching all to seek the

spirit "that would reconcile and unite all the children of our heavenly Father together."

Then followed an appointed meeting that lasted from six till eleven in the evening, and to which all of both persuasions were invited. It proved to be one of the outstanding religious experiences of William Savery's life. Many besides the visitors took part:

"I marveled at the clearness with which they expressed themselves, the Lord graciously condescending to favour in a very remarkable manner with his blessed presence. All hearts were humbled and the high, untoward will of man brought down & the spirit that loves contention & delights to have the superiority was cast out, and through mercy, the meek, teachable state of little children appeared to predominate in most present. We were opened with clearness to set before them the nature of our holy profession, the love of Christ, the good Shepherd, to us all & the necessity of dwelling in that charity, which instead of magnifying each other's weakness & entertaining groundless jealousies & surmises of one another, would cast a mantle of love over them, remembering that we also were weak & liable to be tempted.

"A truly contriting & heart tendring time it was and most of the company were melted into tears. * * * Both sides freely and in great tenderness, confessing their readiness so to do and to begin again under the direction of the heavenly Master Builder in an united labour for the edification & building one another up in the most holy faith. They rose, embraced and saluted each other with manifest tokens of unfeigned love & thankfulness. * * *

"We parted at almost eleven. For my part I thought myself amply repaid for all my exercise, the long journey & the long voyage & the trying separation from my dearest natural ties, by being made a witness to the love of God poured forth, I thought as in the beginning of Friends. We went to rest sweetly refreshed in spirit and did not marvel that my mind has been so remarkably turned to this place before I left home."

Thereafter followed the reorganization of the Monthly Meeting, which had been neglected. Officers and Committees were appointed, in real Quaker fashion; the better education of their children was taken up, in connection with a gift of £30, left them by John Pemberton for the purpose, and when the Friends left they had the satisfaction of knowing that a well regulated Monthly Meeting was functioning at Pyrmont.

"The parting was one of the most affectionate I ever experienced. Divers of the dear young people held us by the hand, would scarcely let us go & testified their affection by many tears."

The Pyrmont community was interesting in itself. The Friends were well esteemed by the Prince of Waldeck, whose palace was at Pyrmont. Four years earlier, the Prince had given a little valley, a mile and a half from the town, to Lewis Seebohm, to establish there a factory for edged tools. He had improved the place very much, had built his factory and named his valley "Friendenstall," or "Peace-dale." It was "a quiet, sequestered, fertile spot" and a real haven for the four families who inhabited it. The Seebohm family, consisting of the three brothers, Lewis, Frederick and Diedrick, and little Jacob, of the next generation, were pillars in the community. Lewis had a good library and spoke both English and French in addition to his native German. His service as interpreter to the Friends practically all the time they were in Germany was one they constantly appreciated. Even little Jacob was of use, as he wrote out Scripture texts in German for William Savery to give to visitors, in keeping with the custom of the country.

After the reconciliation at Pyrmont, the Friends turned toward Minden for a similar purpose. At Minden there had been no regular meeting, but there were a number of people in close sympathy with the Pyrmont group. As many as sixty had formerly been accustomed to meet together, but the schism that had affected Pyrmont had also depleted Minden to a handful of five or six families. The meetings were usually held in Frederick Smith's home, a mile from the town, but the Friends also held meetings in the Orphan School, as has already been narrated. At Kiepshagen, near Minden, lived Christopher Reckefus and his brother Deitrich, while the home of John Lazarus Rousseau, nephew of the great Jean Jacques Rousseau, was also open to the meetings. Lewis Seebohm's father-in-law, Counsellor-Director Borjes, a "man of note and influence," also lived at Minden. His attitude toward the Friends was distinctly cool during their first visit. He was not a Friend and, as a politician holding office, had much to lose by too warm a reception. As a fair was in progress, the hotels full and the people preoccupied, the Friends stayed only three days on their first visit.

Between the two visits to Minden came the circuit through Herford, Ufeln, Bielefeld, Lemgo, Hanover and Hameln, to which reference has already been made. This circuit marked a time of deep, spiritual travail and exercise of spirit, as the group could not divine which way its duty lay. For a fortnight, they went on, day by day, with no certainty of destination beyond the next city. As they approached the Dutch border, Amsterdam seemed very enticing,

"but after solid consideration, all seemed closed for the present with respect to Holland & our minds were most easy to proceed in the faith towards Hanover,—directly back. Oh! when shall we get out of Germany!"

At Bielefeld William Farrer and William Savery visited Charlotte Laer, another of the German Friends who had undergone much for her faith. Her father lived at Bielefeld, although the daughter had been much at Pyrmont. Her family was a distinguished one and the father had formerly driven her from his house as a protest against her religious ideas. He received the visitors coldly, but more respectfully than they had anticipated, while his wife was very friendly and pleased to see the travelers.

Another incident on this circuit has application today, when the message of Quakerism is again being borne to parts which heretofore have not known it. One of the new converts "having been led into some singular paths we had a free conversation with him. * * * He is a zealous, solid man & we cannot marvel that some in this country, who are lately brought forth, into testimony they were formerly so entirely ignorant of, should sometimes overshoot the mark. But the bottom of sincerity that appears in him and others, we hope in time, will be the means of bringing them to walk in the midst of the paths of judgment."

The catholicity of William Savery's spirit and his unwillingness to judge harshly were even more strikingly exemplified upon meeting with Emanuel Brown, the fomenter of all the trouble among German Friends, at Hanover. He appeared

"to be a solid, valuable man; looks like a Friend & has past through many exercises. He was loving & tender; was glad he had met with us & we also that we had seen him before we left this part of Germany."

Another interview followed the next day, when both George Dillwyn and William Savery met him. They found him "very loving & freely acknowledging the doctrines of Friends." They seemed to be at one on most subjects, though Emanuel Brown approved of celibacy for religiously minded people, and did not wholly eschew the sacraments, thinking

"as we also do, that those who used that ceremony with sincear hearts were at times partakers of a blessing, but it was not obligatory. * * * (He) professed much love for us and we cannot but entertain a hope he may become strictly united and useful to the cause of truth in this country."

Later they returned to Minden for a week and were as successful in reconciliation as they had been at Pyrmont. Upon the return, although they did not arrive until 8 P.M., Benjamin Johnson and William Savery at once visited John Lazarus Rousseau and his wife, who received them kindly. The next day a meeting was held at their home, attended by a score of the people.

Following the meeting at Rousseau's, some of "the

friendly convinced people" came to see the travelers and desired "to be more strictly united with Friends at Pyrmont and enjoy the privilege of members." The close associations and relationships between the two communities augured well for such connection in the future. Then ensued in the evening another meeting, attended by over two hundred people, including "divers people of note and officers of the army," which held for three hours and ended triumphantly, "so that we apprehended such meetings were never held before in Germany."

After a few calls upon Counsellor Borjes and his two daughters, who were "people of high stile and character," they too began to melt toward the Friends and the old gentleman invited them several times to dine with him. They had much religious conversation, and Lewis Seebohm had the gratification of stating that his father-in-law had never before received Friends so cordially. It was a fortunate circumstance, for the trouble with the Consistorial Rath, narrated in the previous chapter, very soon ensued and ended happily.

As a parting gift, Borjes sent the Friends six bottles of English beer, a hare, some apples and a German Testament, William Savery having left his Testament behind at Hildesheim. Borjes told Lewis Seebohm, much to the latter's delight, that he would be glad to spend twenty-four hours with William Savery on religious subjects, his conversation in German being so free. Their final parting, practically the last intimate scene in the German ministry, was a very loving one:

"Evening at 4, drank coffee with Counsellor Borjes, and afterwards had some religious service, wherein the Lord favoured and a humbling tendring time it was. The old man embraced us over and over again & said he had not words to express the thankfulness he felt for our visits. We took very affectionate leave of them all, the father following us to the gate. * * * Some of these partings in Germany must remain with me as long as my memory."

## CHAPTER XIX

# HOLLAND AND FRANCE DURING THE REVOLUTION

The French Revolution lasted from 1792 until about 1799, when Napoleon overturned the Directory and established himself as First Consul. William Savery, David Sands and Benjamin Johnson were traveling in Holland and France from December 21, 1796, until May 15, 1797. While they were in Holland, William Farrer was with them, but his British nationality prevented his obtaining a passport to France and he therefore returned home. It was therefore the France of the Directory that the travelers saw,—a Directory of five men, who, under the Constitution of 1795, shared the executive responsibilities, by turns, during their term of office.

As the journey in Germany ended, William Savery and Benjamin Johnson set themselves seriously to the study of French. The former had undoubtedly had some previous knowledge of German, but neither of them had a vestige of French. They kept at it pretty constantly. In Amsterdam, they took a lesson every day for two hours, under a tutor, and devoted the evenings to it when opportunity offered. While riding, they conversed with willing fellow travelers and learned much from amiable Flamanders and Frenchmen in this way as they crossed Holland and Flanders.

Friends were by no means unknown in France. The American Consul at Dunkirk, a Frenchman by birth, advised inserting in the passports the fact that the travelers were Friends or Quakers, which, he thought, would insure more respectful attention to them. Later, in Paris, when the passports were to be viséed, the Friends did not remove their hats in the presence of the municipal officer who was to seal them. William Savery relates the incident:

"We told him we were of the people called Quakers, who did not use that compliment to any. He appeared warm and said it was no matter what we were; no people could be admitted before them with their hats on, and came toward us, we supposed to take them off. But one of his companions in office, observing to him that we made a religious scruple of it, he withdrew, and growing more mild, said, he always paid respect to religion, and had no more to say, if that was the case. He sealed and signed our passports and we parted friendly. A law of France which obliged all others to appear uncovered before the National Convention, exempted Friends from this obligation by a special clause."

All of the Friends had approached France with trepidation, fearing what might be required of them under the revolutionary government. These fears were not allayed as they traveled in Holland. When they had entered the Hall of the Dutch National Convention at the Hague, the doorkeeper requested them to remove their hats, which they refused to do. To avoid difficulty, they immediately left, surprised, because the Convention was sitting with hats on at the time. It was here, too, that the first objection to William Farrer occurred. They had been courteously received by John Quincy Adams, then American Ambassador to the Hague, and at his introduction, by the French Ambassador, who, though willing to serve them "de bon cœur," said he had no authority to give a pass to an Englishman. Most of all, the Friends dreaded the National Cockade, of which they had heard much, in anticipation. Though determined not to wear it, from conscientious motives, they were vastly relieved when assured by the American Consul at Nieuport that no cockade would be expected of them. As it happened, they traversed the length of France to Nîmes before they were questioned

about it, and then their explanation was entirely satisfactory.

In the two large cities of Holland,—Amsterdam and Rotterdam,—William Savery noted many interesting things,
distinct from the French and German customs. Belgium
did not at that time exist, the territory being known as
Flanders. The Dutch were largely Protestant and the
Flamanders, Roman Catholic. In the Dutch cities were
numerous Jews, 30,000 of them in Amsterdam alone, confined to a Jewish Quarter, well equipped with synagogues.
With these, William Savery was quite disgusted. Beggars
were everywhere in evidence, besetting the travelers in
troops as they alighted from their carriage. In the Jewish
Quarter especially,

"the misery, nakedness and dirtiness of the beggars exceeds all I
have ever seen in any place. In Berlin, I was never asked charity."

With the exception of the beggars, everything in Holland
was in the pink of neatness and orderly decorum. This,
too, was in contrast to the more slovenly German habits and
proved to be a veritable tonic to the feelings of the Friends
and especially of David Sands. Prices generally, and especially hotel charges, were much higher in Holland and
France than in Germany. The innkeepers did not scruple
to assess their charges, the rates at the Hague being "very
high a Florin or Guilder, about 20d sterling, a man for our
beds, 1½ for dinner, &c., and firing high." The firing was
very novel. Although it was winter, fires were rare, except
foot stoves for the women. Such local fuel as there was
consisted largely of clippings from the trees, along the
canals, or of turf.

"In Holland it is not customary for women to draw near the fire.
This is the privilege of the men only. * * * The custom is to furnish
the women with little wooden boxes with basons of coals or turf in
them, to put under their feet and they sit at a distance from the
fire. We think it much colder here than in Philadelphia. The hair
of the men is frose white with their breath as they pass the streets.

The firing, which is dear, is chiefly turf, some few coals from Germany and England and a little small wood to light with. They keep very small fires and having very few stoves, the rooms are so cold, that we keep our thick great coats on most of the day."

William Savery found Amsterdam "the handsomest and most convenient commercial city, perhaps, in Europe." The houses were high, built of very tiny, chocolate-colored bricks, making very handsome walls. The upper stories in the Dutch cities projected over the street, making a coving that reduced the light and air below and increased the fire risk. While the travelers were in Rotterdam there was a fire that jumped across the street, due to the coving of the walls, and four houses on the opposite side were consumed. To their admiration, Rotterdam had a paid fire department:

"The rest of the citizens trouble themselves but little about it. Indeed, they are not permitted to be active. They fix pumps in the canals, and by means of leather pipes, convey the water to the engines, so that they use but few buckets."

Few things interested William Savery more than the canals. Most of the principal streets were canaled in the middle, with fine trees on the banks.

"The people are exceeding fond of scaiting on the canals. Here and there are many little slays, which are pushed by a man behind, that convey women and children from one part of the town to another, but few with horses, except coaches with slay runners."

The canals also served for drinking water at Rotterdam and in an emergency at Amsterdam. They were dangerous in foggy weather. Due to recent accidents, when three hundred people had been drowned at Rotterdam, the number of lamps had been much increased and ropes were stretched from tree to tree.

All told, things seemed to be progressing in Holland. There was liberty of conscience; the countryside was flourishing with good crops and the war was far enough away to leave the Dutch largely immune from its intimate terrors, while they tasted the fictitious prosperity, that modern generations have learned to associate with war-time.

In France it was even more so. The Revolution had carried the people to the top of the wave and they were riding it with all the abandon of their natures. Perhaps in no other way was France more differentiated, in William Savery's mind, from Germany than in this enthusiastic, volatile effervescence of spirit that he saw and noted in many sections. And he was well qualified to judge. He and his companions entered France at the extreme north and traversed the country twice, returning by a different route. In the journey to the south, they went through the cities of Dunkirk, Lille, Cambrai and Paris, thence via Fontainebleau, Nevers, Moulins, Roanne, Lyons and Montélimar to Nîmes. On their return they journeyed through Valence, Lyons, Villefranche, Mâcon, Châlon-sur-Saône, Avallon, Auxerre, Melun, Paris, where they hardly tarried, and thence through Clermont, Amiens, Arras and Armentières to Dunkirk again. It is difficult to list so many cities without emulating the train-caller; it is still more difficult to pass over the narrative in the effort to give the spirit of it rather than the intimate detail.

In all these cities France was in evidence,—the France of the Revolution, but still the France that could not break, entirely, even under convulsions, from her past. Everywhere the villagers and peasants seemed to be in carnival. At Fontainebleau, in carnival time, prior to Ash-Wednesday,

"The villagers, being dressed in their best clothes, appeared very lively in their wooden shoes, which they wear universally. Some were attending the places of worship, but more, diverting themselves in the fields. They appear not to be deeply impressed with trouble for the miseries of war. * * * The people everywhere full of mirth, some wearing masks, and young and old, dancing in rings in the fields and streets of the villages. They are certainly a light-hearted people, yet many of them live very hard. * * * The people still celebrating the carnival, and travelling the streets, singing and dancing and exciting each other to music."

Another similar description, although from the north of France, near Béthune, follows:

"The villagers appeared very numerous, amusing themselves in a variety of ways a la mode de France. One would hardly suppose this country had passed through many afflictions and scourges; the natural vivacity of the people seems to rise above them all."

The prevalence of fête days in France was amazing. Church holidays were observed, though the solemnity had largely left them. On Easter Sunday, at Saulieu, the very fine evening found the people of the town assembled in their best clothes, amusing themselves according to the customs of France, "which are all activity and vivacity." Mayday in Dunkirk was another fête occasion:

"Garlands of flowers, curiously wrought in a variety of colors, hang by ropes fastened to both sides of the streets, suspended in the middle. This day is foolishly observed in France & spent in a licentious manner. The people of this place however, paid not so much attention to it as I expected in the morning, tho troops of young women & girls were in different places, dancing under the garlands."

At most times the French appeared, as at Paris, "a gay and dissipated people, many of whom, making light of all religion," gave the Friends much serious thought, in keeping to their simple testimony. The middle class Frenchman was more inclined to be serious and sensible, although, in common with the peasants, tending to loquacity. The people near Roanne, a manufacturing town, proved remarkably friendly, which led William Savery to generalize:

"Indeed the frankness of this nation does not suffer us to remain, more than an hour, strangers, after our arrival. They see few strangers, especially from other nations and they are curious in their enquiries."

This urbanity put the Friends upon their guard, as they penetrated deeper into the country, feeling, in the Southland, "it is not good to enter too freely into conversation about things which has little or no connection with our main business among this people. We often find it best to withdraw, for they are a people very fond of talking."

As in Germany, so in France, the life of the public houses made much impress upon the Friends. Quaint word pictures there are of these inns, some of them large, like the hotel at Mâcon,

"one of those immensely extensive inns which we have found in many places on this continent, exceeding for size any I have seen in England or America. (The inn) * * * was so far from the kitchen and other offices of the house, that we obtained what we had need of with difficulty, tho the girls seemed active and ready to oblige us, when they knew our wants, which indeed is the case at most auberges in France."

Of these inns, "perhaps the largest we have seen in Europe, forming a hollow square of about 200 feet a side," was the "Celestin," of Lyons, which was then the second city of France with 140,000 inhabitants. Their reckoning at this auberge was "a very unreasonable one."

Among the few names given are the "Sign of the Falcon," at Villefranche and the "Café de Boston," at Paris. More remarkable still was the "Hôtel de Bourbon," at Lille, a name that must have persisted in spite of circumstances, as did that of the "King of Prussia" Tavern, in Pennsylvania, during the Great War. More enlightening as to the political changes, was the aubergiste near Chipy, who had taken possession of the ancient ditched castle of a cidevant nobleman, and converted it into an inn. William Savery's comment: "Of course (he) was a good Republican," is symptomatic of the times. At La Palisse, the two inns were kept by a father and son, whose agreement in restraint of trade mulcted the traveling public "at least 50% higher than the best inns or carriages in America."

The Friends were in a condition to test the hotel accommodations of France, both coming and going. William Savery was sick and very much discouraged in mind all the way from Paris to Nîmes, and in the return, Benjamin Johnson succumbed and gave his fellows great concern over his condition, until they arrived in England. Under these trying circumstances, the agreeable auberge at Sennecy tempted them to stay over a day, during which they had their clothes washed and mended and Benjamin Johnson was "somewhat recruited." The next evening, however, all the good vanished "at a very sorry inn" at St. Emiland, at which a driving rain forced them to stop. Of all their trying experiences, the chief occurred here. Benjamin Johnson's saddlebags were stolen while they were at their very poor supper. All search and inquiry proved unavailing.

"After wearying ourselves much, we went to bed, the rain coming down on mine thro the thatched roof. The people coming in and going out frequently, the idea I had reason to conceive of the badness of their characters, and the loss of the saddle bags, which I was afraid were irrecoverably gone, altogether kept my mind in a try'd situation. I got very little sleep, but lay tossing and longing for morning."

The bags contained most of Benjamin Johnson's clothing and all his papers and his Journal. As he was sick, William Savery turned detective. In spite of the annoyance, he got some humor out of the situation which rapidly developed from "tant pis" to "pis et pis." The morning proved clear and he went from house to house, telling of the loss and received lamentations, and learned of the ill repute of the aubergiste, but little else. He then declared he would ride back to the next town for police assistance and "had procured a horse with much ado." A native philosopher "sitting by the fire" detained him, as the bags were undoubtedly in the town, and suggested the local magistrate. After more ado, he was found, and although he "was far from making a figure of importance in the world, (he) appeared to be a man of integrity." William Savery offered a reward of two louis and to ask no questions, whereupon the magistrate dispatched a man through the village, beating a drum and telling the tale. Within an hour a man came to the auberge, "his countenance evidently marked with guilt and confusion," bringing the saddlebags, which he said he had found in a distant stable, covered with hay. William Savery did ask one question, —"whether, as he had found them so easily, he insisted upon the two louis, or not. He said we might give him what we pleased, so, all the company agreeing it was sufficient, we gave him a louis, and prepared to leave a place we were heartily tired of." This episode is the more interesting as it conforms in some of its details with William Savery's advertisement for a thief in his Philadelphia tanyard, as already narrated.

On the return trip at Lyons, the postilion, without definite orders, took them to an excellent hotel, opposite the Grande Promenade, and here Benjamin Johnson, with his daily chill and fever, received the care of a motherly old woman, "solicitous to do all she could." The care was appreciated for he was getting extremely weak. Had it not been for his illness, it is probable that the Friends would have gone to Geneva, instead of returning directly to Paris.

War rates and prices were everywhere in evidence; profiteering was the order of the day. William Savery complained bitterly against the extortion of the publicans:

"The innkeepers very extravagant in their charges; their provision tolerable, if it were cooked in our manner, but they make use of no vegetables, except a salad, after the meat is taken away. The common red wine, which is almost the universal drink, is very poor and the taste, to me, not agreeable. Their beds are, in general, full four feet high, so that it is difficult ascending. They are tolerable when you are got on to them, though they are the reverse of the Germans in their beds as well as almost everything else. In Germany they sleep sitting almost upright; here we find no pillows and but a very low bolster. Their linen is clean; they do not salt their butter and make use of but little and we can seldom get any milk; indeed there are but few cows or goats."

**Later at St. Giles his**

"bed exceeded in height any I had yet seen. * * * I could not ascend it but by the help of a chair. It must have been 4½ feet."

In one place at least, near St. Rambert, on the Rhone, the innkeepers were very modern in their methods. Upon the arrival of the evening boat:

"The keepers of the auberges rushed down to the shore; almost compelled us to enter their houses, each one speaking highly of their own and perhaps twenty girls and boys waiting to carry our baggage, which they contended for with great earnestness to earn a few sous."

And so the story continues,—"the innkeepers charges enormous, but very civil and attentive, helping us out in our bad French" and "our reckoning at Lyons, a very unreasonable one."

"We are liable to continuous impositions and the travelling amounts on the whole to 3½ guineas a day, though we often have no full meal but supper. We content ourselves almost all day with bread and cheese and smoked herring, with some apples, nuts and wine of a poor quality here, to accompany them, sometimes some tolerable beer."

The liquors in France did not seem to suit William Savery's taste. He records that

"the country appears to abound in wine. Little else is drank, tho I cannot say I am fond of it. It is generally a very light claret."

Naturally at Paris rates were at the peak:

"Sat down to a dinner from the traiteur, which without drink, cost us 20 livres or 16s 8d sterling, and nothing extraordinary either. 5s sterling for a roast fowl."

Although they used all the "œconomy" possible, their accommodations at Paris cost them on an average upwards of two louis a day.

One may well be surprised at the extent of the hotel business of that day when traveling was by no means as common as it is today. In France, however, the roads were much better adapted to traffic than they were in Germany. William Savery had nothing but praise for the French roads, although, as will be remembered, he was explicit in his complaints at the German roads. In spite of the good roads, speed seemed impossible:

"There is scarcely any such thing as travelling fast in France,—tho the roads are generally pretty good, their poor little horses, mules and asses seldom travel more than three miles an hour."

And later, in the extreme south of France,

"Horses are very scarce but they have excellent mules for their wagons; sometimes a little ass of 3½ feet high is leader of a team of four or five mules."

Between Sluys and Dunkirk, in Flanders, the only mirey road in the whole French narrative is mentioned, and that gave way, in five miles, to a paved road, whereupon the third horse was discharged and the travelers proceeded with two horses, to a carriage like an English postchaise. The road was paved all the rest of the way to Dunkirk, save for the part where they went over the strand by the sea, at low tide. From Lille to Paris, 150 miles, something in the nature of expresses ran. A cabriolet, or carriage, when all the seats were bespoken, made the trip without stopping, day or night, the roads being paved all the way. The time was advertised as thirty-six hours, but William Savery soon surmised that they would not make it, as they rarely maintained four miles per hour. The present day can hardly picture the heavy lumbering coach, carrying "a great deal of goods," with eight horses, two postilions and a director for the seven passengers; nor can we well imagine the tedium and discomfort of two days and nights of such a moil, without stop, save to change horses and take refreshment, but such was travel de luxe in the days of the French Revolution.

From Paris to the South like conveyances plied. The coach is more minutely described as a "cabriolet national, a heavy carriage, more calculated for carrying of merchandise than passengers, having eight horses and two postilions. However, it had a kind of coach body in the center, with glass in the doors, and there being no other passengers, but ourselves, we sat down quietly to improve in the French."

In spite of the good roads, the cabriolet was so heavily laden that it made but about three miles an hour, with no night travel. This conveyance took the travelers as far as Moulins. From there on they were forced to take a

"chariot de post or potache, which is nothing more than a small cart, without sides; at each end, a basket & in the middle a straw bed for passengers to sit on, which they do, back to back, with their legs in the baskets & carry 4 persons; have a little horse or a mule & a postilion and these appear to be the only carriages that travellers can obtain in France, except they travel in the National Cabrioles with 8 horses or have their own carriages,—then they may obtain post horses."

In approaching Nîmes the postilion forced two women on the three Friends, William Savery at the time being indisposed. Naturally the five passengers, postilion, trunk of books and personal baggage, with "only a very little horse and a poor mule" for motive power, traveled very slowly.

They tired of the rough potache at Lyons and took a boat thence down the Rhone, one hundred thirty miles, for twelve livres apiece, for Avignon. On the boat, among the twenty other passengers, was a young merchant of Carcapone, who proved a friend in need to them as they went. He had his coach aboard. The river trip was decidedly restful and the pilgrims enjoyed watching the boats, laden with wine, coming up the stream, sometimes three and four lashed together and drawn by twenty horses against the current, "which in some places is as rapid as the River St. Lawrence in Canada." With the snow-covered Alps about eight miles distant to the east and the nearer mountains planted to their very tops with vines, interspersed with olive, almond and mulberry trees, the countryside began to appear like a paradise. Unfortunately the water in the Rhone was low and the boat grounded twice in one day. For such emergencies, a little boat was towed behind, carrying two stout horses, and with the help of these, an hour's labor floated the passenger boat in each case. Finally the low water and contrary winds forced the captain to lie by at Montélemar, and the Friends availed themselves of the invitation of their young companion, the merchant of Carcapone, to accompany him in his coach. They traveled with him for a day, and he then halted, owing to reports of robbers and assassins, in the mountains. These reports had assailed the travelers all the way from Paris and the young merchant was peculiarly susceptible to them. In fact, there was a general alarm among the people. At a "large town closely environed by mountains," probably Tarare, the Friends slept in a room that also served as a passageway for others. During the night, rough people were passing to and fro, and these, with the current reports, gave the travelers a poor rest. When they finally arrived at Nîmes, it was not until candle light, and some French itinerants chided them for assuming so great a risk, as the mail had been robbed two days before and several people murdered on the same road. These evidences of wartime crime and lax civil control made the Friends doubly thankful for their safe arrival.

In the Southland, among the French Quakers, William Savery recounts many rides among the mountains, on horse or mule back, writing of the mounts as "bidets," the colloquial word for pony or nag. One scene is well worth quoting, relating the journey between Congénies and St. Gilles, along paths in places inaccessible to vehicles:

"We mounted David (Sands) on a bidet, me upon a very poor little mule, L. Majolier and Pierre Benezet, having two asses between them, accompanied us. I rode about a league on my mule, which kicked and flounced about and shewed so many obstinate airs that

I was willing to exchange for an ass, but had not rode two leagues more, before the little animal stumbled onto his knees and slipped me over his head, without damage. I remounted my mule, but soon after arriving at a village, where he had a mind to stop, he kicked and refused very obstinately to go on; at length, however, with the assistance of the spectators, I got through the village, and he behaved with more decorum afterwards, during the journey. David thought if our friends in America had seen us travelling in the manner we were equipped, and at the rate of 2½ miles an hour, it would have moved some of them to laugh and others to cry. Our whole business on this Continent having one tendency to learn us patience, we shall be poor scholars indeed, if we return with as poor a stock as we came."

The cost of traveling in wartime France was, as might be expected, very high. In Flanders, for the thirty-seven miles from Bruges to Dunkirk, the charge was eight Crowns for a postchaise and two horses and half a Crown extra to the postilion, and that, too, over a flat, populous country. At normal rates this amounted to seven cents a mile per person. The diligence rate between Dunkirk and Lille, thirty-six miles, was seven and a half livres a seat, or about four cents a mile per person. In the south, the travelers paid a louis d'or, normally worth about four dollars and fifty cents, for a closed carriage, or voiture, to convey them the three and a half leagues from Nîmes to Congénies. The use of the gold coin is interesting in itself, for we learn from numismatic records, that the louis d'or was worth only twenty-three francs, and as its normal worth was twenty francs, there could have been little inflation and small object in carrying gold, in preference to the smaller coins of silver.

So heavy was the expense and so unsatisfactory the service received from the public conveyances in the trip south that the Friends decided to buy their own cabriolet for the journey north. At Nîmes they were offered a coach and two good horses to take them to Paris in twelve days for twenty-four louis d'or. They preferred their own cabriolet with post horses and bought one for seventeen louis. "It was too small and confined for us, but we saw none that suited better, except such which came too high and we were obliged to study economy."

William Savery had a sense of humor, but he did not indulge it in recounting their adventures with that cabriolet. The second day out the comedy began. Arriving at Montélemar, they "took a small repast of cold turkey and a bottle of small wine, for which they charged us a French crown," and while so doing,

"a smith in the neighborhood, without our orders, apprehending he saw a flaw in one of the wheels, took the opportunity, while we were in the auberge, to put a piece of iron round it. When we came out, he demanded three shillings sterling for labour, but as we had not hired him, we endeavored to shew him the unreasonableness of meddling with our carriage without consulting us & obliged him finally, tho not without a great many hard words, to take it off again, as we saw it would rather injure than help the wheel. The postilion that had brought us there also demanding an unconscionable fee, we were obliged to dispute the point with them all for about half an hour. Many people gathering round, we felt unpleasant & rid ourselves as well as we could by sacrificing some of our argent for the sake of peace. It is not uncommon to have a host of this kind of people to contend with, in France and other places where we have travelled on the Continent, which among other things, makes it almost everywhere very exercising for Friends to travel. So that we need a double supply of meekness and wisdom to pass along to keep a conscience void of offence."

The very next day a similar experience occurred with the next postilion. After a long and ineffectual dispute, David Sands and William Savery took him to a magistrate, only to find the latter away:

"The postilion making such noise & drawing the attention of the people, I thought best to give him some money and quiet him. It is often very exercising to me, travelling in these European countrys, at least on the Continent, as it subjects us to so many impositions. We must either contend or suffer and sometimes both. We cannot make use of the same means of opposing them that many travellers do."

There is a little sermon in itself, in this avoidance of a double standard,—refusing, in Rome, "to do as Rome does." The Friends set themselves to a consistent line of conduct and unhesitatingly kept to it as a part of their message to the people. It involved inconvenience and at times, tried their faith. We shall never know what were the meaning and import of that cryptic sentence that William Savery penned of "The Sign of the Falcon," in Villefranche,—

"There was something singular that happened to me at that place which I shall not soon forget. Our way is strewed with circumstances unusual to Friends."

Still another unwelcome discovery awaited them the next day in entering Lyons. Though they had made only four leagues in the day they paid double rates for the last two, "it being established by law that the last post entering in & the first going out of Lyons, Paris and other great cities, travelers shall be subject to that additional price, the fixed rate in common, being thirty sous for each horse for two leagues. In our circumstances of carriage and number, the law requires us to be furnished with three horses and pay for four, but they generally incline to go with two & take pay for three and a half."

One can but admire the French adroitness in anticipating not only the efforts of the Society for Prevention of Cruelty to Animals, but the subterfuge of time and half time, applied to horse and half horse, long before labor unions had been heard of.

Almost a week passed and then at Chipy they halted an hour for a minor repair to the carriage, only to break a spring upon going the next mile. They returned on foot, "to the joy of the aubergiste," and "set the mareschal to work to repair our cabriole." At Sens, the next day, the incident was repeated, as "the rough pavements of France are very destructive to carriages."

"The mareschal or blacksmith took half what he asked for his labour and got three times as much as he should. It was the same yesterday, where we got our carriage mended, the man took 12s 6d sterling, for two hours work."

At Paris, trouble again, and they demanded a smith "to raccomode it." The same day, at Chantilly,

"our carriage was again badly broke and demanded immediate repair. We * * * sent for a mareschal who asked us two louis to raccomode it, but we afterward got it well done by another for two crowns. Voila the extortions upon strangers in France,—the last man was paid too much."

So far as recorded, the cabriolet lasted the rest of the journey to Dunkirk, but what the travelers did with it is not stated. The carriage used in Germany, as already stated, was shipped to America, but probably the battered cabriolet was little better than junk.

One cannot escape the impression, in reading the Journal in France, that the French were in much better economic and social condition than the Germans. This was reflected, too, in spite of the fact that William Savery was exceptionally low-spirited upon entering France and did not recover until the cordial welcome of the Friends in the south dispelled his homesickness. Both he and Benjamin Johnson were ill much of the time, the indisposition of the latter lasting till his return to England. A cheerful reaction under such circumstances is the more remarkable. The French, says William Savery,

"do not appear to be as laborious people as the Germans, and they generally live better. * * * In short, the manners of this people baffle all my powers of description."

There was much hard work, but it was not taken as hard. The levity of spirits and the village and folk dancing, in which nearly all of the peasants indulged, alleviated the appearance of toil. This lightheartedness was undoubtedly a reflection of the feeling of emancipation that followed the excesses of the Revolution. For the first time the French peasant felt his importance. According to the philosophers, freedom was being ushered in, with "liberté, égalité and fraternité" as the watchword and the National Cockade the symbol. The intoxication was so recent that the people were not yet disillusioned, nor were they to be until after the collapse of the Napoleonic military splendors.

In spite of the volatile French temperament, there was the inevitable poverty and beggary on every hand. They were the background of William Savery's discursive notes on Douai,

"famous for the translation of the Catholic Bible, contains abt 25,000 inhabitants, not remarkable for its buildings, but much so for the beggars, who beset us in troops, abt 20 surrounding the carriage at coming out and going in. It cost us many sous; they were very importunate."

In Dunkirk, every Friday was open season for beggars,

"they swarm in abundance, stopping one constantly and entering almost all the houses. There are not many to be seen the rest of the week. Most of the inhabitants give them something on Sixth Day. It has been a custom for time immemorial."

Another variety of begging in Dunkirk emanated from a large prison near the market,

"The prisoners put out several shoes, tied by a very long string & hird boys to carry them through the market to a considerable distance, begging sous. They could draw them in at their pleasure. This is a new way of managing the matter."

The south was as addicted to the habit as the northern cities. Between Valence and Vienne, on the Rhone,

"we were attacked by many beggars on the road, who when we approached them fell down on their knees and held out their hats. This posture had an unpleasant effect on my mind, and I checked some of them for it. We generally throw them a sou, which appears to satisfy them."

Near Lyons,

"we met with a new species of beggars. The peasants and villagers send their children out early into the fields to gather nosegays. After they have made a number of them of violets, &c, they lay wait for travellers who travel genteely. * * * As they pass along these young applicants throw their nosegays into the carriage, for which they expect a sou. Sometimes they follow us for a consider-

able distance, without being able to make one lodge in the carriage.
* * * All over Europe there are a vast variety of ways of begging."

There is more color in the narrative the further south
the travelers went. The women of Dunkirk

"generally wear long, camblet cloaks, with hoods or bonnets to them
& look as plain in the color &c, as Friends. There are however,
some exceptions. Some are gay and dressy,—a striking contrast in
their persons to the people of Magdeburg."

In Paris, "the people, especially the women (are) remarkable for the richness of their dress, but not gaudy." Near
Mâcon, the villagers and peasant women wore small hats,
not over nine or eleven inches in diameter, while in the
extreme south, although really only a few miles away, their
hats were at least two feet across. Still another type prevailed near Joigny where they

"wear little hats of wool, some with ribbons, &c. They are about
six inches diameter & have a smart appearance, with flat crowns,
just stuck on their heads. * * * Here again the people seems to be
scattered in flocks, all over this beautiful country, round the city as
well as in, in dancing &c."

Food seemed plenty everywhere. Perhaps the cause of
the illness of the Friends may be partially attributed to
the better diet they received in France. Sausage and wine
and the groaning tables of the southern Friends loaded with
nuts, grapes and olives contributed much to revive their
spirits. At the other end of France, in Dunkirk, the "meat,
fish, vegetable and fowl" market was visited. Like all the
European markets it was in the open and both buyers and
sellers were for the most part women.

"In a very large open square were a vast number of booths, with
goods of many kinds for sale and a quack doctor haranguing a
multitude on the virtues of his medicine."

Vegetables were to be had in great abundance,

"especially potatoes and turnips which I think may be bought for
about 10d sterling a bushel. Apples are also very good & in greater
plenty than in America at this time of the year, (February) about

five for a penny or sou. In short, this place abounds in the necessaries of life & good. * * * Their oysters are small and coppery as in England and elsewhere in Europe. The fish not excellent, at least such as are for sale now."

This astringency in the taste of the oysters was one of William Savery's chief reactions to French cuisine. One might judge that he was something of an epicure from his frequent mention of the bivalves and his satisfaction in finding that the coppery taste was eliminated when they were roasted in their shells. Around Dunkirk, at a later visit in May, were many kitchen gardens to supply the city with vegetables, but one wonders from the prices how the truckers were paid for their efforts. Radishes, the size of a hickory nut, apples, "with a rough, yellow skin, like our Pearmains," a plenty, at "three for a sou, less than an American cent." Eggs "uncommonly large, for twelve sous a quarter of a hundred," butter about 6d sterling a pound, "excellent, good beef, veal, &c, about (torn) sterling a pound and their small, but well flavored oysters for fifteen sous a hundred." Nearly everything in the south of France was sold by weight, even to live eels, which being weighed "in a shallow pair of scales, they had much difficulty to keep them in." Here the greatest attention was paid to grape culture and wine. The Friends around St. Gilles were in the very heart of this industry, and produced some of the "finest wine in all Languedoc." Their river bottoms were small, but extremely fertile, and yet it was upon the apparently dry and gravelly hillsides that the highest value was placed, for there grew the vines that produced better wine than the rich lowlands.

On an early morning in January, William Savery took one of his solitary walks to a hilltop, above St. Gilles, and there saw the panorama of the "fine, extensive valley, with a canal in the middle on the side next the Rhone. I thought it as handsome & rich a spot as I had seen in France." It was not so highly esteemed by the natives.

"The valley was too rich and too damp for wine & two acres of it would be given for one of vineyard, * * * nor did it yield half the profit of the hills of gravel."

The grape was the outstanding feature of the southern landscapes, covering the high hills, even to their very summits. Interspersed here and there with olives, almonds in blossom and mulberries, and with the snow-covered heights of the Alps, only a few miles distant beyond the river, this southland wrought wonders in the spirits of the travelers. Timber in this section there was none for two hundred miles. The peasants used the trimmings from the vines, the olives and almond trees for firing, buying them by weight.

"The vineyards endure a long time; do not arrive at their most fruitful state in less than 15 years and I have seen several from 100 to 150 years old, which are highly esteemed at present. They trim them almost to the stump every year."

There was also some wheat and rye in evidence in the rich river bottoms, "which," said our Journalist, "looked fine." The agricultural resources,—now the "beautiful verdure" of the wheat, near Saulieu, and again the "very fine country of wheat," north of Joigny, and the wheat fields and pasture land near Arras, all gave evidence of a high state of cultivation and prosperity in France, superior, one would judge, to the Germany of poor soil and barren scapes that the travelers had just left, although it was a winter Germany that they had seen.

In other districts sheep raising with the attendant shepherds or shepherdesses and faithful dogs were in evidence. The dogs were a novelty to the Friends. The following was written of a scene near Paris, at Chantilly,

"The sagacity and attention of the shepherd dogs is admirable as there are few hedges in France & no fences except a few stone ones. Where there are intervals of pasture or grass on the side of the road, the dogs let the sheep pasture along the borders of the grain, but are continually watching them at all quarters. If one or more transgress the bounds, they immediately bring them to order. The shepherds have so much confidence in them, that they sit down on the side of a bank, &c, and work at making baskets, &c, leaving the management of the flock very much to the dogs."

It was in the Southland, however, that this pastoral life reached its loveliest expression. Two of the Friends in that section might very truly be said to "vie with some of the ancient patriarchs for riches in flocks and herds." David Ventigole, "perhaps the richest, called a Quaker, in France," owned 1800 sheep, 50 oxen, 50 horses, 17 mules and 10 asses. He gave employment to 100 to 200 employees, according to the season. Another Friend had as many employees and specialized in sheep, having flocks aggregating 2700 head. About half of the flocks were ewes and were milked twice a day by the shepherds and shepherdesses, at noon and midnight. They afforded slightly less than a pint of milk apiece.

One is tempted to linger over these pastorals, as they seemed to fit so exactly into William Savery's temperament, in allaying his homesickness. They are redolent with the perfumes of the Mediterranean and bright with its balmy winter skies. One could dream and believe great things after penning as charming and innocent a scene as the following:

"The weather being very fine, the almond and peach trees in blossom, and the olives, figs, &c, put out into leaves, the mulberries and grape-vines just putting out. We took a long walk in this very delightful valley. The peasants, who appeared generally to be a harmless, civil people and little accustomed to strangers, were trimming their vines, both men and women. They looked at us with curiosity and respect. I never was in a country where there was more unaffected simplicity than here, shepherds and shepherdesses scattered here and there tending their flocks and knitting or spinning at the same time."

The activity of the French was not confined to agriculture alone, by any means. In the north, near Lille the greatest density of population appears to have been. The

Journalist noted a point in that vicinity whence forty-four walled cities could be seen. "A more populous country I have not seen." In these metropolitan districts manufacturing was in evidence to a certain degree, though not nearly to the extent that we shall later find in England. In fact, the predominance of England in the wars that were to follow can be largely explained by her greater industrial development. For the first time in history, wars were to be decided as much by the industrial preparedness, behind the lines, as by the weight of metal and number of men. England long antedated France and Germany in industrial development.

Among the first of the industries to excite William Savery's admiration was that of the Gobelin tapestries at Paris. He wrote enthusiastically of their beauty and the ingenuity of their makers. It was the only factory of its kind in Europe:

"They weave strip hangings of the richest colours and in all sorts of figures, portraits, landscapes, etc, which are equal if not superior in their shades and beauty to any of the finest paintings of Europe, and sell for one hundred livres the square ell."

Lest he overdo it, William Savery curbed his admiration for the Gobelins, stating,

"This fabrique is a great curiosity, yet our business in this country, being of a weighty and serious nature, does not admit of our taking much delight in these things."

The most prevalent articles of manufacture in France seems to have been muslin and silk. The travelers ran across this industry at several places, but the chief was at Moulins on the Allier River, two hundred miles south of Paris. Contrary to what the name would imply, the muslins were not made in mills. It was, in very sooth, manufacture, this muslin, "which the women spin, walking all over the streets, upon racks." Hand knitting was also a side issue with the shepherdesses, who near Charitie "sit all day on the sides of the rocks and mountains, tending perhaps 12 sheep, 6 hogs and one or two goats, on very barren pasture. They spin with a rack in their hand all day long, and follow their flocks."

Still farther south the industry increased, it being the chief occupation of the 140,000 inhabitants of Lyons, the second city of France. At only one place, and that was probably Bagnols, though the name is not accurately given, is there mention of a factory in the modern sense. There the travelers visited a silk manufactory, "the machines of which were very curious." Finally at Nîmes, their chief destination, a city of 40,000 inhabitants at that time, the silk manufacture was again the chief business. It is possible, in fact, probable, that machinery was used in most of these larger cities, though the account does not clearly distinguish between hand and machine production save in the two instances above mentioned.

Of the manufacture of earthen and iron ware, slight mention is made at the ancient city of Nevers, but it was not until the return trip, at Chantilly, when the delay in repairing their carriage brought the travelers into touch with Christopher Potter, that they saw much of the beginnings in France of industrialism on a large scale. The incident is so full of side lights upon French life and Revolutionary conditions in the metropolitan district around Paris, that it is well worth quoting in full. While their cabriolet was being repaired:

"a man arrived in his own cabriole & servant from Paris. Supposing us to be Englishmen, he accosted us. He was an Englishman of genteel appearance; had been in France about ten years; told us he lived at Chantilly; would be glad to have us at supper to-night, which we agreed to. * * * Our friend, Christopher Potter, for that was the name of our English acquaintance, sent a young man who had spent some time in Philadelphia & other places in America, but a native of England. We were received with great frankness and well entertained. Potter is a man of ability. Spending most of his fortune in obtaining a seat in Parliament for Colchester and came over to France to repair it, in which he has succeeded marvellously. Before he could command any business to his mind, he had reduced his purse to about 25 Louis or Guineas, but having a genius for manufactures, he has established an extensive one in china and yellow, or Staffordshire ware; has two grist mills and one saw mill, supplied with plenty of water, and also a wool card manufactory; is also concerned in the printing business at Paris, and on the whole, says he gives bread to about 600 people.

"He lives on part of the place once belonging to the Prince of Condé. His wife and three children remain in England. She has a fortune to maintain them. He is a very communicative and hospitable man. Invited us to breakfast to-morrow morning and we returned to lodge at the Auberge.

"6th day 4th mo (21st, 1797) Breakfasted at Potter's, after which he took us to promenade about the former delightful seat of the Prince, which for magnificence & extent exceeds by far anything we have seen in Europe belonging to a subject, though at present its grandeur is greatly defaced. The mansion house, stables, greenhouses and other buildings are, in their extent and otherwise, such as I have no talent for description. The beautiful forests, (extending?) in many directions with avenues, one of them said to be 72 miles long, the gardens, fish-ponds, canals, cascades, & fountains are said to have been in their best condition, preferable to anything in Europe. We walked about three miles; saw the largest perch, carp, pike, etc, in abundance in the ponds, which Potter is privileged to take at his pleasure, as he appears in some measure to have stepped into the Prince's place, though the estate is not yet sold. He thinks when times are more settled, he shall buy the buildings and some of the land & employ them in manufactorys.

"Nightingales were numerous in the woods & gardens and appeared to enjoy a delightful morning. These ruined palaces, once replete and surrounded with all that could please and gratify the voluptuous inclinations of their former inhabitants, are some of the monuments that the world can afford of the instability & vanity of all earthly enjoyment & brings with them, to a wise, reflecting mind, an antidote against setting our hearts on any terrestrial thing and cast a melancholy shade over all human glory.

"* * * The Prince and his family, who formerly, it is said, had above 1000 people that wore his livery, are now wandering emigrants in the dominions of an Emperor, whose predecessor, Joseph, was entertained with the utmost pomp and splendor, who, invited his royal guest for supper and to a hunt in his forest, which for miles round was illuminated with flambeaux and lamps on the occasion. What a scene of human extravagance & weakness!

"Potter took us through his porcelain & yellow, or Queens ware manufactorys. The china especially, was entirely new & very curious to us. He has carpenters, joiners, wheel-wrights, smiths & most tradesmen that are necessary, all within his extensive concerns, which the Englishman who had been in America, was Superintendent of. In short, Potter is a very extraordinary man of this world and no doubt is of great use in employing the poor in his neighborhood, yet one thing is lacking, a thousand times more than all else he can ever acquire, which is a desire more ardent after that Peace of God which passeth all understanding and that riches which will never perish.

"* * * Potter desires to obtain some Andover iron to make an essay of it for steel; is to write to America."

This last memorandum is the sole reference, in France, to the iron and steel industry, which was already blackening the landscapes of England. Industry, in the modern sense, was but beginning in Revolutionary France.

In those days, as in these, France was not France without Paris, although William Savery cordially disliked the metropolis. "It has little to satisfy the soul longing after celestial riches." It was interesting to the travelers because different from other cities, having "everything to satisfy the eyes of the curious, the desires of the voluptuous, the talents of the learned and the dissipation of the gay and fashionable world." It was about two-thirds the size of London in population. The apartment dwelling had, so early in urban life, made its appearance.

"Many of the houses are five and six stories high, different families living in the several stories and hanging out the various signs of their merchandise, trades, etc."

It is interesting to find so many Parisian sights that were familiar in 1797 and still are. The Champ de Mars, the Hôtel des Invalides, "as fine a building as any I have seen," the Pont Neuf and Pont Républicain, "the bridges over the Seine are handsome." There, too, was the Palais Royal, "about twice the size of the squares of Philadelphia," built by the Duc d'Orléans, with a piazza and shops which our chronicler did not attempt to describe,—"I will content myself with saying, the sight of it much astonished me." More interesting still, was the Panthéon, then two years under construction, and "not near finished," although it already contained the tombs of Voltaire and Rousseau. Street scenes were different, however. Many of the boulevards were broad, one encircling the city being two hundred feet wide.

"It is perhaps, take it all in all, the most extraordinary street in Europe, containing abundance of shops and stalls of every species of goods, many places of vain amusement and handsome walks with seats and is almost always crowded with passengers."

Street lighting was in its infancy, with lamps suspended by chains from posts on the sides of the street, so that they could be let down or hoisted with ease. Traffic was fast and reckless, especially on a street along the Seine, "more crowded than Cheapside, London, or any street in that City." Pedestrians took their lives in their hands:

"There are no foot-ways, or very few in any part of the City, so that at the approach of carriages, they fly in crowds into the houses and shops adjacent."

William Savery was anxious to leave Paris as soon as possible.

"All the mind grows perfectly wearied with these objects, desiring rather some peaceful, quiet retreat, even in the interior parts of America, than to dwell in a city like Paris; at least, this was entirely my case. It made me sad and disgusted at the ever-lying vanity of a delusive and uncertain world."

And so, the travelers tarried but a short time and shook the dust of this Babylon off their feet at the first opportunity.

## CHAPTER XX

# RELIGIOUS LABOR IN HOLLAND AND FRANCE

The Friends had considerable service in Holland, especially at Amsterdam and Rotterdam, where still remained the vestiges of the meetings established early in the history of the Society. John Vanderwerf was the mainstay of the Society in Amsterdam. There were a few Friends in the city and these gathered to the meetings held while the visitors were there. Apparently John Vanderwerf lived in the house belonging to Friends. It had a meeting room with a capacity of four hundred people. The attendance at all of the meetings was about fifty. Near the door of the room a box for the receipt of coins for charity had been fixed. The Friends objected to this in a Friends' meeting house, but John Vanderwerf stated that it had always been there and that the people were used to it, although visiting Friends from time to time had objected to it. "We repeated our uneasiness several times but doubt whether it will yet be taken down," says our chronicler.

The form of a Monthly Meeting still existed, although John Vanderwerf and one Sanderman were the only attenders.

"Their principal business for several years appears to have been to meet and make a minute that they did so and once a year to transmit an account to Friends in London of the state of the estate of Friends there, as the house where J. Van^r lives, in which the meeting is held, belongs in part to Friends of England and part to Friends of Holland. There is also about 400 pounds Sterling left by a Friend for the entertainment of travelling Friends and conveying them to Rotterdam. There is also some other monie belonging to the meeting. The books for 130 year back, both minutes of the Monthly Meeting, records of births, burials and marriages are still preserved in very neat and decent order. By these it appeared that from about 1670 to 1720, there were a considerable number of Friends, 60 to 70 signing their marriage certificates. Since the last date there appears to have been a gradual decline, till it came to what it now is,—the two antient Friends being all that keep up the Monthly Meeting, who appear concerned what might become of the property if they should be taken away. * * * At the same (time) there were Friends at Emden, Utrecht, Harlem, Rotterdam and other places in Holland."

At Rotterdam, the itinerants found no Friends. Shadrach Jones and Cornelius Lloyd were both of Quaker extraction, but belonged to other faiths. They were unceasing in their hospitality, however. The former, though an Englishman, had lived some years in Philadelphia. The latter had been the last to contribute to the Friends' meeting in Rotterdam. The old meeting house had been converted into a carpenter's shop. At the request of the Friends, it was at once cleared out and made ready for meetings. The house was rented and the return from that source and a small stock in hand was available for keeping it in order and to supply candles, although most of the funds to the extent of 25,000 guilders belonging to the meeting had been lost through the failure of a descendant of Friends, some years before. The Friends remained in Rotterdam about three weeks, holding many meetings. The attendance was good, varying from sixty to one hundred and fifty, and though there were no actual members there, William Savery thought Rotterdam a more promising place than Amsterdam for future service. The Friends' house eventually proving too small, "the Episcopal Worship House" was offered and accepted. It had been built by Queen Anne for the English residents of Rotterdam, but had been closed when the "priest" and many of his congregation had left to avoid the effects of the war. The service of the Friends in Rotterdam gave earnest of much expansion. The people came to the meetings in increasing numbers but still the call to France would not down. The Danish Consul, who was very friendly, whimsically told the Friends he would put them under arrest to detain them for longer service.

Moving on to Dunkirk, several Friends were found there, although like the groups in Amsterdam and Rotterdam, they were mostly of English extraction. A number of meetings were held there before the travelers went on into France.

The work in France differed from that in Germany for a very good reason. There was little possibility of direct communication with the people.

"There can hardly be a more exercising service than we are engaged in to minds like mine. We frequently feel as though there were some religious people in the places we pass through, but how to select them or be of much use to them, if we could, as none of us have sufficient of their language, is what we are often tried about. We conversed however at times freely & sometimes disperse books. * * * At present we feel rather a spirit of heaviness & mourning than any pointings of truth to gather the people to the true standard. Probably the time is not now."

For this reason, there was little religious work, if any, among the French people except among the so-called Friends, in the south, on whose account, in reality, the strenuous journey was undertaken.

Deferring, for the moment, that phase of the work, some observations upon religious conditions in Revolutionary France should be noted. France, before the Revolution, had been essentially a Catholic country. As in Germany, so here, the wayside had been ornamented with crosses and crucifixes, but in France these, and in some cases, the chapels over them had been demolished with Republican fervor, leaving only the scattered fragments as evidence of the past. "This indeed is the present picture of most parts of France." Religion was very evidently in a decay, though at the same time the innate religious sense of the

common people was unchanged. They still flocked to their
"mass houses," but no services were allowed, save those
conducted by priests who had taken the national oath. Over
many of the chapel doors appeared the inscription, "La
Nation Française reconnaît l'Être Suprême et l'Immortalité
de l'Âme." Of the worshipers there were more men than
women, very few of the latter being among the crowds
that were going in and out of the churches all day long.
The solemnization of marriages had been taken out of the
hands of the clergy and made a municipal function. In
spite of this it was quite customary for couples to go early
in the morning to the church for the religious ceremony
before the civil one. The number of priests had greatly
diminished. At St. Gilles, a town of 6,000 inhabitants,
there was a very large and ancient chapel, that had
formerly had twenty-nine priests attached to it. Since
the Revolution and the separation of Church and State,
this force had been reduced to two priests, needless to
say, of the "constitutional" type. At places there
were refractory priests, who had refused to take the
national oath, and who had to remain in confinement,
assisted by the charity of the pious. These held mass
in private.

The Friends were often taken for priests themselves, so
frequently, in fact, that William Savery chronicled "as
usual," toward the end of the journey. This was not always
so, however. In riding toward Lille, in company with a
young officer and two women, one of the latter objected
strenuously because the Friends ate some cold meat, it
being Friday. Her

"zeal (was) raised pretty high. She called us pagans & heretics
for eating flesh on a 6th day, but the young officer defended us &
requested we would eat what we pleased."

The decay of religion in France was very apparent to
William Savery. The continued fidelity of the peasants

was sharply contrasted with the independence of the upper classes:

"The great mass of the people, tho at present turned out of their old channel as to exteriors, remain attached and rivetted to the religion of their education; yet the superstition & extravagance of that has received so great a stroke that it is scarcely probable it will ever rise again to the same degree as formerly. There are many pious people mourning in secret & desirous of seeing the depraved manners of many of the people reformed."

It was in noticing this contrast between the superstition of the masses and the superciliousness of the educated, in this age of reason, enthroned and deified, that William Savery penned a very broad and catholic reaction. He had been watching the crowds going in and coming from the Notre Dame of Dunkirk:

"tho many appear to be ashamed and are accounted as ignorant people for so doing by others that have less religion than themselves. I could not help feeling a love for these devotees, tho I cannot own their superstition. I believe they will be accepted according to the sincerity of their hearts, when many wise philosophers will have nothing to yield them consolation."

He also found great charity in those he met for the opinions of others. In Dunkirk, where a number of Friends still lived, the magistrates had taken steps to shield them from military service during the siege, when all able bodied men had been called out.

"To screen the men from taking arms they sent them tickets that they were enrolled among the standing company, which we find in most of the cities on the Continent for extinguishing fires, which exempted them from arms. Several illuminations have been from time to time in this city. At such times the Mayor, &c, sent guards to their houses of his own accord & put lights in the streets before their windows. Thus they treat them kindly on all occasions."

Later when he himself witnessed the celebration of what proved to be a false peace rumor, when this same Dunkirk went wild with joy, there was doubtless a ready recollection in his mind of the troubles experienced by Philadelphia Friends, at the time of the American Revolution, because they refused to illuminate; but, said he:

"No insult was offered to our Friends. England and America behave very differently on these occasions to Friends, to their reproach. Friends enjoy more freedoms in France than in either of the two."

Evidently conscientious objection and ostracism therefor, are not as entirely a product of modern warfare as we of the present generation are prone to believe.

When the Friends reached Paris on the return trip, David Sands and William Savery quite unexpectedly ran across Tom Paine in a coffee house. The present generation remembers little of Paine, save as a free thinker of a most pronounced type. His real significance lies not therein, but in his political ideas. He was born a Friend, at Thetford, Norfolk, England, in 1737. His pamphlet "Common Sense," published in America in 1776, whither he had come in 1774, was one of the classics of the American Revolution. It was in that pamphlet that he wrote, "The United States of America will sound as significantly in the ears of the future as the Kingdom of Great Britain," using the expression "United States of America" for the first time in history. He returned to England in 1787, and in 1791 published the first part of his "Rights of Man." It had a strong republican tinge, and was written as a direct answer to Burke's "Reflections on the French Revolution," a reactionary document that declined to admit any development in British political life since the Settlement of 1689. In 1792 the second part of "Rights of Man" appeared, advocating a full democratic and republican régime for England, the abolition of all hereditary rights of Lords and King, direct election, by poor as well as wealthy, of both houses of Parliament, the abolition of livings and pensions, the education of all at the State's expense, the adoption of graduated income taxes, and old age and maternity benefits. In spite of the fact that very few of his propositions remain unadopted today, this second part of his book was at once proscribed as seditious, and was suppressed by the Government. Paine, forewarned of his danger, fled to France. He was elected to the French National Convention in 1793, imprisoned in 1794, the year his "Age of Reason" appeared, and narrowly escaped the guillotine for trying to save the life of Louis XVI. He dubbed himself and in one sense he was, a "citizen of the world." He had no national adherences at all. Within a few months after his chance meeting with William Savery and David Sands, he was in full concord with Napoleon, the then champion of republicanism, and advising him upon the best means of invading England.

His "Age of Reason" was probably the extreme expression of the religious unbelief of the French Revolution. It was surely the anathema of religious people, both in England and America. It was read by some of them, but not with the eagerness that had made his two earlier political works the most discussed of contemporary books in England and America. Paine not only differed from people in his beliefs, but he shocked and repelled them by the impolitic presentation of his ideas. In the hour and a half that William Savery and David Sands spent with him, his manner "had much more the appearance of passionate railing than argument." He was most abusive in reference to Moses, the prophets and Jesus Christ and termed the Bible a vile and lying book. He told the Friends that he was about to publish the third part of his "Age of Reason" which "would be more convincing of the justice of his sentiments than what had gone before," and hoped to return to America in the summer.

"He acknowledged he was educated a Friend and was of the opinion that they came nearest the truth of any Society, * * * (but) said we could not enlarge his information with respect to the principles of Friends."

Paine was a regular habitué of this Parisian coffee house, in the evenings. It was a social center of the early type, the profit of the publican and the interest of the guests coinciding in the sprightliness of the discussions. As there were several present who understood English, the Friends

"remarked to him what was then given us. I felt zealously opposed to him, but believe nothing was dropped by my companion and myself that gave him least occasion to triumph, but bore our testimony against him firmly."

As was at other times the case, William Savery's Journal does not give the only available information. Once again Sarah Rawes' account, penned after conversing with him, is spicier:

"Himself and David Sands were at Paris and walking about a hundred yards from the hotel where Thomas Paine lodged, they felt a concern on their minds to go to him. They went and requested he might be informed that two citizens of America wished to speak with him. They were desired to go to him and shown to the room where he was. He was sitting alone with his bottle of brandy before him (which the man at the hotel informed the Friends he usually finished before night) he drank it out of a glass, unmixed. As W. S. wished to lose no time in coming to the point they had in view, he began by telling him,—'I knew thee, Thomas, when thee lived a few doors from my Father, when thee wrote the book, entitled, Common Sense, and if thee hadst left off there, perhaps thee mightest have been set down as a man of understanding, but since—' 'Ah,' said he, 'I see you have been reading *that Book*. My writings have spread much farther than that (part illegible). You need not tell me of your principles, for I know them well. I remember my good mother used to give me a great deal of advice and I believe she meant well.'

"They told him the Society did not thank him for the compliments he had paid them in his book, but had much rather he had omitted it. Wm told us that they felt as standing in the place of the Society or for Friends and they did not feel disposed to give way, as he would soon triumph over them. David was wonderful in argument with him. Wm said he never knew his equal,—he twisted and twined about him in such an artful way that it was surprising.

"Thos Paine put out foolish questions, merely to confuse and perplex and to draw into a labyrinth, as,—'How many acres of land do you suppose that man and his wife had to cultivate in the Garden of Eden?' and 'When and where were they driven, when they were turned out of the Garden?' They asked him if he believed that man *was* created? 'Yes,' he said, 'how could anything create itself?'"

In the passage of time, Christianity has weathered much more serious storms than Tom Paine ever engendered, and the above seems laughable because the Friends took the occasion so much to heart. It was not, however, a light matter in those days, when religiously minded men and women thought the foundations of everything they held most dear were being blasted. In a very real sense William Savery and David Sands thought they were standing at Armageddon to battle for the Lord.

One does not marvel at William Savery's apostrophe to this land, late in his journey:

"O France, how dissolute and thoughtless are many of thy inhabitants, who have certainly not learned the things which belong to their peace, though their chastisement has been heavy."

Turning now from the general religious atmosphere of France as the Journal records it, there is a distinct relief in the charming tale of association with the simple and hospitable Friends in the ancient Languedoc. As before stated, these people were the real cause of the long, tedious and dangerous journey. Their early history and connection with Friends is a long story that has never been adequately recorded, though much material on the subject exists.

From the time of the Revocation of the Edict of Nantes, in 1685, the south of France had been a Protestant stronghold. The Camisards of that period had resisted with arms the encroachments of the Catholic armies and in time won a degree of tolerance from the weariness of both sides. Of the successors of the Camisards, the most spiritually minded were termed "Inspirants," believing in immediate revelation of God to man, and of the personal nature of the Holy Spirit. In time they also became pacifists and refused to bear arms. During the American Revolution, and the French participation in it, a British privateer took a French vessel as a prize. A Friend of London was part owner of the privateer and being conscientiously opposed to the vessel's occupation, declined to appropriate his share of the prize money. He segregated it, however, and after the war went to Paris and advertized for the owners of the French ship and cargo to come forward to be reimbursed to the extent of his share of the prize money. Through this advertisement the Inspirants in the south came into contact with English Friends and received visits from some of them. A closer approximation to Friendly principles resulted, although it cost much by way of trials and even imprisonment. William Savery had the story from Pierre Robinel, a man of seventy years, to whom many of the details were very familiar.

The party of Friends arrived at Congénies, near Nîmes, at candle light. It was with considerable apprehension that they thus completed the arduous journey, for they knew not what kind of welcome awaited them. Alighting at the inn, "the people looked pleased and friendly" and judged at once that the travelers were Friends, as they recalled the Friends who had been there six or eight years before. They inquired for Louis Majolier, who the people of the inn said was "un bon garçon." He came in a few minutes, and, wrote William Savery, "from the time I saw him, I felt my mind grow more easy than for many days." After supper at the inn they went to Majolier's to lodge and found there a number to meet them. "We went among them and they received us with strong marks of affection and joy. Slept better than for several nights past."

From that time on, all doubt as to the rectitude of their mission vanished. The next day the people flocked to greet the visitors, "men, women and children saluted us with tears of joy." The halting French which William Savery and Benjamin Johnson had acquired served them well, in simple inquiries and answers, so that the second evening a little meeting was held where they "offered some sentences in much brokenness, which they received like the thirsty ground," and then old Pierre Robinel, "worthy Magdalene Benezet" and Louis Majolier all added their part, so that the meeting lasted late into the evening.

From that time on William Savery trusted more and more to his own French, although the natives spoke a patois of "bad French and Italian mixed," rather than the classical French. At first Louis Majolier translated, but William Savery soon recorded:

"Can perceive my facility in speaking the language, as well as Benjamin's, to increase and yield us much satisfaction."

This ability developed fast. In a fortnight, when leaving the Friends at Congénies, William Savery's parting sermon, "Louis mending it in some places," ended "with the words of Paul, which I remembered perfectly, 'Ma freres & seurs-rejouissez vous- Soyez parfait, consolez vous- ayez un le meme sentiment, vive en paix a le Dieu de charities a de paix- sera avec vous,'" from which we may realize that his French was better by ear than in writing, although his mastery of it for preaching alone was sufficient to indicate great linguistic ability. Later at St. Gilles,

"I thought best to speak without assistance of Louis and by attending to my concern and speaking deliberately, I found myself more relieved and satisfied than since I came into the South."

The Friends lived not only at Congénies, but at Calvison and Fontaines, a short distance away, and also at St. Gilles, a village farther off. The Congénies Friends were the most open to receive the message of the visitors, although Samuel Brun and his family at Fontaines were excelled by none in the "kindness, simplicity and genuine hospitality" of their house. The St. Gilles Friends were more sophisticated, wealthier and more preoccupied in the affairs of their business and community than the other groups. In all of them, however, the visitors met with unaffected cordiality.

There was no scarcity of provender among these simple folk. Jean and Magdalene Benezet entertained the Friends at Congénies and William Savery "marvelled at the variety of the dinner." And well he might. It consisted of

"boiled beef, pork and soup, roast fowl, roast rabbits and roast lamb and sausages, but little or no vegetables. For the second course custards, made in a peculiar manner, some cakes and butter and afterwards the fruits, common to the place, as grapes, in fine clusters about half dried, excellent figs, walnuts like English, olives, raisins and almonds with some preserves, I think made of mangoes, stewed in the sweet wine * * * such as is commonly drank here as Americans do cider, and is not stronger."

Menus of similar elaborateness awaited the travelers when they were guests of David Ventigole at St. Gilles, and at the table of their old "landlord" who, though his name is not given, was reputed to be "the richest, called a Quaker, in France."

At Congénies, a more exact description of village life was given, William Savery having visited all of the seventeen families, with Louis Majolier. They were

"peasants in wooden shoes, mean houses and little land * * * mostly employed in vineyards or cultivating olives and making oil of them, or raising silk worms. Some however are weavers of silk and some of wool and linen for the use of the villagers, one shoemaker and one taylor. They appear to have but little in the world and yet are contented, as much so as I have seen any people on the Continent. Their dispositions and manners evidently different from the other nations we have visited. The village contains about 150 houses and 650 inhabitants, all of whom have been civil and respectful to us. There does not appear to be any person of high character or riches among them. A remarkable equality reigns throughout the whole. In all the village of Congenies, I believe there is not one shop for the vending of any kind of goods, either wet or dry, yet the simple wants of the inhabitants seem to be supplied"

Later acquaintance found a most versatile individual who was omitted from the above catalog, a physician, who was called in to attend Benjamin Johnson, but he proved to be a repairer of watches and a barber also, and had "but little medicine and probably but little skill to apply it if he had." By incidental reference we also learn that Louis Majolier kept school.

He was easily the leading member of this group of French Friends, if such they might rightly be termed. He accompanied the visitors in their round of all the villages and interpreted for them and introduced them in all the households. Pierre Robinel and Magdalene Benezet, of whom mention has already been made, were other choice spirits with whom the Friends had close fellowship. They and Pierre Marignon were frequent in the ministry. Pierre Robinel also accompanied the Friends in their visits. At St. Gilles, David Ventigole the patriarch of the flocks, and his daughter Mary, were the leading spirits, the latter being in the ministry. Of her preaching William Savery wrote:

(she) "bore a lively and tendering testimony, in much humility. I thought I had not heard the Gospel preached more in the demonstration of the Spirit in France."

One other Friend of St. Gilles deserves mention, Jacques Broun, who also bore testimony in one or another of the meetings:

"a lame man, a taylor and sells cloth &c. This man appears a steady religious Friend; says he never asks one price and takes another for his goods."

It is easy to realize why William Savery in the midst of these folk could say:

[252]

"Our love increases to the people here the more we know of them. * * * This people are remarkable for their hospitality and spare no pains to entertain us. * * * I felt myself very happy in their company. * * * O, the sweet simplicity and innocence of this poor, industrious, but apparently happy people. No strangers ever attached me to them more suddenly nor more strongly than they do."

The main business before the Friends in their undertaking was the reëstablishment of some sort of business meetings among the French Quakers. The situation among the French, in this line, was very similar to that found among the German Friends. The visitors in each instance gave proof of excellent organizing ability, but one may doubt whether the French and German religious genius was suited to conform to all that the English and American Disciplines considered necessary. William Savery at St. Gilles found some of the young women wearing gold crosses around their necks. While they removed them at his reproof, they did not attain to uniform clothing in the sectarian sense that was so important to the concerned Friend of that day. In fact, their temperament appeared too mercurial even to William Savery, fond as he was of them:

"Our friends here have not yet banished that lively activity of spirit and quickness of imagination so characteristic of their nation, and may be in danger of carrying it into their most serious concerns. They do not appear to possess that visionary disposition and desire of penetrating hidden mysteries, so observable in the Germans. Indeed, the two nations appear to differ in almost everything."

In spite of this handicap, the visitors labored loyally in all of these French villages to instill some sort of order and routine. As in Germany, so here it was done very intensively. After a few meetings for worship at Congénies within the first week of the visit, a group of eight or ten men and seven women were gathered together, "the most noted among them," to consider

"establishing some order and discipline and a monthly meeting which had been dropped for some years and never was of much account."

This work with the "pillars" proved successful, for two days later a large meeting was held and an organization effected with Louis Majolier as clerk. In scanning the minutes of the old Monthly Meeting which had fallen into desuetude, William Savery was agreeably surprised to find how accurately they had transacted business in the early days, and how nearly their practice had conformed to the English model. He found there recorded the certificates of Friends who had visited the community before,—Robert and Sarah Grubb, George and Sarah Dillwyn, Ady Bellamy, John Elliot and Mary Dudley. He thereupon noted in his Journal a memorandum to send them a copy of the Discipline, a work which at that period was much rarer in its distribution than today, being then reserved for the Overseers only. The final result at Congénies was to recommend to the Monthly Meeting the holding of two meetings on First Days and one in the middle of the week.

Much the same method was pursued at St. Gilles. For them William Savery

"wrote out some thoughts for the relief of my own mind, respecting worship and the solemnity in which all our meetings ought to be held,"

which, being translated into French, was read several times in the various villages. A conference was held after meeting at St. Gilles, at which Louis Majolier suggested the desirability of establishing a Monthly Meeting there as well as at Congénies, to which there was some assent, but, wrote our Journalist, "We thought best to say nothing on that head." It was with no small gratification that each of the Friends afterwards received, at Dunkirk, whilst awaiting their passports, a returning certificate, over the hand of Louis Majolier, from the Monthly Meeting at Congénies, "the first of the kind ever attempted in France." They must have made interesting reading upon the traveler's return, in old North Meeting, Philadelphia.

And so, after working among these simple affectionate folk from March 13 to April 6, the visitors departed

"in heart-felt sympathy and affection, with many tears and pious wishes. * * * We were mounted, David and me upon two little horses, our two Friends from Congenies and D(avid) V(entigole) and Jacques (Broun) from Gilles had four asses between them; five men Friends accompanied us a mile or two on the road on foot and appeared affected at the thoughts of parting. * * * After dinner our dear Friends from Congenies and Gilles * * * took a most affectionate leave, such as, I trust, will not soon be forgotten by any of us."

Then began the long return journey already described in part. At the end of it our Friend wrote:

"For my own part, weak, feeble and unworthy of any employment in His holy hand, I see but little or nothing towards the promotion of this great work that has been answered by my being among them, yet as I came here under a simple apprehension of duty, not to seek my own things, but the things that belong to Jesus Christ and his Kingdom, after all my weak moments and divers things in the course of this deeply exercising journey which had better have been omitted or might have been better performed, I submit all into the hands of my tender, merciful Father and ask nothing more than to spare me from being followed by the arrows of condemnation and such a portion of peace and assurance in Him, as in the riches of His love, he may condescend to grant me, who, in my best estate am unworthy of the least of all His mercies and a poor, helpless and unprofitable servant."

## CHAPTER XXI

# NEW WINE IN OLD SKINS

No one would have denied his possession of political wisdom more quickly than William Savery. He would have claimed that his was a Gospel errand and that he eschewed all else beside. Though he was witness to the political and economic changes around him that were ushering in a new era, he evidently thought that his sole concern was for the religion he preached. In reality, however, he was vastly interested in the transition and vaguely aware of its significance. More than any Quaker intinerant minister, save Penn, did he record events, men and circumstances, collateral to his religious work. He combined the saintly, introspective and mystical type of religious experience with a quick and eager appreciation of the practical and economic features of everyday existence. He was a splendid example of that combination of business man and preacher, saint and savant, which the Society of Friends, with its unpaid ministry, has from time to time raised up.

He nowhere directly mentions the Constitution of the United States and the French Statement of Rights of Man, both of which emanated from the year 1789, and which were the outstanding liberal or radical political events of his generation. And yet he was aware of the new spirit; he partook of the altruistic concern for the poor and furthered the charitable efforts toward ameliorating their lot.

Beyond this he did not go. He was by birth and training peculiarly a conservative. He was used to and satisfied with an authoritarian philosophy in politics. He did not know,—in fact, we of today are only realizing the significance of the middle class ascendancy that was everywhere being ushered in. Middle class rule, democracy as it is now called, was a novel, untried and idealistic innovation. It was as cordially feared, scorned and despised in the Europe of 1790 as Russian communism is today in the Western World. William Savery knew the essential poverty of lower and middle class Germany, the effervescence and volatility of France, the wretchedness and squalor of Ireland and the teeming industrial busy-ness and distress of England, but he did not see them as kindred problems.

And why should we expect it of any man of his time? History records no politician or seer of that period who rightly descried the signs of the time. Wilberforce, the hope of nascent Liberalism, appealed strongly to our traveler, but his political creed was remedial rather than prophylactic; Paine, whose influence William Savery distrusted and feared, went the full cycle of radical belief, but was rather harping on political theory to justify events than shaping events to meet the new essentials of which he was never to plumb the depths.

It is a sad commentary upon human shortsightedness that our trusted prophets are too frequently those who skillfully summarize or explain to us what we *are* doing, rather than indicate what we *should* do. Events, under such circumstances, of necessity shape themselves and the next generation reaps the whirlwind of the fathers' expediency or neglect. Of those true seers, who seeing, dare to tell and not to quibble, the shadow of Calvary always and inevitably lies athwart the path.

The period of William Savery's European tour (1796-1798) was within one of the most momentous decades that human history records. Between 1789, the year of the United States Constitution and the French States General, and 1799, when the French Directory gave way to the Consulate, there was a strong possibility of a true internationalism. France was the storm center and the nerve center. When Louis XVI for the first time since 1614 convoked the States General in 1789, he raised a wraith he could not lay. Not only did he call the Tiers État, as he supposed, but he evoked the spirit of the populace of France,—the vast, teeming, illiterate, dirty, cursing and careless populace, which, though not summoned by the King, became, back of the middle class Tiers État, the most potent and terrible factor in that kaleidoscopic tragedy. Came the French Constitution of 1791; too moderate! Enter the National Convention in 1793; exit the King to the guillotine,—then a new Constitution, and the Terror, followed by a third Constitution (1795) and the Directory of five men in executive control. The Directory lasted till 1799 when the Corsican toppled it over into his Consulate and the decade and the Revolution proper went out together.

In this brief period France was truly cosmopolitan and with an intense fervor. In 1792 her Convention (with Louis XVI yet alive) offered aid to all the oppressed peoples of the Earth, with the same abandon as that with which the Russian Bolshevists renewed the offer of succor in 1918. And be it said, the comfortable portion of the world shivered instinctively at each offer. French sovereignty had entered its third period. The feudal, personal sovereignty of Le Grand Monarch, whose "L'État, c'est moi" was no arrogant assumption, had passed first. Next came and went the territorial sovereignty, the geographical type, when a delimitation of land, bounded here by a river, there by a sea or by mountains, constituted the State. But France by her Revolution crashed through in a decade into the popular or third type of sovereignty, that of the people, toward which England had, slowly and with manifest uncertainty, been evolving since her bloodless Revolution (1688) and

the Declaration of Rights (1689). Little did they reckon
in their feu de joie,—these garlanded townspeople en fête,
the villagers singing in the streets and the shepherds and
shepherdesses dancing in the fields,—little did they foresee
the next fifteen years and the burnt out meteor that Mos-
cow, the Peninsula and Waterloo were to leave to them.
Their philosophers had told them that thus they were to
return to nature and so they were returning. The aristocracy beyond the Rhine, the King guillotined, the estates
confiscated,—why not dance and sing in a revel of first
principles?

But then the shadow of Potter and his ilk and their
industries, the six hundred poor who owed their bread to
him! Industrialism and middle class ascendency, nationalism, new-born and virile, and its younger brother, imperial-
ism, still to come,—why worry! The Prince of Condé is
gone and Potter is here. Dance on and sing, wave your garlands and justify the poets and philosophers in covering
France with swains and shepherdesses, happy in the pseudo-
innocence and mirth of their pretty pastorals. The Corsican
is yet to come!

For this brief period (1792-1798) almost exactly coin-
cidental with William Savery's visit, France was the liberal
apostle to the nations. With the fervor of the Crusaders
and the fanaticism of the Prophet combined, the Alps, the
Pyrenees, the Rhine and the Channel became false im-
pediments to the progress of the spirit of liberty and en-
franchisement, which the French were privileged and bound
to carry to the oppressed beyond them.

And then, into this apostolic France of William Savery's
period, there broke the dominant political factor of the
next century,—a factor as disruptive of altruistic idealism
as it was novel and untried. The French armies went to
the Rhine, and, as we have seen, harassed the Prussians
beyond it, but the oppressed populations did not welcome
the troops of the Directory, as philosophical theory would

have surmised. Splendid victories resulted; French prestige and self-esteem increased apace; but with opposition the altruism first began to abate, and then ebbed away with the irresistible undertow of a receding wave. First of all the great nations, France burst full bloom in that period into the self-consciousness of Nationalism, with those racial and restricted implications that are still the dominant and most potent factors in the experience of the Great Powers, as each in turn, in the intervening century, has acquired the status.

What we can appreciate as history, William Savery and his contemporaries did not, and in sooth, humanly could not foresee. Events happened around them as around us. As we drift, busied about our little affairs, so they drifted, worried perhaps, concerned certainly, those of them that realized, but as impotent, as are we today, either to suggest the remedy or to initiate the means to it.

It may be God's plan that humanity shall only work its way upward, through turmoil, labor and pain to the attaining of its collective triumphs, and that in the process, His love shall be so nearly eclipsed that humanity shall lose sight of it. It may also be His plan that in such times a few beacons shall pierce the darkness with the light of His Gospel, and as such, the labors and travail of William Savery and his fellow pilgrims in a war-ridden and desolate Europe may be counted as gain. Our work of today can claim little that is superior to theirs.

That they did no more; that they failed to assuage or to mollify the misery and suffering they witnessed should be more of a stimulus to us than a criticism of them. We stand, as did they, at the beginning of an era,—yet with far greater possibilities of appreciating the current and significance of events than were available to them. Perchance the present is dissipating in a renewed blind economic surge the opportunity of a century to cement peace between the nations on the only Foundation available then and now. The prospects of world rehabilitation, that budded fairly, in the contrition of a dubious victory in 1918, came full bloom red in realization of the completeness of Germany's collapse. The altruism of President Wilson's "Fourteen Points" evaporated before a hostile Senate as quickly as did that of the Revolutionary French for the oppressed masses of other peoples. Reform, then and now, even if accomplished, and whether in a social, political or economic endeavor, or all three mixed, is of little value, without a leavening or confirming spiritual change. Without such, the apparent settlement is too often merely a shift of emphasis under which men change their tactics to the same ends by revised methods. Such in the event have proved to be the three great Congresses of the Nations since,—Vienna (1815), Berlin (1878) and Versailles (1918). Spirituality in the practical affairs of the world has invariably been ignored, relegated to a place of incidental import, or attuned to an hypocrisy little short of blasphemy as in the fulsome platitudes of the Holy Alliance. Power, whether in politics, business or society, constantly runs amuck, and will continue to do so, until it be harnessed with or tempered by the power of the Gospel of Christ Jesus, which was William Savery's sole remedy for the ills of the world.

In that spirit could our Journalist write at Dunkirk, with the tricolor waving from upper windows and the streets a shifting maze of riotous men and women, celebrating a false report of peace:

"Instead of a vain shew of joy, full of tumult and confusion, it appears to me to be a matter of reverent thankfulness and secret gladness of heart to the merciful Author of every good work, who appeared to be disposing the Powers who have stained the Earth with so much human blood, to stay their hands. But oh! how can they recompense the thousands of unhappy widows and orphans who are mourning in secret places their irretrievable loss, all over those nations we have traversed. Oh! when will men be wise; when will they suffer the peaceable Kingdom of the Redeemer, whom they profess to adore, to come on earth as it is in Heaven,—how have the great of this world always resisted the coming of that glorious day, which they pretend to intercede for in their prayers!"

## CHAPTER XXII

## IRELAND IN DISTRESS

William Savery's experiences in Ireland coincided almost exactly with the period which stands out of all others as the most dramatic and the most terrible. Centuries of active misrule came to a climax in "the '98," as the insurrection of 1798 is called, and it was in 1797-1798 that the Quaker preacher twice toured the Island and noted with concern the political and economic troubles of the Irish peasantry and the doctrinal difficulties among the Friends which also resulted disastrously for the cause of Irish Quakerism, soon after his departure.

Since the Battle of the Boyne, in 1690, when William of Orange had defeated the Irish and French armies in County Meath, Ireland had remained in the desperate silence of cowed and sullen peace. The Treaty of Limerick, of 1691, which followed the Battle of the Boyne and the siege and surrender of Limerick, had banished 10,000 Irishmen and had promised to the Catholics "such privileges in the exercise of their religion as were consistent with law, or as they had enjoyed in the reign of Charles the Second." In the category of "scraps of paper" the Treaty of Limerick is entitled to notorious preëminence. For well nigh a century the political disabilities heaped upon Catholics were only tolerable, because they were also imposed upon all Protestants, except Anglicans, although the latter constituted but a twelfth of the population. The influential Presbyterian population of Ulster, in the north of Ireland, and the Quakers of Ulster and Leinster were also denied, until 1780, every vestige of political power.

It is rarely understood, in these times, that the early Irish troubles originated largely through Protestants, in a new protest against the crushing barbarity of Anglican laws, originating in London, and accepted by Dublin, under the absolute control of English landlords. There was no essential political significance in the religious opinions of Irishmen, either Protestant or Catholic, until after Vinegar Hill, in 1798, when the Catholic priest took to politics as a last resort. The "United Irishmen," of whom William Savery wrote, and who, in his time, and since, have meant Catholicism in politics, were originally "united" irrespective of religious affiliation, and had been, in fact, at first largely Protestant. The "Orangemen" of later significance, had not yet evolved as counterparts to the Catholic "Defenders" and "Peep-o-day Boys."

Much of the economic hardship resulted from restrictive legislation from London, directly and openly hostile to Ireland. Westminster adopted the frank policy of ruining Irish commerce and dominating Irish agriculture, in the interest of English predominance in both respects. The export of Irish cattle and sheep to English ports was forbidden and the export of wool to any port was interdicted, lest it might compete disastrously with the English wool trade. Add to these external disabilities the internal exploitation by parasitic office-holders, battening upon all sorts of bounties, pensions, preferments and sinecures, and the cause of part of Ireland's century of woe is apparent.

As in all other parts of Europe, the American Revolution had both a practical and academic effect. The entry of the French into the American War found England unable to garrison Ireland against a possible French invasion. London thereupon called upon Ireland to prepare for her own defense, with the result that 40,000 troops, all volunteers, officered entirely by Protestants, were raised. Of these a great number were Presbyterians but the Catholics were notably represented in the rank and file. The result, however, was a demand that London had not anticipated. Grattan, the popular Irish leader, demanded, as a reward for this show of loyalty, that Ireland be granted independence.

And independence, of a type, she was in fact granted in 1782. But truly, it was of a type. It meant in the event independence for the Protestant rulers of Ireland to complete their political investiture of the distracted Island. Without even the slight restraint from the Privy Council in London, which had in the past had a small, but altogether salutary deterrent influence, the Irish rotten boroughs, yielding a majority in the Irish Commons to the small handful of "undertakers" who returned members from them, ruled Ireland with a reckless disregard of insular welfare that completed the full measure of Irish woe. The flood of bitterness had been accumulating for a century. Just at the time of William Savery's visit, it was ready to overflow, in the wrath, futile to be sure, but terrible in its futility, of a down-trodden and brow-beaten populace, desperate to the point of despair.

At this time also entered as a main factor the religious question to remain a curse, insoluble for the English for generations to come. In 1782, when Lord Rockingham had yielded to Grattan's demands for "independence," the Catholic soldiery which had served loyally as a part of the Volunteers demanded the franchise and other civil rights, on a parity with Protestants. The claim was denied. If it had been granted, the now ancient, but then inchoate division between Catholic and Protestant, between the "Defenders" and the "Orangemen," between Scotch-Irish Ulster and the south of Ireland, might never have developed. The history of those years is the epitome of English failure to understand Irish psychology,—a grudging and tardy compliance, when too late, in demands, which, if granted in time would have avoided the bloody scenes, of which Irish history is full.

In 1793, after the outbreak of the French Revolution, a belated attempt was made to stem the tide by granting the franchise to the Catholics, but, even then, they were not admissible to Parliament. The concession, as always, came too late and the "United Irishmen," which originally stood for a nationalistic conception, irrespective of creed, changed rapidly into a Catholic organization and the most hesitant of the Protestant land-owners, aside from the Quakers, threw aside their neutrality and joined the Orange lodges. The lines were set, hard and fast. The struggle for supremacy was on.

It is a truism to say that the political discontent was but a reflection of the economic distress. Ireland was not only undergoing the throes of the Industrial Revolution, as was England also, and even she with profound malaise, but she was also undergoing systematic exploitation. Americans fondly think, at times, that England learned to govern her colonies from her experience in the American Revolution. There is something in the theory in some regions, but it has assuredly never applied in Ireland. Ireland was the despoiling politician's paradise. There was every opportunity to loot and small restraint upon the looters. Says William Savery:

"Little as the trade of Dublin is, its superb Custom House has 300 clerks who receive salaries the whole duties are hardly able to pay them. But a clerkship is granted as a douceur for other services. One-tenth would probably do the business."

It was not the political graft, however, that was most apparent to the casual visitor. The terrific discrepancy between the rich and poor, everywhere in evidence, both in country and city, was the appalling and sinister factor of Irish life that William Savery could not escape:

"Yet after all the opulence of the City of Dublin, there is no comparison that I have seen in Europe, for wretched habitations in the alleys and back streets, which are filled with human beings, who in their present filthy mode of living, nakedness, depravity of mind and morals, are really the most affecting sight to a humane, feeling mind, that perhaps any city in the world can exhibit."

In the country it was as bad. Descriptions as terrible as these appear in many places in William Savery's pages, as he recorded the day's progress in visiting these abodes of pitiable distress. In County Antrim, in the country near Lisburn, North Ireland, he went among the cottages with his hostess, Lucy Condrun:

"The women spin, and the men weave linen, muslin, &c., but are very poorly clad, their children next to naked (in November). Their houses very cold, with little light but what comes in at the door. Walls of mud & straw, roofs thatched, floors of earth, small fires of turf, for which they pay dear to the landholders, a straw bed or so with some stools, a table, a few bowls, &c., make up their furniture. How would a sight of these poor, oppressed people make many, even of the poor, in Pennsylvania, thankful for their blessings."

Repulsive as these descriptions are, they visualize Ireland, as it then was. Belfast, in the Protestant north, disappointed our traveler

"in almost every way. Streets are everywhere dirty, the people, especially the poor, as dirty as the streets. Without shoes or stockings the women, and children of both sexes, tramp through the mud, now in the 11th month. The men have stockings and there are a few well dressed people mixed among them."

Once again in Dublin, at "Mud Island," near Summerhill:

"there may be 100 poor houses, many of them mud. And many miserable inhabitants we found. Some without any fire at all, the day, cold and damp and the floors of the houses earth & quite wet. They appeared universally to lay on straw and were miserably provided for that. Expended about eight guineas among these poor, almost naked people and visited about 100 families today. Came again to the Widow Forbes; purchased about 100 loaves of bread at 4d each, for which we soon had plenty of customers, not more than one loaf for each person."

As a result of these labors, William Savery contracted a heavy cold, but the next day two young men, not Friends, who were members of the Committee for the Relief of the Poor, called upon him, and with them, he

"turned out again, visited and relieved many truly miserable human beings. The memory of these visits cannot soon be effaced. May they teach me to be humble and thankful for the blessings I enjoy. Oh! my dear country folks, could many of them that live in ease and abundance, far removed from these affecting scenes of wretchedness, behold them, profitable impressions might be made for life. To see a mother and daughter, the youngest of them 60, almost naked, without fire on a damp, earthen floor, lying upon a little straw and only their tattered rags for covering & very little to eat, how must every feeling heart be touched! In another place two widows with seven children, two of them blind and nearly naked, and one of the mothers, racked with rheumatic pains, having no fire and not two ounces of bread in the house."

In these visits, which he was constantly making to the poor, William Savery gave away large sums of money, which had been entrusted to him for the purpose by Friends in many parts of England and Ireland. In one place when their carriages were surrounded by beggars, he took up a special collection from Friends on the spot for this kind of relief. It was, as he himself realized, utterly inadequate:

"Seeing about ten miserable beggars sitting around a Friend's door, sent for ten two-penny loaves, but before they were distributed, thirty appeared, and every one had the same quantity. This is the way in Ireland. There is no coming to an end of the business."

Though he had come to Ireland as a minister of the Gospel, and primarily intent upon preaching to those outside the fold of the Society of Friends, his heart was so stirred by the conditions he found that he devoted much time and thought to remedying them, feeling therein "as usefully employed as if laboring in the word and doctrine." He mentions giving fifty guineas in cash, bread and coals, in Dublin alone, and at various times. The larger part of this was given through the Committee for the Relief of the

Poor, and cash was given only "to the most worthy, as they were pointed out to me." Time and again, they "received a profusion of blessings. . . . Most of the poor being Roman Catholics, their benedictions are often very singular."

With the halting knowledge that we of today have on the subject of unemployment, it is easy to acquit William Savery of superficiality, in not grasping the fundamentals of the situation. We, with more experience, still hesitate to enact provisions for unemployment insurance, in spite of the great growth of paternalistic legislation. He realized somewhat the connection of the economic ills and the political spoliation, and he labeled as "absurd," the "prohibition of any artisans going for America, where there is labour and provision enough." He would have been no less than a political seer had he clearly analyzed the evils of absentee landlordism, and the blighting effect of discriminatory tariffs, as the economists of the future were to do, and he never posed as a politician. As far as his personal responsibility was concerned, it went no further than the doles of money and food, which he himself knew to be futile for permanent results.

He attributed much of the distress, and probably rightly so, to the dissolute and improvident habits of the people. Of these the lotteries and drink held the chief place, among the degrading influences, and as adducing causes of the unemployment. He describes the lotteries minutely; their "offices in the City which make a most splendid appearance after candle-light"; and their doors, "continually surrounded by poor, half naked people, who lay out their shillings and six-pences, which perhaps, they have begged, in hopes of gaining by their chances." The usual lottery issued 50,000 tickets and was forty days in the drawing. The rich took guineas, the poor pooled their shillings. The collateral betting and gambling on the drawings often involved more than the amounts in the lottery itself. The wealthy occasionally purchased insurance upon numbers undrawn at a given time, either enhancing their gains or decreasing the loss of their deposits.

Of equally evil import, by which "many are exceedingly hurt," was drinking the "pernicious spirits, made of malt rye, &c, called whiskey, of which an immense quantity is distilled in Ireland." Some of the Friends in Ireland were brewers. There was no excise upon beer at that time in Ireland, but on barley or malt there was a tax of 3s/9d per hundred. "They brew good porter and excellent strong ale, which the retailers sell as low as 2s/2d per quart," chronicles our traveler.

But below and beneath these, in William Savery's estimate, still remained the problem of unemployment. "Yet the most judicious men I spoke with, were not able to devise anything to set them at work," and the work-house in Dublin was over-full with 1,700 inmates, and not nearly maintained by the labor performed in it. "Till some employ can be found for them and they, by some means brought to labour," he could see no cessation of the dire distress of the 20,000 to 40,000 wretched people in Dublin alone, who suffered "many through their own folly and wickedness, and yet not a few merely from want of employment." Most remarkable of all, there were in the Ireland of that day, subject though it was to tithing, no Poor Laws, to force upon the Parishes even the public doles that England provided, with all their questionable social results. Private charity, functioning in bread and coal rations, constituted the sole approach of sympathetic people toward the immediate relief of the stricken populace. Political and economic relief was too remote and too long in coming for the emergency, but of that we shall see more later.

With the spread of the modern idea, that the right to labor is one of the inherent boons of citizenship, it is easy to see in the retrospect, what was not then so apparent, even to deeply concerned minds. Ireland was rich in resources, but false economic ideas and basely adverse legislation, not only deprived her of her own produce, but prevented her excess population from emigrating, as it did in the greater famines of the forties. The soil of the Island was rich almost throughout. "The Counties of Limerick, Cork and Tipperary are so rich naturally that much of it wants but little manure." It produced food products on a large scale, "cattle, horses, hogs and sheep" crowding the market in Belfast, on a fair day; food was cheap at Lurgan,—8d the pound for butter,—a shilling for a pair of fat ducks and fowls,—beef, 3½ to 4d the pound; at Belfast, a shilling the Winchester bushel for potatoes and at Antrim 9d the bushel of 56 pounds, with eggs, 4d Irish, the dozen, and "pork by the hog, 37/6 to 40/ per 120 pounds." At Cove of Cork prices were very low, although foodstuffs were much in demand for provisioning ships. Eggs were 5d a dozen, ducks 15d a pair and "fowls somewhat lower." Fish was cheapest of all,—haddock at 2d and "sprats for ½ a woodin box that will hold a quart." "Turkey pouts" greeted the traveler for supper, when he landed at Donaghadee, and he found them very common in Ireland, along with saffron pudding, boiled ducks and geese and "young crow pye, esteemd excellent."

The export of food stuffs constituted a vast trade, especially from Cork, in beef, port, butter and grain. It is significant that the great activity in these exports seems to have been from the south of Ireland where the discontent was sharpest. At Waterford,

"pork is 28/ and beef 30/ Irish, per hundred weight of 112 pounds. The hogs are drove to town alive & the salters of the provisions kill them in their warehouses. Notwithstanding the great abundance of provisions that appear everywhere, this place, like most others in Ireland, abounds in poor and beggars and all the suburbs for a great ways, are poor, thatched cabins."

The other side of the picture, offsetting the bounties of

the productive soil, appears in the rent and wage scales. In South Ireland "women, as house servants, 50/ Irish, per annum," in Antrim, "men's labour, 6½d per day & meat, 1/ without provisions." The same rate prevailed also in Clonmel, in Tipperary.

Landholdings and taxes varied according to localities. Thomas Bradshaw, near Newtonards, in County Down, had three hundred acres, clear of tithes and paid a tax of 4/ per acre. Near Limerick, three Friends, William Mc-Allister, James Fisher and Joseph M. Harvey, had taken forty acres of land on the Shannon, on perpetual lease. Of this, Joseph M. Harvey had twenty-eight acres, standing him about £180 sterling forever. Besides being extensively occupied in the grain and salt provision trade, in Limerick, Joseph M. Harvey was agent for the large estate of the Marquis of Lansdowne, on the opposite side of the Shannon. Here was absentee landlordism at its best. He rented land for about £4 10s per annum per acre.

"Some of the poor in this neighborhood give six guineas or more a year for an acre of potatoe ground, when manured by the landlord. The earning of this six guineas takes a great deal of the year in labour for their landlord at 6d or 8d per day & food—so that the state of the poor is indeed a very hopeless one in this country. It takes them considerable of their time to cut & dry their turf & in some places they now pay high for the privilege of the bogs and many of the poor have no way of getting it home, but as the women carry it a long way on their backs."

Practically the same rates prevailed in Antrim in the north, where potato land rented for 40/ per Irish acre (about 1½ English acres), but in Tipperary, at Clonmel, nine guineas the year was the rate.

"This takes a long time to pay for their acre of potatoe ground, then the Episcopal Priests take their tenth, and they pay ye Roman Priest beside."

This potato culture of Ireland has always been of great interest to Americans, because of its introduction from the

States. William Savery was traveling those parts in the digging season, and the fields swarmed with women and children, universally barelegged and barefooted, and men, as usually shod. With his remarkably inquisitive habit our traveler noted the culture "in ridges about four feet wide, with trenches on each side," and in Antrim, did not think the quality equal to the American potato. Upon inquiry, he was told that one bushel of tubers from seven yards in length, of the ridges, was counted a good yield,—surely not a prolific one from modern standards. Potatoes, "with a little oatmeal, sometimes milk, and now and then a bit of meat, make up their principal food."

The only other industry of the peasants to which William Savery refers was the weaving of linens, upon the cottage system. In Antrim, the raw flax, fresh from the swingle, cost the cottager about 6d or a trifle more, presumably by the pound, although the quantity is not stated. This the country people took and the women would spin and the men weave the linens and muslins, that to this day, vie with potatoes, as synonomous with Irish life. Once a week, in the principal towns, markets were held and to these the country folk flocked with their week's production. It was still in a very raw, crude state, and required bleaching. At the markets the green linens were sold and bought, and the professional bleachers took up the next step in finishing the product for the trade. Many Friends in Ireland were bleachers, and William Savery soon found it out of the question to appoint meetings, in the vicinity of these markets, on a market-day, as few of the men Friends would be in attendance.

If such may be taken as glimpses of the poverty, wretchedness and toiling of the peasantry of Ireland, the wealth of the masters of the land was equally apparent. It was probably this factor of wealth, of which the Friends partook in no small measure, that obscured the causes of poverty, and emphasized the dissolute habits of the poor, as the cause of their misery. If some could prosper, why not all, if they were but thrifty, sober and industrious? Belfast, with 30,000 inhabitants, was a dirty, unattractive town, but Dublin the Capital, with its 250,000 people, was "certainly a very fine city" with streets,

"many of them wide and elegant built, perhaps Sackville Street is not excelled by many, if any in Europe. (It) is 120 feet wide and that and other of the good streets have lamps before every door. Indeed Dublin is the best lighted city I have seen. The houses many of them four or five stories high, principally of tolerable good brick. The best streets very uniform and straight, with good flagged footways, not so well watered as London, but in the same manner. The public buildings are grand, exceeding those of London, especially."

The description of the back streets and alleys has already been quoted, in contrast with the apparent opulence of the city, many of whose inhabitants, says the Journal, "roll in luxury." This contrast constantly recurs, "The country (approaching Mallow) fine, very rich land, handsome gentlemen's seats here and there, and abounding in wretched cabins for the poor." Another touch of the landlord at Hillsborough, in County Down:

"The town is small. The Earl who takes his name from thence is building an expensive and grand house there, though he has been latterly so obnoxious to some of the people, that he does not now visit his seat, but resides in London."

Near by also was the seat of the Earl of Moira, and so all over the Island. In Dublin, William Savery drank tea at the home of Elizabeth Coates:

"a very rich woman. I had a good deal of conversation, exciting her to have the pleasure of seeing 3 or 4,000 per annum do good in her life-time. She appeared to take it kind. Her and her daughter live in high style; could spare much to the hungry and the naked."

And so the age-long agony of Ireland was approaching another crisis in its history, rich and poor drifting, either carelessly or recklessly, ignorantly or knowingly, into the whirlpool of civil war. Ireland was at another of the peaks of her distress.

Although the actual outbreak, known as "The '98," did not occur until after William Savery and William Farrer had left the Island, there were ample premonitory signs. The day of their landing at Donaghadee, they were forced to remain there the night, as "no persons were permitted to enter any town in Ireland after 8 o'clock till 4 next morning." A few days later, in approaching Lisburn in North Ireland, they passed through a small town which

"had been much abused a few days before, the windows of many houses broke to pieces & some doors. The sufferers were such as are called United Irishmen. This part of Ireland has been long famous for rioting."

The travelers were afterwards regaled at Dublin, by an attorney and his son from Youghall, with "shocking accounts of the murders and plunder of the United Irishmen in the South within a few days." They were subjected to summary treatment, if detected. At the mouth of the River Suir, in Waterford Harbor, as William Savery sailed out to Wales, lay "a large Dutch built ship, which was the prison of about eighty United Irishmen."

In the South, Friends were sincerely troubled at the signs of the times. Though they had much to make them comfortable,

"the confidence of many is much shaken from their earthly riches, and many have been seriously tried & afflicted. May all things work together for good."

Friends estimated the preponderance of Catholics, south of Dublin, at from three-fourths to seven-eighths of the population.

"They are an oppressed people. It is thought two out of three of them don't eat meat six times a year, have but little milk & indeed, scarcely anything but potatoes and salt. They are at present very uneasy, commit many riots, robberies and murders, refuse to pay tithes of the few potatoes, &c, which they raise and seem to be almost lawless. Many of them are daily taken up and put in prison, but it is hard to say where it will end."

So apparent was the impending trouble that the Society of Friends as a precautionary measure, recommended that all members who had guns or other weapons should destroy them, in order, as the Yearly Meeting stated:

"to prevent their being made use of to the destruction of any of our fellow creatures, and more fully and clearly to support our peaceable and Christian testimony in these perilous times."

About three months afterward the Government required all arms to be surrendered, and it was a cause of gratification that few Friends had any in their possession. In the Monthly Meeting in Antrim in November, 1797, a case was presented of a young man who had given his gun away, instead of breaking it up. Upon the proposal of William Savery and William Farrer, his disownment was postponed for a time and the final decision is not, of course, recorded in the Journal.

Another form of the same testimony was met in the National Half-Year's Meeting's deliberations at Dublin, in 1797:

"Divers members having obtained the freedom of cities by taking an affirmation to keep a gun & bayonet in their houses & a few others being at present contractors for the army, took up much of the time. * * * The first is a thing of many years standing & but lately taken notice of in a Society capacity. Divers active members are in that circumstance. Some have sent in to the Corporations a resignation of their freedoms."

The troubles increased in intensity as the summer of 1798 wore on. William Savery was once more in London, but he heard frequently from Ireland. The French, at war with England upon the Continent, were only too willing to promise succor to the Irish, and the latter were as anxious to receive it. Memories of the American Revolution, where the French had been a decisive factor in establishing independence, had great weight with the leaders of the United Irishmen. With revolution in the air, it did not seem to be the harebrained thing that the event proved it to be, and so in the spring of 1798, the looting, pillage and burning increased. The Government had few troops available to send to Ireland, and called upon the Protestant citizenry, as it had done before, to defend themselves and the Government. It was the beginning of the acute situation between Catholic and Protestant that has not since been laid. The Orangemen formed and the rebels gathered in great hordes in the South, armed with crude weapons. The worst scenes of the revolt occurred in Wexford, the southeast county of Ireland, where the Friends had long been numerous. The chief encounters were at Ross and at Vinegar Hill, both near Friendly centers.

In London, William Savery heard:

"a Friend of Ross writes, all Friends in the town, of which there are but about six families, were preserved from injury in person or property, during the great slaughter & burning, that have been there lately. (He) could count 250 dead bodies at once in the streets from his own window. 'Tis a special mercy and favor from the Lord that Friends have been so preserved."

At Ferns and Enniscorthy, in Wexford, the revolt came even nearer to the Friends, and many authentic accounts of fidelity to pacific principles have been written. Vinegar Hill was hard by Enniscorthy. Here gathered about 15,000 of the rebels. Friends remained at their homes, as a rule, and received into them both factions, as the tide of war swept around them. The respect paid by both Catholic and Protestant to this apparently suicidal neutrality was most remarkable. It constitutes one of the most thrilling tales in Quaker annals. The homes of numerous Friends were burned and their estates otherwise ruined, but in many cases threats to burn, murder and pillage were unfulfilled. At Enniscorthy and Ferns, both near Vinegar Hill, the insurgents threatened to burn the meeting houses and preparations to do so were made. Friends gathered notwithstanding, at Enniscorthy finding the pillagers in the galleries as they convened. Delay ensued, however, and at Ferns some of the insurgents, fleeing from their defeat at Vinegar Hill, sought refuge and asylum, while meeting was in session, in the house that a few days before they had prepared to destroy. Similar experiences and preservations, little short of miraculous, are recorded of Friends in the counties of Westmeath, Kildare and Antrim, so general were the disturbances. William Savery's correspondents wrote him and he records:

"Several have suffered at Enniscorthy & elsewhere, Jacob —— being almost ruined and his house wrecked. Many Protestants, it is said, have adjured their religion to save their lives. Friends have also been required to embrace the Catholic religion in some instances, as the insurgents said there should be but one religion in the country. Yet no violence was offered to any member on that account, but two young men who had latterly appeared under convincement and attended Friends' meetings at times, declared they could neither take an oath nor deny their faith, suffered death."

This reference is to the brothers, Samuel and John Jones of Kilbroney, in Wexford. They were not actually members of the Society of Friends though closely attached to it. They were offered immunity if they would accept the Catholic faith, and upon declining, both were shot. Samuel Jones's wife supported him throughout, and held his hand as he was shot by the side of his brother.

"One also, a member, whose name was Gatchell of Rathangan, having departed from the testimony of truth and associated with others to oppose the insurgents, so called, was, with all the party, about twenty, killed. A son of J. Woodcock, (was) shot at behind his master, J. Pim's counter, at Rathangan, and badly wounded, but likely to recover. He was shot at by mistake, being an innocent young man, but taken for another. The Quarterly Meeting was held at Enniscorthy next day but one after the great slaughter &

burning of that town. Friends had to remove the dead bodies out of the way of the carriage wheels."

Dublin Yearly Meeting in 1801 addressed Philadelphia Yearly Meeting, stating:

"It was a cause of grateful acknowledgment to the God and Father of all mercies, that in retrospection to that gloomy season, when in some places Friends did not know but that every day would be their last, seeing and hearing of so many of their neighbors being put to death, that no member of our society fell a sacrifice in that way, but one young man."

Vinegar Hill was stormed in June, 1798, by Royal troops, and the rebellion came to an end. The French arrived about a month later, a force of one thousand landing in Mayo, and defeating thrice their number at Castlebar, but finally surrendering when faced with 30,000 troops.

The revolt was thus suppressed, but Ireland and the Irish were worse off than ever. "The '98" was largely religious in its significance, a feature which drove lines of cleavage deep into Irish life and history. The Friends in London were aroused by a letter from Dr. John Davies of Lurgan, which was laid before the meeting for Ministers and Elders of London and Middlesex Quarterly Meeting on June 25th. Dr. Davies requested London Friends to lay before Government:

"the necessity that appeared to him and many others, of more mild and gentle means being used to put a stop to the insurrection before the country was totally ruined, which he feared would be the consequence of the present measures."

Four Friends, including George Dillwyn and William Savery, set off at once to see Pitt and Wilberforce by coach to Old Palace Yard, but found Pitt unwell and Wilberforce out of town. A note to the latter, however, elicited an invitation to meet him at "Broomfield," his house on Clapham Common, and thither they repaired two days later, and "drank tea with him & his wife and the Dean of Arklowan, Irish emigrant, who, we found, had represented the state of the poor in Ireland in far too favourable a point of view; said there was scarcely one in 500 families who had not a cow, which was diametrically contrary to my observation. We retired into the library with W. W. Read him an extract from J. D's (Dr. John Davies) letter, which with our sentiments seemed to give him much satisfaction. We spent about two hours and returned to London, having much reason to believe our visit would not be wholly lost. He mentioned his thoughts of uniting Ireland and England together as in the case of Scotland, being the best expedient to promote the peace of Ireland."

This last sentiment, expressed thus in 1798, is chiefly interesting because it was upon this very union of England and Ireland that Pitt wrecked himself and ended his long ministry in 1801. That it had been in mind, as a practical move, so long, and that Wilberforce, of the Ministry, knew of it, or perchance originated it, and even divulged it to others, would indicate that it could not have been as much of a surprise to George III as that astute individual chose to consider it, when presented by Pitt with Catholic emancipation, the commutation of tithes and "an effectual and adequate provision for the Catholic clergy." It is freely conceded by historians that the Act of Union could never have been carried in the Irish Parliament, if it had not been for the counter-proposition of Catholic emancipation. As it was, Pitt had to buy, by weight of pure gold, a million and a quarter sterling, enough votes to put it through, and in addition, to create new peerages lavishly. The bill passed and one hundred Irish members took their seats in the House of Commons and thirty-two peers in the Lords; taxation was proportionally assessed between the two peoples and commerce and trade between the two opened on equal terms. Truly it began to appear as if better days were in prospect for Ireland.

Then came the blast from the King that dissipated the rest of the salutary program. "I count any man my personal enemy," quoth he, "who proposes any such measure" as Catholic emancipation and payment of the Catholic clergy. Once again, as always in regard to Ireland, England stopped short; the bigotry of the King prevailed, Pitt resigned and terminated that long and remarkable ministry, one of the most momentous and glorious in substantial achievements, in British history.

Without emancipation, the Union was a sad betrayal, for since 1792 the Catholics had had representation even though farcical, in their own Parliament, but with the new Constitution, no Irish Parliament and Catholics absolutely barred from Westminster, arose that desperate and despairing merger of Catholicism and Republicanism, that at the time of the next famine of the forties, sent Irishmen to the four corners of the globe, carrying with them a deep and insatiate hatred of England, that has not disappeared with the passage of time.

## CHAPTER XXIII

# THE SOCIETY OF FRIENDS IN IRELAND

With all the poverty and distress around them, it is surprising to read, in William Savery's Journal:

"Indeed, Friends of Ireland seem to live like princes of the earth, more than in any country I have seen. Their gardens, their horses and carriages and various conveniences, with the abundance of their tables has often appeared to me to call for much gratitude."

These expressions were largely elicited by the residences of John Strangman, of Waterford, and of Robert and Mary Dudley and Richard Sparrows, near Clonmel, in Tipperary. Of the latter's stables, dairy, brewery and coach house, William Savery remarked, that, though not yet finished, they were in a grand style, more like a nobleman's than a Friend's, and "I told him I thought it was quite too much so, which he acknowledged, and said, if it were to plan again, it should not be such as it was now like to be."

The same ample appearance seemed to mark the houses of Friends throughout the Island. At Youghall, he saw many poor huts, "but none of them belong to Friends. Their houses as usual in Ireland are large and their stores and warehouses too." It is probable that William Savery saw only the larger and more elaborate homes, and that his comment cannot be taken for universal application, fitting all Friends. Irish Friends were wealthy, but they also had their poor. The insurrection of 1798 also ruined some of them but it is noteworthy that subscriptions were taken from Friends all over the Island to reimburse these losses and that the amount necessary was oversubscribed. Offers of aid from English and American Friends for a like purpose were declined.

William Savery's first journey in Ireland, with his faithful companion, William Farrer, extended from November 5, 1797, to May 9, 1798. They entered the country at Donaghadee in the North and visited Friends generally in many parts of Ulster. From the North, they went directly to Dublin, for a considerable stay, mostly devoted to visiting the poor, and then across Ireland, largely by canal, to Mountmellick and Limerick. South from that city brought them to Mallow and Cork, where they had some labor and then to Clonmel and Waterford. The journey was much in the winter time. Two trivial features appealed especially to the travelers,—the greenness of the Irish fields, as green as those in Pennsylvania in April, and the prevalence of fires in their bedrooms for their comfort.

"We have several times spoken of it as giving our Friends unnecessary trouble, but it is their custom and no Friends in any part of the world are more hospitable and kind."

Irish Friends at that time did not constitute a Yearly Meeting, separate from London, though the matter had been mooted to a considerable extent. Due to the political disturbances and their own doctrinal differences, Dublin

"Friends recommended their representatives not to urge a conclusion in the Yearly Meeting of London upon the request of a separate Yearly Meeting for Ireland. All Friends who spoke thought it was no time to break any connexion, in which I much united."

The business pursuits of the Irish Friends were, naturally, very diversified. They were among the leaders of their communities, and apparently headed up many important enterprises. Many of them were bleachers of the Irish linens that were brought "green out of the loom," into the town markets from the homes of the poor country people, and there sold for the pittances that their labor commanded. Many Friends were also in the grain business, with its accessory, the brewery. Jonathan Pym and his son, Abraham, of Mountmellick, had an extensive tannery in connection with their brewery. The Strangman family of Waterford, including Joshua Strangman and his three sons and two sons-in-law, were all concerned in the corn and provision trade and in a very extensive brewery. "They brew good porter and excellent strong ale." Another Quaker enterprise at Waterford was William Penrose's glass house, where a flint glass was produced from a "fine whitish sand, salt peter, red lead and pearl ash all melted together." The product was chiefly mugs and tumblers.

At Limerick, Joseph M. Harvey and W. Fisher conducted a vast grain and salt provision trade, the latter referring to the salting of salmon, caught in the River Shannon, flowing through the town, and of pork and beef, brought in from the country around.

In southern Ireland, several Friends were operating mills on the River Suir. Of these Richard Sparrow's at Clonmel, was the most extensive and modern:

"They have just got the American elevators to work, contrived by Oliver Evans (and) supposed to be the first introduced into Ireland. Mills in Europe in general (are) inferior to Pennsylvania."

This effusion of justifiable local pride was further buttressed by the fine bridge at Waterford, across the River Suir "about 300 yards long, built of American oak, by one Cox, who built Boston Bridge and several in this country."

No slight feature of Irish life was the association with the Roman Catholics, who predominated in numbers throughout the Island. As has always been the case Friends, though further from them in religious views than any other Protestants, were tolerant of others' opinions and thereby gained and held their confidence and esteem. This fact enabled Friends to become in a real sense, mediators between the factions. The Friendly garb was an earnest of protection. In County Kildare, during the insurrection, a

Catholic Priest availed himself of a Friend's coat for a disguise to save his life and strangely enough, near Enniscorthy, a Protestant minister vainly sought the same protection.[1]

While William Savery found that "the Catholics are walled around and it is hard to penetrate them," he only learned of active opposition at one meeting, held in Dublin, by Deborah Darby and Rebecca Young at Meath Street while he was holding one at Sycamore Alley. The Meath Street neighborhood, being inhabited by "many of the lowest class of the people," they

"crowding in, disturbed it much and it proved a time of great exercise to Friends and broke up in a very noisy manner. It was not doubted but the Romish priests had a hand in the disturbance of the meeting as some of them had enjoined their miserable flocks not to attend such meetings."

To offset this single instance, the liberality of some of the Catholic clergy was evident by the attendance of one of them at another appointed meeting at Sycamore Alley, and later in a great meeting held at Waterford, at which "many of the upper rank of the people were present, * * * they were mostly Roman Catholics." Throughout the country, the travelers met no discourtesies, due to religious differences, and William Savery records, of families living remote from Friendly centers and in the midst of Catholics, even in those troublesome times, that they "meet with no insults from them." Friends were careful, however, to give no cause for misunderstanding. In the case of a funeral at Waterford, the corpse was not brought into the meeting, but left in an adjoining room, "lest, as they were surrounded by Roman Catholics, they should take up an idea that Friends were of an opinion it might be profitable to the departed spirits to pray over them." In the same city, an old Friends' meeting house had been sold to the Catholic Church and was "after much purgation by the

[1] Hodgson: *Historical Memoirs of Friends,* 386, 387.

priests," used as a Roman chapel. All such incidents point
to very good feeling and much charity between the two
religious fellowships, and well it was for both that it was so.

Irish Friends were much absorbed in completing their
school system patterned upon Ackworth. At Lisburn, not
for from Belfast, was the Boarding School for Ulster.
After tea at Jacob Hancock's, the party "with the help of
lanterns," went out to the school, where they found fifty
boys and girls, at supper of potatoes and milk. "They
looked healthy and were decently dressed." The following day, William Savery had some service among the
children "which they were much affected with."

As in all these schools, William Savery's primary purpose was to obtain ideas adaptable to Pennsylvania, and
the Westtown School that was to be. The Lisburn School
"pleased me as much as anything I have seen of the kind."
He describes its extensive prospect and fine air, ample
grounds and commodious apartments.

"The Nation subscribed £4000 towards, and the Province of
Ulster raise an annual subscription of about £300 for its support.
This with some little income beside, enables the Institution to board,
educate and clothe 56 children at £3 per annum, from eight to fifteen years of age, they bringing from their parents, or monthly
meeting, if poor, one good suit and one common one with them. All
that have yet applied have been admitted. The whole expences is
for one scholar about 13£ Irish, per annum."

At Mountmellick, he visited the Boarding School for
Leinster, finding about fifty boys and girls in the Institution, and between twenty and thirty in the separate girls'
school. With the one, he had "a truly tendering opportunity" and under like circumstances, the girls were "much
broken into tears." The work in Munster was just starting
at Newton, where the palatial residence of William Penrose,
lately deceased, had been recently purchased. With meticulous care, justified because of his intimate interest in such
projects, our Journalist recorded the purchase price at

£1530 Irish, subject to leasehold at £200 per annum. To bring the residence into Friendly simplicity a great deal of the ornamental work,—the stucco on the ceilings, and the costly marble chimney pieces were being removed and plainly replastered. Ornamental shrubbery from the grounds had been sold for £130 and the whole cost of repairs and alterations had been covered by this sum and others realized from disposing of superfluous parts of the building.

Irish Friends were also interested in education for those beyond the limits of the Society. In Dublin, a school was maintained, with Friends as the chief promoters, for about eighty boys and girls, ragged in appearance and many without shoes and stockings, but "kept in pretty good order." It was supported by annual subscriptions. In Cork, a Foundling Hospital claimed a visit, though Friends were not the dominant influence in it, and its support came largely from a tax on coals. William Savery's preaching, as usual, was very effective with these children who were "attentive, tender and some in tears." He left a guinea to buy them some cakes and was much pleased with the system of instruction, leading from the cradle to apprenticeship at sixteen. The need for the Hospital was forcibly brought to his attention by the leaving of a newborn infant that same evening at his host's door. It was promptly confided to the Institution. Once again, at Clonmel, was a charity school, of which Friends bore most of the burden. "It is supposed the townspeople, not Friends, are so careless it must have been dropt." It was held in the old meeting house and accommodated one hundred fifty poor, ragged children who were taught reading, writing, knitting and sewing, at a cost of about 3/6 a quarter, per child,—certainly not an expensive project.

Traveling in Ireland in those days was beset with even more excitement than in England. Extortionate rates, both by water and land, were in evidence and sincerely deprecated by the travelers. At every turn, they were over-charged by scheming publicans, obdurate postilions or obsequious, albeit exacting post proprietors. From Limerick to Cork, about sixty-three miles, cost the two Friends four guineas, part of the way being at 1/6 per mile in addition to turnpike toll and postilion fees. When off the turnpikes, "the roads were as bad as the Pennsylvania (roads) in the Spring, at breaking of the frost," a description that in those days meant even more than the same would now. It was quite customary for the local Friends to set the travelers on their way by private conveyance, with outriders on horseback, to assure company and safety.

The accounts of breakdowns sound more amusing, probably, than the experiences were at the time. In an eventful trip from Rathangan to Mountmellick on a stormy December day, Joshua Wilson's chaise was placed at the disposal of William Savery, William Farrer and Jane Watson, the latter being a local Friend previously known to the travelers, who accompanied them. Near Portarlington, one of the fellies broke. The trio walked into the town and hired a postchaise, which, in turn, broke down "in a very dirty place," less than a mile from the town, with all three Friends in it. "Jane jumped out of the window with the activity of a girl of sixteen, and W. F. and myself followed," says our chronicler. As it was still raining they took refuge in a wretched, wayside hovel where though warmly clad, they shivered for an hour, in the presence of the poor family without shoes or stockings. "I thought we ought not to complain but give thanks." In the predicament, James Pym, of Mountmellick, who had joined them, went back to Portarlington, took another chaise, and by evening, in spite of high waters, which caused a détour, all the travelers were hospitably received into the home of Jonathan Pym.

Two peculiarities of Irish travel evoked William Savery's comment. The low wheeled "cars," with baggage space in the middle, and side seats, where the passengers rode back to back, excited his curiosity almost as much as the canal facilities. The "canal coach" in Dublin, called upon appointment at 7 A.M. and transported prospective passengers to the boat. Between Dublin and Rathangan were twenty-three locks in the twenty-six Irish miles, and the voyagers enjoyed the novel mode of traveling and the scenery en route:

"These canal boats are drawn by two horses, have two cabins, very convenient with fire and a kitchen in them. The two apartments differ considerably in price and the passengers breakfast and dine in them if they chuse, which we did. We having but about five or six passengers, men and women, in the best cabin besides ourselves and some children, passed the day agreeably."

From a religious standpoint Irish Friends were at this time unhappily circumstanced. They were, at best, a small group in the Protestant minority, and in the South particularly, their pacific principles differentiated them even from the other Protestants. Mention has already been made of their troubles in the impending political disturbances and they were as uneasy also over doctrinal and theological differences among themselves. The doctrinal difficulties that were to divide and weaken the Society for the next century and longer, were generating at that time, for the first among Quakers in Ireland.

Religion is never so remote from economics and politics as to be immune from influences that affect them. At this time the economics and politics of the world were undergoing fundamental revision, just as they are today, as the concomitant and aftermath of a great social upheaval. It was then, and it is now, inevitable that men's religious attitudes and modes of thought should undergo reëxamination and revision. In America, where the political storm broke first, the religious irregularities did not appear in acute form until two decades after they had been aired in Ireland and, to a less degree, in England. But in both America and

Ireland, where political and economic changes were most fundamental, the religious differences in the Society of Friends were most disastrous. On either side of the water, and irrespective of the personalities involved and the time concerned, they were a part of the same general movement. The "deism" which William Savery, David Sands and Thomas Shillitoe everywhere found and preached against, and the rationalism which they lamented in John Hancock and Abraham Shackleton, in Ireland, were easily associated with the atheism and infidelity which the two former had met upon the Continent. Granted this association, and the general unrest evident in every other phase of human activity, it was easy to designate labels and formulae, even in a creedless sect, and then to classify orthodoxy and soundness in accordance with these, without allowance for variations.

William Savery, by early training and associations, was of the Quietist type, with the mystical element profoundly prevalent in his religious experience. He was broadly cultured and well read, as such things went in those days, but in his Irish and English ministry he was encountering, for the first time, a phase of religious experience new, not only to him, but to the religious world at large. Rationalism or "deism," as he termed it, meant anything from the atheism of Paine to the quiet, unobtrusive and entirely honest scepticism of John Hancock. With the latter, William Savery abode and fraternized, little dreaming that in a few years this gentle minister would be separated, by his own resignation, from the flock among which William Savery found him.

Over against this rationalistic conception of religion was pitted the new evangelical movement of the Methodist revival,—a movement different in many of its tenets and much of its emphasis, from Anglicanism and Quakerism alike. But one type of emphasis it did share with Quakerism, and that was the lay ministry, with little or no pecuniary recompense. The influence of Methodism, along this and similar lines, upon Quakerism itself has never been sufficiently appreciated. It appealed to Friends because of the power it developed in its great sweep of converts, so similar to the early Quaker movement. In it, certainly, William Savery found a virility fit to combat deism; but, ardently evangelical as he was, he discounted the noise and ranting of the Methodist assemblies and lamented, upon occasion, the introduction of like methods into the sessions of Friends. Moreover, his Journal and printed sermons do not reveal the elaborate evangelical phraseology of a generation later.

Only as a result of sore trial and tribulation have we of today found that Christianity is too catholic to be labeled and formulated. With the legitimate mingling, within the Quaker fold, of mystical types, evangelical types, quietist types and some rationalistic types, there is general acceptance today, for some of the things that were considered heresy in the successive Barnard, Hicksite, Beaconite and Gurney controversies. Likewise, other things have been rejected, having been proved wanting from the tried standpoint of spiritual experience. This process has enabled a creedless sect to absorb shocks that, though they have riven Quakerism into factions, have probably preserved for the Society the best life and thought of all, and have thrown into the discard unbending ecclesiastical and doctrinal certainty, on the one hand, and vagaries, excesses and unsound extravagances, on the other. There is no justification in reviving these ancient difficulties and dissensions, unless by so doing, we can precipitate the truth with the acid of the controversy and so prepare ourselves historically and spiritually for a degree of Christian urbanity and catholicity, sufficient to meet like crises in the life of the Church, if they should arise today.

At the time of William Savery's visit to Ireland, Abraham Shackleton was the best known of those whose irregularities were causing concern. He and William Savery had had some correspondence, but had never met until the latter came to Waterford in January, 1798. There is some indication in the Journal that William Savery would have been glad to have avoided meeting Abraham Shackleton. Certain it is that he had no expectation of going to Ballitore where the Shackletons for three generations had kept school. But Abraham Shackleton came a distance of forty-two miles to him one winter night, just as he had settled himself for an evening's writing at his lodgings. With the visitor came Robert Greer. They ensconced themselves in William Savery's room and a lengthy conversation ensued. Most of the difficulties of this period centered in the effort to harmonize the Old and the New Testaments, particularly regarding the God-inspired wars of the Hebrews. Abraham Shackleton and his associates were unable to give credence to the historical narrative of a God who commanded and directed the conquest of Canaan and the extirpation of the enemies of Israel, to the bitter end, in contrast with the loving Father of the New Testament. He therefore rejected the first five books of Moses. In the New Testament he believed the Evangelists were poor historians and that "Paul brought much of his Epistles from the feet of Gamaliel," in consequence of which "they are rabbinical stuff, in many places." With a consistency, more analytical than practical, he saw "little if any need of books of any kind on religious subjects. They only darken the mind and keep it from turning itself wholly unto God, the Fountain of all Light and Life." He especially disliked Friends' Journals and

"had but a light opinion of ministry and discipline and all secondary helps in general. * * * Christ was a good man, the Leader of the people, because he was wholly obedient to this Light, which he was, in an especial manner, filled with."

Abraham Shackleton made a deep and very troublesome impression upon William Savery,—deeper than he liked:

# THE SOCIETY OF FRIENDS IN IRELAND

"I perceived all this was accompanied with a pretended looking towards a far greater state of perfection and redemption than our Society has yet arrived at. For my part I could not see eye to eye with him nor unite in his extraordinary expressions and opinions, and I really feel a fear they will produce much hurt, if he and others in this nation are not greatly on their watch, in deep self abasement, his talents and morality making error in his hands more dangerous. We separated without reaping much satisfaction, at least on my side."

There ensued for William Savery a night, mostly sleepless, "musing on the conversation," and when he slept:

"I thought or dreamt that I saw a man in a field, who appeared plucking out a few tares that was growing among choise wheat. But he pulled up more wheat than tares and trod down abundance of it under his feet. I thought he had far better have left them alone until the harvest."

The next day Abraham Shackleton sent a letter to William Savery "in which he appears lovingly disposed towards me, but evidently wrong, so far as I am able to judge, in some of his opinions." After two days another letter followed as Abraham Shackleton set off for home, of which last fact William Savery records,—"and I am not sorry; he has given me much exercise."

In 1797, near the close of William Savery's labors in Ireland, Hannah Barnard, an American minister, liberated by New York Yearly Meeting, appeared in Ireland with religious opinions nearly in harmony with those that had caused the body of Friends concern. She was a woman of strong convictions and fearless perseverance in them. She had had some difficulty in obtaining her certificate, the Committee to which it had been referred in her home Monthly Meeting having withheld it for nine months before its issuance. In Ireland, however, she felt strong unity with the views of the radical Friends, and grew in their belief faster perhaps than any of them did. David Sands was all the while in Ireland, mourning over her fallen state with a heartfelt pathos that refused to find consolation. If he had been less persistent in combating Hannah Barnard she might have caused less trouble. As it was, she was closely followed by several ministers and by a Committee of the Yearly Meeting appointed to visit the Quarterly and Monthly Meetings. She remained in Ireland until the spring of 1800 and then went to England, where she was finally requested to return home. She appealed from Devonshire Monthly Meeting, which had pronounced this judgment, to London and Middlesex Quarterly Meeting and then to London Yearly Meeting, in each case having the judgment of the subordinate meeting sustained. She was finally disowned by her Monthly Meeting in New York.

In 1802, the Irish meetings declared their disunity with the doctrines that had been so thoroughly discussed during the past several years and disowned many members.

"In the Province of Ulster, all the Elders were displaced from their station; and a considerable number of Ministers and Elders in various parts were disowned from membership." [1]

And so the sad story ran on, to be duplicated and enlarged in America a generation later, in the great and most disastrous Separation of 1827-28.

One can but feel that all these things might, by Christian charity, have been avoided. Many, nay most, of the doctrines that caused concern have since evaporated. Much of the divergence of opinion may well be attributed to variance of definition, rather than to fundamental difference, and even in basic beliefs, where there was undoubtedly an unsound trend, the spirit of the times and the unrest that actuated men's minds and hearts might have been the earnest of a broad spirit of forbearance, through which, if appreciated, both in Ireland and America, much of the toil and moil of dissension and separation might have been avoided. The unavoidable stigma attaching to

[1] Hodgson: *Historical Memoirs of Friends,* 395.

the Quaker opposition to all wars lies in the fact that in our own affairs "irrepressible conflicts" and "manifest destinies" have found us at war among ourselves to the degradation of that Truth which each faction has invariably claimed as its sole and exclusive possession.

## CHAPTER XXIV

# ENGLAND AT THE CLOSE OF THE EIGHTEENTH CENTURY

With the termination of hostilities between England and America, the fraternal bonds between the two groups of the Society of Friends on either side of the Atlantic were reëstablished with alacrity. Though interrupted by non-intercourse, cordiality of relations between British and American Friends had not suffered from wartime strains. The decade following the declaration of peace witnessed a remarkable interchange of itinerant ministers across the Atlantic.

William Savery went purely from religious concern to preach the Gospel, especially to those not of the Society of Friends, and to visit the families of Friends. It so happens, however, that this period constitutes one of the most momentous decades in European history. All unwittingly, the American ministers of the Gospel who toured Europe in that decade were witnessing conditions and changes of which they saw and recorded the effect, but of the real meaning of which they were as ignorant as the rulers and statesmen proved to be. From every viewpoint,—political, social, economic and religious,—it would be difficult to find a more precipitous decade than the last ten years of the Eighteenth Century. It was a period both of consummations and beginnings, a transition stage between two eras. Posterity, with the evidence all in, can judge, weigh and evaluate, where the actors could but guess and surmise, or at the best, experiment. We know now the event; they only knew events. We can study cause and effect; they were so close to facts that they lacked the perspective by which to judge them.

Even in so long a period as a decade, it is difficult to assign a definite date for world results, long in germination. The French Revolution of that decade was really inaugurated by the American Revolution of 1776 and the consequent wars lasted in acute form till Waterloo in 1815. The Industrial Revolution of that decade had no dramatic climax, to which a convenient date can be pinned. It was simply growing,—accumulating a vast burden of intolerable conditions upon the backs of a people, between 1782 and perhaps 1819, when Peterloo dramatically revealed to unwilling England the appalling situation of her submerged populace.

Religiously it was the same. Dissent had been assaulting the Establishment throughout the entire Century but the growth of Nonconformity and its serious recognition as a factor in the life of the nation awaited the efforts of the great Methodist preachers, Wesley and Whitefield, culminating in the last decade of the Century.

In addition to these internal transformations, Britain was involved in a constant series of Alliances or Coalitions with Continental Powers, fighting France for twenty years from 1795 to 1815. In that period she saw every phase of human passion exemplified in the maelstrom of Europe, and herself partook of the reaction that is the inevitable reflex of revolution. Desperately hugging her insular isolation, her foreign policy evolved from paying foreign mercenaries to fight her battles, to the development of a Continental army of her own, fit to cope with Napoleon on the Peninsula and in Flanders, while her navy fought its way from the Nile to Trafalgar and the supremacy of the seas.

So much, therefore, of consummation and so much of beginnings did this decade of 1790 contain, but most of all of beginnings. And it was these beginnings that the pages of the American Quaker ministers of the Gospel, itinerant in those times, record with a deeply sensitive appreciation of the wretchedness and misery about them and a devout and utter dependence upon a Higher Power to bring peace and happiness once again into the land. Of these Journals, William Savery's account is the fullest and completest, in references to social and economic conditions; as to political and military affairs it is important, but in a purely incidental way. Naturally, its ripest expression is with reference to religious life and conditions. I propose, therefore, to take up the subject from the two main aspects which he treats, and to weave into the account the others, so far as pertinent, so that the narrative may have the setting, as far as possible, in which William Savery penned it.

## ECONOMIC ENGLAND

Eighteenth Century England was probably the happiest example that can be found in history of a conservative society, admittedly based upon what has been well called [1] the "harmonizing" rather than the "equality" of classes. The changes of the past few generations had been momentous, even fundamental. A bloodless revolution had been effected, religious revival had awakened new life in the nation and great wars had been fought in America and India,—in the main, to the credit of British prowess. These events had, however, little effect on the real life of the people. To the small farmer and yeoman it mattered little whether a Stuart or a Guelph sat upon the throne; his squire was the same and his rents were collected just as inevitably under either. Nor did India and America especially appeal to him; his lot as a free-born Briton, with an unwritten Constitution and under social conditions hallowed by the tradition of centuries, was all-in-all to him and needed no change. He accepted the superiority of the

[1] Trevelyan: *British History in the Nineteenth Century.*

county families, gentry and squires, as unhesitatingly as he did the system of livings and advowsons that gave him his ease-loving parson and his respectable, but penniless curate. Britain was solid and content to the core.

About 1760 began, in a small way, the series of inventions and changes in methods that galloped along through the next seventy years, uprooting old ideals and foundations, waxing hotter and hotter in their pace as the Century waned, until by 1800 England was in the throes of the Industrial Revolution, so-called, and neither statesmen, philosophers nor philanthropists could predict its course or accurately interpret its meaning. The last decade of the Century was a vast, accelerated swirl of political propaganda, actuated by the French Revolution, unemployment and poverty. The unrest was due to the transition from home work to factory and machine production. Pauperism, stalking gaunt over the land, was but slightly alleviated by the poor rates.

Both farming and manufacture had been upon a cottage basis. The "cotter" had had more than a Saturday night fame and usefulness in England and Scotland. He, himself, tilled the small plot, adjacent to the Common, where his cow was pastured, and to the woodland where he could, under strict surveillance, lest he shoot or snare a rabbit or partridge, obtain his winter's supply of firewood. Hard by was the Manor House, where his rents were paid and his loyalty, often of several generations standing, ungrudgingly bestowed upon his squire.

The cotter's wife and daughters were the manufacturing end of the enterprise, with his assistance in winter and at odd times. They spun and wove, in addition to their household duties, and the product was regularly gathered, by itinerant factors, with long trains of pack horses that were able to brave the deep roads of the period before Macadam taught England the feasibility of a hard surface. There was much poverty, much deprivation and much suffering, but, though far short of the ideal, England had been passably happy and truly loyal to superior breeding. It was the last ray of a setting feudal sun, and its brillance was greater than its warmth. Wealth, so far as it was known, was still in lands.

The country landscape of the England of today, which so readily excites the admiration of Americans, was literally created at the end of the Eighteenth Century. Ancient England from the time of Piers Plowman had been projected into the Georgian period, with little substantial improvement. The accredited type of production was carried on by small farmers living on a cluster of houses along a street, or around the Church. Around and to the rear of the village, stretched the open field, unditched and unfenced, but divided into many dozens or hundreds of strips, relatively minute, and not unlike, in arrangement, the plots in the modern school gardens. Invariably the immemorial custom of crop routine bound the tiller and precluded enterprise and innovation.

The first general Enclosing Act in England was not passed until 1801. For many decades before that date special acts, fitting particular cases and at the instance of promoters of definite projects, had been passed frequently. The aim of all enclosing was to combine the little strips and to oust the independent cotter, in favor of the small proprietor or tenant farmer, under the great landlord. Readers of Bulwer-Lytton's "The Caxtons" will recall Trevelyan as one of these "improving" or "enclosing" landlords in fiction that was true to the day. The result was undoubtedly favorable to production. The French privateers had made the foreign grain supply, small though it was in those days, very precarious, practically preventing importation. Agriculture, during the last quarter of the Century, became very profitable for the capitalist. Enclosing was definitely getting under way. The hedges and ditches of the England of today began to appear. Between

1793 and 1809 four and one half millions of acres were added to the tilled area of England and Wales.[1] So prevalent had enclosing become that much of the smooth ground, available for hunting and for the cavalry tactics of the Wars of the Commonwealth period, had yielded to the inevitable hedge and ditch.

William Savery's incidental comment upon this phase of British life in 1798 is interesting:

"Newmarket is remarkable for horse-racing. There were many horses training, round the extensive plains, the smallest legged ones, I ever saw. The town itself is but small and poor, except at the time of sporting, but has very good Inns. From thence, we rode on through an open country, without hedge or ditch, and very few farms on the road, to Boune Bridge, and there dined. From thence, having five miles more of heath to cross, we saw many sportsmen and their horses, with servants and a great company of hounds, coursing for a poor hare, but they had not then found any."

It is most remarkable that a minister in the Society of Friends of that period should deign to notice and record such worldly sports. Such entries in the Journal were strictly out of accord with common practice of the time, when itinerants, superficially at least, kept their recorded observations unsullied by mundane references. On another occasion, William Savery mentions both hunting and the absence of enclosure.

"We passed again a great deal of commons and heath in Cambridgeshire. Another party were hunting a poor buck they had turned out. I never saw so much open ground as in Cambridgeshire, in any part of England together; a vast deal of it might be cultivated."

It is easy to surmise from the concluding phrase that William Savery was in full accord with the enclosing policy and the economic reasons back of it.

In some sections, notably near Bath, in Somerset and in the Vale of Cluyd, Denbighshire, Wales, these hedges were

[1] Traill: *Social England*, V, 458.

of sufficient antiquity to constitute a timber supply, "as good as any I have seen in England." He took especial delight in this productiveness,—"the fields and meadows, luxuriant in their produce and abounding in timber trees in the hedges and in clumps." But even more did he delight in the cattle. In the hills and valleys of Cumberland were many small sheep, "said to be the sweetest mutton in England." This small breed "almost all with black faces and black legs" also abounded in Lancashire and Westmoreland. In Suffolk and Norfolk they were larger than in Cumberland, but it was in Warwickshire that he found them "as fine as any in England. They will weigh from fifteen to twenty pounds per quarter and carry from seven to ten pounds of wool."

In the midland counties the cattle were abundant, "generally without horns, not large, but round and fat. Several droves of them were going to London." The rich pastures of Warwickshire seemed especially adapted to the "large, handsome cows" of that section, but they did not surpass the cattle of the damp pastures in the Cumberland valleys. Of the latter, he wrote:

"They keep fine cows, who give from 10 to 20 quarts of milk a day apiece. Milk unskimmed is abt 2d a quart in Kendal; skimmed abt 1 penny, ½ penny. Butter abt 10d, meat abt 5 or 6d, except beef 8d. Milk is brought to market in things like our churns on each side of a horse, with a brass cock at bottom, very handy. Their cheese is but small like Pennsylvania farmers."

He also states the weight of these cows in North England to have been from eight hundred to one thousand pounds when fat. In Cheshire they were noticeably smaller.

Later when in London, a visit to the Smithfield Market, with Joseph Savory as guide, revealed to William Savery the ultimate destination of much of the livestock. He describes it as follows:

"It was one of the market days. There were abundance of fine cattle. The cows generally larger than ours, but the oxen about the same, from six to ten hundred weight. The sheep much heavier wooled than in America, but not so much larger as I expected to have seen; pigs and calves of all sizes—it was worth seeing."

As one would expect from the prevalence of cattle, hay was the most mentioned of crops, although wheat, oats and barley "all at one time ripe," had a prominent place in the damp husbandry of Cumberland, where it had rained almost continuously for a month when William Savery visited that section in September, 1797. Much of the wheat had sprouted in the shocks and a good deal of hay had rotted in the field. In other sections, notably in Warwick and near Ackworth School, in Yorkshire, haying was toward under better weather conditions. More women than men were in evidence in the hayfields. Ackworth's eighty acres were mostly grass-land, "on which they keep a number of fine cows and make much hay."

Londoners of the present day would hardly recognize the pursuits described by William Savery in the vicinity of the City:

"Went out at half past four in the Newington Coach, with my friend, Nancy Capper and some others to Newington. It was high hay-making time and a very fine evening. The lots about London seemed alive with people, making and getting in hay. Men have 2/6 per day and beer and women 1/6 for hay-making and 4/0 per acre for mowing. Visited Jonathan Hoare and family and viewed his vast improvements, his piggery of about 200 fine hogs and pigs. His dairy is also large, and extensive hen houses for raising fowls, which as well hay and other produce of a farm and abundance of garden vegetables, he intends raising for London market. He has laid out within a twelve month in order to pursue his scheme of farming, in improvements, in buildings, &c, perhaps £10,000; has about 72 acres of land; hopes it will yield him 8 or 9 per cent profit upon his expenditures. This is farming with the rank of a nobleman, everything around him in the highest stile of elegance."

William Savery does not record, in England, the distress in the rural districts that he found in Ireland and in the London slums. He seems more impressed with the amazing production that the new type of farming was yielding. The French privateering had forced the situation, and William Savery's visit coincided with the first appreciable effects thereof. England perforce settled down to as near self-sufficient production as possible. It meant literal starvation to many in the cities, but it swelled the coffers of the capitalist farmers, almost as much to their astonishment as to that of the economists of the time, who themselves were at a loss to explain the situation adequately.

The agricultural boom saved England in her extremity and enabled her to turn her attention to the manufacturing that, in the end, was the undoing of France. But it was at a terrible cost in depleted man power in the country, and, as we shall see, in sweated women and children in the cities. For enclosing and migration to the towns were concurrent processes. Each was both a cause and an effect. In the towns the result was child-labor, sweating and slums. In the country the change was no less marked, because the former cotter became the farm laborer, or the dependent tenant farmer. "An able farmer," wrote William Savery of T. Cropper, a Friend near Wigan, "tho not on his own land; few in this country are." Rentals, too, in this north country were high. Lord Lawnsdale (Lonsdale), formerly Sir James Lowther, whom we shall meet later in coal and shipping, was landlord to many, and oppressive at that. His tenants paid from thirty shillings to four pounds an acre annually with the privilege of some commons on the mountains. William Savery adds, however, in extenuation of the noble Lord, that, "having the right of tithes, he never suffers distraint upon Friends, consequently they come free." In that day, such leniency was praiseworthy.

It was only the most able of the farmers that could make the shift from small owners, divested of their holdings and commons, by the enclosing, into the upper class of tenant farmers. In most instances they were given utterly inadequate compensation for divesting them of their rights in commons, entirely too little to enable them to purchase enough land or equipment to set up independently. Naturally the only recourse was to hire out as a laborer. In spite of the migration to the towns, so great was the excess of rural labor available that wages fell to insignificant amounts and the usual condition of the agricultural laborer in the decade under discussion approached pauperism, with doles from the poor rates. So acute did this situation become, that, in spite of war prosperity for the upper classes, the poor, both in town and country, in 1795, were actually facing famine. William Savery noted the improved methods, palliatives though they were, of relief,

"Walked to the soup-house in Spittalfields, where a few Friends were busily employed in distributing about fourteen hundred quarts of soup, which they do in about two hours,—the poor people bless the Quakers and seem very grateful for this relief."

A recent generalization summarizes the situation well:

"Hollow-cheeked, ragged, housed in hovels, the peasantry of England degenerated year by year under the eyes of men who were doubling and trebling their rents, and who tried to silence Cobbet as an 'incendiary' because, when no one else dared, he pointed out the contrast." [1]

Enclosure had worked a vital change in the English social system by the time of William Savery's visit. Its full effects were not even then apparent and the alleviation of the evils incident to it was to await the agitation of two generations later, when Cobden and Bright toured the country again and again in the fight against the same class of landlords and farmers that had begun to batten on the sweat of the poor in the closing days of the Eighteenth Century. The evils of the Corn Laws were then patent to all but the privileged who profited from them. Even then, Bright and Cobden, with some degree of appreciation of the economic causes of the distress pressing on the consciences of the people, had to wage their fight before an electorate,

[1] Trevelyan: *British History in the Nineteenth Century*, 149.

far more representative of the privileged than of those crying "Give us bread."

As the ancient commons were furrowed by the plows of the new type of agriculturist, and the derelicts of the farm drifted more and more to the industrial towns as a refuge, with them, perforce, went the children. Frequently the children were in demand when the parents were superfluous. The exploitation of tiny hands was more profitable than the hiring of their elders, and the adults, defeated in their efforts, by their very superiority, turned to the paupers' dole, and fed their children more and more into the maw of the new monster that had first deprived them of a trade and then of a living.

Population in the newly developed industrial towns increased by leaps and bounds, and new markets for produce developed rapidly to feed the city dwellers. A new division of labor became apparent, as the artisan and his family ceased to raise any of the food they consumed, and, dependent upon their industrial callings alone, bought their food from the purveyors. The farm and the city became interdependent just as their denizens became class conscious enough to develop a friction, evident in the suspicion with which both producers and consumers began to view the factor or middle-man.

Along with the shift in population came the inventions. Watt's steam engine first operated in Manchester in 1789 and in Glasgow in 1792. Cartwright's power loom, by means of which the weaving process at last caught up with the spinning in speed of production, was first effective in 1789. For long before, the spinning "frames" and "mules" of Hargreaves and Arkwright had been too speedy for the weaver. The workers resented the new speed and the reduction of hand labor. A Manchester factory, where four hundred of Cartwright's looms had been installed, paid the price of initiative, in 1791, when it was burnt to the ground, with every indication of incendiarism.

And with the other factors of change came the shift in wealth. Not only did property change in kind,—from land to personalty; it changed even more fundamentally, from one class to another. Society and social status slipped like a landslide, depleting the old and enriching the new locality and class. Shropshire, Staffordshire and Warwick took on, as manufacturing centers, the importance that had previously attached to Sussex, Kent, Essex and Surrey in agriculture and foreign commerce. The Friends of William Savery's time and he himself had a reverence, almost approaching obsequiousness, for the gentry. The attendance of the nobility or office holders at the appointed meetings is sometimes noted in a manner that modern Friends would hesitate to use. Many of the Friends were merchants, a class that for generations had been despised by the landed class, but for whom this decade of transition was already preparing the middle class ascendency, in business and politics. The shift of wealth to the new class of manufacturers and merchants was even then in full progress, but it did not attain formal recognition till it swept in the new and out the old, in the Reform Bill of 1832.

It is hard to realize that society of 1800 knew very little of stocks and bonds and even mortgages in their present ubiquitous sense. Few people saved anything, as there was little to invest in but gold or land. The former was precarious from robbers and bore no interest; the latter was impossible to any but the rich. The new wealth, however, came from "profits," as distinguished from the "rents" of old. Aggregations of capital were even then creating the new and lusty monster of modern industrial and financial life,—the joint stock company or corporation. With it, investment became popularized and open to all on a small or large scale, yielding dividends or bond-interest. Even though restricted in its activities in those days, the London Stock Exchange presented some features of modern frenzy to William Savery:

"Pasd by the Stock Exchange on my way home, they acted like people who had taken leave of their Senses."

The celerity of the change was astounding. Gone were the packhorses. Gather the factory output in a dray and store it. Concentrate the "hands" in vast charnal buildings, dark, damp and often filthy; sweat them, of all ages, into a tumultuous production of the "goods" that England may supply the antipodes and garner the wealth of the seven seas in return. No more of the self-sufficient villages, supplying all their own needs and producing little surplus. The new over-production requires new territory, and commerce must depend upon inland transport to the sea, and beyond it, to the primitive communities that know not industry. Strange indeed, and full of portent for the next century and beyond! In these industrial beginnings abode the war-wraiths of the future, with commercial and colonial rivalry intensified into a fierce struggle for spheres of influence, places in the sun, mandates and open doors.

The commercial and industrial activity in England did not escape William Savery's observant eye. His close inspections and minute descriptions indicate that he was interested in the changes, although neither he nor anyone of that generation realized how drastic they were. In Shropshire he

"passed by a great number of furnaces and forges at Ketly and round about there, many of them belonging to W. Reynolds, son of Richard Reynolds, which with the coal pits and smoak from many steam machines, etc, made the country appear black for many miles, covering all the trees, shrubs, houses, etc, which with the blackness of the people, and many fires for charing the stone coal, altogether formed an extraordinary scene."

Sheffield, where "the most curious cutlery (perhaps in the world) is made," was a fit rival for Ketly, it being "a very busy place in a valley covered with perpetual smoke." As in most early manufacturing towns, so at Sheffield, the coal pits were hard by the furnaces. Transportation of coal was little thought of save by carts overland or by water routes. Says our observer:

"The coal pits run far under the town. The blackness of the houses with its numerous poor manufactures and the continual sulpherous smell, make it altogether no desirable place to live in."

Near Brosely in Shropshire the valley of the Severn for a mile or more was filled with iron works.

"It has a very dark appearance, even the trees and bushes are quite blackened with the smoke; and in the night the fires have a terrific appearance."

Similarly at Manchester, where D. Holt employed about four hundred men, women and children in spinning cottons:

"the machines for which really astonished me, being beyond anything I had conceived wonderful. Men and women earn here from 15 to 18d a day, and find themselves, and children from 4 to 9. They make the thread for velvets, fustians, thickest yarns, &c. Two machines are tended by a man and two children and spin abt 80 threads at a time. The whole of the works turn by two steam engines. They spin the cotton so fine for muslin that one pound makes a thread abt 100 miles long. The force of steam is amazing. Coals are cheap here and the whole works use abt 40 bushells a day, which cost abt 20/ sterling."

Another visit, just outside Manchester to Thomas Hoyle's mill, revealed much the same situation. He employed about one hundred hands, almost all men, in a steam and hydraulic factory. Being a finisher of velvets, jeans, calicoes and all cotton stuffs, he ran practically everything, even fine muslins

"over a red hot cylinder, in order to smooth them. Their dyes are mostly beech or birch bark and logwood, both of which they grind to powder."

The modern dye-works has not progressed in its essentials much beyond the hot cylinder and the powdered dyes, justifying William Savery's summary:

"These manufactures exceed in ingenuity, expence and number of hands employed, anything I had hitherto seen."

At Whitehaven, Cumberland, in the far north of England, we get another peep at the coal industry, in the first stages of monopoly, with no fear of prosecution for restraint of trade or unfair competition:

"Whitehaven's trade (is) coal, with very little else, which Lord Lawnsdale engrosses much to himself and suffers no ships to load but such as take their iron work and cordage at works he is concerned in. And all the coals in the neighborhood but his are inferior in quality and are brought far by land, which makes them come higher. This is a sample among many in this country of the arbitrary powers, exercised by the rich and great over others. * * *

"We visited several coal pitts that were at work, some by means of horses and others by steam engines. Several were 120 fathom or 240 yards deep and were working a considerable distance under the sea, where large ships ride at anchor above them. In them are horses and asses, with little carts and men, women and boys at work for small wages. The steam engines hoist from abt 10 to 12 ton per hour, which, being on high ground, they load 30 hundred in a cart with iron wheels which runs upon iron sleepers down to the ships that are loading. The horses are only wanted to draw the empty carts back again. Firing for a family much cheaper than in Philadelphia, abt 12 Winchester bushells for 4/0 delivered at their doors. Two fires a year cost abt 4½ guineas."

And so the Journal continues. The cloth mills of Kendal, the pins at Worcester, the check linens, coarse woolens and hats at Carlisle, and the serges, hats and tanneries of Cockermouth, attest as well the scope of William Savery's travels as the intimacy of his observation. It was, however, in coal and iron that the new wonders were being wrought; in them that the novelty of the thing lay. In the villages about Wolverhampton the iron workers wrought on a small scale, in their modest smithies, unlike the works at Ketly. At Birmingham, there seem to have been both, in the "several handsome streets and divers very black ones, crowded on every side with iron manufactory or smith shops." At Birmingham, William Savery was entertained by Richard and Elizabeth Cadbury, the latter a sister of Ann Warder, wife of John Warder, of Philadelphia. The Cadburys received the traveler with the full intimacy and affection that existed between the two families in Philadelphia, so that he was given more than usual opportunity to see the main features of the city, both charitable and industrial. Here was a factory for making paper japanned ware, "as elegant as any in England," buttonboxes, servers, fruit trays and tea chests; here, too, was a factory for plated goods, carried on by one Robeson, "a Friend with one leg," whose process for plating silver upon iron "to me was curious, having had no conception of the manner it was done before."

William Savery saw both types of manufacture in and around Birmingham,—the cottage production and the factory production:

"In these manufactorys, men, women, girls and boys are all employed and the surprising facility, which by the help of curious machines, they expedite their business, is not to be conceived without seeing it."

As to the cottage manufacture, he was disillusioned. Says he:

"The goods sent abroad called Birmingham, Sheffield and Manchester wares, are a great part of them made in the villages and country places round about those towns for many miles, and the poor workmen bring them in to factors in the towns once a week, and just live, as the saying is, from hand to mouth."

Northamptonshire was the center of straw goods manufacture. At an inn in these parts, many curious articles in straw were on exhibit, and for sale through the waiters, who, like their predatory successors of the present day, "took care to allow themselves a large per cent for vending them." This work in straw was on the cottage basis, all the villages round about being occupied in it, and many hundreds getting their bread by it.

In London, Joseph and Thomas Foster conducted calico works on the collective factory system at Bromley. A number of visitors drank tea there one afternoon and then inspected the works. They employed "many people and could print between seven and eight hundred different patterns from the plates now in their possession. The machinery is curious and the expedition very great." Friends were active in many other lines of business in London, of which more will be said later, but manufacturing was not so prevalent among them in the metropolis.

The Society of Friends did not understand the crushing nature of the wage slavery that was beginning. No more did the economists and statesmen. If society as a whole had been seriously concerned, more blame could be bestowed,—nay, if we of today were more alive to present industrial conditions, we could the more consistently criticize. As it happened, England was still operating under the old Elizabethan Statute of Artificers (1562) requiring seven years apprenticeship for entrance upon a trade, an act strenuously upheld by the master mechanics and craftsmen themselves and under which they partially regulated each trade. Beyond that, the new doctrine of laissez-faire was supreme. Poverty and misery were universally attributed to natural laws, as inevitable, and due to defects of character, sloth or laziness. Religion was cited, not to show a better way in this world, but as a hope for another world, where the iniquities and inequalities, inevitable in this, would be abolished for all who accepted their lot meekly. This strange doctrine was common, both to established and dissenting thought, and was even more obnoxious, to modern ideas, in the application of charity of a direct and degrading type. A dole of money, with a religious tract and a pious adjuration to rest content in that station where God had placed the unfortunate, were, all too often, the extent of relief, even if they were not told, as was a dying pauper in an Essex workhouse,—"And thankful you ought to be, that you have a hell to go to." [1] In visiting slums, prisons and workhouses, William Savery often records gifts

[1] Frederic Harrison, in Bury; Freedom of Thought, 223.

of money to the poor and squalid, sometimes with a suggestion in the prisons that they buy beer with the gift. Large sums were given him for this sort of distribution by rich Friends, who trusted in his discretion in application.

Even in the enlightened circles of earnest people, like the More sisters, and in the political conscience of Wilberforce, decent living for working people, as a whole, was considered a millennial and wholly impractical thing. Higher wages would simply mean more children, and the increased expense thus involved would defeat all prosperity and foster broods of the unfit and ignorant; hence alleviation alone was possible, prevention never.

By Acts of Parliament of 1799 and 1800, with Wilberforce working as an eager aide to Pitt, in the last year of the latter's ministry, the so-called Combination Laws were passed, forbidding trade unionism. England was feeling the iron in its soul, under the duress of foreign war, and was ripe for any restrictive or repressive legislation that seemed to oppose Jacobinism and Democracy (which were the Bolshevism of those days). No clearer instance can be found in history of war's effect in postponing liberal and forward movements in a nation's progress than the collapse, for a full generation, of the enlightened legislative program that the young Pitt had in preparation in 1792, when the storm of the French Revolution broke over Britain. Not until 1824-5 was trade unionism legalized, and not until 1833 was any kind of Factory Act passed to alleviate the intolerable conditions of the child-consuming and woman-destroying Molochs of British industrialism.

## CHAPTER XXV

# RELIGIOUS ENGLAND

To Americans, the history of Non-conformity in Great Britain in the Eighteenth Century is puzzling. With no experience of an Established Church and the system of tithes, advowsons and livings, incident to it, and with very little experience of tests and judicial or dynastic oaths, it is almost impossible to realize that the Dissenters from the Anglican Church were, throughout the entire Century, subjected to inconveniences, indignities, distraints and levies that were likelier to the system from which Protestantism came forth than of established Protestantism itself. Be that as it may, the political features of dissent during the entire Century present an unvarying effort, seemingly fruitless, to set aside the disabilities still attaching to non-Anglican Protestants.

The political importance of orthodox belief was sealed during the days of the Commonwealth by the Corporation Act (1661) enabling only those who participated in the Lord's Supper, according to the rites of the Church of England, to hold office. The Conventicle Act of 1670 forbade meetings of non-conformists of more than four people beside the family. It imposed heavy penalties. The Test Act of 1673 soon followed, aimed more at Papists than Quakers, but intimately involving the increasing numbers of the latter. It required that an official-elect must sign a declaration against the doctrine of transubstantiation and produce a certificate of sacraments partaken under Anglican forms.

The Act of Toleration of 1689 left the earlier Acts unrepealed, but annulled the penalties of the Conventicle Act and allowed non-conforming worship, under strict surveillance, and upon the due registration of the meeting houses. From this arose the distinction between church and chapel on the one hand and meeting house on the other; a distinction that even to this day connotes a difference between formality and simplicity of worship. The Conventicle Act was not finally repealed until 1812.

In the Eighteenth Century there were four separate attempts to alleviate the disabilities attaching to dissent. An early attempt in 1717 was only succeeded by three others in 1787, 1789 and 1790, the last being aided by the powerful eloquence of Fox, the great forerunner of British Liberalism. All of these attempts failed and immediately afterwards came the French Revolution and the terror in England, incident to it. From that time, liberalism, reform and tolerance were relegated to the background, and for forty years England wallowed in a slough of distrust, suspicion and bigotry. In the earthquake of the Revolution, as we shall see hereafter, the institutions of England took on a sanctity by reason of their establishment that ignored, resented and suppressed criticism of them, however just. The Establishment was *the* Institution, par example, and to it clung all the conservatism of England with a desperation that would seem ludicrous, had not the present generation witnessed a popular stampede, as wild and as unreasoned, in the red terror following in the wake of the Great War. Not until 1828 was the Test Act of 1673 repealed. At that time England had again caught her stride and could look with some degree of complacency upon the events that from 1792 to 1815 kept her in constant warfare with France, and killed at the source any attempts toward liberalism in politics or toleration in religion.

In the face of all these negative disabilities, Dissent flourished. The number of meeting houses registered from 1731 to 1740 was only four hundred forty-eight. But in the period from 1791 to 1800, the period during which William Savery was active in England, 4,394 meeting houses were registered. The vast majority of these were in all probability very humble affairs, and mostly of the Methodist type. Therein, however, lay a deep significance, and one of more importance to the Society of Friends than is usually realized.

The old type of non-conformity of the Baptists, Presbyterians and Quakers of the Commonwealth was, by this time, largely a tradition. Going no further than the Friends themselves, the difference between the spiritual fervor and abandon of the First Publishers of Truth and the cultivated, well educated and respectable Quaker ministry of 1790 is apparent upon the surface. To the former, open-air preaching, whether from a barrel top in a London street or among the fells and moors of Yorkshire, brought the adherence of all classes. The fishmongers and kitchen maids were as readily reached and convinced by the lay preaching as were the scholars. There had been to it an urge, a stimulus or momentum that smacked of the open air, free from glass, incense and priestly rites; and England had been psychologically and spiritually ready for just that manifestation. In the century following the Commonwealth, that momentum had eased off just in proportion as the creeds, forms and respectability of the dissenting sects became more definitely set. They too, then, had their regular places of worship, their own clergy or recommended ministers, in short, their own organization, well formulated and concrete, but, of course, lacking the connection with the State.

The particular controversy, in the last decade of the Eighteenth Century, centered around "deism." While it really belongs more to the religious philosophy of the early Nineteenth Century, its roots ran far back. William Savery frequently mentions its baleful influence on religious life, and attributes to it much of the loss of religious fervor. In its devotion to a religion of nature as all sufficient, and in its efforts to rationalize and explain all the Biblical narrative, it was the exact opposite of the early Quaker mysticism, with its intuitive certainty of spiritual things and the new evangelical doctrine that was sweeping England.

The dispute began in theological circles alone. It passed thence to philosophy, as such disputes are ever wont to do. Butler and Berkeley, of the orthodox group, found early favor among the Society of Friends. After them came Hume, who, as historian and philosopher, shifted the issue to far more subtle grounds of skepticism. History and natural science were ushered in anew, with their bearing on religion and theology. Rationalism in philosophy and science, attaching through them to religion, brought them unfortunately into disrepute and suspicion from the religious standpoint. A generation later, Huxley, Darwin and Wallace revolutionized scientific thought and method, and precipitated the controversy between science and religion that raged during the rest of the Nineteenth Century. In a sense, the "deism" of William Savery's time was the forerunner of the later unrest, the vague stirrings of discontent at the antiquated forms, arid theology and grafting politics of a bishop-ridden church.

By far the greatest favorite, among the orthodox writers of the period, among the Society of Friends in America was Paley, whose "Evidences of Christianity" appeared in 1794. It was long a standard text-book in Friends' schools and colleges. It would be hard to designate any other book, originating outside the Society, that has had a profounder influence upon the ethics and philosophy of the Friends. It was likewise a direct counter-blast to the deistical doctrines which Methodism, Anglicanism and most of Quakerism were opposing.

Fortunately for the Friends, their lack of creed and their rigid formlessness preserved them from some of the eccle-

siastical tendencies which barred other old forms of dissent
from the approach to the poor and lowly that had been the
especial stronghold of early non-conformity.   In the matter
of preaching, the Friends occupied a peculiar position also.
While other sects, both Anglican and of the Dissent, were
stressing ecclesiastical training, Friends still clung to a lay
ministry.   This feature brought them nearer to the populace, though the tendency toward a tacit segregation of
"recommended" ministers, as apart from the "priesthood of
believers" and holier by reason of the recommendation, was
well on its way to draw them, too, away from common
people.   The ancient institution of tithes in support of the
Established Church was still alive in some parts of England,
though not universally enforced.   When William Savery
visited York, he found in the Castle there seven Friends,
imprisoned for refusal to pay tithes.   They had a large
room to themselves and spent their time knitting purses
and weaving laces, gartering, etc.; were in good health and
well used.   Ten days before Wiliam Savery's visit:

"the poor curate who belonged to the parish they mostly came from,
(came) to York to complain to the Archbishop of the Priest who
put Friends in, who would not pay him for preaching.  He paid
Friends three visits and they said he was more affected at seeing them
than any that had visited (them). * * * those poor curates who do
the drudgery of the Priests for abt 30 or 40 £ per year, are really
to be pitied in many parts of England.  Their profligate superiors
pay them badly."

The great Methodist movement, under Whitefield and
Wesley, both of whom had been trained for the Church,
dominated the dissenting element in the latter half of the
Century.   To them came the fresh inspiration of the living
faith in a living Christ, that had actuated Luther in his
Treatise on Galatians.   With that faith, in its utmost simplicity, they approached again with apostolic fervor the
poor and downcast and the victims of the economic strin-
gency.   Wesleyanism became the dominant following of the

era and swept England as Quakerism had done in the previous century.

In fact, they had much in common. Whitefield revived the open air preaching which, common to the itinerant Quakers of the previous century, had been abandoned as they acquired meeting houses. Wesley too, after delay and hesitancy, employed lay preachers, finding them, in their power of close approach to the people, a most cogent instrument in the work of the new movement.

Whitefield died in 1770 and Wesley in 1791. At the latter date, there were two hundred seventy-eight ministers in connection with the Wesleyan movement, but there was no organization apart from the Established Church. Wesley died regarding himself as a member of the Establishment and praying his followers never to leave it. And yet by 1795, the year before William Savery began his preaching in England, so swift had been the revolt from ecclesiasticism, that the Wesleyans finally separated themselves from the National body and began holding services at the same hour and place.

Although Methodism was the most active and successful of the dissenting sects, the others shared in the revival of religious life that was everywhere apparent in the country. The Society of Friends was more deeply affected by the movement than is superficially evident. A generation later, headed by such English Friends as Joseph John Gurney and Isaac Crewdson, for their respective parties, the evangelical type of Quakerism, somewhat on the Methodist model, precipitated fresh divisions and was destined to find its fruitful soil in the middle west of the United States.

The immediate effect on the Society of this renewed religious life in the nation at large was apparent in a way that was peculiar to it alone. Prior to the revival, both Non-conformity and the Establishment had suffered acutely from an Arian deadness of form without spirituality; the evangelical call infused the new life of the Spirit into the men and women that it reached, but strangely enough, the ancient aversion of the Church, in any age, to carry the new vision into social practice, thwarted the movement by applying it to personal sins and vices only and leaving the social ills untouched.

It has ever been the genius of the Society of Friends (and be it said in all humility) to apply its doctrine and inspiration to the world in which we live. There had been much of sincerity in the attitude of many denominations, in their stand for a gospel message only, leaving to an omnipotent God the responsibility of drawing from men's hearts the application in their everyday lives, without it being necessary for the Church to carry the work further. There was also in this attitude, at times, a smug effort on the part of the Church to straddle, and, while preaching the truth, to wink at the infraction of it, by the "practical people" who as laymen were not hedged about by clerical safeguards. Being a "Society," and the only denomination that has so designated itself, the Friends' group has never been inspired with a great conviction, from personal standpoints, without seeking individually to apply the conviction to social and community matters.

The great revival of the Eighteenth Century fired the lives of the Quakers of both Continents and the fervor of the inspiration overflowed in a renewed visitation of power. But the effort was not alone in preaching on personal vices. It was applied to the slave-trade, the prison system and to a less degree, the economic order.

In the first two it went straight to the point. It decried the wickedness of slavery wherever it raised its head and in the other it worked indefatigably to reform the stinking, rotten system with which the Friends of former generations had been all too familiar. In neither effort did the Quakers work alone. Clarkson and Wilberforce in their anti-slavery efforts were close to but not of the Quaker fold, nor were Howard or Dickens convinced of the evils of the prison system by Friendly means, but the early agitation, in the days when such agitation meant social ostracism and estrangement, was largely upon the shoulders of the Society of Friends, both individually and as an organized group, and the example wrought powerfully, on both sides of the Atlantic, for the right in the struggle over slavery that was to shake the two Continents sixty-five years later.

Toward the other problem, then acute for the first, the Society felt and still feels grave responsibility. No branch of the Christian Church has yet so seriously attacked the evils in the social order as to claim any particular shibboleth for their solution. The spirit of John Woolman is today perhaps the strongest element from the purely religious standpoint, working toward social amelioration, just as the saintly and dignified figure of Elizabeth Fry stands preëminent in connection with prison reform. The Society of Friends cannot afford, however, to rest upon such spiritual eminence today to solve the peculiar problems of the social order, and the time is ripe for sacrifice and example to rivet the attention of the world to the essentially religious character of the undertaking.

The populace at large in England was considerably chastened in spirit during the wars at the end of the Eighteenth Century. The main activity toward social uplift was on that account, as it often is today, identified with charitably inclined groups, without denominational cohesion. As a consequence, the Church, then as now, got little resultant benefit from movements which it did not initiate or promote. Many of the philanthropic schemes were for merely temporary relief. Others, and notably those for thrift, savings and relief, have persisted to this day; the business side of them having given them a twofold impetus.

The religious conscience of the world is not yet tender enough to assume its share of responsibility for the economic iniquities, that, though modern, were in a very sure sense arising from the Industrial Revolution at the time of William Savery. A century and a quarter has not even yet aroused the Church to its full sense of responsibility, in spite of prophets like Rauchenbusch, who are true lineal successors to Woolman. In Savery's time, as we have seen, there was almost no comprehension of the fundamental difficulties. Alms-giving and preaching were about as far as Christian people went, for many decades, after the turn of the century, in applying religious concern to social ills. Nor can we of today, well afford to criticize their lack of appreciation of the task, when we ourselves, educated to the evils and comprehensive of their origins, are so lamentably weak in sufficient efforts to meet the situation.

## CHAPTER XXVI

## SOCIAL ENGLAND

It is only possible to visualize the England of 1800, even in the partial way it is described by William Savery, by realizing that it was a war England.   Once again the sense of trembling possibilities and the sickening feeling of unfulfilled opportunities haunts one in reading of the time, either in private journal or public record.   In economics, capital was putting the irons on labor, reckless or ignorant of the discords that all the decades since have brought about; in social life, aristocracy was persecuting or disdaining the liberal tendencies toward the democracy that England now boasts, but which then she damned; in religion, Dissent was waging battle royal with the Establishment, and both were united in horror of and opposition to deism and agnosticism. And each was inextricably bound up with the other.   It is impossible to understand properly the rise of the Liberal Party, without an appreciation of the enormous part that religious dissent played in it.   And one can no more understand these two unless they are coupled with the economic emergence of the great and powerful middle class of manufacturers and merchants that toppled aristocracy into a figurehead.

The decade from 1791 to 1800 was as productive of change in a social or political sense as it was in an economic.   By the time William Savery landed in England, in 1796, the acuteness of the war hysteria had somewhat subsided.   Its effects were, however, still apparent.   One feels, all through the Journal, a tacit restraint from any broad comment upon public questions.   He carried this manuscript Journal, in small volumes, with him on most of his travels. If any written comment by an American traveler, who had traversed Germany, France and Ireland, had been adverse to the British cause, or even critical of British policy, it might very easily have been considered seditious, to the detriment of the writer. Such precedents had not been wanting in the few years previous.

At that time when the United States was a despised experiment in democracy; when the red cap in France was the symbol of republicanism, and when the aristocracy of England had not yet realized the significance of the social and economic upheaval then well under way, it was a parlous undertaking for an American preacher to travel around with any but a circumspect message. William Savery was asked by both King George and his sister, the Princess Elizabeth of Brunswick, about the democratic experiment in America. Curiosity was rampant about it. Reports regarding it were as unsatisfactory and as definitely "inspired" as any reports circulating these days about events in Russia and Poland.

Moreover, Dissent had been unpopular, through an unreasoning hatred, in the early years of the decade. In 1791, the scientist, Priestley of Birmingham, was raided for his reforming views, his house and scientific instruments destroyed, and thereafter like outrages were perpetrated upon the houses and chapels of others in dissent. Anti-Jacobinism became the accepted order of the day, and the only sure indicator of patriotism. It was not, however, the indicator of independent thought, either in religion or politics.

The sweetening influence, during these years, was Wilberforce. There were no Friends in Government. In England as in America they had no interest in politics, though in England more because they were excluded from the charmed official circle than from voluntary retirement, as had been the case in America. Wilberforce had been bred in the choicest social medium in England, had been the favorite child of that society and yet, through his wife, had close affiliations with Methodism. He became the mainstay of the progressive thought and action, both within and without Parliament. Next to Clarkson, he became the most beloved by the Friends of all Englishmen in the public eye. William Savery met him several times and became very fond of him. He had recently married "a sweet young woman who is rather inclined to the Methodists and dresses plain for her station." It was in conversation with Wilberforce that William Savery gave the only reflection upon the war that he records outside of his printed sermons,—the only entry, in fact, that has much bearing upon the greatest factor in English life at the time:

"Our conversation was very friendly and much freedom was used by us all. He assured me Minister Pitt was sincerely disposed for peace and all the Cabinet with him lamented it could not be obtained. He said he thought if I and two or three of my friends would undertake to bring about a negotiation upon amicable terms, between the two nations, he had not a doubt but it would succeed. He thought us the fittest people in the world to make peace. I told him in the present state of worldly policy, Friends were quite shut out, from the nature of their principles, from any interference, but one thing I thought was worth considering and that was not to appoint men as negotiators for peace who were lovers and promoters of war. That, he said, should be always attended to. * * * A member of Parliament came in and sat down to table with us and spoke to him (Wilberforce) of the subscriptions for carrying on the war, going on rapidly, and that one dissenting meeting had subscribed £800. I told them I believed Friends must content themselves with being in the rear in that business, which W. W. did not say anything to, but the other supposed it perfectly consistent with our principles, as much so, he said, as to insure our ships from the dangers of the sea, etc.; it was only giving part of our property to secure the rest from depredation and robbery. W. W. smiled at his logick, knowing we did not unite with it."

Such candor was possible with Wilberforce, while it would not have been safe with less responsible, but more blatant patriots of the Tory régime.

In his travels he met with the soldiery at intervals. At one time the presence of noisy and half-drunken troops in a town prevented the holding of an appointed meeting; at another time in approaching London, he ran into a troop of two thousand of the City Militia, parading near Islington, and going toward Moorfields. His chaise was drawn into the "amazing concourse of people, escorting them into town," and so he rode alongside of the ranks of soldiers. Still later, the Gentlemen Volunteers of Deptford drew the people away from the Friends' Meeting by reason of a parade to their Church for the consecration of their colors. Beyond these trivial incidents there is practically no mention of the war, after entering England, although it must have been on every tongue.

It is possible that the small amount of building of houses was due to war conditions. William Savery mentions this condition in several places though without attributing it to scarcity of man power. At Cockermouth, rents were remarkably low. "Such a house as mine would not bring more than 9 pound Sterling a year." And Isaac Robinson told him that but one new house had been built in Cockermouth in thirty years, except where some few old ones had been pulled down, which, says the Journal, "is much the case in many towns in England." At Bristol, economic conditions had been so bad that there were "several handsome rows of houses . . . that have been covered in for several years, but are decaying without finishing," gloomy as they appeared. For a different reason Whitehaven had a similar unfinished building operation,

"On the side of one of (the hills) Sir J. Lowther, now the Earl (of Lonsdale) had built, some years ago, abt 300 small stone houses, about 10 feet front, in three rows above each other, which are all vacant at present, never was finished, but stand there as a monument to his folly and the great expence he went to to obtain a seat in Parliament, having intended to give them to 300 poor familys & by that means to qualify them to vote for him at elections, but the scheme by some means fell through and the houses are left to go to ruin."

There are a few more sidelights upon the gentry. Some of them were frequently in attendance at appointed meetings. In fact, there was still a considerable dissenting following among the gentry and county families, though less than in the early days of religious unrest. Westminster Meeting in London frequently had "some of the first rank in the west part of the town" in attendance. William Savery was much impressed, in many places in England, with the magnificence of the country seats of the wealthy. Even in those days, the vacation habit had fastened itself upon the British people. For the clerks of London the Thames was the pleasure ground. For the wealthy, more distant resorts were already popular. In the north of England were numerous handsome country seats, notably along Lake Windermere. Near Ambleside, at the head of the Lake:

"There were many gentry from different parts of the country come to spend some weeks amidst the mountains and lakes of Westmoreland and Cumberland, as they do annually. The English have many places to ramble to in the summer, which they seem to be immoderately fond of."

He describes a similar scene at Keswick, where the demand for horses was so great that they had difficulty in obtaining a pair. Around Bath and London particularly, there were many "very elegant and delightful spots indeed." At Bath, in January, the nobility were present in crowds, to drink the waters. They

"make a splendid appearance and live in great dissipation to the disgrace of religion and morality. The public rooms of amusement are spacious, 1000 attended the concert last night."

William Savery partook of the waters himself. His account of the famous resort is as follows:

"I had time with some of my friends to visit the pump room where the numerous visitants to the waters go to drink them. Two waiters are always stationed within a bar, inclosing the pump. These serve all that come in with water. I drank some. It did not appear strongly impregnated with mineral. The heat of the Bath waters is surprizing, amounting to 105 degrees of Fahrenheit's thermometer; would almost cook an egg. Everybody making a decent appearance are privileged to walk in the spacious pump-room, from dukes and duchesses down to decent tradesmen."

The hot wells near Bristol were also in high favor.

"Though called hot (they) are scarcely as warm as river water in the summer. There are no baths the waters being only drank by invalids that visit them; have nothing peculiar in their taste and yet are much celebrated and frequented, and several hands continually employed in bottling it for exportation."

Another glimpse of the nobility was had at Windsor, where the travelers caught sight of the Queen

"who appeared above one of the windows, with a low head dress, and looked like a pretty, domestic woman. The King was gone ahunting, though they had only come from London this morning. We rode through the forest where they were hunting; saw many servants and some of the nobility, but not the King."

It is interesting to note that the King was accustomed to walk on the terrace at Windsor, every Tuesday, to receive petitions and addresses from his subjects, an opportunity to which Wilberforce referred some Friends who asked him to present a memorial to the King, on the slave trade. This would seem to be a late survival of the direct appeal to the King's conscience, a function largely assigned, long before, to the Lord Chancellor.

The new fad of sea-bathing came under William Savery's observant eye twice in his travels. At Weymouth, he

"took a long walk along the sea-side. This being a famous watering place, where the King and royal family reported annually, were now expected in three days, many great people were there and some of the royal family. There were many machines on wheels to go into the water for bathing."

Later, in the same summer of 1797, in approaching Liverpool, by sea, the boat skirted the shores of Lancashire. Says the Journal:

"Was surprised to see the numbers of people, men, women and children, bathing for two miles below the town, many hundreds coming in at this time of the year from the country, as they do also to most places round the coast of England. The English people are passionately fond of bathing in the sea water, and meeting in companies at those places. The present scene appeared to me rather indecent, as men and women, though with some cloaths on, were bathing very near each other."

The water played an important part in English life from the transportation standpoint also. The packets, of which, in the English Channel, and between England, Ireland and the Isle of Man, William Savery saw much, were the main arteries of passenger service. Between Dublin, Ireland and Holyhead, Wales, five of these packets regularly plied in 1798, one scheduled to sail from either side of the water each day. They were peculiarly undependable, as they could sail only when the wind was right. Many delays were due to adverse winds. For shorter trips, they served better. Between Liverpool and Chester the water trip was made nine miles up the River, on a packet "not so handsome & convenient as the stage boats on the Delaware," to a canal, for another nine miles in a canal boat:

"having two large apartments at different prices and a kitchen in the middle. Those who choose it sit down to a good dinner cooked on board. The passage from Liverpool to Chester which is reckoned cheap in this country is 2/6d Sterg for the cabin and best rooms higher than in America. The Canal has twenty stone bridges across it in nine miles. We passed along about four miles an hour, through a fine country. The weather being fine, the passengers sat on the top of the room outside."

Another water scene that William Savery describes at Liverpool is redolent of the salt in those early days of British commercial supremacy:

"A large fleet of West India ships arrived, upwards of twenty, whom the people crowded to see, expressing much joy. They looked well, coming up under a fine breeze and tide. The bells rung most of the day."

The arrival of such a fleet, after running the gauntlet of the French privateers, was something of a maritime event, and the sight would naturally kindle the blood of any Philadelphian of that time, who, as a boy, had seen the shipping on the Delaware bringing in the products of every quarter of the globe.

In London, the Thames was much used as a waterway, both for business and pleasure. Two references, particularly, convey the tang of the ancient water front. When a party of Friends were inspecting the *Amicable*, as a possible conveyance for William Savery to America,

"the tower guns were fired while we were on board and we being so near, startled the women much at first, but no harm was done. The Captain ordered an arm-chair slung and swung us all over the side of the ship into a water-man's boat, who landed us at Billingsgate."

The other entry describes the Thames on a warm night in June, 1798:

"London feeling oppressive, went towards evening with J. & M. Savory, their little Mary, & N(athaniel) Pryor, of Leeds (&) wife, M. P. (Mary Pattison Pryor) to Queenhithe Stairs, above London Bridge and took boat for Chelsea. No vessels with masts, except a few that can lower them, are above bridge, but a vast number of flats of different kinds who ply up the river to many places with coal, timber, &c, and many wherrys for passengers. A great many people were of the same mind with us and were come out to catch a little air. * * * Went ashore at Chelsea to a Coffee House and took a little refreshment. It was called Don Saltero's & had a large collection of curiositys to amuse visitors. Returned and met a large number of boats with company, going to Vauxhall, Ranleigh, &c, which were now lighted up with lamps as it was growing dark. Passed under Westminster & Blackfryers Bridges and landing at Blackfryers Stairs, took coach for Finsbury, where we arrived finely refreshed & cool enough with the air on the river."

Perhaps as great a contrast between then and now existed in the roads. Traffic was just commencing on a large scale through the demand of Industrialism for adequate facilities of transport to the sea, although railroads were still a generation distant. There were some good roads, but relatively few. Most of the back roads still exhibited the ruts and quagmires of former years, but the through routes, though frequented in places by highwaymen, were passable to the swirling coaches and Royal Mails, that swelled the horse-loving heart of England with pride, as they bowled along at incredible speeds, between the growing industrial towns and the Metropolis of 700,000 inhabitants.

Bristol to London in fourteen hours, by the mail coaches! William Savery made the same trip twice, in a two-passenger postchaise, in 1798, in eighteen hours,—once via Newberry, Marlborough and Calne, one hundred and sixteen miles, and returning via Reading and Slough, one hundred and twenty miles, putting on "from stage to stage" and with nothing to eat but "cold mutton, cheese and beer" at Reading. A call was made upon the astronomer, Herschell, at Slough, while the horses were changing, he having just completed "a second enormous telescope and is almost constantly taken up with his favorite study." Shorter trips, London to Portsmouth, seventy-three miles, and Bristol to Birmingham, eighty-six miles, were by no means unusual in the swinging coaches, with six passengers inside and one or more on top.

As early as 1792 sixteen mail coaches left the General Post Office daily, with five passengers and an armed guard. Their departure was one of the sights of the City.[1] When William Savery strolled into the General Post Office in 1798, to send a letter via Falmouth, to his "Dear Sally" in Philadelphia, it cost him 1/8. He was "astonished at the multitude of clerks, apartments and offices and the names of different countries over each door or window."

[1] Traill: *Social England*, V, 347.

The start for these long trips by postchaise, of which William Savery took a many, was always early. In the winter, breakfast by candlelight; in the summer, the gray, early twilight of the English latitude, saw this "Herculean traveler," as his London intimates dubbed him, on his way time and time again, by three or four o'clock, and once as early as two A.M. The roads near London were good and traffic moved fast. Besides the postchaises, with postilions, and stagecoaches for the public, there were private conveyances of all kinds,—many of them very luxurious. William Savery, himself, occasionally traveled on horseback, the steed being supplied from place to place by the Friend who was his host for the time being. Between Newington and Hyde Park Corner, a commuting coach ran every hour for the public after eight in the morning. At week-ends, the exodus from London to the towns up the Thames was tremendous. From Bagshot and Brentford to London even then was almost a continuous town, and along this road William Savery and his party met, on a Saturday afternoon, twenty-one regular stage coaches, loaded within and without, besides a great number of postchaises and private carriages. So dense was traffic that it took their vehicle forty minutes to go from Hyde Park Corner into Finsbury, where lived Joseph Savory, host to and cousin of William Savery.

The scene on another week-end is thus described:

"We amused ourselves at meeting with a vast number of Londoners going out of town to spend the First Day, for fresh air, in almost every kind of conveyance, as gig-whiskeys, post chaises, one-horse chaises, taxed carts, on horse-back, on foot and in the inside and outside of coaches, most of which had from seven to ten outside. Of that kind we met near thirty between Slough and London. It is to be sure a surprising scene to see what thousands pour out of London on all sides on Seventh Day evening and indeed the unremitting attention that many continue throughout the course of the week to business, in confined places, almost impenetrable to wholesome air, seems absolutely to require it."

Such a wholesale, headlong vacation habit is but another of the many tendencies of a people at war. Moreover, the admiration of the American, used to wide Philadelphia streets, for the handling of traffic in London, was evident then as now:

"Rose before 6: it was dark, the streets yet in the possession of the watchmen. Joseph Savory kindly went with me to Jasper Capper's town house in Gracious Street. As we went along, the streets began to thicken with people; the day was dawning. There soon appeared to be as many stirring and coaches and carriages running in Bishopsgate Street as in Philadelphia at noon-day. This London baffles all my power of description."

The present-day reader can but smile at such statements, even while sympathizing intimately with the Journalist when he writes,—

"The bustle of London is too great to be endured long together."

In places away from London, the roads were much more of a problem. Deep in mud in the wintertime, they either stopped vehicular traffic or required extra horses. Every inn had horses for emergencies and postilions to ride and return with them. The détour, of unsavory motor repute today, was in evidence in those days but under another name, French names being in ill favor. William Savery describes as "the quickest I ever rode in England," a run from Hertford to London, in a postchaise with Jasper Capper, twenty-one miles in less than three hours, including a stop, to change horses at Waltham Cross. The roads in the growing and busy industrial centers in Staffordshire, around Wolverhampton and Birmingham were also good and travel over them very fast.

An interesting, though perhaps not important feature of this traveling was the gossip between fellow-passengers. Frequently these wayfarers are described and their conversation, weighty or trivial, recorded with appropriate comment. On one occasion, after George Dillwyn and

William Savery had visited the King and Queen, a large number of Friends were drinking tea at Thomas Foster's in London:

"One of them had been in a stage-coach lately, where a gentleman told him he understood that Mr. Savery, in the presence of the King, had foretold that the close of the 18th Century, would exhibit a general peace with all the European powers."

The incident was very embarrassing to William Savery, as he had said nothing of the kind, and had been beset with other erroneous bits of gossip as to what had transpired at the audience with George III and Queen Charlotte, an account of which, from a source unknown to him, had appeared in the newspapers. The visit is described more at length in a subsequent chapter, but the incident was evidently of news value in the stagecoach.

Occasionally there would be an annoying incident like the occurrence at Derby, although the event was not always as favorable. The throng of post passengers at Derby on a fine summer day in 1797 was so great that horses were at a premium. The traveling Friends had no sooner got their baggage into a chaise than "some high people, two men and a woman, came and claimed it as their right, having come in first. With some reluctance we suffered our things to be taken out." After a half hour's wait, another chaise was procured and they proceeded, only to find the "high people" lamenting their chaise, broken down three miles from the town, whither they had sent for a substitute. Philosophically, the gentle spirit of the minister recorded:

"Everything that appears to us like misfortunes at first, do not always prove so in the end."

On another pilgrimage, when he, two women and a young Jew were traveling companions, they took up "two very lusty women, the most incessant talkers I have met with for a long time," and all the occupants were relieved when they were put down at Shoreditch. Even more whimsical was an incident, in the water passage from Port Patrick, Scotland, to Donaghadee, Ireland. William Savery's own account is worth quoting in full:

"One (of the passengers), who had the appearance of what is called 'a gentleman from Ireland,' who was very drunk, disturbed the company much; said he knew many Friends in Ireland, and was not far from being one himself. But his conduct was vile and his language very prophane. He called me his friend, Obadiah, but was very officious to get me a good seat; said he respected my cloth. A young Scotsman, from Norfolk in Virginia, seemed glad to find I was an American, but before we got to Donaghadee, got as drunk as the other, and they fell into high disputes of religion, and contention for the honour of the countries that gave them birth, which I was afraid would have ended with some mischief, but the more sober and decent expressed their disapprobation of these men's conduct and tried to soften them with some effect."

In another ride from London to Ipswich, the party, besides William Savery, consisted of a "young, vain and assuming parson of a regiment, a decent young woman of Ipswich, Sir Thomas T——, of the same place" and two other men. With these dramatis personæ, our traveler managed to amuse himself from 7 A.M. till 7:30 P.M.:

"The young chaplain kept singing catches, talking very lightly to the young woman, who was much more serious than himself, and whistling to the disturbance of our quiet, much. His regiment was at Ipswich, where he said the soldiers had committed their souls to his keeping; that he preached to them every Sunday and prayed for their salvation, and supposed he was of use to the Creation, but he could not conceive what use the young woman was of. He thought it was no matter to the world or anybody, whether she lived or died. She made him some good replies to his impertinence. I also threw in a little."

It is perhaps appropriate to end this chronicle of travel in the quaint words of the Journalist himself,—

"I may here make some remarks on the travelling in England which may serve generally."

Then follows the résumé of costs and customs:

"The price of a seat in the stage coach from Weymouth to Bristol, 65 miles, is 26/6 Sterling, besides about 2/0 to coachman. The price of post chaise is everywhere 1/0 per mile for three persons, the charge of turnpike 4/0 this day & 1½ a mile, sometimes more, to the postilion. Breakfast, tea or coffee, with bread & butter or toast, 1/0; a common dinner about 2/0. The Inn keepers and servants are attentive and obliging, for which the servants always expect something,—the chambermaids, some places 6 and some 9 for the bed; Boots and waiter on table, each about 6 apiece for every traveller; many give them more. This all mounts high and I should suppose, upon the best judgment I can form, travelling and accommodations in England cost about as many shillings a day, Sterling, as the same distances in America does Pennsylvania currency."

The Friends of London were at that time very much alive to the enormity of the criminal laws and to the lawlessness that is always the concomitant of wars. Instead of a decrease in capital punishment, as one would expect, after the beneficent example set by Penn in that regard a century before, the time of the first two Georges saw an actual increase in death dealing laws. At the period of William Savery's visit, there were two hundred offenses for which the gibbet was the penalty. Justice was even handed, as far as convictions were concerned, but detection was anything but consistent or dependent. It was long before Peel developed the metropolitan police system that gave his myrmidons of that age the name of "peelers." The night watchman, "going about with a bell in his hand, crying the hours," was all the protection from depredation that William Savery mentions. In that instance, the watchman was in Hitchin, where the minister was the guest of John Fry. He also mentions the watch in the City itself, and no doubt would have welcomed company when, on one occasion, he "felt a little alarmed, crossing Moorfields so late at night,—but all went well." Pickpockets were a frequent nuisance. A kindly disposed person once warned William Savery of this menace, "observing my mind was more employed upon the subject before us than my pockets."

Executions were still conducted in public and this feature strongly disgusted the tender sensibilities of this man who, as we have seen, did not hesitate, in his youth, to attend the criminal to the scaffold. At Wimbledon Common, he chanced, one day, upon a "noted highwayman hanging in chains,—a disgusting spectacle, seldom met with but in England." So differently are things done in these days, that the following description reads more like the times of the Inquisition than of the turn of the Eighteenth Century:

"A vast crowd of people were collected and poor Norton with a young priest of some sort and the executioner, standing together on a scaffold at the prison door. He spoke to the people in a humble, penitent manner, but low. The Sheriffs of London rode round the scaffold with drawn swords. They left him and a trap door immediately fell and he was left hanging. This being the only hanging I had seen for several years, it affected me much and though I had hope poor Norton went well, I could not but lament the sanguinary laws that took his life. What was observable at the gallows, confirmed me that it had a bad effect upon the people."

William Savery had not attended the execution from mere curiosity. The day before, he with Thomas Pole, Joshua Smith and Jane Fry had visited the condemned, whose offense had been the taking of bank notes out of letters in the Post Office, where he had been employed. They had had a satisfactory religious opportunity with him and his wife in Newgate Prison, and had left him somewhat comforted. Newgate was then better than the prisons of the times of the early Friends, but even at that, was anything but adequate, from the modern standpoint. Our Friend visited it several times, and with other Friends was readily admitted by the Keeper upon permit from an Alderman. He describes the

"many dismal apartments and several iron gates, where we were obliged to pass many wretched fellow creatures who thronged about us for half pence."

and adds significantly, that they had left their watches, money, etc., at a Friend's house in Cheapside.

On another occasion, after four men and one woman had been hanged in one week past for forgery or passing counterfeit bills, William Savery's mind was so overcome with the enormity of the practice that he solicited the company of S. West, William Crotch and David Dent and repaired to Newgate to visit several more under the death penalty for that week. These were three younger men, Wilkinson, Reeves and Adamson, all convicted of forgery of a kind that seems to have been customary in those days of war fever and speculation, "most people say hundreds are or have been in the same practice for years, but being able to pay their notes when due, no notice is taken of them." All these men were of high type, and one of them had been religiously inclined as a follower of White-field in his happier days. He knew William Savery, who had held a meeting in the house of his father-in-law, at Bethnal Green. The other, who had "lived in high style and kept his coach," had evidently overstretched his conscience under stress of war prosperity. Their respectability and contrition and the agonies suffered by their wives and relatives made an impression upon William Savery and his companions that released the floodgates of religious exercise. All partook of prayer and finally

"the poor man broke forth in a flood of tears, in which all present joined, and such another baptizing season I never remember on a like occasion, * * * a most extraordinary affecting scene which I have no language to describe, but true—I shall never forget. * * * Oh! when will these legal murders cease!"

These unfortunates and the commercial extension that was an inducing cause toward their downfall so deeply impressed William Savery that he frequently, thereafter, would gently reprove individual Friends, sometimes even when they were his hosts, for too elaborate a ménage or too tense an interest in business to the exclusion of other and

higher things. The apparent rudeness of such suggestions
was tempered by a knowledge of the results in the cases of
the Newgate prisoners.

As they left Newgate, they passed through one of the
many yards and

"were surrounded by a group of perhaps sixty, some half naked and
all wretched looking men, yet mostly under middle age. They
begged hard for half pence. William Crotch desired them to stand
at a little distance and began to preach to them powerfully, which
they received, some with a kind of astonishment and others were
tendered but all very still. I made some addition, and then our
company, putting about 12/0 together gave it to the turnkey, to lay
out in beer for them, for which they were very grateful and blessed
the Quakers. We had yet another yard and group to pass through,
who with the turnkeys at every gate, emptied our pockets of near all
the silver and copper we had."

One can but wonder whether any of the beer ever got past
the turnkeys to the prisoners.

Other humane concerns, besides the visiting of prisons,
occupied publicly inclined Britons at that time. It was the
period when many societies, with long, and sometimes
ludicrous, names were being organized. A group bearing
the euphonious name "Association for Improving the Situation of Infant Chimney-sweepers" was flourishing for a
time. Public zeal, in keeping with the attempt of the
churches to realign religion with humanitarianism, favored
such enterprises. One of these, "The Humane Society for
ye Recovery of Drowned and Suffocated Persons," was the
especial hobby of William Savery's friend, Dr. Lettsom.
For his efforts in this direction he had been awarded a
"most curious gold medal, enclosed in crystal and worth a
great deal of money." It is perhaps permissible to suggest
that the good Doctor might better have exerted his efforts
at an earlier stage than the name of the Society would
indicate.

Dr. Lettsom was a very interesting man. He had been
born on a small island near Tortola, and coming to Eng-

land had won the patronage of Dr. Fothergill, who introduced him to his own gentle circle of patients. In time Lettsom succeeded to Fothergill's practice and at this period William Savery met and became intimate with him. In the narrative is considerable detail of the Doctor's affairs, of which a few of a medical nature are interesting. Besides his "extensive practice of physix," he was an indefatigable writer on medical subjects. Most of the writing he did in his carriage, riding to his patients. Save for the numerous patients from whom he took nothing, he seldom visited under a guinea. Some of the nobility had given him "incredible sums for his attendance," as a result of which and his books he had acquired a great estate. Although a Friend, he, and particularly his wife, were "gay," in the Quaker parlance of the day. He was remarkably cordial to William Savery, who, in spite of the differences between them, reciprocated the feeling. After his friend's death, Dr. Lettsom wrote a biographical introduction to an English edition of William Savery's sermons, to which reference will be made later in connection with incidents not elsewhere recorded.

Medical care was much on the mend at this time. There is even a reference to such modern treatment as getting "electrified for numbness in the leg." At Bury St. Edmunds, William Savery, "being much unacquainted with the nature and power" of a "paregorick elixir," was given some for a toothache by his "affectionate hostess." It gave him relief, but upon awaking in the night, he took more and finally swallowed some. His friends, on measuring the vial, found he had taken eight teaspoonfuls. In spite of being sick, pale and chilly, the next morning he took warm brandy and water, topped off with strong coffee, and then traveled on thirty-five miles during the day. It was several days before he entirely recovered from the opiate. Another interesting sidelight of a dental nature relates how

"G. Bott (of London) drew 16 teeth out of one woman's mouth, which was all she had; then made her two compleat jaws full, as white as ivory."

Institutional care of unfortunates was also well under way in those days. With Richard Chester, one of the Governors of the Institution, William Savery visited "Luke's Hospital for Lunatics." His description of the inmates parallels modern cases of insanity, varying from mild excitement to "deep, melancholy silence" and "the most horrid state of frenzy and violence." A few were handcuffed and chained to prevent them from injuring themselves:

"Their apartments and persons were kept clean and decent, beyond anything I have ever seen of the kind, except the Retreat at York. * * * The whole was conducted in a manner exceeding almost, or perhaps quite, everything of so extensive a nature in Europe, far exceeding Bedlam, both in numbers and economy."

Another institution at Hackney was the Boarding School for Deaf and Dumb, where already, in 1798, the pupils were taught to "articulate so as to be understood, and to read, write and cypher well," and where William Savery had "a comfortable visit." Such institutions betoken most commendable care for these unfortunates.

Social change, social and religious reform were in the air. The war had much to do with it, and much of the new piety was, perhaps, ephemeral, as was the case under similar circumstances in 1914. Much of the change had, however, come to stay. In dress, more than in any other visible manifestation, the change was working itself out. The rigidities of wartime financing necessitated considerable adaptation in apparel. Scarcity of flour and the consequent tax imposed in 1795, upon toilet powder, effectually discouraged indulgence in powdered wigs and the egregious "mobs" of the women. Much the same abandon in dress, with a studied négligé, apparent today, as a post-war mania, was then evident among the British of all ages. Court dress and swords gave place in Parliament to top boots and great coats. Men's styles, especially, changed quickly. Knee breeches, with buckles, first lengthened to meet Hessian boots and later blossomed into the pantaloon, often strapped under the instep. Tail coats also made their advent along with high hats, replacing the skirted coats with vast pockets and the three-cornered hats. The chief significance to Friends in these changes in dress, lies in the fact that Friends refused to change with them, and deeply lamented them.

A more fundamental social change working in Britain as a whole, and profoundly affecting English Quakerism particularly, was the shift of political power and social respectability to the manufacturing and merchant class, in which Friends soon proved the peers of any. There had always been wealthy members and gently bred, in the Society, but the rank and file had included many of the lowly and even uncouth. The early Society regarded itself as a cross-section of society in general; master and servant of the same faith. With the Industrial Revolution and the Friends' adoption of advanced educational methods, the Society continually developed its personnel in business, to whatever degree of advancement was possible for each individual. "Education for the duties of life" spelled opportunity for commercial or professional advancement. A few poor remained, but the Friends' schools, far in advance of their time, began to turn out a standardized product that became a counting house clerk, a shop keeper or a captain of industry according to his capacity.

The Society of Friends has so remained ever since. English Friends of late years have attempted, with more or less success, to reconstruct the affiliations with other classes than the professional and commercial, but in America, where the same process was under way, the vast laboring class and the problems it feels are unknown, as far as personnel is concerned, within the limits of membership of practically all of the Yearly Meetings. Whether for good or ill, this tendency became established at this period, and the results are with us in undiminished force today.

## CHAPTER XXVII

# THE SOCIETY OF FRIENDS IN ENGLAND

We are accustomed these days to think of the discipline' and practice of the Society of Friends as of long and un-varied standing. As a matter of fact, the middle period of Quakerism shows many anachronisms which have since been corrected. At the time of William Savery's visit, London was the prevalent factor in the life and policy of the Yearly Meeting. The distances, though now compara-tively small, were then considerable, time for travel between points so long, and journeys so tedious, that it was probably essential to concentrate in a few centers where many Friends resided, the chief responsibility for the continuous admin-istration of the Meeting's affairs.

The same situation then existed in Philadelphia, where the weighty Friends of the City meetings practically ab-sorbed the control of the Yearly Meeting's affairs. Friends in New Jersey, and in Delaware, Chester and Bucks Coun-ties, Pennsylvania, prior to the Hicksite Separation, were so remote that they had to operate through Representatives, who in those days had functions that today they do not have. The democratic tendency of that time in society at large contributed far more than is often realized to the Separation. The theological differences, so frequently stressed as the sole cause, were often of minor importance in communities where the social, financial and educational superiority of the Philadelphia Elders found less com-munity of interest than did the homely simplicity and native eloquence of Elias Hicks.

One can but suppose that the greater homogeneity of

Friends in England, the absence there of very great distances and a broadening of the fellowship before it was too late, prevented the schism that Samuel Bettle, Clerk to Philadelphia Yearly Meeting at the time of the Separation, stated might have been prevented in Philadelphia.

Certain it is that the same sort of trouble was brewing in Ireland and England in 1798 as that which later precipitated the Separations in America. Time and again William Savery inveighs against "deism" as a corrosive element in the religious life of the nation. Especially was this true, as we have already seen, in Ireland, where the Society was already in a parlous situation over theological questions. In England the Society was practically united in its opposition to tendencies of this kind from the outside, and as the future proved, there was sufficient statesmanship and forbearance in London, when the test came, to avoid the consequences that ensued in other places.

William Savery spent much of his time and effort in and around London. He "traveled out," however, a great deal and the sketch of his journeyings upon the map looks like a spiderweb, centering upon London. In 1796, after landing at Liverpool, he spent only seven weeks in England before sailing for the Continent. Returning in 1797, he spent one summer month in London and three in the Channel Islands, the Isle of Man and the Isle of Wight. In 1798, he traveled nearly six months, visiting most of the important Quaker centers, and Scotland, Ireland and Wales. It was in this period that he crossed and recrossed the midland counties of England, with their great diversity of life and conditions.

In these side trips away from London, William Savery recorded some very interesting observations upon the Friends' communities of England. Most notable of all the generalizations regarding English Friends of the period was the paucity of men Friends in the ministry and the number and power of the women ministers. British Friends depended almost entirely upon women, at this time in the ministry and the intimation which William Savery received that it would be most acceptable to London Friends if he would close out his business in Philadelphia and live in London was seriously enough considered for him to write his wife Sarah Savery, about it. This feature was the more remarkable because, as already stated, the men ministers of Philadelphia Yearly Meeting were at this time in the preponderance, forming a galaxy probably unsurpassed, in gifts and consecration, by any time before or since.

As William Savery was about to enter Scotland he met a young man, recently returned thence, who had seen a notable group of women Friends then active in service in Scotland. They were Sarah Harrison, Sarah Birkbeck, Sarah Talbot, Sarah Shackleton, Deborah Darby, Rebecca Young, Mary Watson, Mary Sterry, Ann Alexander, Martha Haworth, Priscilla Gurney, Phebe Speakman and Ann Crawley. William Savery's comment on this imposing list of devoted women is:

"No man Friends in the ministry, but T. Scattergood & myself in this part & D. Sands, possibly in Wales. There are no other men Friends that I know of out on religious service in England at this time. What hath hindered and what doth hinder them but the too great attachment to the pursuits of this world. Oh! what a pity in such an abundant field of labor as this country affords! Lord, loosen our Society more and more, that they may be ready to enter the field Thou art opening in Europe."

In spite of this entry, the Journal mentions many men who were ministers in local congregations, although their call and their influence reached no further. They were not "public Friends," in the true significance of that obsolete expression, and it was the itinerant type, traveling under a well defined concern, that William Savery missed in the work.

His incidental references to some of the Friendly localities are sometimes of interest. Bristol Meeting, with ninety families in membership, was the largest meeting in England, with Devonshire House, London, next, and Kendal, third. There were at that time two meetings held in Bristol, although one was so small that "Friends seem uneasy about it and think it had better be dropped." The large meeting house was said to seat fourteen hundred people, but it would not contain the crowd desiring to attend a public meeting held in the evening, after the regular meeting in the morning. Bristol was a favorite stopping place of William Savery's. He was frequently there for short stays, en route for other destinations, and was the guest, on each occasion, of John Lury, who with his family were most affectionate and attentive hosts. It was a city of 80,000 inhabitants, accounted to be the second in England, although its trade was already much decreased, owing to the wars.

At Kendal, with its twelve thousand inhabitants, the Society was prospering. One gathers from William Savery's expression, that the spirit of that meeting was a strong factor in the life of the community:

"Indeed, Friends here appear to live in a great deal of harmony and brotherly love, which makes it very pleasant to be with them. They are an open-hearted, respectable company."

As he was laboring under a very heavy cold, during his stay in Kendal, William Savery appreciated the more the kind attentions of the families of George Braithwaite and George Stewardson. The home of the former is referred to as "a very kind house," which through its mistress, D. Braithwaite provided for the cold, "an emulsion, made principally of almonds," while the "good girls" of the Stewardson household, Anna and Dorothy by name, "seem as if they could not think they do too much." Their remedy for the cold was a warm foot bath and a "paregorick elixir." They were the more endeared to him because George Stewardson was the father of Thomas Stewardson of Philadelphia, a close intimate of William Savery's and one of the men who kept a watchful oversight of his tanning business during its owner's absence. At Kendal three meetings a week were then held, on First, Third and Sixth Days, with a midweek attendance of about one hundred. In the evening public meetings, the attendance ranged from one thousand to fourteen hundred.

And so the account continues about one community after another. At Leeds they had "one of the nicest and most spacious houses I have seen in England, except Devonshire in London"; at Liverpool, there were two houses, an old and a new one, though the latter, being under repairs, could not have been very new. At Chester there were but few Friends, but about sixty were in attendance at the regular session and both at Liverpool and Chester, the public meetings were very largely attended. At Hardshaw, twelve miles from Liverpool, there were but two families of Friends but the large house was the Monthly Meeting center for the countryside, so that two hundred Friends gathered for the session. At Wigton, the one hundred in attendance were "mostly decent looking Friends (although) there were a few other professors." Carlisle contained thirty-two families of Friends and, as usual, the house was crowded to its capacity of one thousand at the evening meeting. It was here that an old Presbyterian minister, "a strong predestinarian," attended and that doctrine being "treated on, some thought the old man bore it quite as well as they expected, but supposed he wished himself out." At the next meeting he did not appear, it being "supposed he and some of his flock were not disposed to hear any more against their favorite doctrine." The surprising thing in the north of England was the great distance Friends traveled to attend these meetings, William Savery noting it,—"Friends take much pains in this country to see travelling ministers."

The decline in numbers of English Friends was even

then very noticeable. William Savery frequently mentions the desire to emigrate, a subject upon which people constantly inquired:

"But I cannot give much encouragement to Friends who are exemplary and useful in England, going to America, the meetings in many parts of the nation being very small to what they formerly were."

and later, with reference to the same inquiry from a watchmaker of Carlisle, whose business had suffered much, due to the new war tax upon watches:

"was cautious about advising him to such a step, but things look gloomy to many people here in this place. He got 1/0 for cleaning a watch and 2/0 for a clock and 6d for a glas."

One gathers, as a general impression from the Journal, a vague sense of the wealth of a few, and that increasing, and the illth of the many, in a constantly accelerated whirl of taxes and economic changes and shifts of which none knew the possible event and from which many desired to escape by going to other less compromised countries.

William Savery's first attendance at London Yearly Meeting came immediately after his return from France in 1797. The delay in leaving the Continent was very wearying to him and his companions because of their fear that they would be too late for its sessions. He also attended the Yearly Meeting of 1798, after most of his itinerant ministry in England and Ireland had been accomplished. In this intervening year he had become very well acquainted with much of the territory and many of the Friends throughout Great Britain.

There is no very clear account of the Yearly Meeting machinery in the Journal. Most of the work seems to have been done by committees and Representatives. The Yearly Meeting personnel, for business purposes, writes William Savery, was then still constituted in accordance with a ruling, dating from about 1720 or 1730. Under it only those were considered members of the Yearly Meeting who were directly appointed Representatives by the subordinate Quarterly Meetings or who were members of the Meeting for Sufferings and their Correspondents in the country and such Ministers as happened to be in town at the time. William Savery explained this feature further, as follows:

"About seventy members of the Meeting for Sufferings, who are called Correspondents of the several counties, not more than fifty attend, tho they all live in or near London, and there are also thirty or forty, called by some Honorary Members, who having once attended, are still retained on the list, out of respect, though they never attend."

Even this limited membership was somewhat subordinated to the Meeting of Ministers and Elders, which met, at times, to the inconvenience of the Yearly Meeting itself. Besides the regular Representatives there were many Friends who attended for the spiritual and social opportunities afforded. Some of them were poor. An unnamed Friend, in the station of Minister, had walked with his wife about three hundred miles, from Ulverston, in Lancashire. He must have been old, as he had been Sailing Master of a Frigate in the American (Revolutionary) War, and had seen service at the taking of Charleston and in other sea fights. Another Minister, John Thompson, was a servant, but had walked from Cumberland, probably three hundred and seventy-five miles, and "divers others have walked from fifty to one hundred and fifty miles."

All the travelers were not poor, as the following description of the approach to London through Northamptonshire would indicate:

"Numbers of Friends passing this road annually to the Yearly Meeting, as well as divers other roads to London, the people along it have learned to know the time and appeared to look with much pleasure on us as we passed through the villages, about fifty having gone along today. The Innkeeper and waiters are especially glad when Yearly Meeting comes, as Friends generally stop at the best and mostly at the same Inn, in every town they pass. They were hard set today, to find us all post-horses, but were as polite and obliging as possible. We let some Friends have the chaises and go on another stage and two companies of us lodged comfortably at Daventry."

A few years later, Charles Lamb wrote sympathetically of this same approach to Yearly Meeting:

"Every Quakeress is a lily; and where they come up in bands to their whitsun-conferences, whitening the eastern streets of the Metropolis, from all parts of the United Kingdom, they show like troops of the shining ones."

But then, Charles might have been prejudiced, as he had once been in love with a Quakeress.

As a Minister "who happened to be in town at the time," William Savery not only participated in the business of the sessions, but was actually appointed on several important committees. The sessions of the Yearly Meeting lasted for ten days of constant activity. In 1797, the meeting of Ministers and Elders occurred at ten on Second Day morning and the first business session started at four in the afternoon. "Both meetings today, I thought somewhat smaller than those of like kind in Philadelphia." The sessions of the Yearly Meeting were usually held in the late afternoon, around four or five o'clock, and the mornings were largely devoted to committee meetings, in which much of the actual work was performed. The method of selecting a Clerk was peculiar. Apparently the Quarterly Meetings took turns in making nominations, and in 1798, "the Northern Quarters, whose turn it was, named Joseph Birkbeck." The reading and answering of the Queries occupied most of the attention for the first three days. It is easy to realize that they would "take a great deal of time," as there were thirteen Queries and thirty Quarterly Meetings sending up answers. London varied from the Philadelphia practice (which still subsists, namely,—reading the answers from the various Quarters to each Query in turn) by reading the answers to all the Queries from one Quarter, without stopping, leaving a slight pause between the readings from each Quarter, for remarks. In 1798, London and Middlesex Quarterly Meeting sent up a request "respecting the so frequent reading of the Queries, which they considered as a burthen and too formal," but this surprisingly modern attitude was successfully staved off to the innocuous oblivion of "next year," in true Friendly fashion.

On four days during the sessions, meetings for worship were held, most of them large and attended by many "gay people." The meetings for business touched many topics, though few were of a broad type. No better illustration could be had of the narrowly introspective nature of the Quakerism of that time than to read of what was "said about tythes, and the dress, address and manner of living above the simplicity of Truth, training up children, &c." Besides vague lamentations over the hopeless state of the world's affairs and the slight interest in the anti-slavery cause, already mentioned, there was no matter of importance to the outside world before either session of London Yearly Meeting in 1797 and 1798 evidenced in the pages of this careful inside chronicle of activities. There was much room for difference of opinion, even in internal affairs, and at times there were "pretty high disputes." Things waxed warmest when women Friends requested that the men receive a deputation of women. "Above an hour was spent in needless debate, whether to admit them or no, at that time, and at length they were admitted." The women at the end of their sessions had the custom in those days of coming "into men's meeting to make report of the conducting of their meeting which appeared to me singular," wrote our observant Journalist.

William Savery visited the women's Yearly Meeting both in 1797 and 1798. In the former case, it was to report upon the Continental journey, upon a hint that the women had a desire to hear of it:

"The meeting appeared larger than the men's, much like our women's Yearly Meeting. Their meeting house a commodious one. We entered more minutely into our account of the Journey; many were affected and it was a solid and I hope profitable time. A young woman appeared at the close of what we had to say, in prayer at the lower end of the meeting."

In 1798, he went under a concern "respecting the departure from Gospell simplicity in some of the great and rich." Their part of Devonshire House was full to its capacity of twelve hundred:

"A greater degree of consistency in appearance was evident generally than I expected. Friends are mending in this land in that respect, though there were still several powdered heads among them."

It was also in the session of 1798 that William Savery freely expressed his uneasiness at so restricted a membership basis and the topic took such hold upon the meeting that a committee was appointed to suggest modifications. Considerable earnest discussion resulted but apparently unanimity was lacking and the matter was "left for consideration for next year."

Another surprising feature of London Yearly Meeting of that time was a salaried Clerk both to the Meeting for Sufferings and to the Yearly Meeting proper:

"J. A., Clerk to ye Meeting for Sufferings, has his dwelling house and firing, and about 250 P per ann for writing for that meeting, ye Yearly Meeting, Ackworth School, Six Weeks Meeting, care of books and library, &c; is pretty constantly employed, and sometimes has a clerk."

A revelation of William Savery's financial arrangements became apparent in a discussion that was very painful to him and Thomas Scattergood, who was also present in 1798, when the subject was broached. Report was made that about £800 was in the Yearly Meeting's stock, with a recommendation that a liberal subscription be taken throughout the Quarters for the ensuing year.

"Some Friends thought the expences ran high last year: wished to know the items, (but) they were not gratified. * * * Something being said about the expence attending travelling out from among Friends, as many now did, as being considerable, though far from finding fault with it, several seemed to think it was spent to good service. T. S. and myself spoke our minds lest some of the young people should suppose all our expences were paid. Mine had cost me 100 Guineas in Europe besides what Friends had done. Divers Friends were sorry anything had been said to draw forth our remarks and a remarkable spirit of generosity appeared. A few Friends, they said about London, would make up all the money next year without a general subscription. The Country Friends grew jealous of their honor, and so it was recommended to be raised as usual. There is a great deal of wealth and hearts to apply it among Friends in England."

The subject of expenses of traveling Friends subsequently claimed the attention of the Meeting for Sufferings under William Savery's initiative, and a smoother practice seems to have been adopted.

With the presentation and adoption of the Epistles to the various other Yearly Meetings, the sessions of London Yearly Meeting ended, but in 1797 William Savery did not think his service complete, so, in company with Deborah Darby and Rebecca Young, he appointed a meeting for the following evening at Devonshire House, for the youth of the Yearly Meeting. Of his two associates in this labor he penned these beautiful words:

"D. D. & R. Y. are as dear to me in the fellowship of the Gospell as ever they were & I think as dignified & devoted servants as any I have seen in this nation. May their example animate me to increased dedication."

The meeting was filled to overflowing and the women's meeting room proving too small, all moved over to the men's where twelve hundred young people crowded in.

One cannot but feel a regret that none of the tremendous problems of world importance, then before the public, broke the calm of those assemblies, but so it was. Internal affairs were the main topics of consideration. The Society had already entered upon the period when a mode of dress was of over-weening importance as a protest against another mode of apparel. The post-war tendencies in dress, referred to in the previous chapter, affected Friends profoundly and sealed the adherence to a uniform and accepted style, as indicative of a consistent life. From about this time, adherence to the accepted form became the prerequisite for any degree of usefulness in the Society. Perhaps upon no subject can William Savery's true broadness of view be better based than upon this of dress. He yielded to none in his valuation of true plainness, but he deprecated lifeless harangues on the subject, and of them there were many. Of a session of the Meeting of Ministers and Elders, in London, immediately after Yearly Meeting of 1798 he records:

"many remarks were made that were lively, tending to stir up both ministers and elders to their duties; some also upon the dress, address &c of the children of Friends in those stations, furniture of houses, &c, with animadversions upon men's hats, with and without stays. An American, C. C., (Charity Cook) pleaded for hats without stays as plainest, which English Friends controverted, till J. Wigam[1] and myself were moderators. The meeting closed sweetly and in solemn prayer, through Ann Alexander."

That William Savery was instant in prosecuting this concern is frequently evident in his Journal, though it, at times, closely trespassed upon hospitality. He found George Harrison, when his host:

"a sensible, kind Friend * * * but more Gospel simplicity in his children and family would have made my visit more agreeable, which I found occasion to hint at, especially to his lovely daughter."

The throes through which the Society was to pass, in the next century, over this controverted subject of dress, will, in the future, prove one of the least understandable aspects

[1] Another American Friend, then itinerant in England.

of the Quaker polity. Changes there were, from knee breeches to barn-door trousers and then to pantaloons, or from sugar-scoops and beavers to hats and felts, but these changes came so slowly, and so far in the wake of fashion, that each succeeding generation firmly believed itself enveloped in a type of clothing that had not varied from the times of the Protector, and repined over adoption of new Parisian styles, which in turn became the accepted garb of fifty years later. On this topic William Savery maintained, in an attitude that seems distinctly modern:

"No standard could be fixed; that countries differed in some small matters, but that plainness was still plainness in all places; wished Friends to keep to the simplicity without formality."

"Such is the influence of education," he wrote afterwards, in comparing the dress of the Friends in Cumberland and Westmoreland with that of the Southern Friends.

"Two things in their dress I observed, rather differing from Friends in the South. The men wore very generally round-bound hats, inside pockets to their coates, but almost every rank of them, capes to their tight coats, which they consider not a departure from plainness, but think a coat with pocket flaps and no cape, quite reprehensible."

Another peculiarity in the Northern country was that the women rode horseback, "like Friends in America * * * This is rare in England."

Passing from the Yearly Meeting proper, to its constituent parts, many interesting illustrations of practice and discipline are apparent in William Savery's account. London and Middlesex Quarterly Meeting in June, 1798, lasted from 10 A.M. till 9 P.M. The morning meeting for worship was so large that "the largest of the new houses" could not seat all the people. "The meeting for discipline (was) much interrupted by one-half of the Friends going out before it began and straggling in, one after another." A recess gave opportunity for those dinner parties which used to be so important a part of Quarterly Meeting on both sides of the Atlantic. The evening session began at 5 P.M. The Queries occupied the whole of it till adjournment at 9 P.M., the only peculiarity being that the Answers from each Monthly Meeting were read by a Friend belonging to it from his seat, "which," wrote William Savery, "I do not think is a good custom."

Surrey Quarterly Meeting was then held at Wandsworth. It was composed of three monthly meetings, but was at a very low ebb. Morris Birkbeck, Jr., was Clerk. In this session, William Savery, whose homeland was still flourishing with newly established meetings arising on all its borders, and no signs of decay yet apparent in the body of the Society, met apparently for the first time the institution now known as an incorporated committee. "It is a new way of proceeding, but things are very low in Surrey," he says. He mentions with surprise that some women were on the committee for this pastoral care, and that one function of the committee was to assist the monthly meetings in appointing Elders, "but E. Foster said they would not find the right stuff to make Elders of."

At the Peel Monthly Meeting, the list of "such who have been disowned by the others (Monthly Meetings) since last month" was read as was usual in London, to prevent, one may surmise, accepting members disowned from other meetings. The custom was scarcely a cheerful one, but is certainly indicative of the frequent disownments. It is, indeed, a marvelous thing that the Society survived such procedure.

The minutiæ of meeting form were in those days fully developed. The removal of the hat in speaking in meeting was one of these, indicative of the illogical practice, extant in America till 1900 or thereabouts, of sitting the meeting through with hats on. Says William Savery,

"I added a little matter with my hat on, but at using the sacred name was easiest to take it off, though my appearances among Friends seemed to be in so much weakness and so small."

In another meeting, he "made some remarks with my hat on" with no compunctions as to removing it. On another occasion, he desired to enter "Paul's Church," as he termed St. Paul's Cathedral, "but on inquiry whether I might wear my hat, which I found could not be admitted," he stayed outside. A similar experience in entering Parliament House was diplomatically met by non-resistance,—"The door-keeper asked us if he might take care of our hats, to which we making no answer, he took them off."

Visiting Friends were by no means accepted solely upon the merits of minutes from their own meetings, of whatever standing. There were a large number of Americans in attendance at the Yearly Meeting of 1798, and those who arrived just before its sessions were put on practical probation, before their minutes were accepted or returning minutes accorded. Another similar practice, now fortunately in disuse, was a hesitancy in rising, when prayer was offered, until sure that the offering was from a source acceptable to the galleries. On one occasion, at Devonshire Monthly Meeting, the men were passing upon a minute for Mary Sterry. William Savery suggested the words "our friend" before her name, which were objected to as "rather complimentary." They were inserted, however. It is rather remarkable, in this period of punctilious formality, to find William Savery opposing the trend. "I have been affected," he says, "to find these expressions dropt in this country for some of the most valuable Friends." It was a time when long meetings and long sermons were the accepted course of events, though a slight ripple in this situation came from "W. B.," after a session at "Gracious Street," which had been entirely silent, when he was "glad it did not hold longer, to teach some of their gallery Friends not to hold meeting so long, as they often do when there is no service."

In charge of John Bevan, of Charterhouse Square, were moveable forms, or benches, and galleries, to accommodate public, or appointed meetings. For this purpose they were moved as far as Wandsworth and Stockwell, and at another time, when William Savery and George Stacy went to bespeak them for such a meeting, appointed for Islington by Deborah Darby, Rebecca Young and William Savery (a trio who often worked together) they found they were already under requisition by Thomas Scattergood for Ratcliffe. Nothing daunted, John Bevan divided them and sent half to each place.

Ratcliffe Meeting House was new. For a year past the meeting had been held

"over a warehouse fitted up for the purpose. * * * The women sat still and the men moved off by a door they had made into the dining room of the next house, where they (held monthly meeting). It had rather a singular look to see side-board with decanters and glasses, pictures, &c, where Friends were doing monthly meeting business."

Among other novelties presented by the new Ratcliffe house, and by one other in London, then new, were the cast iron pillars, supporting the galleries, a feature probably made possible only recently by the development in the iron business.

There are naturally some interesting sidelights on the London Meeting Houses and their frequenters. Devonshire House was then the largest meeting in England, except Bristol. At a midweek meeting there in 1798, there were two hundred fifty present, which was noticed as "larger than usual," due no doubt to the presence of George Dillwyn, Thomas Scattergood, John Townsend, William Savery and some others in the ministry. Two months later two hundred were present in midweek, which would represent perhaps about the average attendance. The house on First Days was always well filled and on special occasions was overflowing, with doors and passages blocked with people. In all its sessions "divers not members" seemed to attend. The men's monthly meeting was held in the "old house" and the women's "up stairs." On one occasion when a par-

ticularly difficult piece of dealing was toward, four Friends
were appointed by the Quarterly Meeting to assist at Devonshire House, and three of them, Richard Chester, William
Dillwyn and George Stacy, were in attendance. What was
William Savery's surprise and chagrin when he discovered
that the subject of dealing was one of his dearest friends
in Philadelphia. Although the matter had been on the
meeting's books for over ten years and had been sent to
Philadelphia once and returned thence with a report, after
two and a half hours discussion, it was again remanded to
Philadelphia of the Northern District, with what results
the Journal naturally does not disclose. As many of the
individual's descendents are members of Philadelphia
Yearly Meeting today, it is safe to surmise that the trans-
gression was leniently dealt with in Philadelphia.

Gracechurch Street Meeting, or as William Savery invariably called it "Gracious Street," was another of the
very active Quaker centers of that as well as this day. On
First Days it was generally full downstairs and about half-
full in the galleries. On one occasion, having

"no particular draught to any meeting, D. D. (Deborah Darby)
pleasantly laid it upon me to attend Gracious Street, which I did.
It was very crowded and many stood. Many of the gay Friends
and many other professions were present."

Like Westminster Meeting, Gracious Street seemed to
attract many who were not Friends, "though," wrote William Savery, "some of the members of that meeting are as
gay as any other people." It was at Gracious Street that
slight reference was made to the theological unrest in the
"close doctrine delivered, and something like predictions of
trouble approaching. The closing testimony was a healing
one, for which I was thankful."

William Allen was Clerk to the Monthly Meeting, which
merited William Savery's encomium that "their business
seemed to be conducted with weight and dispatch, and
upon the whole, I thought, as well as any Monthly Meet-

ing I had sat in London." It was in this Monthly Meeting, too, that William Savery noted the following:

> "They continue the practice of taking down the names of all that attend, both strangers and their own members, I suppose a very antient practice. They record them on their minutes, every man. There was about 30 of their own members present."

Though he was most thrown with Friends of Devonshire House and Gracechurch Street, William Savery deemed Westminster "the most lively and favored meeting in London." In the ordinary attendance of one hundred fifty to one hundred eighty were many convinced members. It was especially popular with those in the neighborhood, aside from the membership, "who were much accustomed to drop into that meeting, * * * people the most respectable in that part of town."

Horsleydown meeting was esteemed the smallest in London at that time, having about one hundred in attendance usually on First Days. It was within walking distance of Joseph Savory's home in Finsbury, and his family and William Savery at times attended it on foot. Mary Savory, who was the daughter of John and Mary Pryor of Hertford, had followed in her mother's lead as a minister and was heard in Horsleydown meeting occasionally. Horsleydown Monthly Meeting had especial concern for an interesting type of gathering held at the Park Meeting, "for the sake of such servants,—male and female, bankers' clerks, shopkeepers, lads, &c, as cannot conveniently, or not at all get to other week-day meetings in any part of the city." The ministers and elders of the other Monthly Meetings "attend as they feel freedom." William Savery, feeling that "all Friends ought to bring their servants, that are members to the meeting they belong to," could not approve this meeting, but he felt it right to attend twice and found about one hundred twenty men and women, chiefly young, there once, and on the other occasion, a rainy night, only sixty in attendance. The Park Meeting House was the scene of one of the great "public meetings," of which William Savery held so many, and the house became so full "that young Friends were requested to go out, to make room for others." Many of them did so, giving place to "some very gay people about the gallery and two clergymen, so-called." The youths remained in the yard and the aisles of the house were filled with people standing, while the meeting held from 6 till 8:45 P.M.

Peel Meeting, or "The Peel," as William Savery usually termed it, gathered about sixty Friends to an ordinary session of Monthly Meeting in those days. J—— Pym was Clerk in 1798. An unusual incident there was a letter read from one of their aged ministers, Sarah Crowley, which took an acceptable hold upon the meeting. "Their business was conducted with much quietness" summed up the visitor's impression.

At Peel Meeting House was held another of the great "public Meetings" which were the especial concern to which William Savery felt himself called. The house was over-full before the time, and once again the youths were requested to give way to strangers. This

"they pretty generally did by going into the men's and women's monthly meeting rooms and many young men into the yard, though it rained. House and yard at length were filled and it was said some hundreds went away, such readiness do people manifest to attend such meetings. My friends, B. West & wife came and sat in the gallery."

Following the return of George Dillwyn and William Savery from Germany, there was a great revival of interest in the Friends on the Continent. Sarah Harrison and Charity Cook, two American Friends, suddenly conceived concerns to go to the Continent and several London Friends applied to their Monthly Meetings for liberty to accompany the American Friends. The situation gave considerable concern to the London Meeting of Ministers and Elders.

Sarah Harrison had applied to London Friends for a certificate, a request that many opposed, as she was not a member with London. In spite of great hesitancy, the certificate was finally granted, but six or eight Friends declined to sign it. Charity Cook did not apply for a certificate. William Savery was not in unity with the action:

"If our certificates on a journey are unlimited from home, they need no addition. If not, I do not apprehend any other body of Friends ought to enlarge them."

Further uneasiness came to the Meeting of Ministers and Elders by reason of the minutes obtained in considerable hurry by local Friends from their Monthly Meetings, without sanction subsequently by their Quarterly Meetings. A special session of the Meeting of Ministers and Elders was called, as was then possible, upon the desire of three of its members. After sitting three hours and trying four times to break up, it declined to act upon one of the minutes. Said William Savery:

"It was, to be sure, the most trying meeting to me I ever sat, of that kind in London. I was mostly silent and glad when it closed."

No roster of London meetings of that time would be complete without reference to the school and workhouse at Clerkenwell. William Savery visited it several times, attending the meeting for worship there. It impressed him very favorably, and his interest in the Philadelphia project that afterwards developed into Westtown School was stimulated by his acquaintance with such institutions. At the joint expense of the London Monthly Meetings, Clerkenwell was very much upon the hearts of London Friends of all ages. In attendance at one of the meetings there, were "several high people and one clergyman." William Savery found the children as usual very responsive to his ministry. Regarding the institution, he wrote:

"It has been abundantly blessed. Several that have been educated there are now valuable ministers and many useful and promising young people are in Friends' families from thence. After meeting visited the old people in what is called the Work-house, where I believe, however, very little work is done. There are about twenty of them who are clothed and live decently. They appeared pleased with the visit. It was also an agreeable one to me."

Such are some of the unusual features of London Friends' meetings as disclosed in William Savery's Journal. No attempt has been made to portray the constant succession of meetings then as now held in the city. These were in due course and were the backbone of that type of urban Quakerism that was to prove the predominant influence in the Society's life for the next century, when the city was increasing and the country decreasing in Quakerdom the world over. The strong undertone of the Journal is a lament over the affluence and high living of the Friends. Simplicity and plainness were tending toward or had become formal. Elaborate homes and abundant tables had absorbed the artistic creative energy that wealthy Friends stifled in other directions. Business activity presented another outlet to such energy, and the reputation of the men of the Society for shrewd, albeit straightforward dealings was already well acknowledged. Of these and other social features among Friends the next chapter will deal.

## CHAPTER XXVIII

# SOCIAL LIFE AMONG ENGLISH FRIENDS

Although he visited among and called upon Friends of
every degree of affluence or the reverse, and although his
service led him into prisons and workhouses, William Savery's direct social affiliations were with the well-to-do
Friends of London. He was by no means a wealthy man
himself, but he had some means and used them to defray
part of his expenses. He was very well educated, and as
reading went in the Society of Friends in those days, he
had read widely. His very extensive traveling, along the
Atlantic seaboard, in the wilds of America and in the war-
torn countries of Europe, had endowed him with an experience far beyond any of his London associates. He was
a good conversationalist, although his own Journal naturally
does not record any direct hint of that. His power of interesting and holding children and youths would point to
it. When in London, his headquarters were at the home
of Joseph and Mary (Pryor) Savory, of Finsbury, London.
He refers affectionately to their house as "my common
home." In this home he was master of his own time and
engagements. The entertainment of traveling Friends was
no novelty to the Savorys. They kept open house
for all such, and their "prophet's chamber" was rarely
unoccupied. Their home was of the best type of the "plain
Friends."

The great distinction in the Society of that time lay
between the "gay" or "high" Friends and the "plain"
Friends. The formal mode of dress, as we have seen, was
already an established feature, although William Savery
was probably not alone in his desire that Friends keep

"to the simplicity without formality." Dress was an easy criterion to apply, and the adoption of the plain dress was the visible symbol of a supposed inward grace, among a people who, of all others, eschewed any symbols. To it attached much the same sanctity, and from it was derived much of the same guarded piety as mark the religious robes of the Roman Church. Readers of "The Gurneys of Earlham" will recall the mortifying struggles through which Joseph John Gurney and his sister, Elizabeth (Gurney) Fry, who were of the "gay" type, had to go in the sudden adoption of the garb, following their convincements and the consequent gulf that yawned between them and their former associates and even relatives. Emphasis was placed upon the desirability of being a "peculiar" people, as were the Hebrews of old; but in strange ignorance, the vaunted peculiarity was interpreted as "grotesqueness" rather than as "intimacy." In the century and a half since the Society had been founded, so much had been accomplished, as the fruit of persecution, that the formal garb, with the social stigma it so often entailed, became a sort of self-imposed cross, deemed of spiritual value, not only on account of its simplicity, but because of the stigma itself. Fortunately for the future of the Society, there was little hypocrisy in the plain dress. The literature of the time, which may well be taken as illustrative of public opinion, is by no means complimentary to the Friends, where it deals with them. The war riots in London of the period sometimes eventuated in looting bakers' shops and stoning Quakers. Pacifism must have been the chief reason for this, but the unlovely figure of Abel Fletcher, in "John Halifax, Gentleman," is of a type that was fortunately rare.

Mention has been made of the change in social values in England, due to the new industrialism. This social change was of enormous importance to the Society of Friends. Their peculiarity and aloofness had made them self-conscious; their secular ideals in education had intensified their separateness, and these elements, with the tradition of persecution, that at this time was not very far back in the past, gave the Society as a whole, and its individuals in particular, a social timidity and reserve, that were often mistaken for religious snobbishness. Time and again William Savery expresses unfeigned appreciation of traveling courtesy extended to him, or of civilities from clergymen, as if such things were to be marveled at.

This sense of a kind of vague ostracism opened to the Quakers a most peculiar opportunity in the industrial field. Merchants and manufacturers were of inferior standing in the English social scale. Especially was this true of the latter where the "manual" element, then still prevalent, gave the calling a connotation practically equivalent to the "hand-worker" of today. But Friends, having already a sense of some social discrepancies, to which they had accustomed themselves, and being in many places hand-workers, in the strict sense of the word, developed a marvelous ability to become manufacturers, very much by the same graduation that has evolved garages, in modern times, from old-fashioned smithies.

And so, in the course of years, the Society had taken an increasingly prominent part in manufacture and trade, and with these, in banking. Of his hosts and acquaintances, in various parts of England, William Savery mentioned the calling of many. Comparatively few were farmers, except of the gentlemanly type around London. A few instances may be interesting. Mention has already been made of the Foster Brothers, of London, whose calico works employed many people on the seven or eight hundred different patterns in their stock. One of these brothers, Joseph Foster, lived at Bromley, and regaled his guests, after Monthly Meeting in June, with

"the most luscious pine-apple I have seen in Europe, out of his hot-house, also fine blue grapes and strawberries."

[ 367 ]

There is mention of a family named Fosick, umbrella makers, and of Jane Jeffreys, who, having joined Friends two years before, had been turned out of doors by her parents; whereupon she "began a little mercer's shop & mending umbrellas, and her trade is now so increased, that she fears she is in danger of growing rich. She appears to be blessed for her integrity." Pym Nevens of Leeds was "a great manufacturer of cloth"; John Pryor, of Hertford, was a spinner and dyer of worsted; T. Simkins, of Tooly Street, London, a watchmaker; Edmund Fry, a founder of printing types, and John Cash, of Coventry, was a minister, and a manufacturer of "camble callimancoes." It was he who exported to James and Samuel Fisher, of Philadelphia. He told William Savery that he wished all his customers were as good pay as the Fishers were, as he sometimes "lay eighteen months out of his money." Mention has already been made of Robeson, a Friend of Birmingham, who silver plated iron ware, and of John Burlingham of Worcester, who dyed skins and made them into gloves, in which work he employed eight hundred men, women and children. Still more remarkable was the membership, by recent convincement of a young lawyer of Plymouth, named Harding Grant, whom William Savery met at Sparks Moline's. Membership at the bar and in the Society of Friends were hardly considered compatable in those days.

Harder to understand, from the modern standpoint, were the Friends engaged in the liquor business. Matthew Wright, of Bristol, was described as a "useful Friend, largely in the wine and brandy trade." At Hitchin, the traveler took breakfast with William Lucas and his sister Phebe. He was "a brewer and a valuable young man," while the sister was a minister. Richard Bush of Wandsworth, near London, was a distiller on a large scale. The business was evidently very heavily taxed, in the war exigencies, he having paid the incredible sum of £90,000 during the winter and spring preceding, in excise. The

Journal so states very plainly. He was feeling low in mind when William Savery visited him, over the loss, the evening before, of a faithful employee, who had been suffocated by the fumes in one of his vast butts, of three hundred hogsheads capacity. William Savery and he discussed the distilling business, evidently with some concern, the visitor inquiring, diplomatically, of his host, whether "he were not tired of it." Whereupon Richard Bush "wished he were out of it, but did not know how to come at it." This slight critical allusion and the inference already quoted, that a sideboard, glasses and decanter were not harmonious furniture for a monthly meeting room, at Ratcliffe, London, are the only hints of disapproval of the liquor traffic in the Journal. In fact, most Friends of that time interpreted "temperance" literally, instead of meaning abstinence. Many Friends in Philadelphia in times previous had been brewers and practically all Friends partook of some sort of spirits. William Savery constantly quaffed ale, wine and beer, which with tea, in copious draughts, were the indicia of real hospitality. "Bread, cheese and ale" were a comfortable and customary quick lunch in fast traveling. Mention has been made of the purchase of beer for the Newgate prisoners, by the Friends, who, after their visit in the jail, repaired to William Fry's in Mildred Court and partook of cake and wine themselves. Such social customs are appropriately brought to light today rather to inform the present-day Society than to extenuate the practice. When the struggle against intoxicating liquors came in Philadelphia Yearly Meeting, the chief advocates of abstinence were the younger men and the conservatism and weight of the meeting were loath to disturb the comfortable practices of their youth. So it ever is between crystallized practice and effervescent reform!

William Savery saw something of the "high Friends," as those were termed who in British parlance belonged to the "upper middle class." In the spring of 1798, when nature was evidently at her best, he spent a night at Samuel Hoare's, in a fine, open situation, on one side of Hampstead Heath, and commanding a view of London, six miles distant, and the intervening villages. Here, as in other places, he admired the extensive grounds and gardens, "in high stile, much beyond the simplicity of a Friend." He was most graciously entertained:

> "His son and daughters came to me, and though they are quite in high life and gay in their appearance, were as loving and kind as possible. * * * Here seemed to be almost everything this world could wish, and an open reception for Friends, but more conformity to the simplicity would have made it still pleasanter to me."

The London home of Dr. Lettsom, whose wife was "quite a gay woman," but, withal, very hospitable to William Savery, was full of curiosities, collections and bric-a-brac of various kinds. The Doctor and William Savery were the only ones in the household to use the plain language. His country home, "Grove Hill," at Camberwell, was situated in the midst of charming gardens and fields as the Doctor owned "a great part of the land and houses in and about" the village. It being only three miles from London, many citizens repaired thither to walk through his long and delightful grove of elms, furnished with seats, and in the midst of all stood his house:

> "He has a very large museum of natural curiosities, fossils, minerals, fish, petrified into stone and many insects, enclosed in transparent stones, in their full shapes, &c, by nature; the club that killed Captain Cook & a vast number of curiosities that appears as though it would require a man's life to collect them."

Museums, libraries and curios were at their heydey among the well-to-do. Samuel Alexander, of Needham, whom William Savery visited with Jasper Capper, had a combination both indoors and out, that was typical of the wealthy Friends of the period. He had a large, commodious house, open at all times for entertainment, under the efficient care of his two daughters. He, too, had extensive gardens and a farm, adjoining his house:

"He took us into a labyrinth of hedges, such an one as I never saw, which though it covered but about one-half acre of ground, Jasper Capper nor myself could neither find the way to a tree in ye center, nor out of it again, though we spent much time."

Inside the house was a large library and "as much the appearance of affluence as most Friends' houses I have seen in England yet. I do hope (he) has a mind much redeemed out of it all."

Even more sumptuous were the house, gardens and fishponds of William Fry, near Epping Forest. He had purchased some farming land also, making an establishment that gave William Savery some concern. "I reminded him of not setting his heart too much upon it," he records in the Journal.

At Norwich, William Savery wove himself into the fabric of the Gurney family, in a manner to which reference will be made later. Suffice it now to say that at Joseph Gurney's seat, "The Grove," the shrubbery, gardens, house, etc., were "almost in the stile of a nobleman," though the Journalist adds, "he would make a noble man in Society (of Friends) if he was sufficiently willing to take up the cross. He is worthy of much esteem and I hope improving in usefulness," and later, he mentions him as "dear Joseph, * * * whom I loved increasingly the longer I was with him." Of John Gurney and his home, "Earlham," including about one hundred sixty acres of farm land, "in which he takes much delight," William Savery wrote:

"His house, which was formerly ye seat of a nobleman, is very large and magnificent, far from being of a piece with the simplicity of our profession. That, with the dress of his children, * * * and other appearances of grandeur, made me sorrowful, though I saw but little opening to relieve myself."

The affluence of the Norwich Friends was by no means confined to the Gurney families. William Savery mentions the chandelier and the excellent lighting in the handsome new meeting house, with the same curiosity that the cast iron pillars in the new London meeting house had excited. He adds:

"It appears as though a great part of the Friends here kept their coaches. The meeting house yard, which is large was filled with them and others."

He mourned so sincerely over these elaborate and ostentatious ménages, that it is agreeable to find him recording another type of English Friend's home. J—— Hagens, of Wandsworth

"lives in a little old fashioned box, about five miles from London, where he has an acre and a half of ground, garden and stables, in great simplicity, for about 12 pounds a year. * * * This has been the summer residence of his family for several years. I could but commend them for their example of simplicity, considering their wealth, but they said they were sorry to see Friends go so far as they did in their grand and costly houses, gardens, furniture, and equipage."

The summer vacation feature sounds distinctly modern, but the modest rental almost makes one sigh for the times that long have been, even though England was at this time in the throes of foreign war.

Another of the more modest country places described was that of Isaac Bragg, just outside of Whitehaven, in Cumberland. William Savery visited this hospitable Friend in September, 1797, and states:

"He has lately bought a handsome freely estate, clear of tithes or any other incumbrance for 2800 pound. It has an excellent new house, four rooms on a floor, two story, good garden, coppice of wood, stabling &c, 52 acres of land in fine order but not naturally rich. He reckons it very cheap."

There are no descriptions at length of the more modest homes, such as those of Joseph Savory, in Finsbury, London, and of his children in Islington or Pentonville. That they satisfied the traveler's needs and amply supplied that warm hospitality which did much to overcome the homesickness that he suffered in his long absence is apparent in every mention of them, but he does not describe them.

Typical of many of them, perhaps, was the home of the Widow Fearson of Cockermouth, who had "a son in Philad°, Walnut Street No. 7, named Peter Fearson, a member of Society." She and her two sons and two daughters kept a grocery and followed the tallow chandling business. They were very courteous to the stranger, perhaps the more so on account of the son in Philadelphia, and their own desire to emigrate to America, a desire that William Savery could not cordially encourage.

It is probable that William Savery pictured the grander homes in which he visited, because he was more often entertained in such, and also because they pained him with their lavishness. They no more represent the prevalent type of British Quakerism of the time than do the paupers in Clerkenwell Workhouse. Each was an extreme of a Society that was, by and large, prosperous, thrifty and contented, and conscientiously abstemious of ostentation.

Quite naturally, William Savery was in demand at the time of funerals, and he attended several in the months of his service, in and around London. The coffin was then still in use made at times of plain and again of varnished elm. Frequently they were lined with copper and were of great weight. The handles on the sides were like those on chests of drawers, for the convenience of the pall-bearers. The lids fit down over the coffin like the top of a snuff box, and all coffins, both of Friends and others, were plain. Hearses were in use and professional undertakers officiated, but the bearers often had to make long walks to the grave. The coffin was carried, in one case at least, upon the shoulders of the young men. The friends and relatives followed the coffin, two by two, in a burial at Staines, and the sight, as they went through the streets, lined by the townspeople and a number of genteel "cidevant nobility of France who lived in the town," was affecting as well as beautiful. "None but Friends follow their relatives in such order," says William Savery. Funerals were frequently held on the First Day of the week,—on one occasion five in London alone. Burials were made at Bunhill Fields, Long Lane, Winitmore Hill and White Chapel.

In education, Friends then, as always, took a keen interest. It is fair to surmise that the preëminence that the small Society has taken in many matters, in the past two centuries, has been due to the importance so early placed upon schooling. At the time in consideration, there was practically no school system in England. Education for the masses was considered undesirable in some conservative national circles, lest it tend to elevate to tastes beyond the possibility of attainment, and thereby lead to acute distress. In the Society of Friends, there was by no means an adequate school system, but there was a beginning, and a conscious desire to fit all "for the duties of life."

A few of these schools, William Savery mentions. At Ipswich, "a school of pretty lads" attended the week-day meeting. They were from the boarding school, hard by, which "boards, educates, washes, &c, for about 20 Guineas per ann, an addition for French." At Hitchin, was another boarding school, kept by a convinced Friend and his wife, named Blacksland. Thirty of the pupils attended the meeting, among them Jeremiah Head, "the son of dear John," to whom William Savery felt particularly drawn, because of his affiliations with the Heads in Philadelphia. It was a remarkable occasion that the traveler described, one of the many where his power with children was strikingly demonstrated:

"A Friend or two stept in. The lads were collected in pretty order. I found my mind quickly drawn toward them in much affection. Our good Master favored with utterance in a manner which they could understand. Samuel Alexander had a good testimony, attended with power. All the lads and probably all in the room, were broken into tears. It was a time of special favor, I hope some will never forget. Now I thought I saw evidently the hand of the Lord in detaining me here."

A similar school was kept by S. West's wife, at Wandsworth. After meeting, William Savery and William Farrer dined at the school, as "I wanted to be with the dear children," and he adds, "I offered a little matter to them, under which several were much broken."

Mention has already been made of the charity school at Clerkenwell. At Birmingham there was another, founded on similar lines, "a noble institution for the education of orphans, carried on upon a cheaper plan by far than Ackworth, and yet nothing seems to be wanting." It is peculiarly refreshing under present-day educational enigmas to read William Savery's comment at Birmingham, that "some think the servants at Ackworth are too numerous and that the girls and lads, by turns, could properly be employed to save the necessity of divers of them, as is the case in this institution." And the present generation smugly congratulates itself upon student self-help as an original and modern solution for some of the extravagances of school administration and life!

Ackworth School was a most interesting institution to William Savery and Thomas Scattergood, for both of them were deeply engrossed in the plan for a similar school for Philadelphia Friends. William Savery was at Ackworth in July, 1797, at the time of the "yearly meeting," or annual visit of the Committee in charge. He arrived through the "country, full of hills and dales, but handsome," and was glad to see many of his acquaintance from different parts,— "particularly my London friends, with whom I had the most intimacy, R. Chester & wife, G. Stacy & wife, Wilson Birkbeck & divers others, with my friend, W. Farrer, from Liverpool."

The Committee's visit lasted from Meeting time, Fourth

Day, till Seventh Day afternoon, and a momentous time it was for all concerned. At the midweek meeting:

"all the dear children attended in beautiful order and were about 300. There were also about 200 Friends and many of the neighbors, not professing with us. My heart was much tendered at the first sitting down, and it proved, thro divine condesension, a solid, good meeting. 'Study to shew yourselves approved unto God,' was urged to the precious children, who were much melted and broken, especially the giver."

It was a parlous time for the pupils. No sooner was meeting over than two committees, one of men and the other of women, were chosen from the two hundred or more Friends present as "Representatives," to examine the boys and girls. These committees, in turn, were "classed" in eight divisions, and proceeded to work.

"I being appointed and classed, met 22 boys, Joseph Starr, our head-examiner. We got through eleven of them that evening, examining them separately, a paper being produced with their names and program in the different branches of learning last year. They appeared generally to have improved, though one of them was exceeding short-sighted & had much ado to see the letters in the book, and another a very great stammerer, who wept & seemed confused while he was examing. I pitied him much. They spelt, read, shewd their writing, compared it with last year & their cyphering, and were also critically examind respecting their grammar, in which divers were well qualified; then the progress or deficiency in each branch was taken down to serve for next year."

The Friends also

"went to see the dear children sit down at dinner. They have wooden trenchers and are very plainly served. Their tutors sit with them and they sit a little in silence before they begin."

At a meeting of the whole Committee, where the introduction of a new grammar and different regulations for the School were considered, William Savery proposed the entire relinquishment of "corporeal punishment." The topic "had place in the minds of many Friends," but apparently the birch was not forthwith abolished. The classes

[ 376 ]

in session were next visited. The daily regimen is thus summarized:

"The tutors (are) mostly young Friends between 20 and 30. They (the children) all spell from 7 to 8 in the morning, then go to breakfast an hour—then sit school till 12 (and) afternoon from 2 to 5 & sup at 6. They are obliged to give the service of the words they spell, which appears to me worthy of imitation."

It was no small task for the School to care for so large an influx of visitors. "Public Friends and those who were traveling in Truth's service," numbering twenty-four, sat at table with the Superintendent, "dear Jonathan Binns," as guests of the institution. About one hundred eighty others from all parts of England, dined in the Boys' room, and with them William Savery once breakfasted "by request." "They had their dinner at 1/0 each, besides the drink, from the Inn belonging to the institution." Many of the visitors lodged at the inn or in the village of Ackworth, but apparently public Friends were again preferred, as "I had a good bed in the School."

Probably for reference in Philadelphia, the schoolhouse and grounds are described in considerable detail, in the Journal, together with the family routine. On the playground of two acres, William Savery saw the boys under more normal circumstances:

"who I thought not a little noisy and rough in their amusements, though one of the masters is always near hand them. They are decently lodged two in a bed & take turns in helping the chamber maids clean the room. The girls also by turns, help in the kitchen & to wait on table. Upon the whole the regularity, decency and order is good & if in some things they do not come up to my expectation, in others they exceed it & I think it a credit to Friends, but considering the plainness of the diet & dress of the children, am rather at a loss to know how it can cost near 15 Guineas each, as it is said to have done last year."

The closing scene of the Committee's visit is as odd as it is obsolete, from the standpoint of modern charity:

"At 12 a bell being rung, near 200 beggars were let in the gate, who most of them appeared above the stile of common ones, but had been accustomed to come every year the last day of the meeting to receive the cold meat, left by the Innkeeper, which Friends purchased and divide among them & also make a collection of money. They were mostly women, and after arranging them on benches, the fragments were distributed, and to each one from 6d to two shillings in money, after which Sarah Lines and Phebe Speakman appeared in the ministry among them, under which they appeared tender and thankful."

After leaving Ackworth the travelers came to the Retreat at York, an institution for mental defectives that commanded William Savery's admiration. He attributed the origin of the institution to William Tuke's daughter, Ann Alexander, but it was built by general subscription, at a cost a little under £6000, "a sum I think much less than such a place could be had for within one mile of Philadelphia." He admired the handsome appearance of the eleven acre tract with its high situation, handsome garden, and good bathing house, and especially the cast iron window sashes, painted to look like wood. With accommodations for forty or fifty persons, the inmates numbered nine women and seven men in its second year. Four shillings a week was the lowest rate, and those who could afford it paid a half guinea. "Everything seems to be done to prevent the place having a gloomy appearance, as places for that use too generally have. * * * It appeared to me an institution worthy of Friends."

The two topics of social reform in which Friends appeared most interested were slavery and prison conditions. Of the latter, a previous chapter has dealt. In the former the Society did in England what proved impracticable in America. Not only did London Yearly Meeting, through its committees, engage directly in anti-slavery work, but the individual Friends began to agitate outside of the Society and in company with people of other denominations. Wilberforce and Clarkson, though not Quakers, were so closely in accord with the Quaker position, that they almost seem to be so.

The incidental importance of this agitation was twofold. Within the Society were developed independent committees or associations that carried on reform work, whether or not the Yearly Meeting as a whole approved. By this means progress was possible, even though official Quakerdom (which in those days was much narrower in personnel) did not go along, and that, too, in the name of the Society. This method became very common in America where the splits, diversities and divisions were much more pronounced than in England. Only in our own day has the influence of these collateral organizations waned, as they tend, one after another, to merge their work with a willing official body that in less favored days spurned such unauthorized and creaturely activity.

The other important tendency, resulting from anti-slavery agitation, was the reëntrance of the Friends into public activity, but in a new and, as the event proved, a lasting manner. To quote from one of the most readable modern historians, referring to this period:

"Our poets, philosophers and religious enthusiasts, including John Wesley himself, and the Quaker body as a whole, initiated the attack on the slave-trade. Religion and humanitarianism began to renew a connection that had not been obvious during the Middle Ages or the Wars of religion. The initiation of the anti-slavery movement is the greatest debt that the world owes to the Society of Friends. * * * The success of this agitation, then unique in the character of its aims and methods, is one of the turning events in the history of the world. * * * These methods of voluntary organization and open propaganda were directed first to persuade the public and then to bring the pressure of public opinion to bear on the Government. * * * Its methods became the model for the conduct of hundreds and even thousands of other movements—political, humanitarian, social, educational—which have been and still are the chief arteries of the life blood of modern Britain." [1]

Trevelyan: *British History in the Nineteenth Century*, 50-51.

In 1798, William Savery introduced into the Meeting for Sufferings in London a concern that that body should address the Government upon the slave-trade. It had been six years since such an effort had been made and "this serious and alarming time to the nation" seemed to offer an opportunity. A large committee was appointed and as a result of its efforts an address was drawn up and a revived impetus given to the anti-slavery cause, though with what further results the Journal does not inform us.

This activity in the world's affairs was a new departure, but even then it was far more restricted than the Society would agree on today. It is not possible to conceive of a modern Friend, telling a responsible minister of Government, like Wilberforce, who suggested to William Savery, in the passage already quoted, that Friends were the fittest people in the world to make peace, that "in the present state of worldly policy, Friends were quite shut out, from the nature of their principles, from any interference." English Friends were to wait till the Crimean War to find the first faint glimmerings of a world service for humanity, in love and faith, overtopping the bloodshed and the quarrels of nations. In America the vision was not to come till still later, and then through the lessons learned from English Friends and their harsh experiences in the early days of the Great War, until consciously and unconsciously a pattern of "service" was woven, that has stamped for Quakerism for all time an ideal and an incentive. Whether practical or not from the political standpoint, the venture of faith which Wilberforce intimated and Savery declined would be made today by the Society, if the opportunity were offered. There can be no doubting the fact, even though the effort should prove as quixotic as Ford's Peace Ship. The Society, today, is keyed to a different pitch from that of 1800. Its reaction to war and its inbred mission for peace are at once based upon a more intimate knowledge of the causes of war, and a more reckless dependence upon a venture of faith, than the Friends of 1800 had. May it not be well to record, before the atmosphere of the Great War is too far dissipated and while we can yet remember the spiritual heart-burnings and the tempered ostracism of conscientious objection, that those times demanded a spiritual recklessness and abandon that are disappearing with the emergency that called them forth? As the nation sprang to defense in war, and developed unknown energies from unexpected sources, so the Society of Friends, in its own peculiar way, aroused itself to a new and positive pacifism, that smacked somewhat of the spiritual romanticism of the First Publishers of Truth.

The difficulty with the Quakerism of William Savery's period was that it had ceased to be constructively radical. It had lost its early impetus. In the time and persons of Penn, Barclay and Penington, wealth, station and learning had ignored popular opinion and jettisoned reputation in the effort actually to bring in liberal or radical acts as well as ideas. The English and American Quakerism of William Savery's time was highly respectable and well to do, albeit entirely middle-class or below in England. The Friends had lost the intrinsic will to adventure in the social application of the religion they professed, that had so eminently marked the early period. They still hazarded individual comfort and bore the rigors of travel, such as the present generation knows nothing of, but were not girded for a contest, involving social ostracism more fundamental than "peculiarity." The sufferings and the despite which several generations before them had borne, particularly in time of war, had been bred into the very marrow of their narrowing circle of social sufficiency. Moreover, Friends were beginning again to enjoy a comparatively new sense of social acclaim. Particularly in Philadelphia, where the Revolution had greatly discounted Quaker respectability, and where there was no prejudice against merchants and traders, such as existed in England, the Society by 1800 had found something to cherish and develop, with a quiet and consistent persistence, as a basis for the spread of Quaker influence. Much the same inclination is apparent today, when once again, Friends having survived the ostracism, have caught the eye and the acclaim of a busy world. A realization, not only of the strength that such prestige lends, but of the temptations to which it is liable, will go far to help in the present day to a wise and sane attitude toward our possibilities and obligations.

## CHAPTER XXIX

# WILLIAM SAVERY AS A TRAVELER

Mention has been frequently made of the minute and careful observations that William Savery records so constantly in his Journal. It is this feature that distinguishes it from the writings of other Friends of his period. Although he traveled in the ministry, his interest and concern went out to a far wider range of topics. Amusing incidents, scenic appreciation, economic circumstances, and interest in persons and places for their own intrinsic worth are penned with the same zeal that actuated his religious records. In fact, it is not too much to say that he considered them all as a part of his mission. Says Dr. Lettsom:

"He mingled condescension and cheerfulness with animated conversation; and without being obtrusive, the importance of his reflections arrested attention, and the manner of conveying them made them impressive. He had seen much of the world and deeply studied mankind, and his various remarks were no less profound than interesting. * * * His conversation thus tempered, was gratifying to every class of the community; and when he conversed, young people were wont to get near him, to listen to his remarks and to profit by his counsel. * * * However urgently his conversation might have been courted by his friends, his deference to society and his unassuming manners made him adverse from intruding himself, and towards others, attentive to harken and to learn."

His liveliness in social intercourse, the "spark of national vivacity," already referred to, was apparent to others than Dr. Lettsom. It is mentioned in the appreciations of him in the Philadelphia newspapers after his death:

"His open countenance beam'd with the cheerfulness of good-will and the grave deportment that becomes his profession was happily tempered with natural urbanity as well as Christian grace."

Another observer who has recorded William Savery's ease of social intercourse was "S. R.," the wife of William Rawes, in England. At Poole, she and her husband were in William Savery's company at the home of Mary Paul:

"Dear William (Savery) supped there. He was very familiar in conversation with us and as usual, retired to take his pipe. The company by degrees, followed him to the other parlour * * * where we were much gratified by his entertaining converse."

One can well imagine that the conversation of a traveler would be worth while, when it included intimate experiences among the savages on the American frontier, perils by land and water in the American wilderness, and along most of the Atlantic seaboard, in addition to the more recent German and French journeys. He was in the prime of his manhood, being between forty-six and forty-eight years of age at the time of his European experiences. It is probable, however, that his intrepidity wasted his strength and that his death at the age of fifty-four was partly due to his hard traveling.

He was a good sailor, and off and on, saw much of the sea in his European experiences. The voyage from America was in company with a bevy of Friends, Samuel Emlen, Deborah Darby, Rebecca Young, Sarah Talbot and Phebe Speakman. They sailed from New Castle, Delaware, on May 18, 1796. A farewell meeting was held at New Castle before departure. Elizabeth Drinker's busy pen recorded the day before:

"Ruth Rutter, Betsy Foulk and Nancy Mifflin, jun'r dined here. They set off about One O'clock in our carriage, H. D. with them. They intend for Chester or Wilmington this evening, tomorrow to New Castle, where a meeting is proposed to be held before the embarkation of ye friends who are to take shippen there."

There were about one hundred forty Friends who thus accompanied the travelers to New Castle in the middle of the week. They received signal courtesy from the Court then in session, it adjourning and devoting the Court room to the meeting. Judge Basset and many of the magistrates and lawyers remained through the session. The *Sussex* was anchored off shore and to it the wayfarers repaired at eventide. The voyage lasted just a month, much of the time in foul weather and rough seas. Their kind Captain, Philip Atkins, thought the gales harder than he had ever experienced at that time of year, "the sea continually breaking over both the main and quarter deck." Off the fishing banks of Newfoundland the usual fogs were encountered and to avoid the many fishing boats a conch shell was constantly sounded:

"The number of cod annually taken here is astonishing. They fish for them with lines forty or sixty fathoms long, with heavy leads and two hooks; several of these being kept out at a time. Some tend them and others on board split and salt down the fish in bulk, until they are loaded when they return home and dry them. We threw out a line and soon took seven of from ten to twelve pounds weight."

"A mountain of ice," two hundred yards long and forty feet above the water, offered a lull in the monotony of travel on one day, and soon after they were boarded by men from the French privateer, *L'Espérence*, with two hundred men and mounting twenty guns. Being friendly to the Americans, they were not molested and the privateer went merrily on her way in pursuit of a brig. Later, just outside of Liverpool, ten Guinea slavers passed, outward bound. Truly the reflection was justified:

"Those who venture to cross the ocean need to be well convinced that they do it upon a good foundation; such may humbly rest in confidence upon Him who gathers the winds in his fists."

Of William Savery's marine experiences, none was more exasperating than his return from France to England at the end of his Continental mission. He and his fellow travelers had come to Dunkirk, with every expectation of receiving passports, as Americans, to England by the next post. They waited in vain from April 24th, depending upon a Captain Flemming, of Paris, for their papers. He finally notified them that a new law required an additional tax of three livres to be paid in Paris. William Savery was exceedingly anxious to attend London Yearly Meeting and this new delay prompted him to make preparations to go through Holland and thence to England via Hamburg. Finally the Mayor of Dunkirk proposed to give them passports drawn for other persons. It was a sore temptation, and all the more so because nearly every one else was using that expedient. Our Friends declined them:

"Upon sight of them I immediately was convinced my peace, which is better than all riches, would be broken. I have endeavored so far to keep a conscience void of offence on the Continent and feel my mind relieved at present from the pangs of condemnation, though I know I am weak and poor and liable to err from the strait path of duty and I believe it may have been the case in several instances. * * * My hopes now almost totally failed of reaching the Yearly Meeting of London, I retired to my chamber, low and discouraged."

Just how the Friends got away is not clearly disclosed. The sympathetic Mayor finally inquired as to the terms that they would be free to accept and William Savery stated them. David Sands in his Journal states that they

"could not feel easy without letting the Magistrates know it was our intention to go to England, if we could get there; that we would not clear for any port; only wishing to go on board a ship to get out of their ports."

The Mayor acquiesced at once, whereupon all of them "were quite easy with the mode," and left the next day on the *Hancock*, a New York ship, going to England. They were stopped twice near the French coast and their credentials, which evidently did not bear a French visé, examined. Then came the difficulty of landing in England, and once again the temptation to avoid the law. But five ports in England were open to receive passengers from an enemy country, and those nearest were Dover, Southampton and Gravesend. Any captain landing passengers elsewhere was subject to a fine of £200. In spite of the prohibition, the *Hancock*, lying in a fog, put off a boat with some adventurous spirits who promptly lost their way and were only reclaimed by assiduous blowing of a horn. The Friends then took to the boat, deciding to try to land openly at Margate, or if prevented, to go on to Gravesend. At Margate the port officials handed them the King's Proclamation. A long parley ensued and the boatman went ashore to summon some resident Friends. These came down to the quay bringing bread and gammon cakes, but their entreaties could not prevail. The boat put off again and sailed all night with little rest for the occupants, reaching Gravesend in the morning and their troubles were over. The *Duke of York* packet bore the travelers on to London. While on it

"some sailors and bad women soon began to grow troublesome. An old man * * * told them not to swear so prophanely, at which one of the impudent women pertly hoped we had no Quakers on board. I told her I had the honor to be a Quaker and David (Sands) united in it. After some time the passengers mostly gathering into a large room, below decks, those two women came down. D. S. began to speak to them and the two women became much broken. A young man, a Baptist, seconded him in a very feeling, sensible manner and I added my unity with them both and some addition of my own. One of those abominable young women, in a particular manner was bathed in tears. * * * After she had wept much, she fell asleep and remained so till we arrived at Billingsgate Stairs and landed."

Another sea adventure occurred while the *Washington*, on which William Savery had taken passage for America, was lying in the Cove of Cork, daily expecting to sail under convoy. With two lads to row, he attempted to go to Cork.

"It began to rain. I had no upper coat and was in a poor condition to meet a storm. Night came on before we got to Cove and the rain increased. The night growing very dark and waves ran high:

in vain did we search for the Washington, but continued going from one ship to another till the Commodore fired the 9 o'clock gun. Wetter it was impossible for me to be, but fearing the consequences if we remained out much longer, I chose the miserable alternative of going to the town for a lodging. The two lads in the boat were wearied and as wet as myself. We providently landed safe, but not without danger. I gave the lads 5/0 instead of the 3 which we agreed for and they at length, after much inquiry, found me a bed. The people of the house lent me a dry shirt and a great coat. They had no supper for me but a bit of bread and 3 or 4 mouthfuls of cold veal. Took some port wine and went to bed, after hanging my clothes on chairs to dry."

The next morning after a better night than he had anticipated, he donned his wet clothes again and returned to the *Washington*, which lay a half mile off in the harbor.

A peculiarity of William Savery's Journal, which bespeaks the innate genius of the traveler, is the detailed observation of trivial but interesting things. In Ireland he met an infant prodigy, a blind lad of eleven years, named Osborne. His case is so authentically reported that there can be no doubt of the truth. William Savery tested his amazing powers of Scripture quotation, including the ability to tell at once the chapter and verse of any quotation from the Psalms. But such tests of mere memory were insignificant, compared with other feats. He

"has been taught by help of a board, filled with holes and some iron pegs to multiply (as quick as anyone) nine figures, taken promiscuously by two or three others, and give the produce, in hundreds of millions, with the greatest accuracy and expedition.

"But what is the most remarkable and no way to be accounted for by reason,—when he is asked what day of the week, any day of the month in any year for any length of time back happened to be, he answers in a moment. I tried him for the 19th of the 11M, 1778, the day I was married, and the 18th of the 5M, 1796, the day I embarked from America. The first he immediately said was Fifth Day and the second, Fourth Day. I asked him, by help of some very old Almanacks, several questions of like kind, forty or fifty years back. He answered immediately and never missed once. He cannot tell how he knows it; makes no calculation, as he answers in a moment."

Such a psychical phenomenon was not the only one to arouse William Savery's interest. As deism and Tom Paine were the prevalent topics of religious discussion, so in scientific was "animal magnetism," or the "power of sympathy." At William Fry's, in Mildred Court:

"the whole family, except Ellis and Thomas, are great proficients and have performed surprising cures. W. F. Junr can tell by the power of sympathy what part of the body a person disordered is most affected or has the most pain. This has been several times proved, fevers are not a disorder, but the effect of a disorder. All this intelligence was extraordinary to me, yet cannot doubt in the least the veracity of the Friends."

Leaving such phenomena as these to psychical research, other incidents, some grave, some whimsical and humorous, claim places in the general run of comment. Anything out of the ordinary was sure to be noted. At Devizes, in Wiltshire, was a monument in the middle of the street:

"erected to commemorate the sudden death of a woman who told a lie in a solemn manner, in order to defraud. I took the inscription off. It is a solemn warning to deter people (from) frauds and lyes in making bargains."

Like most Friends of his generation, William Savery knew his Cowper well. Reminiscent of the "twice ten tedious years" of the wedded life of the Gilpins, William Savery recorded:

"Passed by the 'Bell,' at Edmonton, celebrated by Cowper in his 'John Gilpin,' the Sign of John Gilpin, with his wig flying off, going full speed on horseback."

Perhaps he recalled:

> "At Edmonton his loving wife
>     From the balcony spied
> Her tender husband, wond'ring much
>     To see how he did ride.

> "Stop, stop, John Gilpin—Here's the house—
> They all at once did cry;
> The dinner waits, and we are tir'd;
> Said Gilpin—So am I!"

The road must have been a fast one perforce. William Savery states that his journey from Hertford to London was "the quickest I ever rode in England."

Another reference is to the White Horse near Uffington in Berks:

"Not far from Calne, we saw on the side of a high chalky hill the figure of a large white horse, of excellent shape and limbs very accurately formed, which was done many years ago by a person in the neighborhood by taking off the dark soil, which is but about a foot thick and thus exposing the chalk in that likeness, which is so large that the outlines of it takes in more than an acre of ground, and is to be seen at many miles distance. Once a year at an appointed time the people come in great numbers to curry the horse, as they call it—that is, to freshen up the chalk and keep up its conspicuity, but it seems they make it a day of rioting."

A half century later, in 1857, the "scouring" of the White Horse was resumed and the legendary origin of the horse far antedating William Savery's information was made available to all by Thomas Hughes in his "Scouring of the White Horse."

One more incident is redolent of antiquity:

"Coming out of Coventry, which is an antient looking town, principally consisting of one street, about one mile long, we saw the effigy of Peeping Tom, which is still preserved, looking out a second story window."

Once again the poet has caught the legend, though in this case Tennyson immortalized the Lady Godiva, years after William Savery's passage through Coventry:

> "Then she rode back, clothed on with chastity.
> And one low churl, compact of thankless earth,
> The fatal byword of all years to come,
> Boring a little augur-hole in fear,
> Peep'd,—but his eyes, before they had their will,
> Were shrivell'd into darkness in his head."

# WILLIAM SAVERY AS A TRAVELER

The statue of Peeping Tom is still preserved (1924) in a top story window near the corner of Hertford and Smithford Streets, Coventry, it having formerly been in the window over a boot shop on the same site.

At places in the Journal occur hasty memoranda, entirely unconnected and evidently penned as fancy dictated. Thus he notes seeing the "heaviest man in England." Of the same tenor is the chance entry in Ireland:

"A woman, 2½ feet high, 25 years of age, perfectly made and handsome, proposes by advertisement, to see company at 1/s each, at Belfast, from 10 to 1 and from 3 to 8 in the evening,"

and

"a blind man with his mother on his back, aged 86, in a sack, led by a faithful dog, solicits charity,"

and in London, the whimsical advertisement caught his eye:

"A porter wanted. He must be a man who fears God and can carry two hundred weight. Apply No 94 Fleet Street,"

and the next item is,—"Insolated, a term much in use," together with the statement, already quoted that

"G. Bott drew 16 teeth out of one woman's mouth, which was all she had, and made her two compleat jaws full, as white as ivory."

England at that time was inquisitive into the habits and customs of the other peoples that for the first were becoming part of her national life. Collections and museums, both public and private, were the order of the day. In the tower of London was at that time a collection of wild beasts, and "many things to gratify the curious." William Savery inspected these with James Phillips, the bookseller, and his three sons, their guide, "a curious man," being a Swiss. Dr. Thomas Pole of Leadenhall Street had a gruesome collection of skeletons that he had gathered in the course of his practice. Dr. Lettsom's two museums at Camberwell and in his Town house in Baringhall Street were probably as elaborate as any of the private ones. Mention of them has already been made. Don Saltero's Coffee House at Chelsea had another collection of curiosities for the amusement of the public. Captain Cook and his exploits seem to have attracted an unusual share of attention in England of that day, as his relics were contained in several of the museums. With William Dillwyn and his son, George, William Savery went to visit

"the Leverian Museum which is an immense collection of the most curious fossils, minerals, birds, beasts, reptiles, insects, with a great variety of Otaheita curiositys & others brought by Cap<sup>t</sup> Cook and a vast number of things, extraordinary both in nature (and) art which come under no particular description; the whole beautifully arranged in a number of rooms and are sufficiently extensive to amuse those who have a taste for such things for months."

At Newington, in the grounds of Jonathan Hoare was a collection of another kind:

"He has the most delightful avion of birds of a great variety of kinds, natives of the four quarters of the globe, that I have ever seen,—the part open to the air and sun, covered and sided with wire net work and planted with shrubbery, in which some of the birds build nests. I could spend a great deal of time in company with these delightful songsters with much pleasure."

The craze had extended to Ireland too. Joshua Wilson and his wife of Rathangan had

"a vast variety of curiositys,—flying squirrel, humming bird, &c, Virginia nightingale or red bird from America, with many other curiositys preserved from the same place. A species of parrot has been 22 years in ye house, a goose 52 years old in good spirit." * * * As they have no children it serves to amuse these kind and worthy old people innocently."

At Clonmel in Tipperary lived worthy Robert and Mary Dudley whose hobby evidently took another tack. They "shewed and read me many curious manuscripts & gave me some of a very antient date." One can but wish that these manuscripts had come down through the generations. These old manuscripts must have made a strong appeal to

William Savery, as he was evidently fond of such things. In London he was a frequent visitor to the book-shops. After a session of the Meeting for Sufferings, in which an effort had been made "to stir some one up, among the many qualified Friends" to edit some children's books, which were "so interlarded with romance compliments of the world" as to be unfit for Quaker usage, William Savery betook himself to James Lackington's book-shop to investigate for himself, and to make a few purchases. It must have been a wonderful store. One can hardly credit the statement that it contained "near 500,000 volumes of different kinds." Darton and Harvey and James Phillips also conducted book-shops that were very attractive to the literary browser, and William Savery spent many hours among their treasures. It was at James Phillips' that he discovered, apparently for the first, the book of his sermons that proved so disconcerting to him.

The instinct of the traveler also took William Savery into "Paul's Church," as he termed the Cathedral, at the time of the annual visit by the children of the London Charity Schools.

They were

"differently dressed in new clothes, received yesterday, most of them plain, decent and substantial. Some of the boys had blue bonnets and some hats, and some of the girls straw hats, plain and some ornamented with a ribbon. * * * All of the children of one parish were dressed alike, and preceded by the beadles dressed in red and lace clothes, and other officers, with rods in their hands, the parson of the parish, etc., and after the children, their tutors and assistants or ushers, male and female. It was to me a very interesting sight and supposed to be about 6 or 7000 in number, but I thought it was too high rated, perhaps there might be 5000."

The sight must have been spectacular. Several thousand people attended, mostly with tickets of admission. William Savery "had some curiosity to see them altogether when seated," and the doorkeeper readily granted him admission as he was a foreigner, but he declined when he found he would have to remove his hat. Mayhap Dickens got some of his "Oliver Twist" from some such scene:

"I contented myself with seeing them in part from the door. The children all sat on scaffolds, one above another, under the dome, and the people promiscuously in all parts of that enormous fabrick, which I apprehend was nearly filled."

St. Paul's evidently thrilled William Savery more than he was willing to acknowledge. He returned the next day and watched the demolition of the scaffolding. He dilates upon the proportion and symmetry of the building, so perfectly harmonized "as to deceive the sight as to the height of the dome." There was no sculpture there then excepting busts of

"the benevolent Howard and Johnson, the author of the Dictionary, but there (were) many colors of different nations, taken in war, hung up as trophies of victory, as the Dutch by Duncan, those taken from the French at Valenciennes, &c. On the whole, though it is an enormous pile of extraordinary workmanship, yet I thought I had seen more magnificence and beauty to a common eye in some great cathedrals on the Continent of Europe."

Such enthusiasm and curiosity about the details of cathedrals were unusual in the Quakerism of that day, and all the more so in an itinerant minister. A similar mention of the Cathedral at Chester which was "so antient the stones outside seem to be wearing away with time," ends with the same comparison,—that "neither its size nor magnificence equal many on the Continent."

Mention has already been made of William Savery's keen appreciation of the scenery of southern France, with its vineyards, olive orchards and Mediterranean landscapes. In England and Wales he was as alive to the beauties of nature lavished around him in his travels,—and that, too, at a time when mere natural beauty was not as much appreciated as it has been since the days of Ruskin and Wordsworth.

# WILLIAM SAVERY AS A TRAVELER

In leaving the "beautiful town and valley about Caermarthan" our traveler lingered over them. They "attracted my eyes as long as I could see them." Later at Cardiff, the seat of Sir Charles Morgan, with its copses of trees, its fish pond and large pile of ancient buildings, surrounded with hills, and the park, with hundreds of deer, sheep, goats and cattle browsing, attracted him strongly. "I thought it the most attractive spot of earth I had almost ever seen." From the high hill above the wells at Bristol, he saw a "most delightful prospect, perhaps as any in England," over Somerset and Gloucestershire and across the Severn, into Wales. His enthusiasm for the hills and valleys of Cumberland and Westmoreland, which he saw later, eclipsed this judgment of Bristol. Lake Windermere, Derwentwater, "about the size of Brandywine," the waterfall near Ambleside and finally Mount Skiddaw, "said to be the highest mountain in England," found him again needing superlatives in his account.

Frequently in his desire to see the country, both in England and France, William Savery would arise early and take a walk before breakfast. At Ackworth School, this cost him a sprained ankle, as he jumped off a wall into the hay field, in the early morning freshness. While he was awaiting the sailing of his ship to America, he spent some nights on shore, and on one of these, at Glenmire, in Ireland, near Cork, where several Friends had country houses, he arose early one morning, and he and "Peggey," the daughter of his host, Paul Abbott, "indulged ourselves with a walk over the hills for an appetite to breakfast," in "the beautiful, winding valley." With or without company, he was very fond of walking, whether in city or country, either for exercise or to relieve his pent-up feelings. In London, "not being able to find any Friend at leisure in this very busy city," William Savery took a long walk alone, "through Fleet Street into Holborn, Snow Hill, Smithfield and along Barbican & Chiswell Street, home."

These walks seem to have given him peculiar solace. When under the heaviest stress of spirits in his foreign service he took refuge in a solitary walk "in some quiet place, out of the noise of the town." Taking coach to St. James Park:

"I walked very quietly alone round the Pond for about an hour. There being but few people walking, made it more delightful, and I enjoyed it much. The bustle of London is too great to be endured long together. This Park and the walks about are very agreeable, with little ornamental, either in the palaces or other buildings near it."

Another busy combination of religion and peripatetics was a certain day in June, 1798. Dining in the Poultry at William Dillwyn's, William Savery, with Thomas Scattergood as companion, soon left and they

"took a quiet walk through Moorfields, &c. His mind seemed low and commanded my near sympathy."

Followed tea at five at Islington with the Savory cousins, and then,

"a long walk afterwards through the fields, over steples, &c, where a vast many people walk; passed by White's Conduit House and garden, which are public for every decent person to walk in, also by Copenhagen House, a tea drinking place & to Highberry, a pretty village, mostly inhabited by Londoners, among whom are some Friends."

William Savery dignified his philosophy of walking, in one of his printed sermons, in these words:

"And this I am persuaded of, that a private sober meditation, and an evening's walk of a wise man, thus informed, is indeed the highest gratification that noble and rational beings, as we are, can enjoy."

Toward the end of his stay in England, William Savery, Mary Knowles and George Dillwyn were received at Buckingham Palace by King George III and Queen Charlotte. Although Dr. Lettsom, who was in good position to judge, attributes this reception to "the deep impression which his public testimonials had produced," one feels that the Continental travels of the two men and their interview with the Duchess of Brunswick, King George's sister, may have been the real motive behind the intimation to William Savery "that his presence would be acceptable to the royal family of the British Empire." The preliminaries were arranged by Benjamin West for the evening of March 10, 1798. It is unfortunate that the manuscript of William Savery's Journal covering this interview is lost, so that the printed edition and Dr. Lettsom's account in the Introduction to an edition of William Savery's Sermons, are all that are available.

The King, Queen and three of the Princesses, with Prince Ernest Augustus, received the Friends alone in a drawing room. The Princess Amelia was absent and William Savery, inquiring for her, was told she was unwell. Princess Mary was, however, sent for her sister and both soon attended, upon which William Savery, according to Dr. Lettsom's account, told the Queen:

" 'I am delighted with thy children and their becoming appearance.' The Queen instantly addressed the Princesses,—'Do you hear what Mr. Savery says of you?' "

Ernest Augustus opened up at once with a line of questions, "but with rather too much rapidity," about affairs on the continent, and particularly regarding Lyons. The King soon joined in. Says William Savery:

"We conversed with the king, queen and children like old acquaintances; and I told them I was grateful for their condescension in receiving us in this social manner—for there was not a single person with us in the room all the time. The king asking me about the situation of things between France and America, I told him I seldom meddled at all with politics, as it was not my business. 'No, no, no,' said he, 'I understand; but as a people you can never form so natural an attachment with any nation of Europe as England; we are united by religion, relationship, commerce, disposition, &c.' I replied that I valued the connection and hoped the family compact would never be broken. And the queen, who had caught a part of the conversation, desired I would repeat it, was much pleased with the idea and spoke of it to her daughters with satisfaction. The king spoke of the Theophilanthropists in France, but had not a right idea of them. I told him I desired to embrace the good as my brethren, under every modification of outward form and profession in the world; to which he and the queen replied,—'A good Christian must do so, for he has the same regard for good people of different professions.' After much free conversation, I could hardly take leave of them without tears. Benjamin West made a motion; the king and queen with the children drew a little back and with gestures of respect, bid us a 'good evening.' I said a few words at parting; George Dillwyn also expressed a little. After we retired, Benjamin West staying a little, heard the king say to the queen, 'Charlotte, how satisfactory this has been.' "

Both to Ernest Augustus in the forepart of the interview and to the King at the end, William Savery dilated upon the horrors of warfare and its appalling harvest in Europe. Dr. Lettsom, writing after William Savery's death of the interview, records the King's inquiries for Americans, "for whom he expressed a continuance of parental regard." Whether the good Doctor's memory was at fault, or whether William Savery's diplomacy outdid his candor, it is hard to say, but George, under either circumstance must have been gratified when William Savery communicated

"to the King the high esteem which the people very generally entertained for him; and that the Society of Friends had always preserved an inviolable attachment to his person and family to the last moment of the American Revolution."

Certainly the forepart of the statement was incorrect, and the latter, even twenty years after the Revolution, was a perversion of the attitude of neutrality, that most of the Society, with rather less than more success, endeavored to maintain.

It was upon surer ground than Buckingham Palace vouchsafed, that William Savery visited two of the Quaker shrines of England and Scotland. In a frame of mind that most Friends, traveling under concern, would not at that time have acknowledged, still less recorded, William Savery visited Swarthmore and Ury. They came in line with religious work, to be sure, but the veneration and awe experienced in visiting scenes, hallowed by historical piety, found the visitor, in William Savery's case, receiving more than he dispensed. The meeting was held at Swarthmore, a quarter mile from the Hall. The house was in good repair and the members composed about a dozen families, living mostly at Ulverston, a mile distant. William Savery uniquely describes them as "good looking Friends." An appointed meeting was held in the meeting house, but distance and rain combined made the attendance only two hundred. The next evening another and larger meeting three hours in length was held in Ulverston in the large Independent meeting house. It was so packed that many were left outside and one woman fainted.

"Going over these grounds caused me to feel serious, I confess, but not superstitious," wrote William Savery, after chronicling the events of the day. He had seen the two heavy armchairs, with elaborately carved backs, used in the meeting by George and Margaret Fox, and the ebony bedstead, left by George Fox for the use of traveling Friends. He describes the premises,—the paved footway between the meeting house and the Hall, and the shaded walk from the Hall to Ulverston. The gateway of rough arched stone, through which Margaret Fox's carriage used to enter, the stone-paved first floor of the Hall and the carving of the wainscoting and chimney pieces of the second floor were the most interesting part of this "large pile of antique building." At Elijah Salthouse's hospitable home in Ulverston, he saw "their antient monthly meet$^g$ book, in the day of G.F. which was curious." There also was the old folio Bible of 1541, with its chain and padlock, by which it had formerly been attached to the wall of the meeting house, for the triple purpose of satisfying cavillers, refuting the charge that Friends rejected the Bible, and for the use of poor Friends arriving before meeting time, which, says the Journal, was

"a far better and more consistent employment than many now are in the practice of before meetings begin, such as conversing ab$^t$ news, trade and politics."

In a similar frame of mind William Savery visited the home of Robert Barclay, the Apologist, of Ury, near Stonehaven, in Scotland. A young Robert, then aged eighteen, had recently come into possession of the estate. "The likeness of Friends seems quite extinguished." The young laird had gone ahunting but his preceptor was most desirous that the visitors should stay to dine with him at four o'clock after his return. Though they declined the invitation, they were courteously shown over the house, which was the same on the exterior as in the time of the Apologist, but had been somewhat modified inside:

"The Library room which was small, was the place where R. B. is said to have wrote his works. There are a great many antient Friends' books, all R. B.'s writings and all or nearly all the pieces in opposition to him, as G. Keith's, &c. There were many other books of a more modern date and on different topics."

The landscape effects outside were admirable, with Stonehaven and the sea in the distance, and a handsome garden, planted round with firs and other trees in the near view. The burial ground, a half mile from the house with a mausoleum over the graves of the Barclays, evidenced their pride in the Apologist, by mention of him on all the stones after his time. The Estate, writes William Savery:

"is said to be now worth 2000 a year but much involved in debt and young R. B. is going away to board in England for some years to save expences & clear the Estate of some of its incumbrance. A considerable part of the land has been long kept in pasture which is excellent and let to a grazier at 30/ P acre; many cattle and sheep on it."

One is tempted to surmise that "young R. B.'s" economies in England would have proved a myth.

The meeting house had not been used for some years. It stood within a few yards of the mansion house.

"The ministers' gallery and some other seats remaining, but appears to be now a place for broken furniture and lumber."

In rather melancholy mood, the Friends wended their way toward Aberdeen, leaving

"the former residence of the excellent Apologist & Defender of our faith with heaviness of mind and reflections upon the impossibility of the best of men conferring grace and virtue upon their descendents."

In this same connection one very conspicuous omission in William Savery's Journal should be noted. No mention whatever is made of William Penn, although William Savery spent more time in the environs of London than in any other section of England. One would think that a Pennsylvanian, of all others, would cherish the memory of the Founder. Strange as it may seem, there is no mention of any part of Buckinghamshire, save in an incidental manner in passing through. Penn had not been dead a century nor had the significance of his life and work been so fully appreciated as they are today. Perhaps the miserable indebtedness of his later years and the failure of his mental power had dimmed for the generation at the close of his own century the luster that history has since acknowledged; whatever the cause, there was evidently not to William Savery the same appeal that exists for Philadelphians today to visit Chalfont, Ruscombe and Jordans in the reverential mood that betokened William Savery's serious, albeit not superstitious frame of mind at Swarthmore and Ury.

When the time came for the return voyage, William Savery experienced a renewal of sore tribulation. England was at war and the seas were rife with French privateers. Practically all merchantmen were armed and none sailed without convoys. He was conscientiously opposed to both cannon and convoys. Long and anxiously did he seek a vessel that would avoid both. Two trips from London to Bristol, the inspection of many ships and numerous requests to captains to eliminate the guns were fruitless. Finally, after weeks of homesick inquiry, he was forced to accept the convoy. He booked on the *Washington* from Bristol, a poor craft, of dubious seaworthiness but carrying no guns. With him sailed Elizabeth Hoyland, a young ministering Friend, wife of John Hoyland, of Sheffield, who was seeking a home in the New World.

We little realize, today, how elaborate were the necessary requirements for a voyage in those times. William Savery mentions placing his stores and provisions upon the ship and erecting the stoves for warmth. William Lewis, a kind Friend of Bristol, noticing a deficiency in the "cabouse," and being a dealer in them, provided "a good and commodious one," of £12 value, with instructions to sell it, either to the owners of the brig or in Philadelphia, the proceeds to go to his brother in America.

At Bristol, the farewell was most tender and affectionate on the part of many Friends, particularly those who had come down from London:

"* * * All proceeded on to Lamplighters hall ab$^t$ 2 mile from where the brig lay in Kings Road. There having an upper room in the Inn, we dropped into a sweet and strengthening silence, during which, that language (was) revived with much comfort on my mind of 'Return thou unto thy rest, Oh my soul, for the Lord hath dealt bountifully with thee.' "

A number of Friends and among them "my tender cousin, E. Savory," then boarded the ship and sailed down the Bristol Channel for fifteen miles, finally leaving in a small boat in a driving rain.

"I looked after them as long as I could well see them, they at times waving their handkerchiefs. Wet as it was, I staid much on deck till evening, the shores of Wales and Devonshire being on each side."

# WILLIAM SAVERY AS A TRAVELER

And so they sailed to the Cove of Cork. In these safe waters the fleet was to assemble to go west under the convoy. No more beautiful seaport could have been chosen, but for once the rocky cliffs, green slopes and islands of the harbor failed to find appreciative record in our traveler's pages. He was weary to repletion. Week followed week and still the fleet did not sail. For more than a month the ships were gathering and in that time William Savery was frequently upon land attending meetings and visiting families. Finally the signal was given and over a hundred sail sallied forth, only to be dispersed by a terrific storm, that blew the *Washington* away from the rest and out of her course into the Bay of Biscay, "a place of much danger with respect to the French." She was not able to rejoin the convoy.

The return voyage was not lacking in the perils of navigation. The *Washington* was leaky and poorly equipped, especially with water and provisions, but the trip was safely made. One incident of thrilling nature occurred in mid-Atlantic, when a ship bore rapidly down upon them:

"Early in the morning the captain came to my room and informed me there was a ship in sight, but he could not yet discover whether it was an enemy or not. * * * I sat down quietly waiting the issue; the prevalent opinion among our people was that she was a Frenchman, and our seamen seemed confident that she was. The suspense and fear lasted more than an hour. I was preserved from fear or disturbance. * * * When they came up they ordered us to lay to till they came on board, which they did being armed, no hats but handkerchiefs tied round their heads, with strong appearances of being neither Americans nor Englishmen; all our people seemed in consternation and dismay, but when their captain boarded us and shook hands with ours, all countenances brightened again, yet with a mixture of fear and doubt. The captain of the stranger said he knew me; had seen me in France and was pleased to meet me again as a friend. They spent an hour with us in a social manner, informed us that the ship was the Camilla, a letter of marque from Boston for Malaga, had fourteen guns and thirty-five men; and ordering his men into the shrouds, they gave us three cheers, fired a gun and parted from us."

## CHAPTER XXX

# FAMILY CONNECTIONS IN ENGLAND

As already mentioned, William Savery's mother was Mary Peters, the daughter of Rees Peters, a Philadelphian of Welsh extraction. For the sake of permanent record, it is interesting to record a family allusion which William Savery penned in his Journal,—one of the all too rare references of this kind. As he and his companion entered Swansea, Wales, in January, 1798, he says:

"We passed by a large house, which we were told, belonged to George Haines, formerly of the house of Haines and Crawford, Philadᵃ, who married my cousin, Kitty Peters. I looked out of the chaise and saw her in the parlour and waved my hand to her. She clasped her hands together, astonished to see me & her & husband invited us to stop, but we went to the Inn and dined, then came to tea with them and took up our lodgings. My cousin and the family highly delighted to have us, spent much of the evening, talking of our friends and dear relatives in Philadᵃ. They live in a stile of elegance, gave each of us a good room and bed and we slept comfortably."

Before leaving the next day, the travelers inspected George Haines' extensive pottery of Staffordshire ware, employing one hundred men, women and children, and turning out a product almost comparable to chinaware. A most affectionate farewell sped the party on its way when they left, and William Savery bore with him pleasant recollections of the visit, which must have been of even more interest to his aged mother. There is no other reference in the Journal to these Welsh connections of the Peters line.

In the *printed* edition of William Savery's Journal there is no accurate mention of the Savory relatives in England. The sole reference to "my cousin, A. Savory," was evidently

MARY (PETERS) SAVERY

inserted by the Editor without warrant from the manuscript, at that place. There are, however, many references
in the manuscript to the London Savory family, conclusive
enough to satisfy the most exacting as to a degree of relationship. Soon after arriving in London, William Savery
refers to his host as "my valued kinsman, J. Savory." The
term kinsmen occurs several times and is even more indicative than the word "cousin," which might, even in those
days, have had its Elizabethan sense of intimacy only.
These references, coupled with the statement of Martha
Yeardley, quoted in Chapter II, would indicate that William Savery and Joseph Savory were second cousins.

Making the best of this slight information, we can learn
something. Very soon after his arrival in London, William
Savery repaired to Joseph Savory's home in Finsbury, and
throughout his protracted stay in London, and on all his
return visits, this was "my common home" and Joseph and
Mary Savory were "my kind host and hostess." It is no
small credit to the hosts that his references to them and their
hospitality grew increasingly affectionate as the account
proceeds. From other sources, we know that Joseph Savory
was a goldsmith in the Strand,—a strange calling for a conservative Friend.

The home of Joseph and Mary Savory was constantly
open, "a house of public resort for Friends," as Mary Savory's mother called it. They entertained many of the American ministers traveling in England, and this intercourse
has made their names familiar on both sides of the Atlantic.
Joseph Savory had married Mary Pryor, in 1786, he being
at that time a widower with four children. His new wife
was the daughter of John and Mary Pryor, of Hertford,
the latter being the itinerant minister of the Gospel, who
was traveling in America while William Savery was in
England. While in Philadelphia, she was entertained by
Thomas and Rebecca (Scattergood) Savery whom she mentions in her letters with affection.

Joseph Savory's first set of children consisted of a son, Ady Bellamy, and three daughters, Hester, Anna (called Nancy) and Elizabeth. There were also three daughters by the second marriage, but of them William Savery mentions only "little Mary" of whom he was very fond. Mary Savory, like her mother, Mary Pryor, was active in Society, appearing frequently in the ministry, both at the Peel and at Horsleydown meetings. She accompanied William Savery on several of his London visits, especially in family visiting, in which he much appreciated her gift. On one of these occasions "several of the young people (were) very tender, especially dear Anna Savory," under the concern of several ministering Friends, of whom William Savery and Mary Savory were two. Anna, or Nancy, was his particular favorite. Young though she was, she was frequently with him in service, and on one occasion,—his return from Ireland,—she was his only companion, having apparently joined him in Dublin. They sailed thence, with many others, to Holyhead, Wales. In their departure, William Savery's leather trunk, containing "all my money, most of the diary I have kept since leaving home, many curious papers and things of one sort or other of value, which I had either bought or my friends had made me presents of," was left behind in Dublin. The other Friends went on leaving him and "poor A. Savory" behind, while he had "never felt so much distressed since coming from home." With indefatigable industry, he spent the day in viewing and writing up Holyhead, "a poor, dull little town," witnessing a Welsh wedding, reading in a poor circulating library and eating a "true Welsh Rabbit or rather rarebit." What his cousin Anna did is not recorded, but he was infinitely relieved, when, at four the next morning, the barkeeper "bolted into my room, saying, 'Mr. Savery, I have glad tidings to bring you. The packet's arrived and your portmanteau is in my possession.'"

For some reason, not clearly disclosed, all of Joseph

Savory's first set of children lived by themselves in the London district, called Pentonville or Islington, for the two names are used synonymously. That their father's second marriage in 1786 was the cause of their removal may be surmised, but even if it were, there was complete cordiality between the two homes, so far as is disclosed in the Journal. In the accounts of this home in Pentonville, whether "to visit my young cousins," or "with J. Savory, to drink tea at his daughters'," or "with the girls," there is an atmosphere of radiant and enthusiastic youth. It was not confined to sociability alone. After dining with them, in company with their father, at one time, William Savery "had a solid opportunity, in which I was favored to relieve my mind of something which had lain on it for some time, on account of these dear young people." Hester, Nancy and their brother, Ady Bellamy Savory, were then at home, and they "left them in much tenderness."

Toward the end of his stay in England, Hester, then twenty-one years old, accompanied William Savery and his friend, Benjamin Rotch, an American sailing-master from Nantucket, Massachusetts, on a journey. A post-chaise to Islington, at four in the morning, then the inevitable and ubiquitous cup of tea, and off they went for Bristol, one hundred sixteen miles in sixteen and a half hours.

Entirely unconsciously, William Savery, with his uncanny habit of being on hand when interesting events were toward, was, all this time, close to one of the minor romances of English literature. The young Savorys lived in the end house of Chapel Street, Pentonville. This little street, only two blocks in length, is today well within metropolitan London. Its dense population and teeming sidewalks have little of the quiet, suburban calm that must have been its attraction at that time. Even less in harmony with that early respectability, would be the evening markets of today, with their stalls, produce carts, baby carriages and bawling hucksters jamming the street from side to side. Not far from there was the Islington madhouse, so-called (though modern speech would give it a milder name) where Mary Lamb was living in 1796. On that account, at the end of the same year, Charles Lamb removed to No. 45 Chapel Street, Pentonville, and later to No. 36, in the same street. Here, after the death of their father, Mary Lamb rejoined him and they lived there together until 1800. We remember from "Old China," that 'twas from Islington that Charles set out, late one Saturday night, for Barker's in Covent Garden, to knock up the old book-seller and to purchase his Beaumont and Fletcher folio, which he then lugged back to Chapel Street. Soon after, Mary was taken ill again, and Charles Lamb moved away, writing to Coleridge [1]:

"My heart is quite sunk and I do not know where to look for relief. Mary will get better again; but her constantly being liable to such relapses is dreadful; nor is it the least of our evils that her case and all our story is so well known around us. We are in a manner marked."

It was in this brief period that Lamb saw Hester Savory and began to worship her from afar. They were both young and he was in deep need of sympathy. Moreover, he was then strongly inclined toward the Society of Friends. Charles Lloyd had visited him in January, 1797, and left, not only a warm impress, but the copy of John Woolman, of which Lamb afterwards wrote, "Get the writings of John Woolman by heart."

On February 13, 1797, Lamb had written to Coleridge [2]:

"Tell Lloyd I have had thoughts of turning Quaker, and have been reading, or am rather just beginning to read, a most capital book, good thoughts in good language, William Penn's 'No Cross, No Crown'; I like it immensely. Unluckily I attended one of his

[1] Lucas: *Life of Charles Lamb*, I, 250.
[2] Lucas: *Idem*, I, 154.

meetings, tell him, in St. John Street, yesterday, and saw a man under all the agitations of a fanatic, who believed himself under the influence of some 'inevitable presence.' This cured me of Quakerism; I love it in the books of Penn and Woolman, but I detest the vanity of a man thinking he speaks by the Spirit, when what he says an ordinary man might say without all that quaking and trembling."

As the neighbors were so well acquainted with the troubles of the Lambs, it is possible that Hester Savory knew Charles Lamb, but certainly not intimately. It is almost too preposterous a pun to attribute even to Elia, but his reference, again in "Old China," to their lunch of "savoury, cold lamb," during the Pentonville residence may have been a facetious coupling of names, personally significant to the writer at least. In 1802, Hester married another man and died in 1803. In March, 1803, Lamb wrote to Thomas Manning [1]:

"I send you some verses I have made on the death of a young Quaker you may have heard me speak of as being in love with for some years while I lived at Pentonville, though I had never spoken to her in my life. She died about a month since."

The verses enclosed were his little lyric, "Hester," slightly stilted, but entirely sincere. They will be read as long as the loves of literary folk interest the public,—and be it said in this instance, with far more tenderness and profit than is often the case:

> When maidens such as Hester die
> Their place ye may not well supply,
> Though ye among a thousand try,
> With vain endeavor.

> A month or more hath she been **dead,**
> Yet cannot I by force be led
> To think upon the wormy bed,
> And her together.

[1] Ainger: *Letters of Charles Lamb,* I, 198.

A springy motion in her gait,
A rising step, did indicate
Of pride and joy no common rate,
 That flush'd her spirit.

I know not by what name beside
I shall it call:—if 'twas not pride,
It was a joy to that allied,
 She did inherit.

Her parents held the Quaker rule,
Which doth the human feeling cool,
But she was trained in Nature's school,
 Nature had blest her.

A waking eye, a prying mind,
A heart that stirs, is hard to bind,
A hawk's keen sight ye cannot blind,
 Ye could not Hester.

My sprightly neighbor, gone before
To that unknown and silent shore,
Shall we not meet as heretofore,
 Some summer morning,

When from thy cheerful eyes a ray
Hath struck a bliss upon the day,
A bliss that would not go away,
 A sweet forewarning?

Thirty years later, Collier, in his "Old Man's Diary" [1] records an incident, indicating that the attachment of Charles Lamb for Hester Savory was still green in the memory of his friends, even though it became the subject of one of the most flagrant of the many poor puns (this time undisputed) attributable to Elia:

"In the evening the Lambs joined the party and Charles was joked about the charming young Quakeress who had lived in the same street in Pentonville where Lamb had lodged. She generally

[1] Quoted in Lucas: *Idem*, II, 342.

wore white, and somebody present called her a 'white witch.' 'No,' said Lamb, 'if a witch at all, as she lived at the last house in our street, she must be the Witch of End-door.' "

And behind that End Door, William Savery had enjoyed no small hospitality at the hands of his young cousins.

## CHAPTER XXXI

# WILLIAM SAVERY'S MINISTRY: METHOD AND EFFECT

Without undue deference to the past, which always seems superlative in either good or ill, it is probable that the Quaker ministers in Philadelphia, in the last decade of the Eighteenth Century, surpassed in power and influence those of any other period or place, since the devoted coterie that followed Fox into the field in the early days.

The names of this later group are still well known in Philadelphia homes, many of them represented by living descendants. The following, culled from Watson's Annals [1] is attributed to "Lang Syne," a gentleman by the name of William McKoy, or McCoy, who was for many years with the Bank of North America and devoted his leisure time to reminiscing on paper. Writing of some of these Friends, he says:

"James Pemberton, Nicholas Waln, Daniel Offley, Arthur Howell, William Savery and Thomas Scattergood were the then 'burning and shining lights.' From the preachers' gallery, as beheld through the 'mist of years,' James Pemberton sat at the head of the gallery—an immovable figure, very erect, and resting with both hands crossed on the top of his cane. Nicholas Waln appeared at all times with a smile of sunshine upon his countenance. An imperturbable severity rested on the dark features of Thomas Scattergood. Arthur Howell always sat shrouded beneath his hat drawn down over his face, and the upper part of his outside coat elevated to meet it—like a prophet 'in his mantle wrapt,' and isolated in thought from all sublunary things. William Savery possessed a mild solemnity of voice and feature, which distinguished him as a preacher above other men; his softer and solemn tones and words

[1] II, 507.

in preaching, like those which may be imagined of the Eolian harp rudely touched by the wind, sunk through the ears down into the heart, as 'the dew of heaven,' falling gently to the earth. The voice of Daniel Offley was as a sound produced by the falling of a bar of his own iron on the brick pavement before his furnace door. Among his dozen hammermen he was always accustomed to raise his piercing voice distinctly above their pattering sounds."

That galaxy of ministers enjoyed, or was embarrassed by a reputation or acclaim far beyond that accorded to the ministers of any other period of Philadelphia Quakerism. They *were* a powerful and saintly group, and the atmosphere of segregated sanctity attached to them while they were still alive and active. William Savery had become a tradition already when he returned from Europe. They became the unconscious objects of a sort of cult and around them clustered a series of stories, poems and witty or pious anecdotes, many of which pass current to this day:

"Where is the race, the Prophet and the Father,
  The heavenly-minded and the zealous-hearted! * * *
Is the die broken and the race extinct?
  Why rise not Emlens, Dillwyns, as of yore?
Stantons, with sympathetic life instinct?
  Drinkers with Gospel and with classic lore?
Is there no Jordan this side Jordan's flood?
  No Woolman a pure standard to exalt?
How watched the Pembertons for Zion's good!
  How mourned a Scattergood for Israel's fault!
Oh for a Savery's large and catholic spirit!
  A Gurney Bevan's wisdom, zeal and love!
A Sands' keen eye the hidden wrong to ferret—
  A Benezet, oppression to reprove— * * *"

Men predominated in this period in Philadelphia, although there were several women Friends, notably Rebecca Jones, who were valuable ministers. In a letter of Ann Warder, written in 1786, she says:

"have often thought of John Pemberton and Sammy Emlen's saying in London, 'the women were the best end of the staff.' Here have thought it reversed with the few who truly keep their place. Thou mayest observe in my records of ministry, seldom females are eminently engaged."

Among those who, to Ann Warder's taste, "kept their place," none surpassed William Savery. Her expressions of approval of his gift became more eulogistic as time went on. Twice in 1787, she wrote of his ministry:

"when my favorite, William Savery, followed him, (Nicholas Waln) and canst thou conceive anyone preferable to all thou ever heard, it is just him,"

and later,

"I wish it was in my power to do justice to his persuasion, tenderness and affection, but the sweetness of his voice render harmonies out of his mouth."

While these expressions seem exaggerated, there can be no doubt that William Savery was gifted with a wonderful voice. In Ireland on two occasions, he himself mentions it,—once when it carried to the street from the meeting house and drew in many, with the sound of his preaching, and again, when a "parson" of another sect, after hearing William Savery preach, told him, "if he had my voice he should be more qualified for his duty." In the vast assemblages which he addressed in England, none but a good voice could have sufficed, and even in Philadelphia, in the afternoon meetings held at the "Great Meeting House," on the Corner of Second and Market Streets, great vocal power was an essential to reach the audience which frequently numbered three thousand, when the Hill, Bank and North meetings combined in attendance.

Illustrative of this early period of William Savery's ministry, Jacob Lindley records an incident during the trip to Detroit in 1793. The party left New York City on the sloop *Schenectady*, but were blown back during the night. William Savery thereupon appointed a meeting for that evening, at which time, the streets being full of people going to the meeting, Captain Lansing sent a call to go aboard. Says Jacob Lindley:

"The strait indeed was great, but William and I agreed, let consequences be what they might, we would attend the meeting."

Returning at 9 P.M. to the boat, they found the

"passengers and Captain in a great heat, but we kept down and it blew over. Captain Lansing told me afterwards in seriousness, he did believe the storm was permitted in order to give us time for the meeting."

William Savery, in the middle period of his ministry, probably appreciated the power of the gift that was his; certainly he did in the later period, when night after night, he preached to houses, packed literally to suffocation, in public halls in England. Dr. Lettsom thus describes his delivery, in public, during those days of London preaching:

"He was easy, clear and impressive; his voice was full, melodious and distinct; his testimonies, always extemporary, occupied usually about the space of an hour; his action was temperate, familiar and interesting."

While he marveled at this power, and was humbled by the manifest evidence of it, he was not averse to analyzing it and applying it in a way that Quaker ministers have rarely had the candor or the temerity to record. His ministry is easier to appreciate because of this element in it. He knew the repute in which he was held, and he consciously adapted his mode of delivery to suit the occasion,—"delivered in much tenderness, with desire to convince the judgment, as well as to soften the heart, and we humbly hoped it had an effect," wrote he, after a meeting in which he had striven mightily against "deism." On another occasion, "cramped myself for my dear fellow laborers, who did not appear," he recorded, and as a consequence, his mind was not relieved of that place without another meeting.

While this would indicate that William Savery was not

oblivious to what might be called the art or technique of his ministry, one should not conclude that his concern was either lightly assumed or mechanically fulfilled. He constantly records the immediacy of it, in that peculiar manner by which a calling may last over a long period and yet be subject to constantly renewed guidance. His preliminary call was to England and the Continent. The detailed prosecution of it was unplanned and always subject to revision. In Germany, he experienced "a day of much exercise, in which my mind has been more tossed and tried about the way of moving from hence than I have ever experienced before and such also has been the state of my dear companion." The solution of the problem came the next morning, "after a time of waiting, under much exercise," although the period of doubt really lasted for over a fortnight. Once when a minister of another denomination in Dublin was to preach a charity sermon for an orphanage, he sent William Savery a polite note requesting

"that I would urge the same subject at our meeting; so little did he know of the ministry of Friends, or true Gospel ministry. However, his request did not appear to be any part of my business to attend to."

With children, William Savery had a very noticeable gift. He visited many of the Friends' Schools, both public and private, in England and Ireland, and in them almost invariably had most acceptable service. At Ackworth, he had an outstanding experience with the three hundred "dear children" who attended "in beautiful order." This experience was renewed at the provincial schools for Ulster and Leinster in Ireland. At the latter place, William Savery appointed a meeting, and soon felt "sweetly opened to them." His power with children was never better exemplified:

"They were soon broken into tears and a more precious opportunity I never remember with children. * * * They took leave of

[416]

us with tears. \* \* \* (I) thought it would be an opportunity long remembered."

Whether in school or foundling hospital or private conversation, this remarkable ability to touch a responsive chord in child life was frequently evidenced by tenderness and tears. At the end of the Yearly Meeting of 1797, William Savery joined with Deborah Darby and Rebecca Young in appointing a meeting "for young Friends, male and female," near London, at Devonshire House. When about half gathered, it became evident that the women's house would not hold the crowd, so the men's room was opened and it was filled to capacity with twelve hundred young people. The service fell upon "Dear D. D., M. Dudley, Sam'l Alexander and my poor self." William Savery's sermon and prayer of that evening are of the few preserved (to his mortification) in shorthand, and are available today in print. The exercise that he underwent was well adapted to youth, though the sermon lacks, as of necessity it had to, the personal or intimate appeal that individual conference would have had.

Perhaps the strangest feature of the English and Irish ministry of William Savery was that his call was not so much to Friends as to "other professors," as he called them. He rarely appeared in the ministry in the regular meetings for worship,—so rarely, that at Chester, late in his service, he commented,—"my mind more than at any other time in England was exercised for our own profession." Time and again he expresses the same strange inability, feeling "nothing to constrain me to minister," or "few besides Friends attending I had not occasion to appear in the ministry." At Gracious Street, "I silent, which seems to be constantly my lot among Friends only," and at Clonmel, Ireland, "I felt something towards them, which not being usual for me among Friends only, I was desirous of putting by, but at length believing it best to submit, I stood. \* \* \*" At the Peel Meeting in London and at Wigton, he had a

few words but so weak that "I did not think myself authorized to take my hat off among them, as indeed I seldom
do among Friends." Sometimes when apparently excused
from service in a regular Friends' gathering, the situation
was changed, as happened at Westminster Meeting,
London:

"I thought I should have been silent as usual, but divers men
and women of other professions, dropping in, I had a little matter
for them at the close, in which I found peace after meeting."

At Cockermouth, toward the end of his journeys out
of London, he met Barbara Drewery, who, evidently reflecting the common report, told him she had heard that
he had only preached five times in Friends' meetings since
he came into England:

" 'I could recollect,' wrote he, 'but four, and two of them would
hardly bear the name of preaching.' "

Of like nature was an unusual statement at the close
of a meeting in Ireland, recorded by Mary Dudley. On
this occasion, William Savery said:

"I feel as I often do in meetings with my brethren and sisters—
not much to say. But I wish them well, and if they are not admitted to the communion table, the supper of the Lamb, it will
not be because they are not bidden guests, but because they are in
the same state as those formerly bidden, not ready;—being full
of or employed too much about other things—lawful in themselves,
but pursued to the hindering their acceptance."

It is possible that this is the incident which William
Savery records as "of a very singular kind," at the close of
a regular meeting at Mountmellick, in Ireland. Jane
Watson and Mary Ridgeway were there and expressed
their approval of the words, though Mary Dudley's
presence is not mentioned. The whole exercise seemed
"foolish" to him at the time, yet he mentioned, after
his return to America, "that he had heard of more

good effected by it, than by his testimony in any of his large meetings where words flowed smoothly and freely."

Such being his usual attitude in the meeting proper, it is also strange to find that he almost invariably arose at the close of the regular meeting for worship and asked Friends to appoint a meeting for the evening, either in the meeting house or quite as frequently in some larger public hall. This request was as invariably granted. "Those promiscuous gatherings," as he termed them, may be considered William Savery's peculiar method of reaching the people for whom he felt his message was intended. So assiduous was he in this concern that he noted on the eve of his departure for America:

"This was only the third evening of a First-day, in which I had not a public meeting, since arriving from France."

These meetings were always well attended, and in many instances they drew large crowds. Almost invariably there were a number of clergymen present. William Savery punctiliously noted their presence, if they were at all noticeable. In some instances they were very cordial to him after the meeting, expressing unity with the sermon or wishing him success and ability in prosecuting his weighty engagement.

Modern fire prevention ideals would stand aghast at the great multitudes, packed into all kinds of halls, sometimes in upper stories with narrow exits. It always took a long time for the crowds to file out after the meetings. The process was often very wearisome to William Savery, upon whom the people would press with appreciative comment, until he was fain to retire to rest. He was frequently much worn by the exercise of the meetings. He records preaching for an hour customarily and for two hours very often. At Whitehaven, a thousand people, in and out of the house, made it "so warm and oppressive for want of air, being an old-fashioned house with small windows, that it was very trying to speak in and exhausted me much."

The crowds at places would stop up the aisles, doors and windows by sitting in them. The whole north country tour was marked by a series of great meetings,—two at Kendal with fourteen hundred and one thousand in attendance, although "it rained very hard." At Carlisle, "the house, which holds about one thousand, would not contain the people," although William Savery did not arrive till five P.M. and the meeting was held at six. It is probable that this meeting was advertised beforehand, as was occasionally done elsewhere.

Comment upon these meetings in the Journal, when collated, is impressive. In several of the meetings women fainted and had to be carried out; in some, the youths of the Society of Friends would withdraw to give room for others; time and again, the crowds were too large for the houses to hold, there being often as many outside as in. Bristol, with capacity for fourteen hundred and Birmingham meeting house large though it was, both proved insufficient.

"The crowd and warmth of the house was very great, yet there was something attended, that preserved the people in great quiet."

At Sycamore Alley, Dublin, the meeting "soon grew exceedingly crowded," many hundreds went away, but a number of "airy young men," supposed to be students, got in, sat near the gallery and "behaved very lightly." To his own credit, William Savery adds, "I felt concerned for them." The meetings at Sycamore Alley were not always peaceful. At one of these appointed evening meetings, with the Mayor and one of the Lord Lieutenant's officers sitting in the gallery by the heads of the meeting, there were "eight or nine priests of different congregations present and many officers." The Journal states:

"I felt my mind opened in an unusual manner. After standing about an hour, two pieces of coal were thrown in at the end windows. I was then speaking to the officers of the army and soldiers particularly. Two officers immediately rose, went out to find the disturbers of the meeting and drew their swords. I sat down for three or four minutes and they returned. The people becoming quiet, I rose and proceeded, touching upon the foolish practice of duelling and war in general."

On numerous occasions these large meetings were held in unconventional places. At Deptford, near London, on a wet evening, between seven and eight hundred people attended in a very large hop and malt house, "seating with deal upon hop bags." On a warm evening in May at Stockwell, five hundred crowded into a corn store and many could not get in.

"The ceiling was low and windows and doors much stopped by the people that made it very warm, yet it was kept very still; no restlessness appeared."

A barn at Stoke Newington housed nearly eight hundred people, while at Bromley under similar circumstances an empty house was used and into the three large rooms and entry crowded five or six hundred people. All of these unusual places were accommodated in part by the folding benches and raised seat and platform mentioned heretofore that could easily be carried from place to place.

After William Savery and George Dillwyn had been received by King George III and Queen Charlotte, his acclaim as a preacher seems to have gone broadcast. Though the Friends were very chary of talking of the visit, their friends, Dr. Lettsom and Benjamin West, both of the select circle, seem not to have been so abstemious in conversation. As a result, William Savery's "public meetings" in London, during the remaining weeks of his stay in England, rivaled in attendance those of the famous revivalists of a century later. The day following the audience with the King, a malt store was again requisitioned for about a thousand people, and the following week "upwards of 2000," including "many of the gay families in and around London," crowded Gracechurch Street meeting house. William Savery

"rejoiced in a hope that truth had risen as high as in any of the public meetings I had had about London."

Still another week later, on March 20, 1798, William Savery appointed what he thought would be the last of his meetings in London, though it did not prove to be so. On this occasion, he curiously enough restricted it, in the call, to the Society of Friends alone. The account does not state in what house it was held, but it was largely attended, a great many having to stand all the time. It proved a memorable occasion:

"It was such a time of cementing union and love with my brethren and sisters in Society as I never experienced in England before. * * * Many were in tears and it was after nine o'clock before I could get out of the meeting house."

In June of 1798, an evening occasion, at Devonshire House, due to the unusual warmth, proved to be a "very spending" meeting. Being low in spirits, William Savery watched "the people collecting in multitudes * * * in much fear," but took consolation in seeing "some Friends from several of the other meetings come in, whom I knew were desirous of bearing part of the exercise." Strong though he was, he leaned upon others.

One can hardly be certain just how widely notice was given of these public meetings. The experience at Carlisle, already mentioned in this chapter, would indicate that a rather definite plan was at times in effect. This is confirmed by the breakdown of several proposed meetings in a series of towns, when William Savery was indisposed and unable to move on to them. A messenger was dispatched to tell Friends to cancel the engagements. The experience at Carlisle was duplicated at Staines, where there had evidently been no advance notice whatever. Arriving in the town at five P.M., William Savery consulted T. Ashby, "an innocent, valuable Friend and minister," and through his efforts, word was immediately sent around and a meeting of two hundred and fifty people gathered by six o'clock, a remarkable accomplishment in days before telephones. A similar method was used in Dublin, where "Friends divided themselves to give notice." At Newtonards, in Ireland, the remarkable expedient was used of requesting notice to be given in the Protestant churches. Thomas Bradshaw left Newtonards morning meeting as soon as William Savery proposed the evening meeting, and went into the town only to find two of the congregations had broken up. The Presbyterian minister, however, gave the notice and offered his "meeting house for the purpose." William Savery "felt no objection to accepting it" and a good meeting resulted. The next evening every place of worship in the town was offered for the use of the Friends in a second public meeting. It was evidently the practice for Friends accompanying traveling ministers in those days to go from house to house, carrying invitations to the proposed meeting. This William Savery thought was "often a mortifying business," and he was thankful to avoid the necessity for it in the Island of Jersey, declining also the services of the town crier and the use of printed hand bills. These publicity measures were in his opinion justifiable only for the public meetings. He very much disliked having Friends invite their neighbors to the regular meetings for worship, simply because he was expected to attend, and all the more if it were done without his knowledge. He was much disconcerted at the Park Meeting in London, when a young man "went out of the meeting to invite them (non-Friends) after I came in." The same thing happened at Rathangan, with the result that the next day, upon arriving at Mountmellick, William Savery "requested

Friends not to notify their neighbors as I found no openness toward them." This very definite distinction in his religious concern between Friends and those of other professions, comported with his feeling that his main calling was almost entirely for the latter.

There was also some newspaper publicity, although entirely unsolicited. The meeting at Norwich on February 4, 1798, the meeting that was to prove so momentous in the religious experience of Elizabeth Gurney, was preceded by the following notice in *The Norfolk Chronicle* or *Gazette* of February 3, quoted from *The Bath Chronicle*:

"Monday evening, the Quakers' Meeting-house at Bath was crouded to an excess, for the sake of hearing a celebrated preacher from America, who for good sense, fluency and even eloquence, formed a singular and very agreeable contrast to the usual style of religious address existing in that community. He has likewise preached to a crouded auditory at Laura Meeting-house and at the Independent Chapel. His name is William Savery, who appears to have assumed the novel character among the Quakers of a volunteer itinerant, or missionary; and in his passage to this country visited France, where he witnessed the persecuted and degraded state of his sect in *that land of civil and religious liberty*. He is a man of prepossessing appearance and address, mild and persuasive in his language and manners, and unusually liberal in all his sentiments. If the Quaker preachers were to imitate the example of this extraordinary brother, instead of distilling a sentence once in five minutes, many an orthodox and dissenting pulpit that is now held in admiration would be powerfully rivalled."

A week later, in the next edition of *The Norfolk Chronicle*, of February 10, 1798, the following report was printed. It covers only the evening meeting for other professors, and does not allude to the regular morning meeting. *The Norwich Mercury* also contained an account, though a much shorter one:

"On Sunday evening last Mr. Savery, from America, commanded the attention of a very crouded and respectable audience, at the

Quakers' Meeting, for above two hours. The subject was generally interesting, founded upon the maxim, that the society which did not revert to first principles was liable to decay, which he with considerable address and seriousness applied to the individual professors of religion, observing that the innovations of creeds and articles, framed and imposed by human authority, or cunning, had produced much infidelity, and arose from a want of adherence to first principles. That the creed of the great founder of Christianity was simple, being directed to promote 'Peace on earth and good will towards men'; he expressed his hope that the turnings and overturnings of the present time would end in restoring the primitive union of Christian fellowship, and that countries assuming the appellation of Christians would no more delight in War, adding, he could not think it an acceptable service to thank God for victory over an enemy. He related with great advantage and perspicuity the advantage he had enjoyed in finding amongst what are called Heathens, men of piety and goodness, who, though they were destitute of a written law, were a law unto themselves, and favored with the assistance of the spirit of the Almighty; very happily illustrating that the salvation published by the Gospel, would be participated by numbers, in the extensive nations of the earth, who never possessed the means of knowing it, while those who rejected its great advantages, would be exposed to just condemnation.

"It is computed that there were near 2,000 persons present in the Meeting, and the serious part of the auditors appeared highly gratified with his discourse, which however was much too prolix, and consequently tautological."

The aftermath of these crowded, stuffy meetings for William Savery was almost always extreme weariness and very frequently, in the winter months, a cold in the head or chest. He learned from experience to take some precaution, but more frequently he was warned by his friends, who at times insisted on taking him away in a coach or other conveyance, to protect him from inclement weather and the throng of people alike. At Carlisle:

"divers polite people of other societies, who sat near me, seemed anxious I should not go immediately into the air, least I might increase my cold. It manifested their kindness."

In Edinburgh, Alexander and Mary Cruickshank, who were "very loving, honest Friends," were even more solicitous:

"They persuaded me to accept two shirts to wear underneath, made of lamb's wool, spun and knit with needles. They think it will be a preventative to my taking cold after warm meetings. I immediately put one of them on, which did not feel very agreeable at first."

It would be hard to decide whether the cold or the lamb's wool would be the worse.

While the Journal does not consciously record effects or results of these great meetings, there are incidental allusions by which one can read between the lines, of the profound influence that William Savery's preaching had upon others. David Sands, in his account of the journey in Germany, tells of the unction that frequently attended the ministry and prayer of William Savery, even in the strange language, stating in one place, "exceeding any that I had ever heard before from him." He attained a similar proficiency in effective preaching in French, toward the end of his Continental experiences venturing alone in the language, and feeling

"I never had been so favored to exercise myself in French before. Great tenderness prevailed and many were bathed in tears: both old and young."

Another incidental reference grew out of one of the large dinner parties of which there were so many, after meeting on First Days in London. Ann Hunt, from near Bristol, took dinner one day with a score of other Friends at William Fry's. She had not been at Bristol meeting when William Savery had attended and preached, thereby stifling an intimation she had had that she should go. The next morning

"a man came to their house and his first expressions were 'such preaching, such preaching!' She asked him where. He said 'last evening at the Meeting house in Blackfryars—Bristol.' He said he had never heard the truth so declared. He was not a professor with Friends."

After a similar testimony from a man in Dublin, whose expressions William Savery recorded, he added, in his Journal:

"I mention this, not to exalt anything I have done or can do, but the goodness of the Lord and the invincible authority of the truth."

He was singularly free from any trace of vanity; rather he marveled as it became evident to him that his ministry had attained such power. In one place he wrote:

"My Friends are far more respectful to me than I deserve, to my humiliation. I wish I were more worthy."

When in London, he was breakfasting at Joseph G. Bevan's with Jasper Capper, and the latter showed him a copy of the Norwich paper, in which the account, of the meeting there, already quoted, was printed. It threw the good man into considerable perturbation, and caused him to record:

"I thank my God who has yet preserved me from being much elated or depressed by the ill or well done of the world. If I can but obtain the answer of a conscience, void of offence to God or man, that is the great object of my concern, and will be enough."

He was also favored at times in individual conversations. Notable among these was his call upon Charles Lloyd's son, James, who had been, like William Savery himself, "a wild, libertine youth." He records that "they were people, great in the world," but when he found the young man "in a very low and reclining state," he had a short talk with him,

"in which the tears showered plentifully down his cheeks, and at taking leave he took my hand to his mouth and kissed it."

In attending a meeting at Bury-St.-Edmunds rather unexpectedly, there were but a few Friends, who had not known that visitors were coming:

"A young woman, who was not of our Society, coming in under some exercise of mind, my mind was turned towards her and I had a few sentences at which she wept."

Another incidental reference to William Savery's peculiar acceptance among young people, is found in the "Memoir of Samuel Hoare" by his daughter, Sarah Hoare. She was at that time a young woman of twenty, and recorded,

"We had a visit from William Savery from America, with whose sermons we were more pleased than with the preaching of any minister amongst Friends whom I remember. The simplicity and genuine excellence of his character made him a delightful companion."

It is interesting to compare this estimate of William Savery with his estimate of the Hoare family, already quoted (page 370), Sarah Hoare having then been one of the gay daughters who were "as loving and kind as possible." One other rather amusing incident, indicative of the esteem in which his gift was held, occurred one morning when he thought he would not attend the mid-week meeting. Changing his mind, he

"put on in a hurry to Devonshire meeting, where for the first time I heard M. Lloyd in testimony, she having alleged at some meeting where we had been, that she could not do her duty if I were present, she was so much afraid of me. Her testimony was lively and satisfactory, to which I added my unity."

Perhaps the most interesting, certainly the best known incident, reflecting the power of William Savery's preaching was the sermon in Norwich Meeting by which Elizabeth Gurney, afterwards Elizabeth Fry, was so remarkably affected. The story of the influence of this strong man of forty-eight upon the adolescent girl of seventeen, and of the consequent right-about face in her mode of life and manner of thinking, is one of the strangest in Quaker annals. It has long been thought that William Savery was largely unaware of the deep impress he had made upon the young mind and heart, but the original manuscript shows a true and well sustained interest in Elizabeth Gurney for long after his visit to Norwich.

William Savery came to Norwich with his intimates, Jasper Capper and John Head. They were to lodge at "The Grove," the home of Joseph Gurney. To their disconcertion, they found that the little Gurneys "were in the measles," so William Savery alone of the trio, remained at "The Grove" and the other two went on to "Earlham," the home of John Gurney, whose seven daughters and four sons composed a large and gay family. The next morning, February 4, 1798, William Savery attended the regular meeting at "the old meeting house" in Goat Lane. He wrote:

"Some not members stept in, there might be 200 under our name, but very few of the middle aged and young that had a consistent appearance in their dress. Indeed, I thought it the gayest Friends' meeting I ever sat in and was grieved to see it. I expected to have passed it through in silent suffering, but at length believed it most for my peace to stand up with, 'Your fathers, where are they, and the prophets do they live forever?' "

He also records that a young man, educated for the ministry, but who had declined ordination, because he could not subscribe to the Thirty-nine Articles, "sat before me with his spectacles on," but he may not have noticed Elizabeth Gurney, who sat "under the gallery," in a row with her six sisters. She had always disliked meeting, referring to "Goats" in her Diary, from time to time in very uncomplimentary terms. She had, however, consented to attend this morning, "because I wished to hear an American Friend, named William Savery." Of the meeting her sister, Richenda, tells in her Diary (for all the Gurney girls, with the sentimentalism of that period, seem to have kept diaries):

"Betsey was generally rather restless at meeting, and on this day I remember her very smart boots were a great amusement to me; they were purple, laced with scarlet. At last William Savery began to preach. His voice and manner were arresting, and we all liked the sound: her attention became fixed, at last I saw her begin to weep, and she became a great deal agitated. As soon as meeting was over, I have a remembrance of her, making her way to the men's side of the meeting, and having found my father, she begged him if she might dine with William Savery at the Grove."

Of this dinner party, Elizabeth herself recorded:

"After a meeting of three hours I then went with Aunt Jane to the Grove. All the Friends dined there and I felt rather odd as I was the only gay person there. However, I liked the manners of the Friend. He was kind and pleasing. He had a meeting at 6 and Uncle Joseph wished me to go with Friends to it. We had much conversation as we went to meeting, but not much serious. Meeting lasted very long. He preached a very excellent sermon. I was very low all the meeting. * * * After meeting I rode home to the Grove with Friend S. We had a sort of meeting all the way. As soon as we got to the Grove, he had a regular one with me. When I got home I mixed too much the idea of growing religious and growing the Quaker. He has caused me to feel a little religion. I have *felt* there is a *God*. I loved the man as if almost he were sent from heaven. We had much serious conversation, in short, what he said and what I felt was like a refreshing shower upon parched up earth that had been dried up for ages."

At the dinner party, William Savery's chief reaction was to lament "the lack of upright standard bearers, left among them." His hostess herself, Jane Gurney, "appeared a dressy woman," but kind and attentive, withal. After noting with approval Lawrence Candler, an elder and "a valuable man," and his wife who was a minister, together with William Crow and Sarah Bland, also ministers, he wrote:

"Several gay girls, daughters of John Gurney, and their father with them, gave us their company, and I rode with Elizabeth to meeting."

The evening meeting was held "in a large meeting house in another part of town," doubtless the Gildencroft meeting house. The crowd was so great that some hundreds were turned away. William Savery preached from the maxim, —"That Society which does not frequently recur to its first principles, is in danger of going to decay." Again he made a profound impression upon Elizabeth Gurney. Says her sister, Richenda, about the return home:

"Betsey sat in the middle, and astonished us all by the feeling she showed. She wept most of the way home."

The sermon must truly have been a powerful effort. Supplementary to the newspaper account, already quoted, is the allusion of a young Roman Catholic Priest, John Pitchford. He was a friend of the Gurneys, and was invited by Joseph Gurney into the Ministers' gallery, a remarkable invitation for that day. He states:

"The name of the speaker was Savery, and his sermon the best I have ever heard among Quakers, so full of candour and liberality. My only objection to it was its excessive length—two hours and a half."

Truly one is attempted to agree with the reporter as to prolixity and tautology.

The next morning William Savery breakfasted at Earlham, and, says Richenda, "preached to our dear sister after breakfast, prophesying of the high and important calling she would be led into." Elizabeth felt confirmed in her own mind:

"My feelings toward Friend S. are unintelligible. I felt no fear, not the least, in his company, as I do with most plain Friends. I loved him as a messenger of glad tidings, * * * and he having been gay and unbelieving only a few years ago, made him better acquainted with the heart of one in the same situation."

Another sister, Louisa, confided her private opinion of these events to her own diary:

"Friend Savery has been here, who seems a charming man and a most liberal-minded Quaker. Betsey, *who spent all yesterday with him*, not only admires, but quite loves him. He appears to me a truly good man, and a most upright Christian, and such men are always loved. To me he is quite different from the common run of disagreeable Quaker preachers. In every society and sect there is always something good and worthy to be found."

As it has never been published before, it may be interesting to add William Savery's impression of the Gurney family, evidencing as it does the realization on his part that some effect had been registered:

"J. G. is a widower. His children seem very kind and attentive to him and he is very indulgent to them; has provided them with an extensive library and every indulgence that Nature, within the bounds of mere morality can desire. They were very respectful and kind to us, and very much regretted, I believe sincerely, our being like to leave them so soon. They are a family very capable of distinguishing, through the grace, what the truth is (and) leads to, but whether, with all the alluring things of this world about them, they will, any of them, chuse to walk in it, time only must determine."

Time did determine affirmatively. Elizabeth took a fling in London, comparable to William Penn's sojourn in Paris. She led a very gay life indeed, going the rounds of the public attractions of the Capital. She met Mrs. Opie and saw Mrs. Siddons in the full glory of her career; she danced and went to the opera, but under it all was a vague and pervasive feeling that she was not in her right element. Once again she confided to her Diary:

"Although I told William Savery my principles were not Friendly; yet I fear I should not like his knowing of my going to the play. I think such religion as his must attract an athiest and if there were many such Quakers as he is, the Society would soon increase."

Time and again, however, she came under the peculiarly tenacious influence of William Savery even while in London. Like Ann Warder, before her in Philadelphia, she seems to have followed him around from one meeting to another, so much so that her sisters teased her about being in love with him. William Savery mentions her half a dozen times during the final weeks of his London service, although he does not appear to have realized the almost sentimental attachment of the young girl for him. On February 25, 1798, Elizabeth supped at Joseph Savory's, after an evening meeting at Westminster meeting house, where William Savery had preached upon,—"Humility goes before honor and a haughty spirit before a fall," whether for her particular benefit or not, does not appear.

It is probable that Elizabeth had previously known Joseph Savory's daughters, as William Savery records that "dear Betsey Gurney" lodged or took meals there several times during her London visit, at one time in company with her father, six sisters and a brother. It was upon one of these occasions that she gave him a keepsake and recorded in her Diary:

"I long to know how he liked my pocket book that I gave him this morning."

On July 25, 1798, William Savery preached for his last time in London at the midweek meeting at Gracious Street meeting house.

"All J. G.'s and R. Barclay's familys there and a number of high friends. * * * Numbers came and took the most affectionate leave of me. * * * Dear E. G. was much affected."

In July, after his sailing, Elizabeth wrote:

"I think a good deal of W. Savery, and I do not much feel for him though he is in a small and old vessel."

A month later she adds:

"Dear W. Savery! May he never fail in the service of his God, but increase in perfection daily. * * * There was a soft, pleasing manner in friend Savery but I thought he had something of the totem of quakers about him. * * * May I never, no never forget the impression he has made on my mind, as much as I can say, I thank God for having sent at least a glimmering and little light through him into my heart."

And a year later, February 14, 1799, she notes:

"It is more than a year since I first knew W. Savery."

Probably nowhere else in Quaker annals is there more worth-while material for the student of adolescent religious psychology, than in this story of Elizabeth Gurney's experience, under the influence of William Savery and later, under the spiritual tutelage of the sweetly devout woman, Deborah Darby. There was truly a warm and fervent Christian love between them, with no erotic implications, and no thought of else than transmitting the experience of the saint to the novice through the process of true, spiritual ordination.

William Savery undoubtedly considered Elizabeth Gurney as the most hopeful of the youth among his many English intimates. Having written her a long letter in April, 1798, in response to one from her, asking his advice, he said:

"My attachment has not been more cordial or agreeable to any young Friend in England,"

and then sympathetically anticipating for her "the world's dread laugh," and stating that no one, certainly not himself, had attained an uninterrupted state of mind, wherein there is no condemnation, and inveighing at the same time against those who "are always exhibiting the dark and gloomy side of religion," he closed with the following beautiful salutatory:

"My dear child, my heart is full towards thee. * * * I would fain take thee by the hand, if I were qualified so to do, and ascend, as our Heavenly Father may enable us, together, step by step, up that ladder which reaches from earth to Heaven; but alas! my weakness is such, I can only recommend both myself and thee to that good hand that is able to do more abundantly for us than we can either ask or think; and bid thee for the present in much Christian affection, farewell.

William Savery."

# MINISTRY: METHOD AND EFFECT

At times we are inclined to ask, what results are achieved from such devoted and selfless service as William Savery rendered? Why are such results not crystalized into some form that will last, more substantial than the fleeting fragrance of a human life spent? Perhaps we must hark back to the first principles, of which he preached, to realize that society, to avoid decay, must be based upon personality rather than crystalized "things," and that the benediction of his influence for Christ, upon Elizabeth Gurney, was a part of the true apostolic succession, in which William Savery planted and that devout Mother in Israel, Deborah Darby, watered, until the personality of Elizabeth Gurney blossomed and ripened into fruition to the bringing forth of spiritual sons and daughters of God in generations since:

" 'I can say one thing,' said Elizabeth Fry, when nearing death, 'since my heart was touched at seventeen years old, I believe I never have awakened from sleep, in sickness or in health, by day or by night, without my first waking thought being how best I might serve my Lord.' "

## CHAPTER XXXII

## WILLIAM SAVERY'S MINISTRY: ATTITUDE
## AND CONTENT

During his London residence, William Savery spent much of his time in his room, at Joseph Savory's, in retirement, reading and writing. It was true sanctuary to him. Time and again he remained in his chamber till close to meeting time:

"I feel public meetings so weighty that I cannot be easy to continue in conversation till they begin, but rather to retire, that I may feel my mind gathered to the Fountain of all good, * * * where all strength and qualification to hold them to the honour of truth, can alone be found, and after all, I think I always have entered them with fear and trembling, lest the blessed cause should, by any means, suffer."

William Savery rarely accepted opportunities to dine out on First Days, though the invitations were naturally numerous. It seemed at times, almost rude to decline:

"Indeed, I wish to have much more retirement than I can enjoy. Friends do not enough consider us poor travellers, when we stop among them or probably they would not croud upon us so much as they do, for though they mean it for kindness, it often amounts to oppression. * * * It is distressing to me to continue in large companies of Friends and conversation till we enter those large public meetings. My mind wants preparation and quiet before I enter them. * * * We have received invitations enough already to dine, as would take us eight or ten days to comply with. This is often trying to me, as I would much rather, when I come into a City, take our Saviour's advice,—'Into whatsoever house ye enter, there abide.' But it seems as if we must, against our better judgement at times, comply with the solicitations of our friends, to avoid giving offence,—at least, I have not always firmness enough to resist, when I ought to do."

The trepidation of spirit, with which William Savery anticipated his public meetings, runs as a steady current throughout all his narrative. He apparently never overcame it, although the reaction, after the meetings, was often as sweet and sufficing as the dread had been acute. The attitude which he had described in one of his early Philadelphia sermons,—"It is in fear and trembling that I address you now," continued as his portion. He was frequently subject to great depression, though that was more usually due to frustration of plans or delay in transit than to spiritual ordeal. On the Continent, among strangers, this feeling took most frequent hold of him. But even in Britain, in approaching London, after he had thought himself clear of further service there, he underwent "tears and dejection." His expressions of attitude run the whole gamut of deep travail. "In much care and fear," he began a sermon, and was unexpectedly enlarged in labor; or again he was given "both matter and utterance, to my own astonishment and thankfulness." In anticipating going to Bath, then a town of much gaiety and revelry and a resort for the nobility, he wrote:

"I dreaded going there, but was convinced the Lord is sufficient for his own work."

Discouragement, humility and "unusual exercise," vary the experience. "Low even to tears and trembling," "spirits sunk as usual," "cast down," and "fear, almost to the smiting of the knees" evince at one time or another the depths to which his soul was sunk. There is no mock humility or pose in any of this. It is the sincere confidence of a deeply tried nature, striving for acquittance from a divine call that cannot be shirked or too quickly fulfilled:

"My own daily feeling of incapacity for any good word or work of myself, and the frailty of my nature which often hangs about me heavily as a body of death, defends me through the grace, from any exaltation of spirit. The Lord be with me and keep me to the end from dishonoring truth."

Surely there is encouragement and solace for Christians
struggling for a better way and more certainty in things
divine, in this humble and dependent cry of a soul, who to
his fellows and to posterity appears fair as one of the saints
of God.

But if he knew the depths, he was also no stranger to that
great boon, the elation and enthusiasm, often quiet and
always decorous, but as precious as spun gold,—the earnest
of the spirit. Those dread anticipations were so frequently
dispelled by a "comfortable refreshing silence" or "recurring peace," or the rebounding "joy" of "revived spirits."
It was at such times when "as much sweet peace * * * as
I remember for a long time past" welled into his heart, that
he was especially wary of "the well or ill done" of the
world. So often, after a great meeting the crowds would
press upon him and express appreciation, that he possessing
then, a quiet mind, freed from the burden of the assemblage,
yearned only to be free and alone, to cherish and nourish
the relief that he experienced.

"Many of the people expressed thankfulness as we went to the
coach, but truly these engagements are not desirable, to the flesh.
I long for a release in the Lord's time. May I be enabled to keep the
word of his patience."

In numerous instances, William Savery wrote the gist
of his sermon in his daily record, noting and analyzing, at
times, his own psychology. He kept close watch over his
audience for signs of approval, tedium or restlessness. In
the meeting at Bath a certain "Sir John" and his wife sat
exactly in front of the ministers' gallery. During the
silence they were very impatient, asking those about them
when the service would begin. After William Savery began preaching, Sir John became very attentive, "scarcely'
taking his eyes off me." At another place he noted the
close attention of the people, "some frequently nodding
assent to the doctrine."

While he frequently started preaching under great labor,

he was often enabled in the course of a sermon to feel a change of circumstances, as he would be led from one topic to another, or from addressing one group in the assemblage to another line of exhortation.

"Light," said he, "appeared suddenly to spring up, and the Lord opening my way, it became through His great condescension and mercy, a time of much brokenness and favor."

The topics of these sermons naturally vary widely. One is reminded of the present day, in reading that

"my mind was led into sympathy with some not of our Society, who appeared to be looking towards Friends, hoping some mighty work would be done to convince them of our faith,"

as an introduction to which he quoted from the temptations of Christ, "If thou be the Son of God, command that these stones be made bread."

Another effort, of less moment today, led him to warn his hearers, on two different occasions against "imagery," quoting Old Testament strictures against graven images. Perhaps his thought followed the same line as that incidentally referred to, one day in a coach, when William Savery had to take the only remaining inside seat, having for company, "three pretty bulky Methodist ministers and two young women." Wrote William Savery:

"One of the preachers began conversation by asking me who that gentleman was that preached at Friends' Meeting last night and told me his wife had been there and was much pleased. She said he had touched pertinently upon the idols of the different Societys which they hung up in their chambers, as John Wesley, Martin Luther, John Calvin, &c."

The subsequent addition of George Fox to that galaxy would hardly have met with William Savery's approval, in spite of the reverential awe, which he later experienced at Swarthmore, where he preached nevertheless upon, "Let me die the death of the righteous."

At Meath Street Meeting, in Dublin, William Savery

felt called to state simply, "There were certain cities which our Lord passed through, wherein it is said, he did not many miracles, because of their unbelief." Immediately Mary Ridgeway took up the theme and after her four others spoke on the same topic.

The Journal contains scores of texts from which William Savery preached, both on the Continent and in the British Isles. In many instances he used the same text twice. At funerals, "Blessed are they that have a part in the first resurrection, for over them the second death shall have no power," was used at least twice. In Ireland, where civil war was rampant, he used texts of peace and security, perhaps consciously in contrast. "My people shall dwell in peaceful habitations and sure dwellings and quiet resting places," was the text at Hillsborough, and again, "The Lord will keep that man in perfect peace whose mind is stayed upon him, because the truth is in him," the quotation not being always exact.

Once in a while he would use an aphorism or old saw, "Time and tide waits for no man," or to the meeting of servants and clerks, in London, "It is no sin to be poor, provided we are honest," indicating a degree of superciliousness that is not altogether pleasant today.

From the great majority of the texts recorded it is impossible to guess what the sermon was. Most of them were taken from the New Testament about equally divided between quotations from Jesus Christ and from Paul's epistles. Paul was evidently a great source of strength to William Savery, as he quoted him in all the sermons which he records as directed against deism. From Ephesians III, 1-4, "For this cause, I Paul, the prisoner of Jesus Christ, for you Gentiles, etc," he drew much comfort and quoted it in two sermons delivered against the current unorthodox beliefs. Most of these Pauline quotations bear directly upon the offices of Christ and the power of the Cross, indicating the Gospel fervor which all William Savery's contemporaries attribute to him as the outstanding feature of the substance of his ministry.

Jonathan Evans, writing years later, said of his ministry:

"I was intimately acquainted with William Savery and esteemed him a brother beloved. His affable disposition, his catholic spirit and his truly Christian principles endeared him to those who knew him. * * * His ministry was generally more of a doctrinal nature than that of many other Friends, accompanied with a fervent engagement that his audience might be brought to an heartfelt experience of the unspeakable love of God, in sending his dear Son, our Lord Jesus Christ, into the world to save sinners; of the efficacy of his propitiatory sacrifice and the sanctifying power of his Holy Spirit, who hath by his own blood obtained eternal redemption for all that come unto Him in true faith. * * *"

Having previously mentioned Joseph Sansom, in his ill-fated activities at his sister's wedding, and as the artist who made the silhouette of William Savery, reproduced herein, it is now necessary to record another project of this versatile young man that brought him into contact with William Savery. He was clever beyond most of his time, in his knowledge of shorthand. That knowledge he put to practical use, twice in February, 1786, at the Bank meeting house, Philadelphia, in transcribing sermons as they fell from William Savery's lips. For a number of years they remained in manuscript.

Another enterprising man, Job Sibley, of London, also had the art of shorthand wrting in 1796, when William Savery spent a few weeks in England, before going to the Continent. He also, entirely unknown to William Savery, took down several sermons and prayers, as they were delivered in London. In an early edition, which he published, now extremely scarce, there were also a few sermons of George Dillwyn, who had preached at the same times.

Upon William Savery's return from the Continent, he went, one afternoon, as he was frequently wont to do, to James Phillips' bookshop, where, says he:

"I found to my astonishment three books on his counter, said to be sermons, preached by myself last year at Devonshire House, Westminster and the Borough Market. Having heard of them some days before, I thought right to look over them, and found them full of errors, from beginning to end, as well in language as doctrine. This added greatly to the exercise I felt before I saw them. Got William Phillips' promise to sell no more."

This printing caused William Savery more travail of spirit than any other of the many untoward incidents of his labors in England. The little volumes contain probably the only sermons ever reported with any literal semblance of that or any prior period of Quakerism. In spite of William Savery's disapproval, they became very popular, the editions growing in bulk as they fell from the press. At least six different collections of these sermons were printed and some of them reached several editions. To three sermons by William Savery in the London edition of 1796, were later added the two taken by Joseph Sansom, in 1786, and this combination ran through many editions—New York in 1797, and after William Savery's death, Burlington, New Jersey, in 1805, Newtown, Pennsylvania, 1805, London (with the valuable Introduction by Dr. Lettsom) in 1806 and finally Philadelphia in 1808.

It is hard to understand, in the light of this evident demand, why William Savery should have been so perturbed. With Ady Bellamy, he visited Job Sibley and

"found him in Goswell Street, a very poor man, a shoemaker, who had obtained some knowledge of short-hand * * * (who) sold the copies to his brother, a printer. * * * It appeared that he was a very illiterate man, who, if he was capable of taking it down in short-hand, could not put that into common sense English."

This visit merely resulted in "more distress than I ever felt in England before." He ascertained that copies had been circulated not only in England and Ireland but that some of them had been sent to America:

"Oh! what a night I past. Slept very little and rose with much headache and unwell. * * * These publications wound me much."

With due allowance for the vagaries of reporting, the English of the printed sermons is well nigh impeccable, and Sibley's qualifications must have been greater than William Savery's warmth attributed to him. He ascertained that Sibley had also taken notes of sermons preached by Deborah Darby, Thomas Scattergood and David Sands. We can but wish that these also were extant today. William Savery informed Job Sibley that the printed copies contained language and doctrines he had never uttered or even conceived,—that he had put in the name of Paine, "which I never mentioned," and that by the omission of two words "he had totally changed my sentiments concerning the things forbidden by the Council of Jerusalem." William Savery's objection reached deeper, however, than the errors, serious as they were to him. He believed the printing alone was wrong, even if the sermons had been correctly reported.

"I marvell much," he wrote, "that Friends should encourage, sell and read them as I found they did, and that all the time I had been on the Continent, they had circulated over this Kingdom and Ireland."

Job Sibley remained obdurate. He stated that his object was more the "spreading the Gospel truths they contained than for gain." At William Savery's second call, he was horrified to find "he had got a third edition of five hundred printed last week. * * * I offered to purchase the whole, if he would publish no more, but this I could not get him to promise." The same evening the imperturbable Job attended Devonshire House meeting, where William Savery felt his "mind enlarged beyond anything I remember before in London," and took down the testimony again, "which I did not expect, after what had passed." To make matters worse, Sibley called upon William Savery later and requested that he correct the proofs of the sermon that he had preached to the young Friends of London, "which, he said, he had entered into obligations to have printed." William Savery looked it over but felt "no freedom to correct it," so that in the Lettsom edition of 1806, the sermon appears as "never before printed."

The matter had become so serious that William Savery laid it before the "Second Day morning meeting" which discussed it for two hours and agreed

"to spread in the approaching Quarterly Meeting a caution to all our members against the practice of taking down testimony, by reading, purchasing, selling or otherways."

William Savery rather curtly records, reminiscent of ancient John Heywood:

"When the steed's stole, we shut the stable door. I am astonished they did not think of it sooner. However, better late than never."

The immediate result was the publication in London of a pamphlet, the only printed work William Savery ever produced, entitled, "Some Remarks on the Practice of taking down and Publishing the Testimonies of Ministering Friends." It was printed and sold by the same James Phillips and Son, who had previously sold the "Sermons." It could hardly have been a convincing effort, even in that day, and surely has little cogency in it to recommend it to the present generation. Its argument is that

"even if it were possible for the most sound and living testimony to be printed with perfect correctness, * * * the benefit arising therefrom would be more imaginary than real." (The transcribers could hardly be accurate.) "The crowds that press them and the inartificial periods of an extempore preacher may, with other causes, combine to frustrate their best endeavors."

The same observations could, with even greater propriety, be applied to the reports of Christ's sermons and those of the Apostles, given from memory, in the Scriptures themselves.

Whether the sermons were reported as defectively as

William Savery thought, or whether he confided to his Journal the wrath that he suppressed otherwise, they remain an invaluable commentary, not only upon him but upon his period. Thankful we can be to Joseph Sansom and Job Sibley for their unwelcome labors, for they have preserved in William Savery a record of broad catholicity and intense fervor that would otherwise be stilled in death and the lapse of generations. In a sense it matters little just how accurate they were verbally. The edition that mentions Paine, associates with him in the same sentence, Bolingbroke and Hume, who were equally anathema to the opponents of deism, and yet William Savery did not state that he did not mention the other two. Probably due to his insistence, Paine is eliminated from the later editions and Bolingbroke and Hume alone remain as notorious examples of spiritual defection.

The two early sermons of 1786 are short. It may be that William Savery never knew that Joseph Sansom had taken them in shorthand, as they were certainly never published till after his death. The minister was then in his thirty-sixth year. The former dealt with the topic, "Truth," and contained little out of the ordinary. The second sermon, preached the same month, on "Wisdom," is more remarkable, although in common with the thought prevalent at the time, William Savery discounts learning so thoroughly that he seems to belie his own excellent education. His early attitude is evidenced in his saying:

"Every true and living minister of the Gospel is sensible that it is a solemn and weighty thing to be true servants; they are often encompassed about with many doubts and fears, feeling their own infirmities, * * * and it is in fear and trembling that I address you now."

Toward the end of this sermon he breaks into one of the Miltonic sentences, rich in experience and full of poetic insight and spiritual fervor, that must have been the type of delivery which, later in life, gave his sonorous voice its chance to carry conviction into the hearts of his hearers:

"According to our devotion and sincerity of heart, we shall know the Lord, the Son of Righteousness, to arise higher and higher; but the unfaithful and those who will not adhere to the openings and breaking forth of the morning light, and in the small ability they have received, travel forward in the light of Christ, these are not likely to be approved, they are not likely to know the day to rise higher and higher: it is a progressive work, Friends, and there is no one present I believe, that dare to say, I have proved the extent and depth of redeeming love."

Curiously enough, there are in these early sermons a few stock phrases that appear also in those reported in England over a decade later, two of them, "an unwearied adversary and enemy of our soul's peace," and "the turnings and over-turnings," having persisted in frequent usage among Quaker ministers until the end of the Nineteenth Century. Two other phrases, "for persuaded I am," and "this is my faith," also appear frequently in both the early and late sermons.

In the later sermons there is a readier distinction regarding education than is apparent in the quotation above. At Houndsditch, in 1796, William Savery said:

"Human learning and science in itself, when properly applied for the purposes which it is fitted and designed for, are by no means to be despised; nay, when those who are qualified by what is called a liberal education, are by the influence of the spirit of Jesus Christ, brought down into a true Christian state, they may be eminently qualified for the promoting of truth and righteousness in their day. So that I would not have you mistake. We make a distinction, it is true; but when the Lord unites them, when he lays his hand upon those that have many advantages in the world, he may make them greater instruments in his hand. But I may also say, that some of the greatest ornaments that ever I have known in the Church of Christ, who I believe were qualified for the preaching of the Gospel in the demonstration of the spirit and of power, have been even among those that have had little advantages of this kind."

But the great underlying theme of all the later discourses that are included in these little books, and we may presume

of most of the sermons that William Savery preached to
"other professors," was a strong, earnest and broad plea
for Church unity and harmony, on the essential basis of
the love of Christ, in God. It seems rather startling, in
these days, when we are prone to attribute Church union
to modern times alone, to find in William Savery an early
and devout believer in it as the means of healing the ills
of the nations. As one reads these sermons, after the lapse
of over a century and a quarter, since they were uttered,
one can realize more clearly why William Savery felt his
call to be to those outside the Society of Friends. His
was no sporadic mission. The sermons and prayers, thus
crystalized for us in type, against his will, show clearly,
more clearly, in fact, than his Journal itself, that his solution for the world disorder, conflict and warfare was simply
the breaking down of creeds and varying opinions, and
allowing the flood of divine love, as revealed in Jesus Christ,
to permeate the individuals and the nations of the earth.

He began broadly. One would hardly know whether
the following was delivered in 1796 or 1918:

"The present is an age of many uncommon events, and the curious observer will not be inattentive to what they tend; and indeed,
many are filled with conjectures where these things will end. It
is a day also, wherein men of science have been exceedingly curious
in their researches; they have brought up some new and before un-
heard of things to view: and probably some of them may be turned
to advantage to their country in ages to come, though they are not
now altogether usefully employed in the world."

Then he would recur to the warfare then prevalent on the
Continent:

"O Christendom! thou oughtest to be a light to enlighten the
heathen, and a glory; aye, the glory of God, to the ends of the
earth! How they must look upon us! For even the Mahometans,
having the New Testament in their hands, how must they stand
amazed, when they come to compare these things with that our
great Leader said:—'By this shall all men know that ye are my
disciples, because ye love one another.' And are there any people

more at discord? Are there any more at variance either in a private or in a public national capacity? O! how this has wounded me! bear with me my friends, I do not wish to hurt any mind present by any means whatever. If thou thinkest not as I think, thou wilt not be judged by my conscience; but by the light thou hast received thyself."

The shadow of warfare lay heavy across his conception of Christendom:

"For sure I am, if the Gospel spirit had been continued to this day, thousands and ten thousands that have died in the field of battle, would not have died in that way, and the carnage and devastations that desolated so many parts of Europe would have been prevented. O the cry of the widows and the tender orphans in the several countries of Europe! Ought this to have been? Or would it ever have been, if men had kept to the principle which taught them not only to love their brethren, but to love their *enemies;* to do good to them that persecuted them and that despitefully used them."

Just before his departure for the Continent, William Savery, at the Borough New Market, London, developed this conception of the Gospel of Christ as all sufficient for the times, in a lengthy sermon, that probably typifies much that he preached in Europe. In fact this sermon had much the same structure as the sermon preached just a week before in St. Martin's Lane, London, and both contained references to the still prevalent taunt of cowardice in pacifism:

"Some may here say,—'What, wouldst thou have us to be cowards?' No: but heroes in the Lamb's army. And who is there that needs be ashamed to be in the Lamb's army, to gain the victory?'"

Then sweeping into his main theme, he delivered this magnificent period:

"For Christ and his glorious dispensation, is not a dispensation of strife and dispute; for when he came, there was even uttered by the songs of angels, 'Peace on earth and good-will to men.' * * * It is as clear to me as the sun that shines in the firmament. He was the Prince of Peace; of whose government the Prophet Isaiah declares there never should be an end. O my fellow Christians, let us with all our souls draw nigh unto and seek for his holy power to influence our hearts; that he may bring us into the bond of Christian charity, and of holy and blessed union, one with another; that he may destroy all that seeks to blow up nations and kingdoms into confusion and that seeks to bring distress upon individuals, nations and countries!"

When one remembers that these sermons were all preached to "other professors," and outside of the regular meetings of Friends, the catholicity of William Savery's aim becomes the more apparent and significant. Such appeals for Church coöperation were the gist of his message, not merely sporadic. He voiced the same at Houndsditch, as recorded in another sermon:

"That all these uncharitable dispositions that are harboured by some, though I hope in this enlightened day, not by a great many, may be removed; God is doing them away, seeking thus his own work; he is abolishing those things which kept us so long at a distance secretly, and will bring them to nought; this is my opinion; and more and more charity will prevail. * * * The peaceable kingdom of Jesus Christ, our Saviour, being established and set up in the hearts of men, would put an end to war and all the horrors appending to it in the world."

Time and again, by cryptic sentences, he would cap a leader of this kind by a reference to Christ as the all essential:

"But the Truth upon which glory, immortality and eternal life depend, is plain, free and simple,—'To know thee, the only true God, and Jesus Christ, whom thou hast sent, is life eternal.'"

Or, in another place:

"But that all men may come to the divine, eternal and unchangeable principle in themselves, that would teach us in all things, * * * the same that our Saviour promised should be with his followers to the end of the world; even his own eternal Spirit, the Spirit of God and Christ."

And finally, to an universal extent:

"For Jesus Christ is 'the true Light that enlighteneth,' not only those that have read the history of his life, death and sufferings;

his glorious and unparalleled miracles and divine doctrines; but also those that have never heard of the name of Christ."

It is natural that William Savery should have approached Church unity from the Quaker standpoint. Such had been his training. But had he stopped there he would have never reached the masses of people to whom he preached. He modestly records the acclaim that greeted his preaching, not only in the few press notices, but even more in the expressions of people coming to him after the meetings. Even from this, one could surmise that his appeal was a broad one. But from the deprecated record that Job Sibley has fortunately left us, there is no need to conjecture. The sermons are full of allusions and references of the broadest kind, all calculated to find and enlarge upon the common denominator of spiritual experience, upon which Christians could unite to redeem the world as Christ's rightful kingdom. "Let no man judge me as a sectarian," said William Savery, in the final paragraph of his last sermon, before going to the Continent, and indeed, he was no sectarian:

" 'We have been variously educated,' he said, 'we have had various prejudices in our minds, and nothing but the divine, illuminating power can make them subside, so as we might have charity, one towards another. I believe there are some of the Lord's true Church in every name and among every nation; and that there are not only these who are professing the same faith with me, and who worship God in silence as I do, but also in other professions there are those who in sincerity of soul offer up their prayers to God. This I desire to believe wherever I may be."

At Peter's Court he dilated still more upon denominationalism:

"It is not systems nor opinions, it is neither high church nor low church that I am speaking about now. There is but one true and living church, the whole world over. Men may call themselves what they please: the world calls me a Quaker—and thee a Dissenter in another form—and thee a member of the Established Church, but what is all this? My friends, these are names, they are distinctions among men: but are they distinctions with God? Does he know high church and low church? Does he descend to inquire whether thou art a Methodist or a Presbyterian, thou a Baptist, thou a Roman Catholic? No: but is thy heart right? Art thou sincere in thy desires to know him and to serve him? * * * So that, my friends, I am not come among you to gather you to *my* party, but that all men may become so inquisitive for themselves that they may be joined to God and Christ in their part. * * * For there are those, I am persuaded in my own experience, among the various professors, whom I can embrace as children of the one great and universal parent, in the Truth as it is in Jesus."

As a practical example of this catholicity of opinion, one could not cite a broader statement from William Savery's sermons than this, culled from his delivery at Houndsditch Meeting house:

"But let every man be persuaded in his own mind; let every man attend to the light of Christ in his conscience, and follow the dictates of it fully and faithfully. If thou believest with all thine heart that it is thy duty in the sight of God to be plunged into water in the name of the Father, Son and holy Ghost, according to thy faith so be it to thee, let no man condemn thee."

He followed that a week later by a similar expression at Peter's Court:

"This is my faith and I do not want you to receive it any further than it may coincide with the best light and knowledge which God in his mercy has granted you. I do not want you to pin your faith upon mine."

In conjunction with this expression, one can but recall William Savery's entries in his Journal, already quoted, regarding the Catholics on the Continent, that "those who partake of that ceremony (bread and wine in communion) with sincere hearts, were at times partakers of a blessing, but it was not obligatory," and the other where he expressed "love for these devotees, tho' I cannot own their superstition. I believe they will be accepted according to the sincerity of their hearts."

It would be only natural that so broad a basis of Christian fellowship as William Savery advocated should have brought him into doctrinal conferences with many outside the meetings. He records the attendance of many ministers and priests at these meetings, and conferences with individuals between times. His references to the Scriptures in his printed sermons are almost certainly the outcome of inquiries or objections stated during these conferences. He grasps and develops the ancient Quaker attitude toward the Scriptures fearlessly, though with a curious confusion as to minute examination and study of them. In two of these printed sermons he says practically the same thing, quoted as follows, from the sermon at the Borough New Market:

"Thou mayest explore volumes after volumes and spend much time in reading many pious books and experiences of many favorite men of God. I do not despise inferior helps. The Scriptures are excellent; they are much more so and worthier to be held in greater estimation than all the books in the world. But the Scriptures point only to that holy, all-powerful Word, which indeed gave all the Scriptures. The whole tenor of the Gospel doctrine is to bring men there—to settle them upon that foundation, where they may build with safety—to the teachings of the holy and blessed spirit of God within them. I know this is a doctrine too much exploded. * * *

Truly the Scriptures do direct us to this glorious principle within us, yet how do men turn them to every purpose! One learned man starts up in one quarter of the nation, and he says,—'Here is a portion of Scripture, and I assure you it means so and so'; and another declares with equal learning, with a great deal of study, and with abundance of eloquence,—'My friends, it is so and so; this way you must believe'; and there is even one gone over to the country of my nativity, who with the New Testament in his hands, is laying the axe by his arguments, as much as is in his power, to the very root of the Christian Religion."

William Savery's solution of this age-old dilemma, as to whose interpretation is the truth, was as broad and fearless as one would expect from the quotations already given:

# MINISTRY: ATTITUDE AND CONTENT

"Well, my friends, do not be afraid of this inquiry; it is the way to truth; it is the way we must examine things; and as I said before, it is a day of inquiry; let us not be afraid of inquiry. Men have been afraid of bringing things to the test. But I believe it will not be sufficient to think so long; and I invite you that are men of freedom, of independent minds, search for the truth yourselves. Let no man lead you in those things which God is sufficient to direct and lead you into himself."

About 1801, in a letter to a correspondent in England anent the Hannah Barnard controversy, he wrote:

"The longer I live, the more unshaken confidence I think I obtain, that the doctrines laid down by Robert Barclay and our first Friends, founded on the New Testament, and still maintained by the Society at large, are invulnerable to the efforts of vain philosophic sophistry and curious speculation, so long as we retain a belief in that most excellent of books."

Nor was he tolerant of bumptious scholarship at Edinburgh. Evidently the King James version of the Bible was sufficient:

"Jas McRay paid us a visit, full of the importance of a new translation of the Bible he had begun; appears to be much puffed up with his knowledge of languages. His visit was so much the more acceptable for its shortness; his object and mine don't harmonize."

In the sermon at Devonshire House on June 1, 1797, appointed for young people, William Savery used the following expression:

"It is not often, nor do I believe it will be at this time, my endeavor to deal out amongst you the terrors of the law, but we endeavor to hold forth an invitation to you in the love of the Gospel. * * *"

The positive attitude of this expression justifies the tradition that has come down by oral transmission alone, according to which Thomas Scattergood asked William Savery why his ministry seemed "to gather" more than his own. William Savery is said to have replied, "be-

[ 453 ]

cause I tell them of the wonders of yielding to the influence of love, and thou threatens them with the terrors of eternal torment if they do not yield." Whether the story, in its details is apocryphal or not, there is certainly in these printed sermons a broad spirit of tolerance and brotherhood that well exemplifies William Savery's own dependence upon the spirit of Christ. The "glorious hope and blessed consolation in the redemption and mediation of our dear Lord and Saviour, Jesus Christ," of which he preached, were not merely a part of an orthodox theology to him, but a living experience. It was, as he said in 1796, "that you may experimentally know that you have need of Christ." There two quotations are all that the printed sermons contain that are couched in the phraseology of the theological disputes of the next generation. There is much of doctrine but little of theology in the sermons. Even the opposition to deism,—the rational attempt to relieve religion of its mystery and superstition, found William Savery far from adopting the Evangelical attitude of making the Bible the sole, complete and finished rule of faith, belief and conduct. While the Deist applied his reasoning faculties as sufficient for every phase of religious experience, scouting faith as little better than superstition, and the Evangelical laid exclusive stress upon the Bible, the close of the Eighteenth Century found Friends still clinging, though in many cases unconsciously, to the ancient, mystical and intuitive knowledge of Christ. As William Savery put it:

"Let every man be persuaded in his own mind: let every man tend to the Light of Christ in his conscience, and follow the dictates of it fully and faithfully."

The two great Separations of the next century are the mute witnesses of the devastation wrought within the Society of Friends by Deism under its later name, Unitarianism, on the one hand and Evangelicism on the other. It is as a mean between what afterward became the two extremes, that William Savery fits. His advocacy of Christ is an experimental advocacy, based upon his personal relation to a crucified, risen and living Lord, in whom he believed, not by dint of imposed theology or Biblical text, but because His humanity and divinity were a part of the believer's life, deeply hid with God. One can feel the appeal of the personality of Christ, glowing in the printed words of William Savery's Journal and sermons, imperfect though both were and are, as means of transmitting the fervor and warmth of his personal experience. What the strength of that appeal must have been, when associated with all the power and strength of a deeply convinced delivery, we can only judge from the results that attended such ministry.

" 'Such was the awfulness of his frame,' said a Philadelphia newspaper tribute, 'in publick prayer, that cold indeed must have been that heart, which was not animated by the fervency of his supplication.' "

His conviction, however, was so blended with urbanity and charity that it drew, rather than repelled; it inspired because he was inspired in delivering it; his hearers caught fire because he himself burned with a zealous flame, being unabashed of his calling. "If I am an enthusiast in these things," he said, "the Lord preserve me an enthusiast to the end of my days." And so, in sooth, He did.

## CHAPTER XXXIII

## LAST YEARS IN PHILADELPHIA

Mid-October, 1798, found the *Washington* nearing New York. It is safe to say that none of its passengers yearned for land more sincerely than did William Savery returning to his native shores after his long absence:

"The consideration of again beholding my native land, frequently filled my heart with gratitude, gladness and thankfulness to the Author of every mercy. But alas! how short lived are our times of rejoicing in this ever changing scene."

The cause of William Savery's lapse from joy to sorrow was the news of the prevalence of the dread yellow fever in his beloved Philadelphia. The officers of the *Camilla*, in boarding the *Washington*, had left newspapers telling of the heavy toll of deaths in the cities of the Atlantic seaboard,— in Philadelphia alone, thirty to forty a day being recorded. When the pilot came on board off New York, he confirmed the gloomiest forebodings, and while their vessel drifted aimlessly for four days, awaiting a breeze to carry them into harbor, William Savery suffered acutely over the situation of his friends and connections at home:

"O, Philadelphia! Philadelphia! thou whom the Lord has known and favored, above all the cities I have ever seen, is there not a cause why thou shouldst so repeatedly, be made to read the roll written within and without, with mourning, lamentation and woe? Doubtless there is, or thy God would still have preserved the walls of salvation around thee, and thy gates would have resounded with anthems of praise."

The scourge of 1798 has come down in history as second only to that of 1793 in its virulence. William Savery after landing, repaired quickly to Philadelphia only to find that his wife and relatives had fled to the country. He joined them at once, but beyond that bare fact, no details of this homecoming have been preserved.

The pall of the yellow fever hung over Philadelphia every autumn for several years after 1798. There were renewed, although less severe epidemics of it in 1799, 1802 and 1803, and in all of these William Savery was active. Ann Warder writes home to England of the noble service rendered the sick in the fall of 1799 by William Savery and Thomas Scattergood, regardless of their own safety. She had gone to Abington, near Philadelphia, for a country refuge, and wrote thence on October 8th:

"Our part of the town so clear that my dear husband has occasionly gone there without fear; indeed such as remained, apprehended no danger. Beloved William and Sarah Savery staid, no doubt under right direction. He seemed not easy to leave the small deserted flock at our meeting. They were both here about two weeks since and though a promised pleasure I had anticipated, yet it ended in a degree of disappointment. Whilst sitting in meeting he was taken with a chill, and in much pain which was succeeded by considerable fever. He set up but little and then had no enjoyment, neither could we have with him, as much fear would arise respecting the result. However, on getting home, his dear Sarah apply'd what was proper, and next day it proved a violent cold only. This is one consequence of remaining in the city, if even not much danger, I should fear every symptom as an alarm of dreadful consequences that might follow."

William Savery entered again actively into the pursuit of his business of tanning, but his heart seems to have gone more into ministrations to the sick, reckless of consequences and "being deeply affected with their sufferings, he was enabled to sympathize with them, and minister to them at seasons comfort and consolation." As he was constantly exposing himself to the virulence of the fever, in sick rooms and at funerals, he thought it most prudent the last years of his life, to avoid practically all meat, in diet,—an abstention that was thought by his friends to have weakened his system and rendered it liable to other disorders. As he was of a full figure, it may well be that this abstinence was wise on general principles, for he finally died of a "dropsical malady."

After his return from Europe, William Savery's life was not very eventful, and the available facts are soon told.

From the printed Journal, we learn that he attended New York Yearly Meeting, under religious concern in 1800 and similarly, Baltimore Yearly Meeting in 1801. No details of these services seem to be available. There are, however, numerous references to him in other sources from which we may learn of his activities.

These appear chiefly in the letters of Rebecca Jones and Ann Warder. Trivial though many of them are, they have a grace that is all their own and the intimacy of the epistolary references is often refreshing after the staid solemnity of the meeting records. Ann Warder constantly forwards the love of William and Sarah Savery to her relatives in Ipswich, England, whom the former had visited. In April, 1799, she surmises that William Savery will soon be off again with a proposed deputation to the Indian nations, far inland, his presence upon the delegation being earnestly sought. This concern persisted, as she writes, July 31, 1801:

"William (Savery) has also been favoured with a long respite, but I believe a journey is contemplating, perhaps among the natives here. As to you, he talks and thinks much about, but there it rests, at present. His life spared, I am often ready to apprehend another voyage will be required of him."

She reiterates this feeling in February of 1802, "he must visit Germany again or I am mistaken," though rheumatism in the head had then confined him for several weeks to the house and perhaps forced a year's respite, in view of the passing of the meetings necessary to forward so extensive a concern to the Yearly Meeting, for its approval.

## LAST YEARS IN PHILADELPHIA

The Warders received a breezy call from William Savery in April, 1800, when he dropt in

"with the acclamation, 'How frail is womankind.' I could not think what he had heard; however, the expected marriage of Reb. Young has surprised him beyond measure. Never was a person more opposed to being joked about anything of the kind, he says, but so strange is the power of persuasion."

Elizabeth Drinker joins the other two women, in noting William Savery's presence at the numerous funerals, where he was usually engaged in prayer, often at the grave, and at weddings, where he seemed to be peculiarly acceptable and "innocently cheerful, as usual." Rebecca Jones, in 1800, reports:

"Our dear N. Waln is poorly; Wm. Savery, a strong man in every way, and D. Bacon remains an upright pillar,—sound and steady."

Though but in the prime of life, he seems to have grown strangely world-weary. "I am worth about (so much)," he is quoted as saying, "and I never expect to be richer." Even more explicit was a letter to Thomas Eddy, the friend of his youth, dated Ninth Month 21, 1803, less than a year before his death:

"Indeed, my dear friend, I think as I advance in life, the desire of being continued in this ever fluctuating scene till very old age rather diminishes, and especially so in my best moments when I reflect on those things of everlasting duration, 'which eye hath not seen nor ear heard, neither hath it enterd into the heart of man to conceive'—compared with which all the joys of this unstable world appear like 'a tale thrice told' and as bubbles in the air."

Some of this weariness may have come from the era of expansion and speculation then prevalent as a concomitant of the European wars. The meretricious nature of wartime prosperity, none too well understood even in this day, was then ignored. Philadelphia Friends were deeply engrossed in trade. The profits from oversea ventures, if the French privateers were eluded, were simply enormous. The business correspondence of Henry Drinker, engaged in the grain export business to Portugal and England alike, are full of quotations of fabulous prices for American products. Rebecca Jones, though far removed from trade, wrote of the times, with reflections, applicable as well to the close of the Great War:

"The spirit for building, for purchasing and selling estates, is amazingly great. Every article in housekeeping is so raised in price that one might almost fancy oneself in Great Britain, and be awake, too,—so that I, with others, are of the mind that the present face of things will be changed, though the time, as well as manner, I desire to leave."

William Savery, of whom the Monthly Meeting's testimonial states that "he was remarkable for punctuality and uprightness in his dealings," and who, in spite of the drain made upon his resources in traveling, and the inferiority with which he esteemed his business, left a considerable estate, was alive to the spirit of speculation. "It is necessary," he remarked to an intimate friend, at this period, "to look to our outward concerns; there are so many reproachful failures."

Another concomitant of the era of expansion was a similar movement within Philadelphia Yearly Meeting. Its members were increasing in wealth, business was thriving and the Society itself caught the impetus. Once again, Rebecca Jones, who, for canny observations was surpassed by few of her contemporaries, epitomizes the situation in a letter to England:

"* * * our great works which are in contemplation,—such as attempting to civilize the inhabitants of the wilderness and to establish a Boarding school, after the manner of your Ackworth; build a large meeting house (after your example) to accommodate both sexes at the Yearly Meeting; admit black people into society fellowship, &c, &c."

# LAST YEARS IN PHILADELPHIA

Perhaps no better appreciation of the growth of the nation and the Society could be gained than by realizing how modern these works of 1800 seem, in comparison with those of the Colonial period of 1750, when William Savery was born. The Indian work was being organized into the Tunesassa School in western New York, the first Indian Committee of the Yearly Meeting (of which William Savery was a member) having been appointed for the service, officially, in 1795. Westtown Boarding School, after years of preparation, was opened in 1799, and the large meeting house was first used in 1804 and is still the center of the Yearly Meeting at Arch and Fourth Streets, Philadelphia.

The reference to the negroes is a curious sidelight upon an inquiry that came up in 1796 from one of the Quarterly Meetings as to whether black people might be received into membership. So extensive had been the work of Friends among the blacks that such an inquiry seems curious in this day. It will be remembered, however, that separate meetings were then held for the negroes, and when any, as was frequently the case, attended the regular meetings for worship, they sat in a section apart from the whites. This custom explains the liberality of sentiment exhibited by William Savery, toward Captain Paul Cuffee, a negro shipowner, who was warmly attached to Friends' principles. He occasionally spoke in meeting and on one occasion:

"he left his seat, walked up into the gallery to a place at the head of the meeting, and standing there, preached a remarkably powerful sermon. At its close, William Savery moved his place and touched his arm, directing him to a seat beside himself, but Paul Cuffee made a gesture of dissent and walked back, down the aisle to his place among his own people."

This incident probably occurred in the old North Meeting House in Keys Alley, though just when, is not recorded. One hardly knows which to admire more, the courtesy of the white man, deferential beyond his time, or the true humility of the negro gentleman. It need hardly be added that the Yearly Meeting of 1796 advised that monthly meetings were "at liberty to receive such into membership, without respect to nation or color."

These closing years of William Savery's life were also the period of great territorial expansion in Philadelphia Yearly Meeting. The query,—"What new meetings established?" was then constantly answered in gratifying figures. There were a thousand families of Friends in Philadelphia alone and the clearing of the forest and the emigration to the west, were synonymous with the numerical strength of the parent meeting.

And yet the elements of decay were already at work. So long had education been confined to a narrow type of elementary instruction, with active distrust of anything smacking of "Oxford and Cambridge" (to which William Savery would have added Edinburgh), that the rank and file of Friends were but slightly educated and many of them were actually illiterate. The survey of a generation later, after the devastation of the Hicksite Separation, revealed that very few families had complete Bibles, and many had not even parts of the Bible. Westtown School was the first effort to remedy this evil, but its scope was too restricted and its initial efforts too feeble to buttress the Society before the whirlwind of religious controversy struck a generation unprepared to resist it. Wrote Ann Warder of the new school, at its opening, with almost prophetic insight:

"This new institution, already much thought of, will enlarge people's ideas more generally upon the advantages of education, and very necessarily indeed, as there are hundreds in the country of Friends and children that can scarcely write their name or read at all."

The great and mute tragedy of that period lies in the constant and reiterated lamentations of the concerned Friends over the waywardness of the youth, and the timidity of these same Friends in attempting methods to assuage the difficulties. "Great works," in truth they were, as Rebecca Jones stated, but they were feeble in comparison with the needs. More than a full century was to elapse after the Indian work corporately undertaken in 1795, before Philadelphia Yearly Meeting, busy with internal dissension, and the letter of the law, was to be able to institute its next attempt, officially, to aid any group outside its own ever narrowing limits. The Russian Doukhobors then broke through with an irresistible appeal for sympathy,—an appeal which fortunately has been repeatedly heeded in still other lines of outside endeavor since. When one contemplates, however, the great movements of that century along religious lines; the battles of faith that were waged in harmonizing the complexities of scientific discovery and scientific method in religious fields, and how pitiably negligent has been the contribution of the Society of Friends in these high endeavors, one wishes that the University experience of Penn, Penington and Barclay had transmuted itself sooner than it did, into the splendid galaxy of Quaker colleges that now exists in America. William Savery's last years at the threshold of the Nineteenth Century, have lessons of intense but painful interest to the attentive student of Quaker history.

William Savery's decline in health was apparently very rapid. During the year 1803 he was ailing from time to time, but gave no great concern to his friends as he was still in the prime of life. His malady increased however, perceptibly. He appeared for the last time in a public meeting on Christmas day, 1803. William Evans, then a youth of sixteen years, was present at the time and has left this account of the occasion:

"I attended the Market Street meeting on the evening of the 25th of the Twelfth Month when he preached, appearing to be in a declining state of health, and which I believe was the last time he appeared in the ministry in a public meeting. What made the opportunity more impressive was his pallid countenance, and the text with which he rose, 'Abraham saw my day and was glad,' and which he uttered with a heavenly spirit and solemn tone of voice. This was the subject of all others which lay near his heart—and he was an indefatigable advocate for the truths and the importance of Christianity."

His ameliorating spirit rather chafed at being unable to attend meetings for worship, stating at one time that he desired "once more to warn the aged who had got into the earth and the youth who had got into the air." He became able to ride out at times, in company with his brother, Thomas Savery, and in the spring appeared to rally. Thomas Scattergood reported to Rebecca Jones that the paralytic affection and the dropsical symptoms seemed less pronounced. "The prospect of losing so valuable a member of our Society is a close trial to his near friends," she wrote.

The end came on June 19, 1804, and the faithful pen of dear old Rebecca Jones once more gives the fullest details:

"This morning before I was up, Ruth Ely sent to let me know that our endeared brother, Wm Savery, departed about six o'clock, very quietly, though unexpectedly at the time, having rode out the day before and seemed rather better. His last words were 'Glory to God!' His remains were kept till 3 o'clock on Fourth-day, when, instead of taking him to the burial ground, he was, at M. Routh's request, taken to our North Meeting House, where M. R. had a short testimony to his worth as a minister, fellow member and fellow citizen, greatly beloved for the work's sake. Elizabeth Foulke appeared in prayer and in a very heavy rain, his body was taken to our ground and decently interred there."

The interment was made in the Friends' burial ground at Fourth and Arch Streets, Philadelphia. As usual in those days, the grave was not marked.

To the above account, Rebecca Jones added an affecting little story of devotion on the part of Jacob Beck, an elderly Methodist who had lost three daughters in the yellow fever of 1802, to whom William Savery had devoted much attention. He was employed as foreman in Peter Brown's blacksmithy, in Front Street, opposite the end of Brook's Court. Soon after William Savery's decease, Rebecca Jones was seated by her open window, when Jacob Beck came up the Court to fill his noggin at her pump,—a pump, incidentally, that was· famous for squares around, for the quality of the water it drew. Jacob Beck remarked:

" 'Maybe you won't have any objections to hearing a hymn I've made, to sing over my work,' adding that it helped his mind to soar, while his hands were engaged in necessary labor. He then proceeded to sing his verses with much emotion, which, with no claim to poetical elegance, contained a warm expression of regard for the virtues and value of William Savery."

One of the verses is quoted in a footnote in the *Memorials of Rebecca Jones*,—a verse as sincere in sentiment as its meter is faulty.

In the old files of the Philadelphia newspapers of the time are found several elaborate and adulatory accounts of William Savery and of his extensive benevolences of deed and substance. They are of a type too effusive to find acceptance today, but with all that, they reflect a true sincerity and depth of feeling and love. Perhaps no heart yearned more over the loss of a strong man called home in his prime than that of his old mother, Mary (Peters) Savery, who died the next month at the age of eighty-two. To her, he must still have seemed young, with his fifty-four years, and young, in very truth he was,—young in the childish simplicity with which he wrote, in those last days:

"I thought I was once strong for the work, but now I am a child, brought back to my horn book, and have nothing to trust to but the mercy of God through Christ, my Saviour."

# INDEX

# INDEX

# INDEX

England, Colonel Richard, 79, 80, 83, 93
Ernest Augustus, Prince, 397, 398
Erskine, Thomas, 159
Evangelical Movement, 34, 290, 318, 319
Evans, Jonathan, 28, 41, 65, 146, 441
  Oliver, 284
  Sarah (See Sarah Savery)
  William, 463

Farmer's Brother, 125, 126, 129, 143, 152, 154
Farrer, William, 165, 183, 197, 210, 213, 275, 276, 283, 288, 375
Fearson, Peter, 373
  Widow, 373
First Publishers of Truth, 3, 316, 381
Fish-carrier, 55, 129, 152
Fisher, James, 272, 368
  Samuel, 368
  Thomas, 118
  W., 284
Flemming, Captain, 386
Forbes, Widow, 267
Ford, Henry, "Peace Ship," 380
Fosick Family, 368
Foster, E., 357
  Joseph & Thomas, 311, 334, 367
Fothergill, Dr. John, 13, 340
Foulke, Elizabeth (Betsy), 384, 464
Fox, Charles James, 156
  George, 204, 399, 412, 439
  Margaret, 399
Frederick the Great, 167, 205
Frederick William II, 167, 171, 172
Frederick William IV, 171
Free Quakers, 25
French & Indian War, 2, 4, 5, 50, 61, 62
French Revolution, 156, 157, 162, 213, 217, 229, 237, 242, 245, 246, 258, 261, 266, 297, 299, 313
Friendly Association for Regaining and Preserving Peace with the Indians by Pacific Measures, 62, 63, 64
Fry, Edmund, 368
  Elizabeth (Gurney), 196, 321, 366, 424, 428, 429, 430, 431, 432, 433, 434, 435
  Ellis, 389
  Jane, 337
  John, 336
  Thomas, 389
  William, 369, 371, 389, 426

Fry, William Jr., 389
Funerals, Quaker, 373, 374

Gaskil, Clayton, 44
Gatchell, 278
George III (of England), 22, 170, 178, 280, 281, 324, 328, 334, 396, 397, 398, 421
Germantown, Battle of, 21, 41
Geronimo, 106
Gibbons, James, 15
Gilpin, John, 389, 390
Girty, Simon, 56, 82, 92, 97, 98, 99, 100, 105
Godiva, Lady, 390
Gobelin Tapestries, 235
Gordon, Colonel, 55, 57
Goshen Monthly Meeting, 14, 15, 16
Girard, Stephen, 115, 116
Grant, Harding, 368
Grattan, Henry, 265
Greer, Robert, 292
Grellet, Stephen, 24, 30, 31, 116, 164
Grubb, Robert & Sarah, 254
Gurney, Elizabeth (See Fry, Elizabeth)
  Jane, 430
  John, 371, 429, 430, 432, 433
  Joseph, 371, 429, 430, 431
  Joseph John, 319, 366
  Louisa, 431
  Priscilla, 346
  Richenda, 429, 431
Guyon, Madame, 190

Hagens, J., 372
Haines, Caspar, 114, 122
  George & Kitty, 404
Halifax, Earl of, 63
Hancock, Jacob, 286
  John, 290
Harmar, General, 53, 54, 120
Harris, Ann, 44
  Mary, 123, 145
Harrison, George, 355
  Sarah, 118, 346, 362, 363
Hartshorne, William, 60, 68, 72, 107, 108, 109, 111
Harvey, Joseph M., 272, 284
Hat honor, 192, 214, 357, 358, 418
Haverford College, viii, 132
Haworth, Martha, 346
Head, Jeremiah, 374
  John, 374, 429
Heckewelder, John, 73, 74, 76, 79, 82, 89, 90, 99, 100, 102, 103, 108, 109, 148
Helm, Peter, 116

[ 469 ]

# INDEX

# INDEX

# INDEX

# INDEX

Elizabeth, 402, 406
Family of England, 6, 7, 396, 405
Hester, 406, 407, 409, 410
Joseph, 302, 330, 332, 333, 361, 365, 372, 405, 406, 407, 433, 436
Mary (Pryor), 330, 361, 365, 405, 406
Mary (Jr.), 330, 406
Nancy (See Anna)
William (the Huguenot), 7, 8, 9
Scanadoe, 153
Scattergood, Thomas, 2, 3, 20, 25, 31, 32, 346, 353, 354, 359, 375, 396, 412, 413, 443, 453, 457, 464
Schwenkfelders, 63
Scott, Captain, 111, 112
Job, 3, 20
Scriptures, The, 452
Sea-bathing, 328, 329
Seaton, Alexander, 12
Seebohm, Diedrick, 209
Frederick, 207, 209
Jacob, 209
Lewis, 166, 176, 194, 195, 196, 201, 204, 207, 209, 211
Senseman, Gabriel, 89, 90
Seven Nations of Canada, 102, 104
Sevérit, 7
Shackleton, Abraham, 290, 291, 292, 293
Sarah, 346
Sharpless, Isaac, viii
Shillitoe, Thomas, 290
Shonning, Anthony, 207
Shutamire, Herman, 207
Sibley, Job, 441, 442, 443, 445, 450
Siddons, Mrs. Sarah, 432
Simcoe, Governor, 56, 74, 79, 90, 92, 105, 120, 132
Simkins, T., 368
Six Nations, 51, 55, 57, 58, 101, 121, 124, 125, 129, 146
Slavery, 34, 35, 156, 320, 328, 378, 379, 380, 385
Smith, Frederick, 209
George, 13
Joseph, 165
Peter, 127
Sparrows, Richard, 282, 284
Speakman, Phebe, 48, 346, 378, 384
"S. R." (See Rawes, Sarah)
Stacy, George, 359, 360, 375
Stage-coaching, 331, 332, 333, 334, 335
Starr, Joseph, 376
St. Clair, General, 54, 88, 119, 120

Sterry, Mary, 346, 358
Stewardson, Anna and Dorothy, 347
George, 347
Thomas, 46, 47, 48, 122, 347
Storer, Charles, 108, 110
Strangman, John, 282
Joshua, 284
Swarthmore, 399
Sword Carrier, 125, 155
Sykes, Thomas, 44, 48

Talbot, Sarah, 48, 346, 384
Tecumseh, Chief, 92, 106
Tennyson, Alfred Lord, 390
Test Act, 156, 314, 315
Thayendanegea (See Brant, Joseph)
Theophilanthropists, 398
Thompson, Charles, 13
John, 350
Toleration Act, 314
Townsend, John, 359
Treaty of Ft. Stanwix, 51, 53, 64, 65, 98, 131, 135, 137, 142
Trotter, "Sukey," 37
Tunesassa Indian School, 125, 155, 461
Tuscaroras, Hopewell Claim, 128

United Irishmen, 264, 266, 275, 277

Vacation habits, 327, 333
Vanderwerf, John, 240
Ventigole, David, 234, 251, 252, 255
Mary, 252
Vinegar Hill, Battle of, 264, 277, 278, 279
Virginia Exiles, 22, 23, 25
Yearly Meeting, 33

Wagus, "Granny," 153
Walking Purchase, 62, 130
Wallace, John, 17
Wallis, Samuel, 123, 145
Waln, Mary, 19
Nicholas, 2, 20, 23, 412, 414, 459
Warder, Ann (Head), 36, 37, 38, 413, 414, 432, 457, 458, 459, 462
John, 36, 38, 310
Washington, George, 54, 55, 56, 59, 60, 71, 117, 133
Watson, Jane, 288, 418
John, 42, 117, 412
Mary, 346
Wawiapieschenwa (See Blue Jacket)

[ 473 ]

# INDEX